Loading . . . Please Wait

●●●●● soltbank 4G 0:00

MEMO END

Aya and her friends managed to defeat the SITE manager Ni, and prevented Sumikura Yuka from becoming a Magical Girl. Their exploit, however, has revealed to them the cruel reality of the situation, as well as a new mystery to solve.

Yuka continued to be bullied at school, and the Magical Girls asked themselves if Yuka was really happier not being a Magical Girl, a question that has a deep resonance and meaning to Aya and the others.

Meanwhile, Alice managed to uncover the identity and confirm the existence of the girl that Ni transformed into as Ochi Shizuka, and that she was once a Magical Girl herself. Are all the SITE managers former Magical Girls...? As Yatsumura Tsuyuno's life dwindled, Aya and the other girls launched another raid on the SITE managers.

Following the rules for finding out when the SITE managers would appear from their earlier encounter with Ni, Aya, and the other Magical Girls split into two teams to take on two managers at the same time. Using Kiyoharu's ability to communicate between teams and coordinate their efforts, they pressed on with the understanding that should one team fail to accomplish their mission, Alice would use her power to turn back time...

However, both raids resulted in failure. The managers, who had become aware of Aya and the group's plans, had countermeasures to use against their attack. Having fallen into the managers' trap, the girls were on the verge of being completely wiped out. And Alice, rather than turning back time...disappeared.

Aya and her friends were in dire straits! But then Tsuyuno used the last of her remaining life to activate her powers...

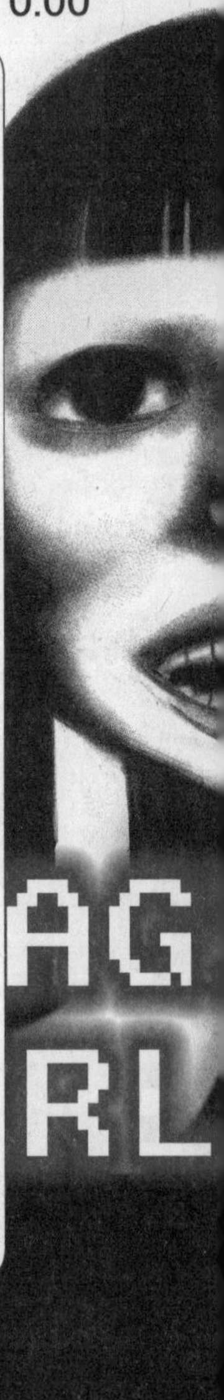
AG
RL

SEVEN SEAS ENTERTAINMENT PRESENTS

MAGICAL GIRL SITE

story and art by KENTARO SATO

VOLUME 9

TRANSLATION
Wesley Bridges

ADAPTATION
Janet Houck

LETTERING AND RETOUCH
Lune Moon

COVER DESIGN
Nicky Lim

PROOFREADER
B. Lana Guggenheim

EDITOR-IN-CHIEF
Adam Arnold

PUBLISHER
Jason DeAngelis

ISBN: 978-1-64275-082-9

Printed in Canada

First Printing: May 2019

10 9 8 7 6 5 4 3 2 1

FOLLOW US ONLINE: ***www.sevenseasentertainment.com***

READING DIRECTIONS

This book reads from ***right to left***, Japanese style. If this is your first time reading manga, you start reading from the top right panel on each page and take it from there. If you get lost, just follow the numbered diagram here. It may seem backwards at first, but you'll get the hang of it! Have fun!!

1
2
3
4
5
6
7
8
9

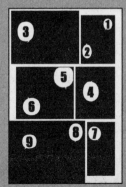

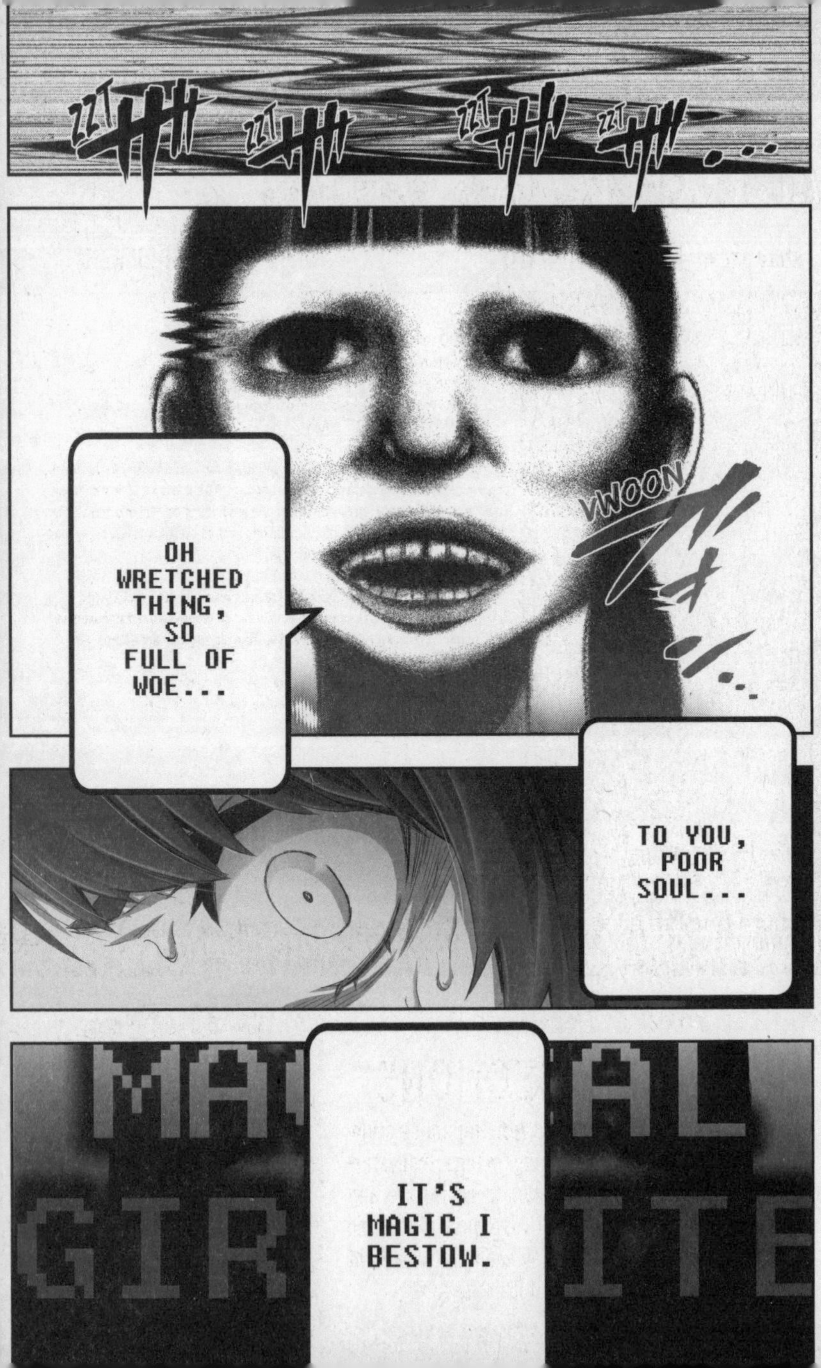
ZZT
ZZT
ZZT
ZZT
VWOON
OH WRETCHED THING, SO FULL OF WOE...
TO YOU, POOR SOUL...
IT'S MAGIC I BESTOW.

ENTER.56 KOMURA KAYO

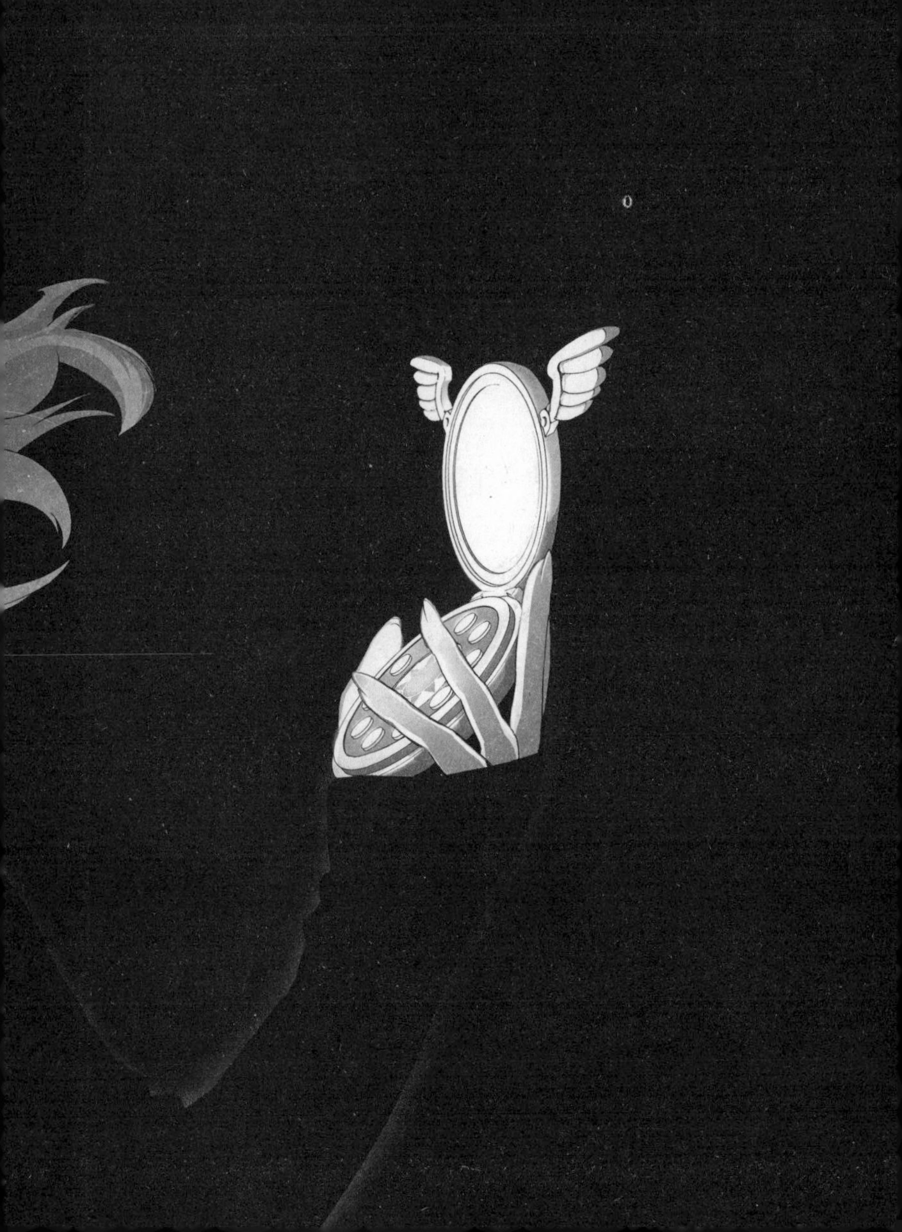

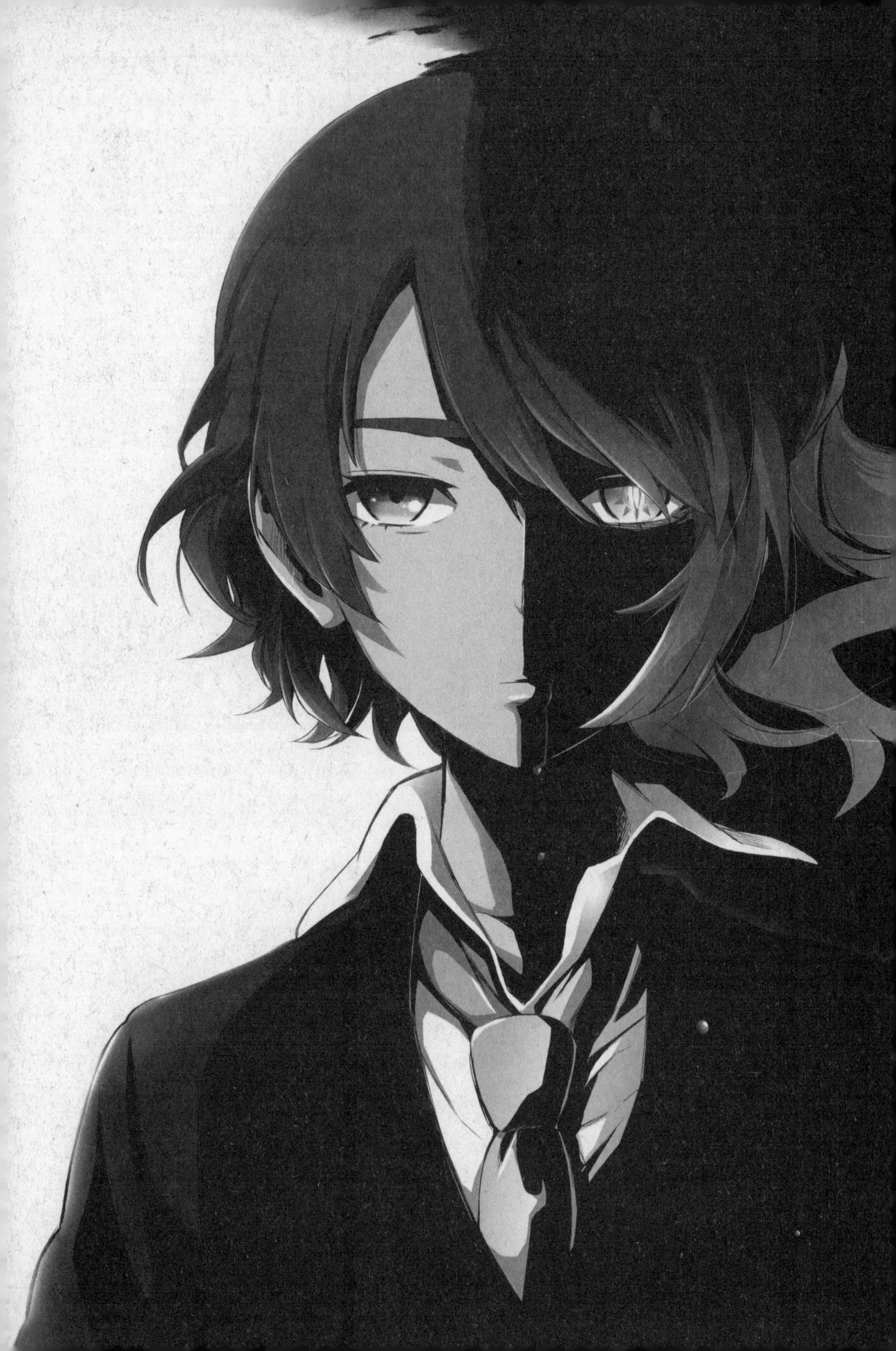

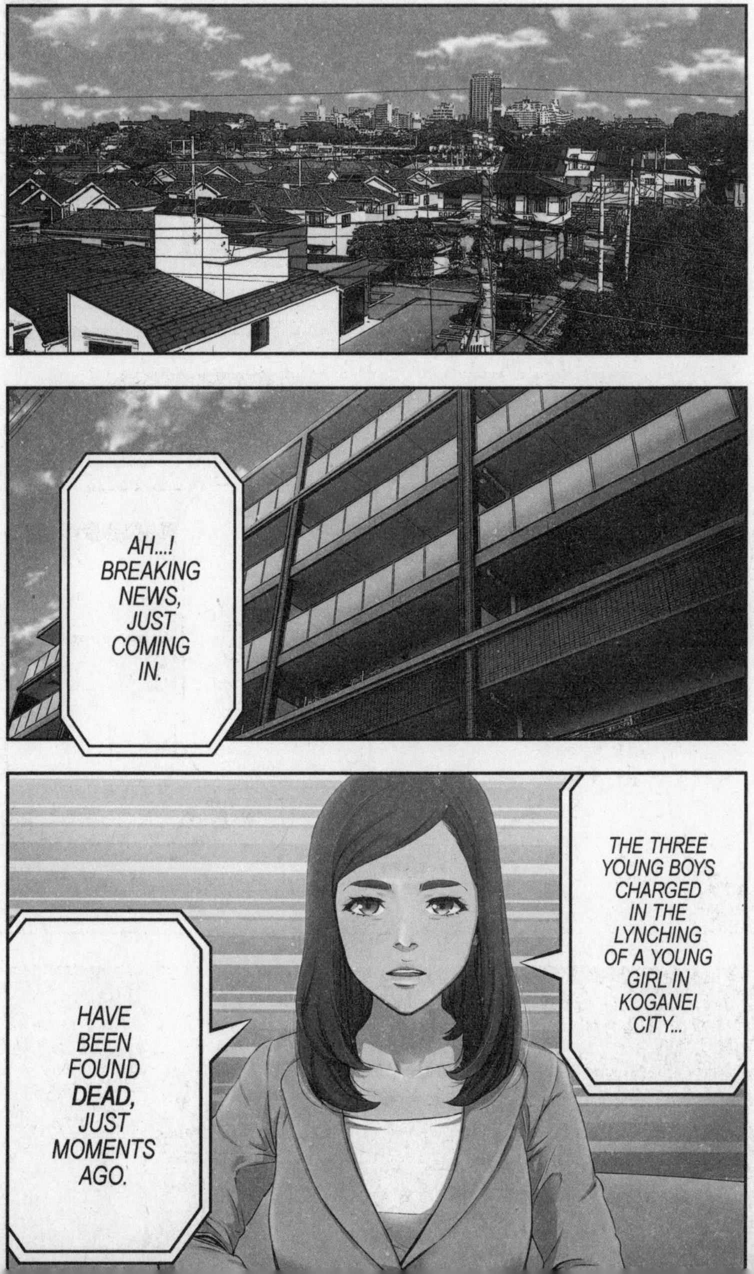
AH...! BREAKING NEWS, JUST COMING IN.
THE THREE YOUNG BOYS CHARGED IN THE LYNCHING OF A YOUNG GIRL IN KOGANEI CITY...
HAVE BEEN FOUND **DEAD,** JUST MOMENTS AGO.

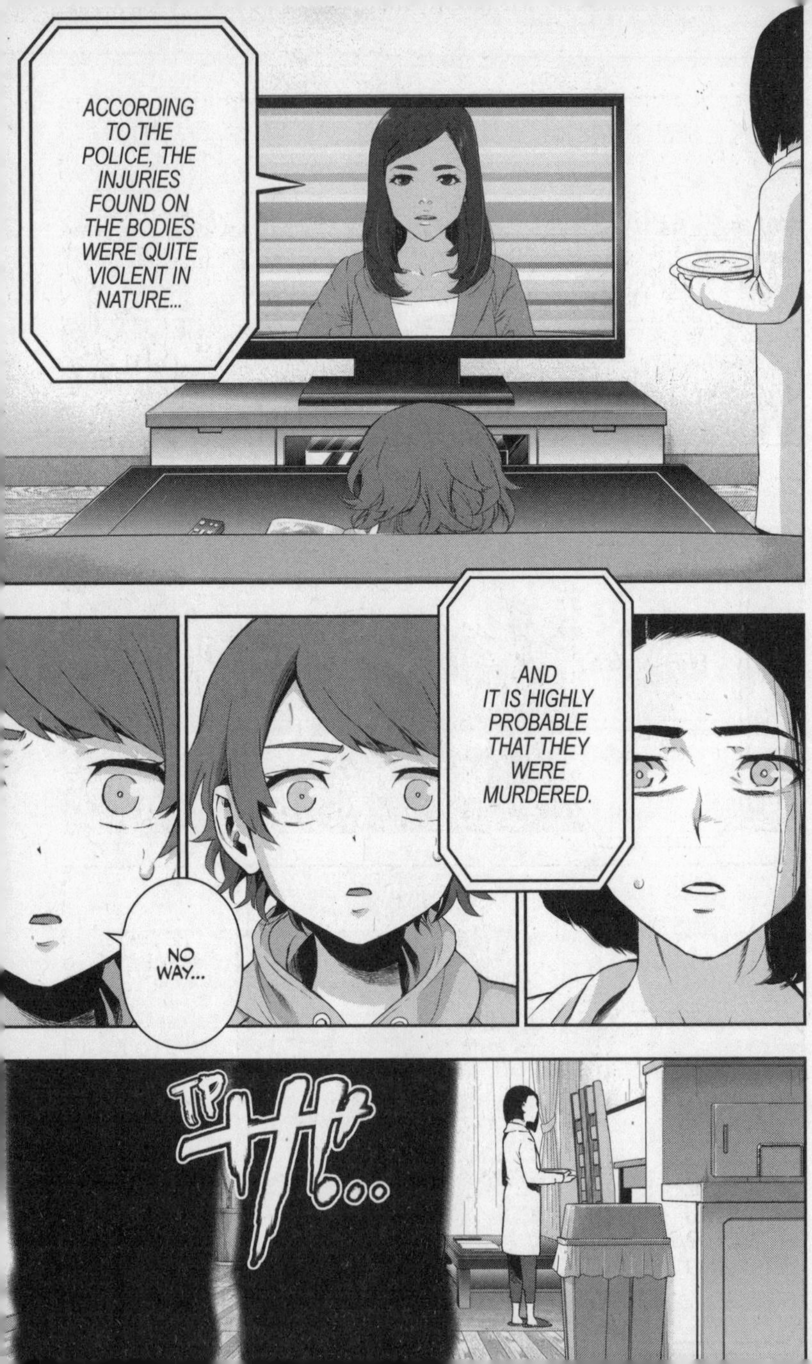
ACCORDING TO THE POLICE, THE INJURIES FOUND ON THE BODIES WERE QUITE VIOLENT IN NATURE...
AND IT IS HIGHLY PROBABLE THAT THEY WERE MURDERED.
NO WAY...
TP

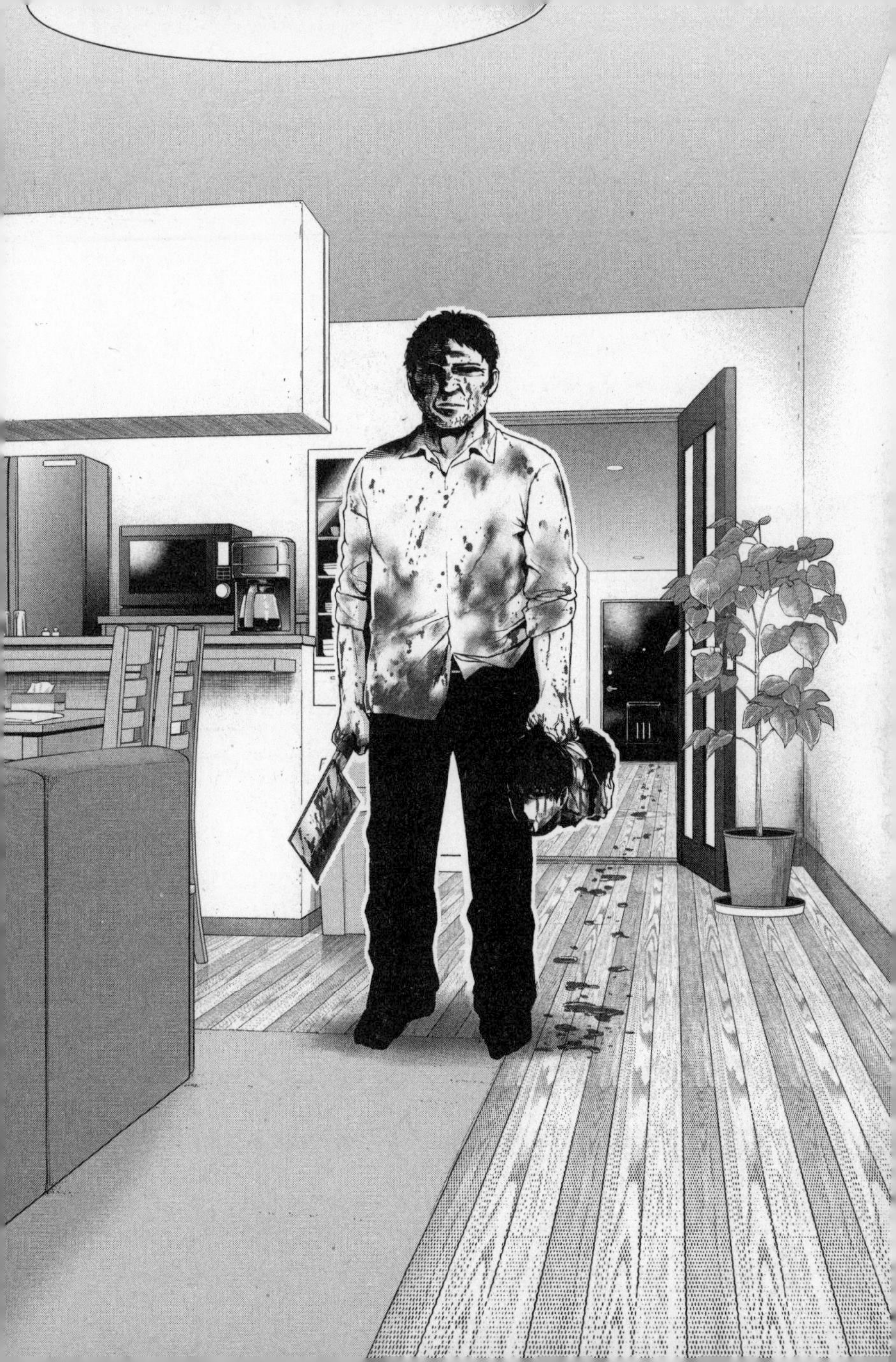

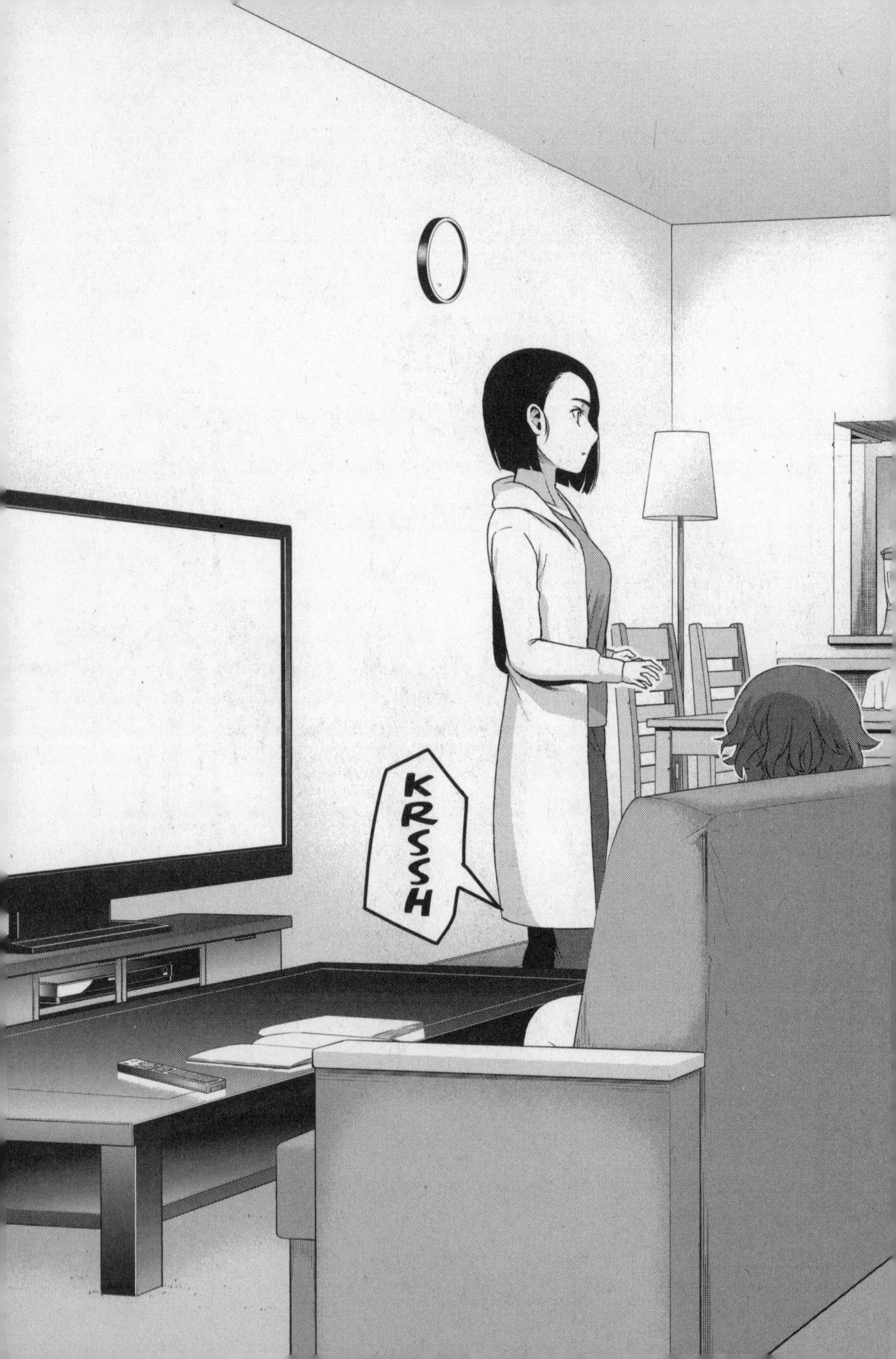
KRSSH

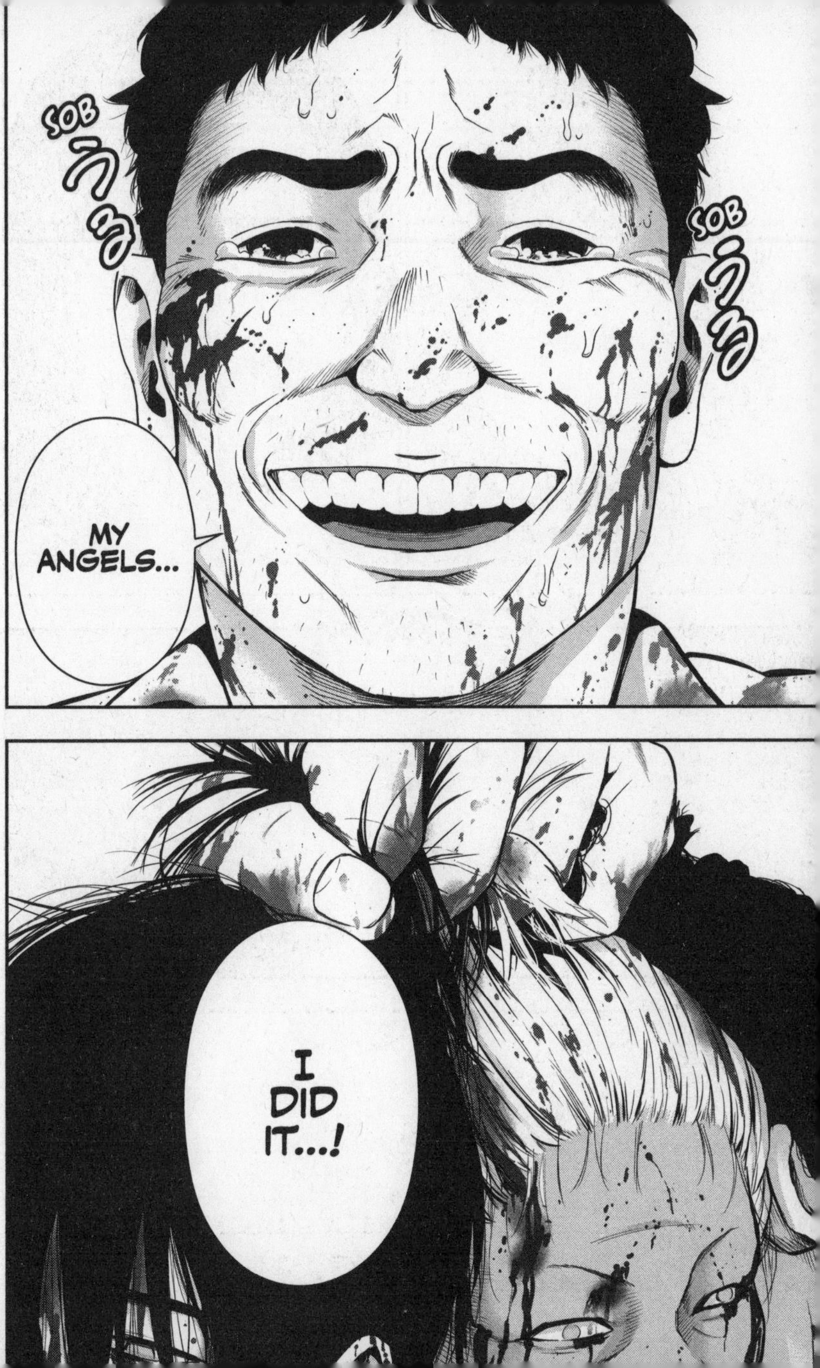
SOB
うう
SOB
うう
MY ANGELS...
I DID IT...!

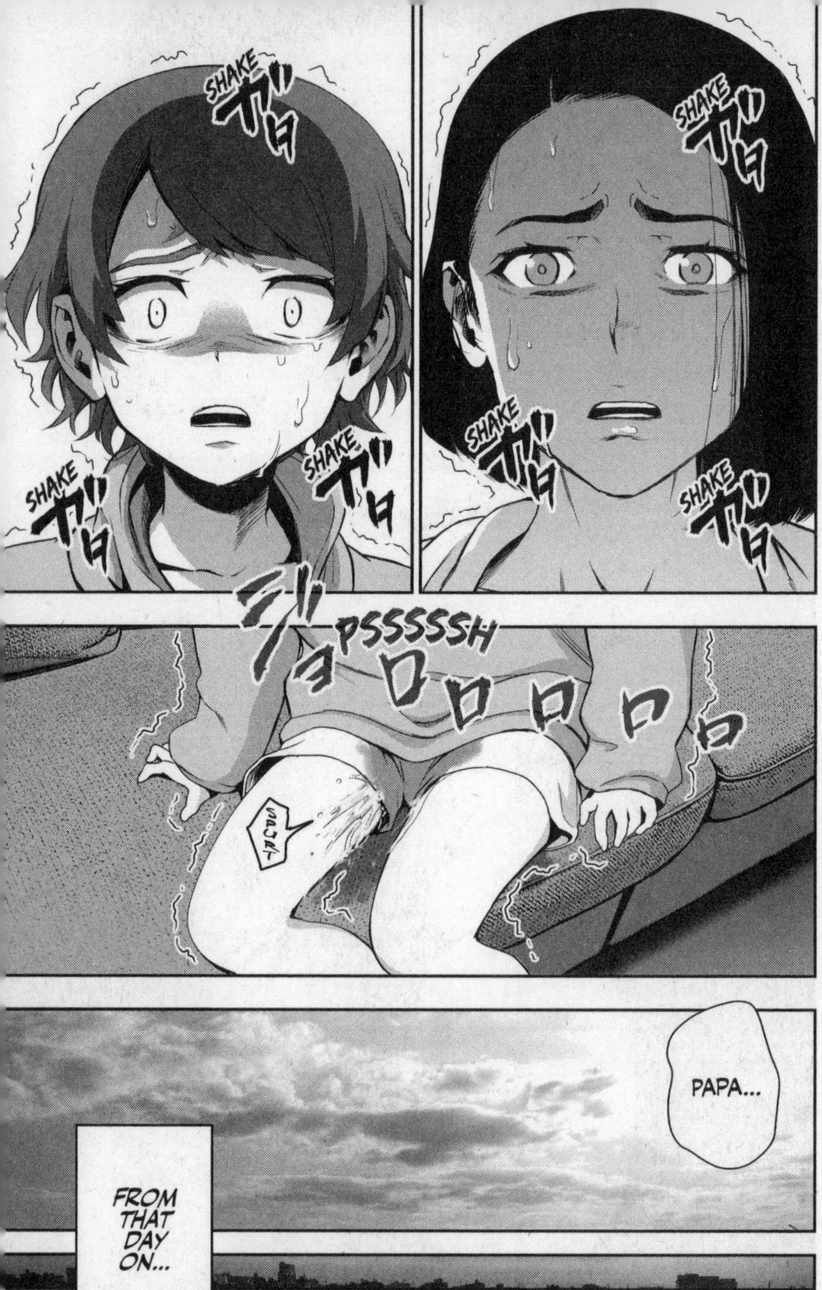
SHAKE ガタ
SHAKE ガタ
SHAKE ガタ
SHAKE ガタ
SHAKE ガタ
SHAKE ガタ
ジョロロロロロ PSSSSSH
SPURT
PAPA...
FROM THAT DAY ON...

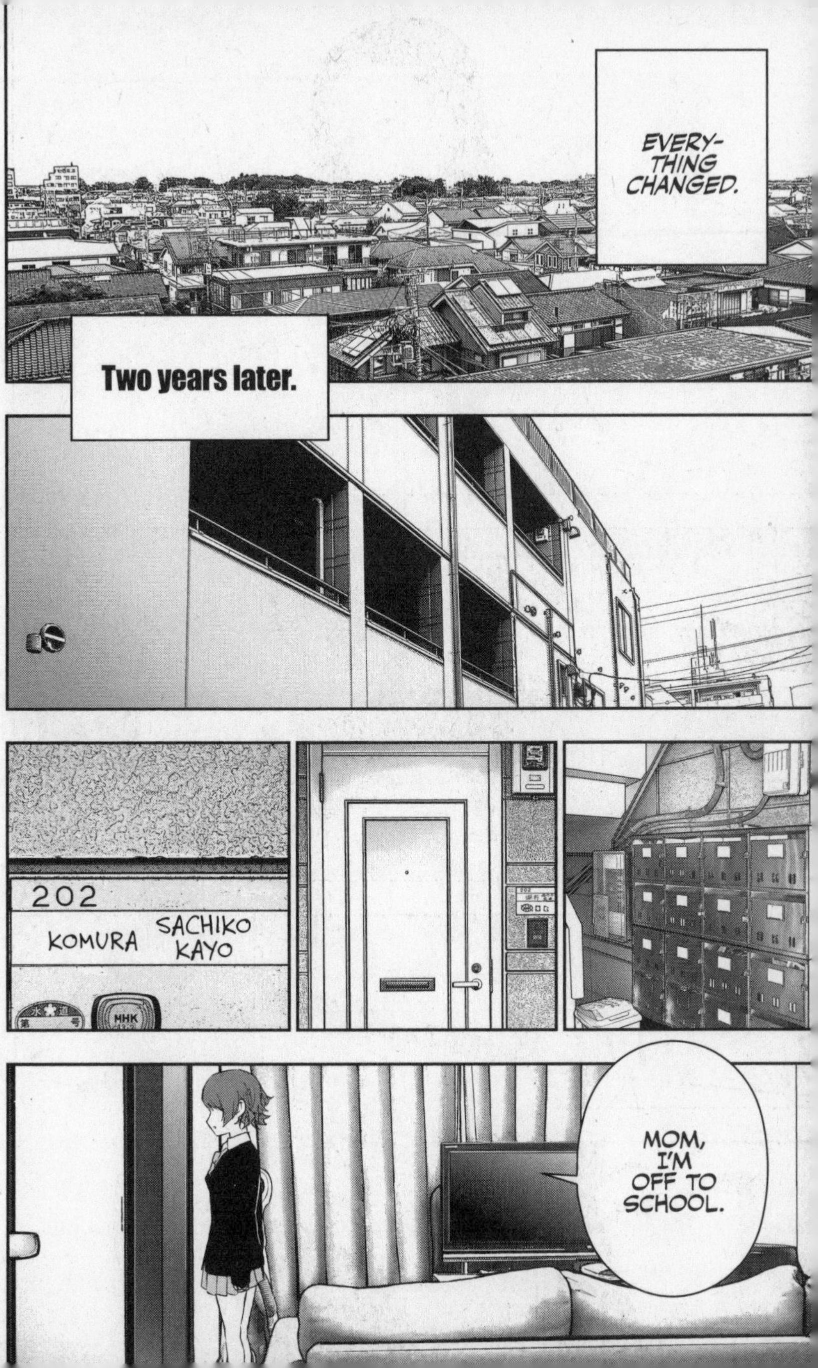
EVERY-THING CHANGED.
Two years later.
202
KOMURA
SACHIKO KAYO
MOM, I'M OFF TO SCHOOL.

I'M SORRY... I COULDN'T MAKE YOUR LUNCH AGAIN TODAY...

I MADE IT MYSELF, SO DON'T WORRY ABOUT IT.

KOFF!

ARE YOU ALL RIGHT?!

DON'T PUSH YOURSELF TOO HARD.

I'M FINE...

KOFF!

KOFF!

17

THANKS...

OKAY, I'M OFF.

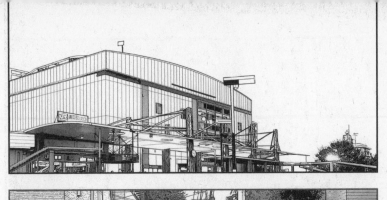

KAYO~!

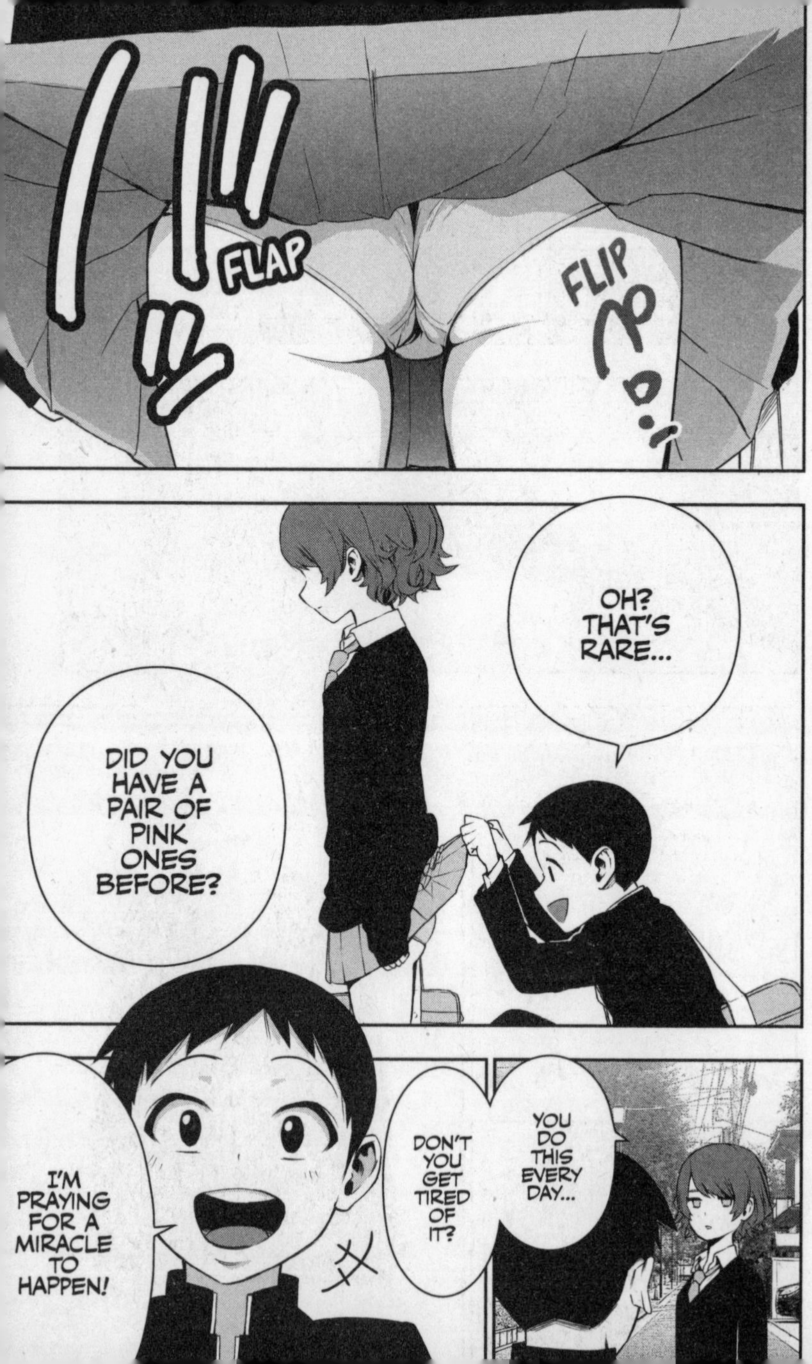
FLIP
FLAP
OH? THAT'S RARE...
DID YOU HAVE A PAIR OF PINK ONES BEFORE?
YOU DO THIS EVERY DAY...
DON'T YOU GET TIRED OF IT?
I'M PRAYING FOR A MIRACLE TO HAPPEN!

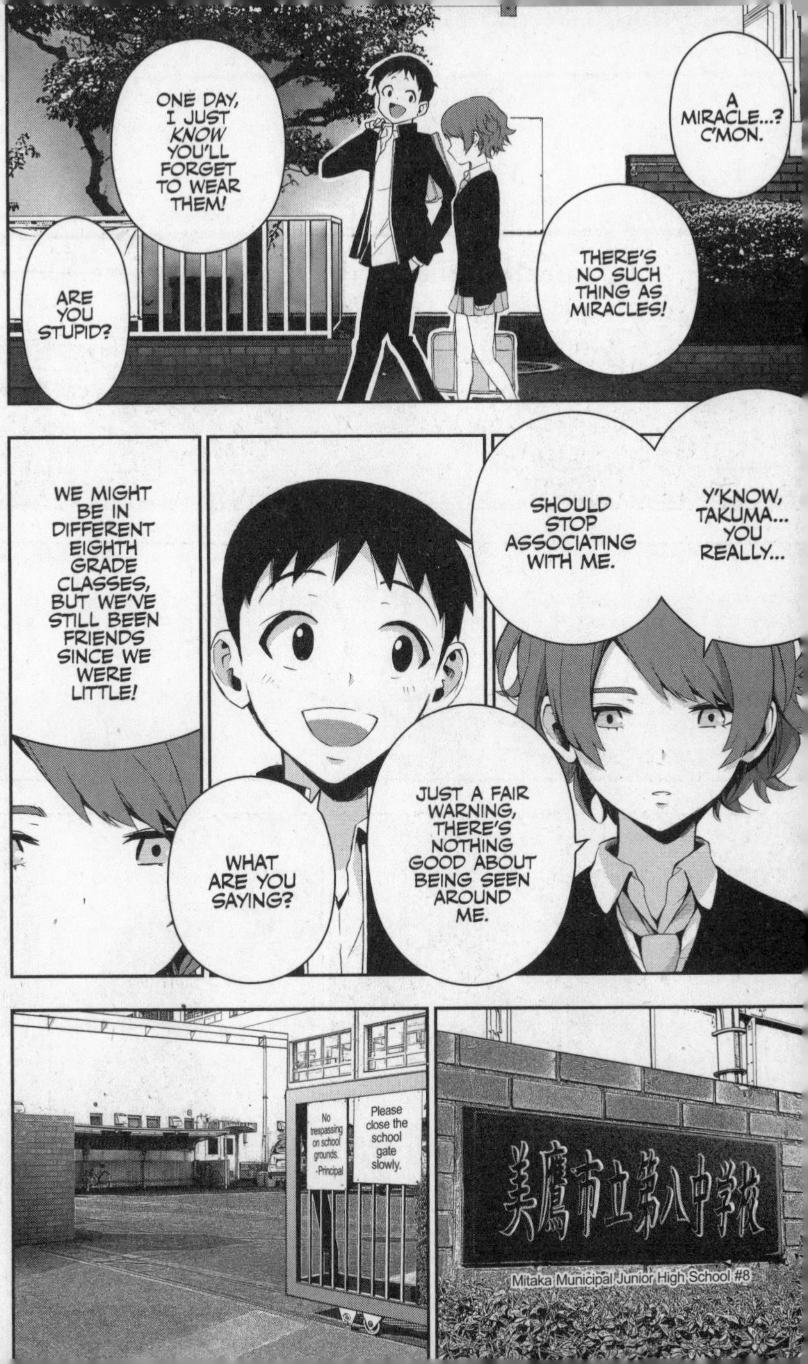
A MIRACLE...? C'MON.
THERE'S NO SUCH THING AS MIRACLES!
ONE DAY, I JUST *KNOW* YOU'LL FORGET TO WEAR THEM!
ARE YOU STUPID?
Y'KNOW, TAKUMA... YOU REALLY...
SHOULD STOP ASSOCIATING WITH ME.
JUST A FAIR WARNING, THERE'S NOTHING GOOD ABOUT BEING SEEN AROUND ME.
WHAT ARE YOU SAYING?
WE MIGHT BE IN DIFFERENT EIGHTH GRADE CLASSES, BUT WE'VE STILL BEEN FRIENDS SINCE WE WERE LITTLE!
美鷹市立第八中学校
Mitaka Municipal Junior High School #8
Please close the school gate slowly.
No trespassing on school grounds. -Principal

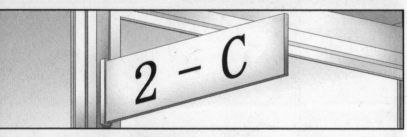

2 − C

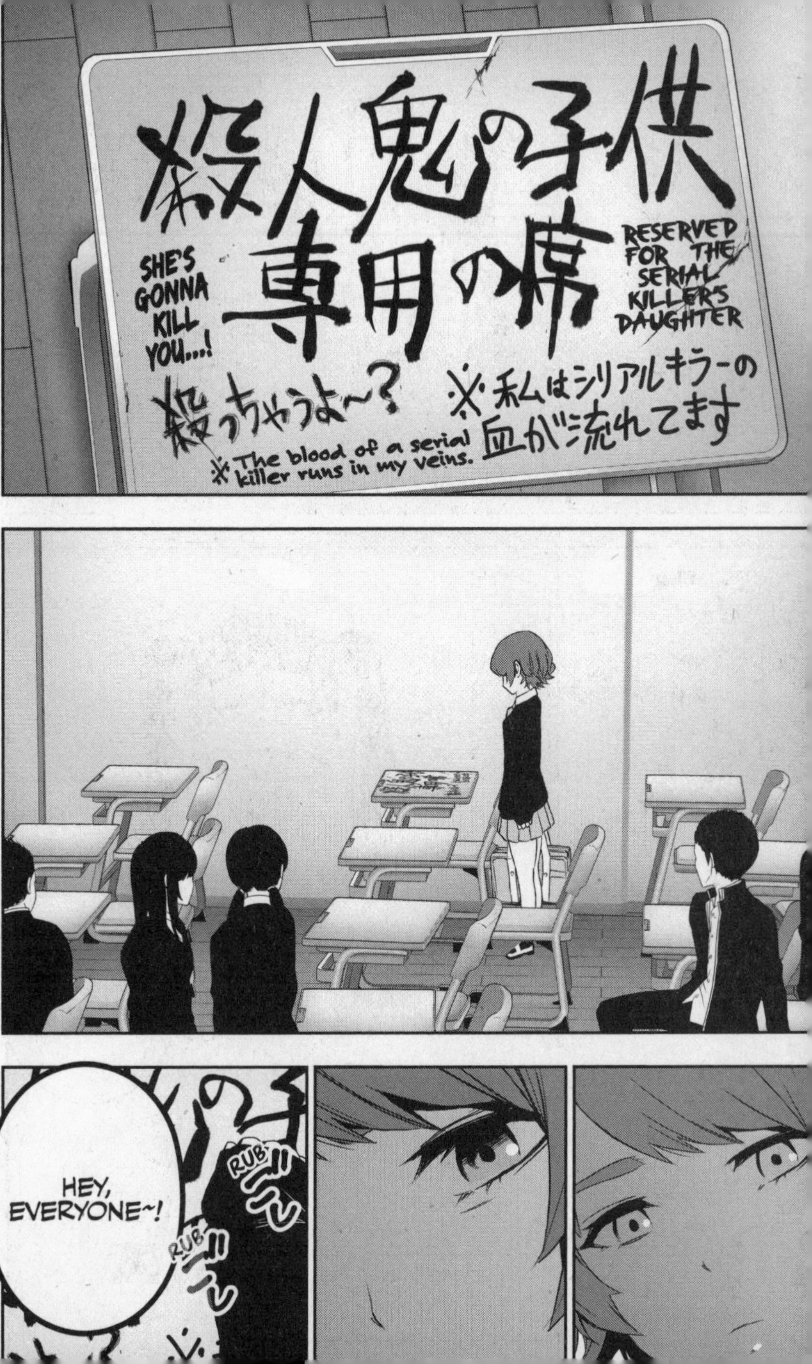
殺人鬼の子供
専用の席
RESERVED FOR THE SERIAL KILLER'S DAUGHTER
SHE'S GONNA KILL YOU...!
※私はシリアルキラーの
血が流れてます
殺っちゃうよ～？
※The blood of a serial killer runs in my veins.
RUB
RUB
HEY, EVERYONE~!

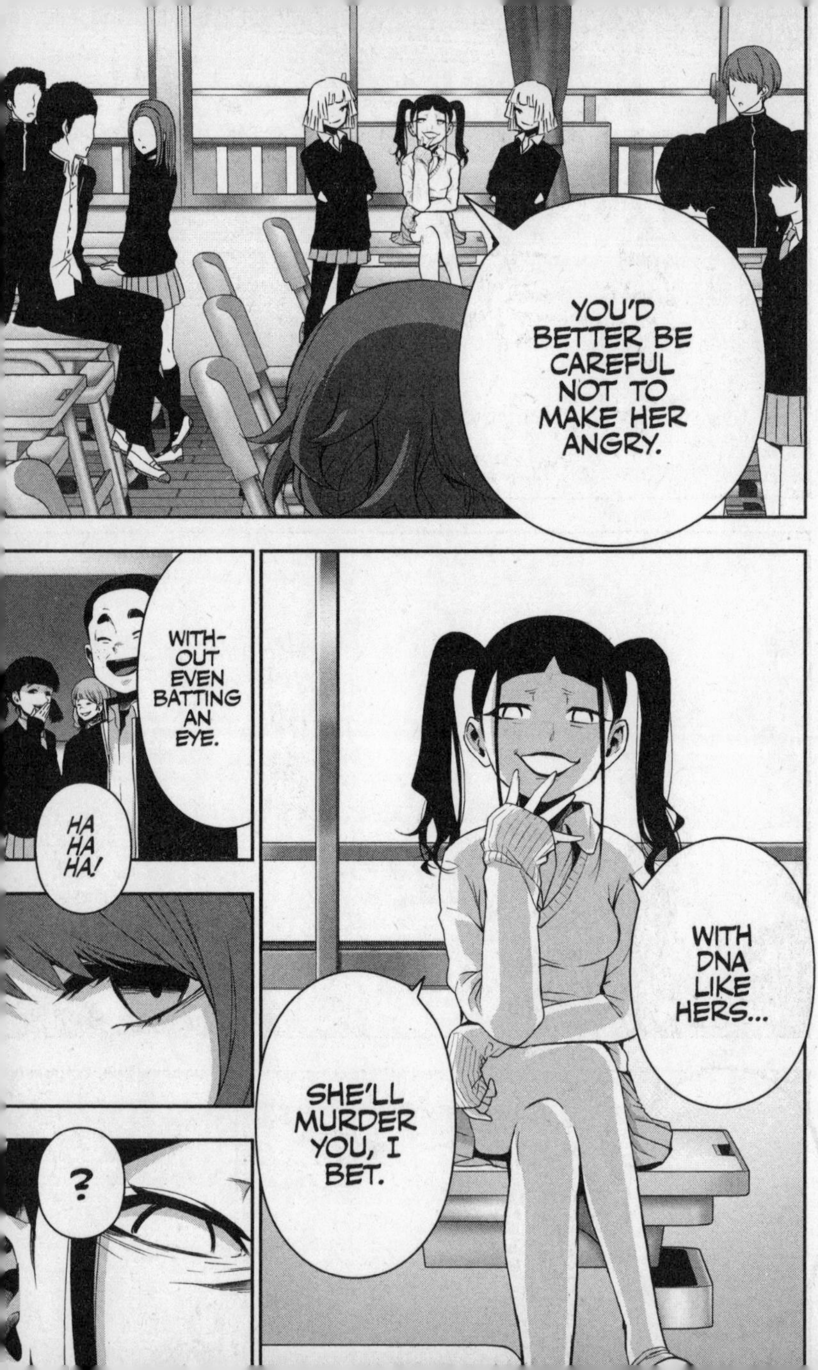
YOU'D BETTER BE CAREFUL NOT TO MAKE HER ANGRY.
WITH DNA LIKE HERS...
SHE'LL MURDER YOU, I BET.
WITH-OUT EVEN BATTING AN EYE.
HA HA HA!
?

YOU'RE SCARING ME.

......!

HEY, WHAT'S WITH THAT LOOK?

MOVE IT!

COME OVER HERE AND APOLOGIZE.

C'MON.

GOOD, JUST LIKE THAT...

GET CLOSER...

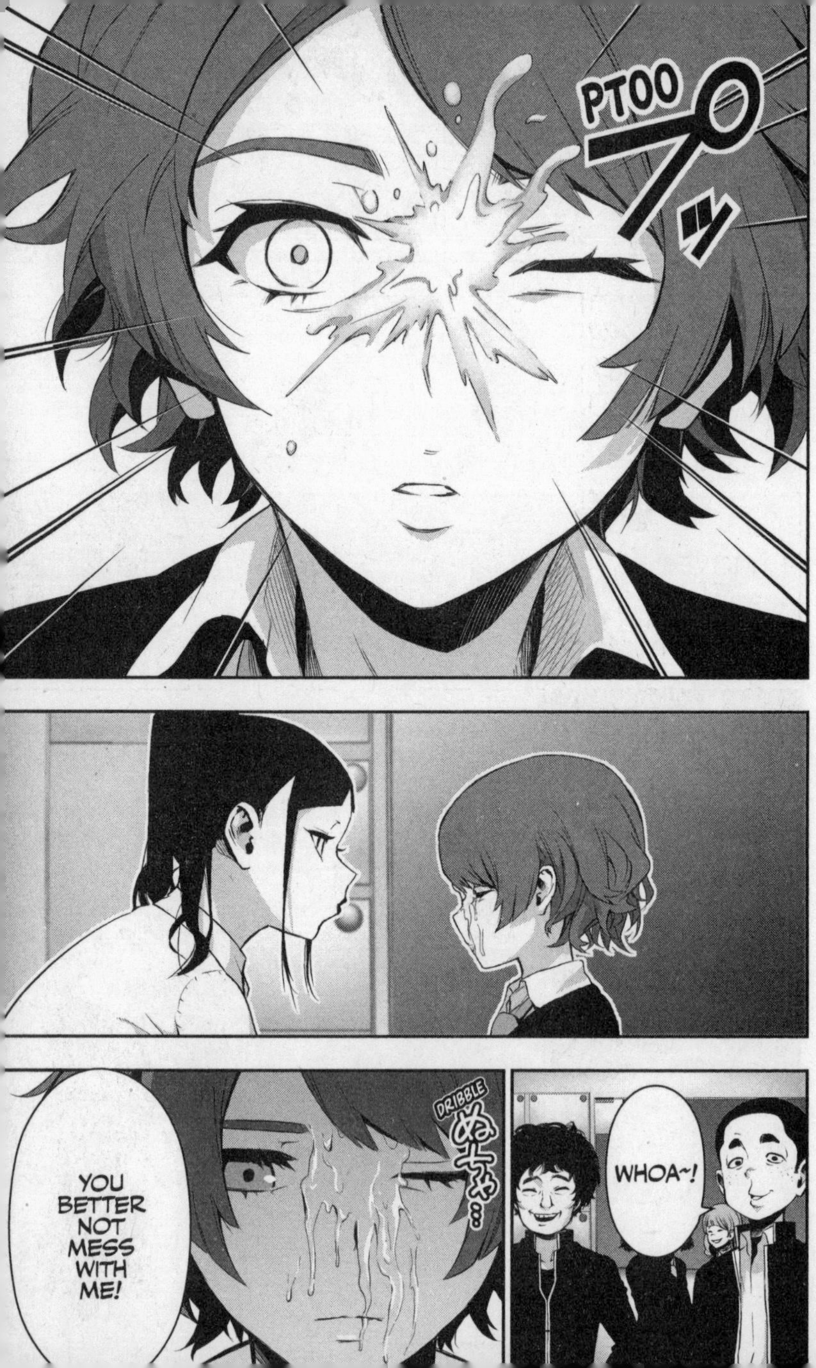
PTOO
WHOA~!
DRIBBLE
ぬちゃ…
YOU BETTER NOT MESS WITH ME!

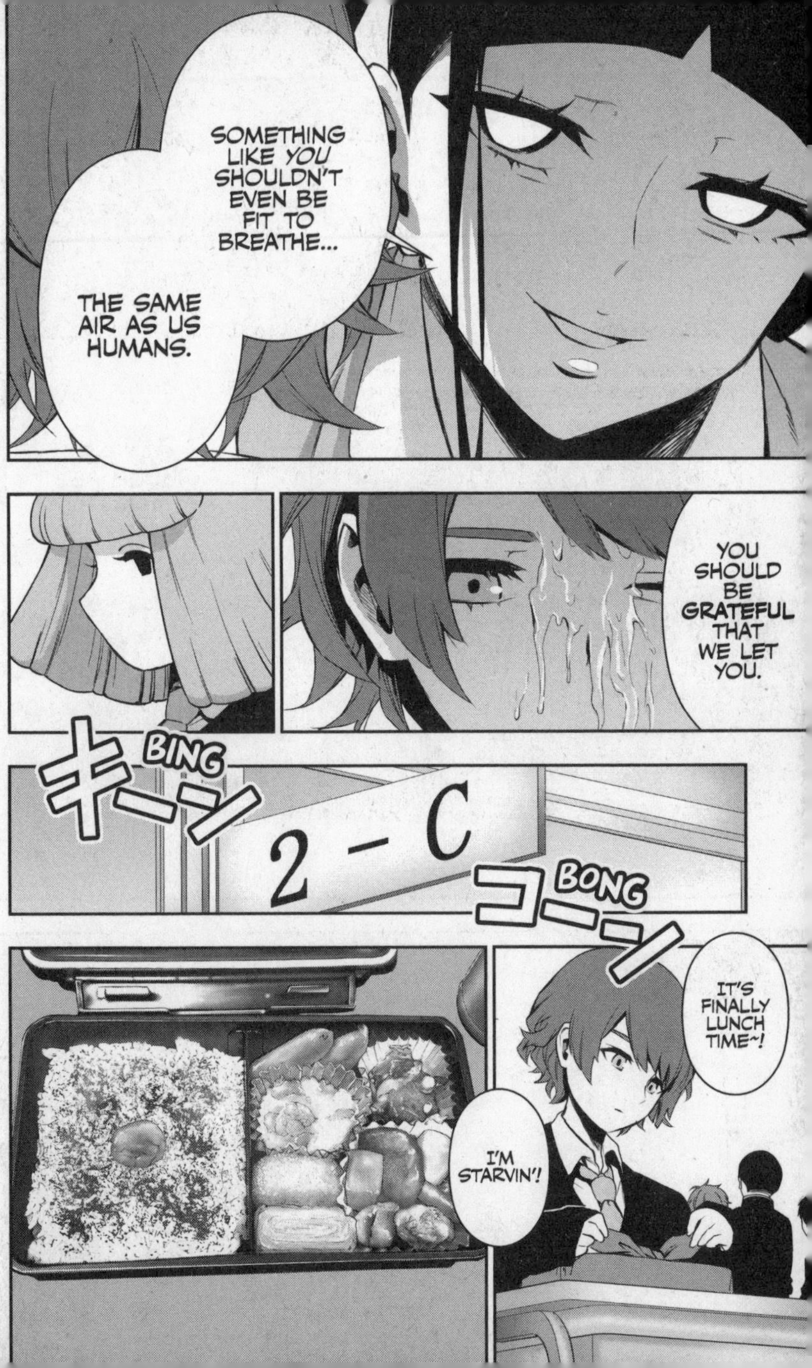
SOMETHING LIKE YOU SHOULDN'T EVEN BE FIT TO BREATHE...
THE SAME AIR AS US HUMANS.
YOU SHOULD BE GRATEFUL THAT WE LET YOU.
BING
BONG
IT'S FINALLY LUNCH TIME~!
I'M STARVIN'!

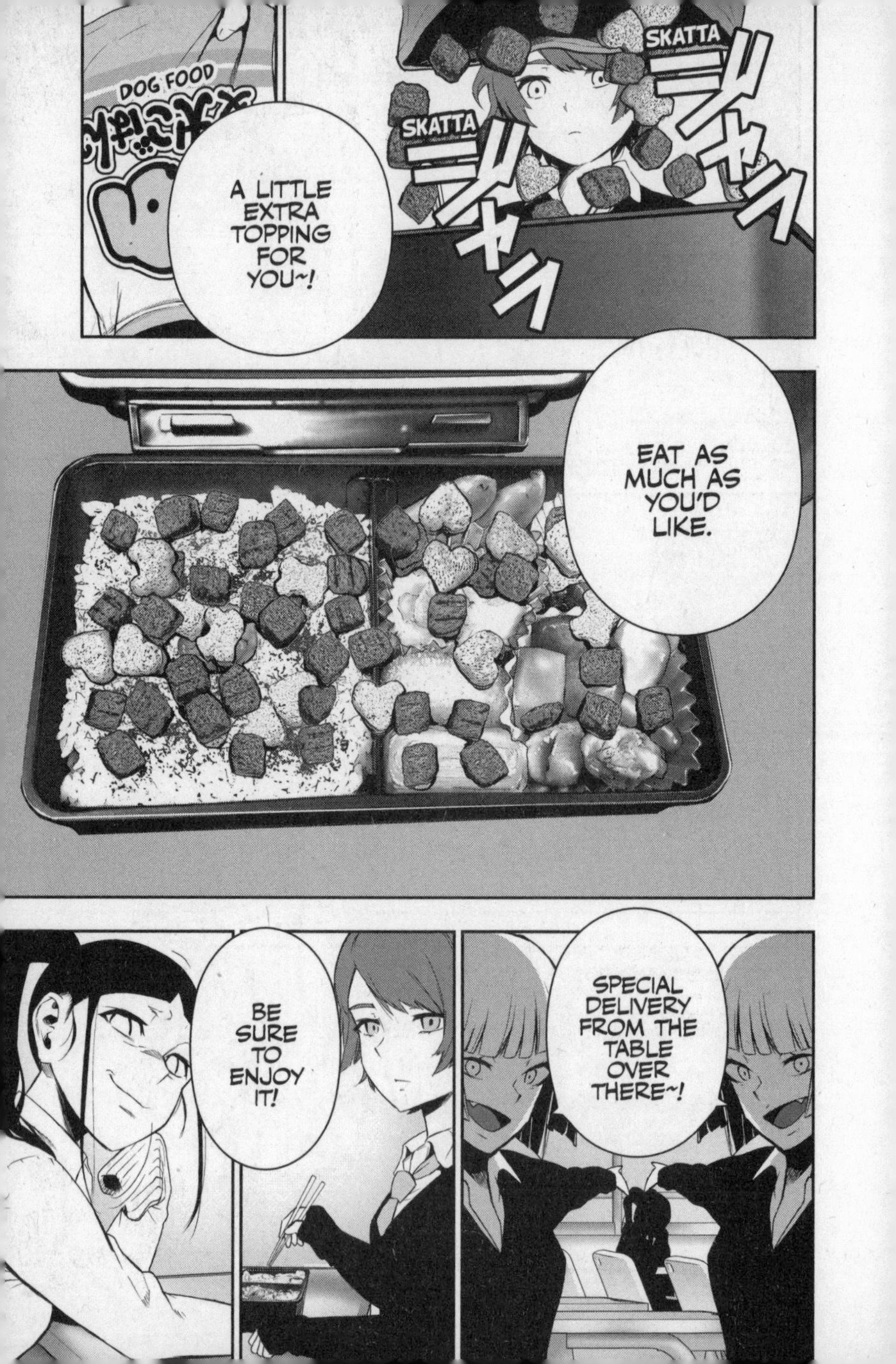
SKATTA
SKATTA
DOG FOOD
A LITTLE EXTRA TOPPING FOR YOU~!
EAT AS MUCH AS YOU'D LIKE.
SPECIAL DELIVERY FROM THE TABLE OVER THERE~!
BE SURE TO ENJOY IT!

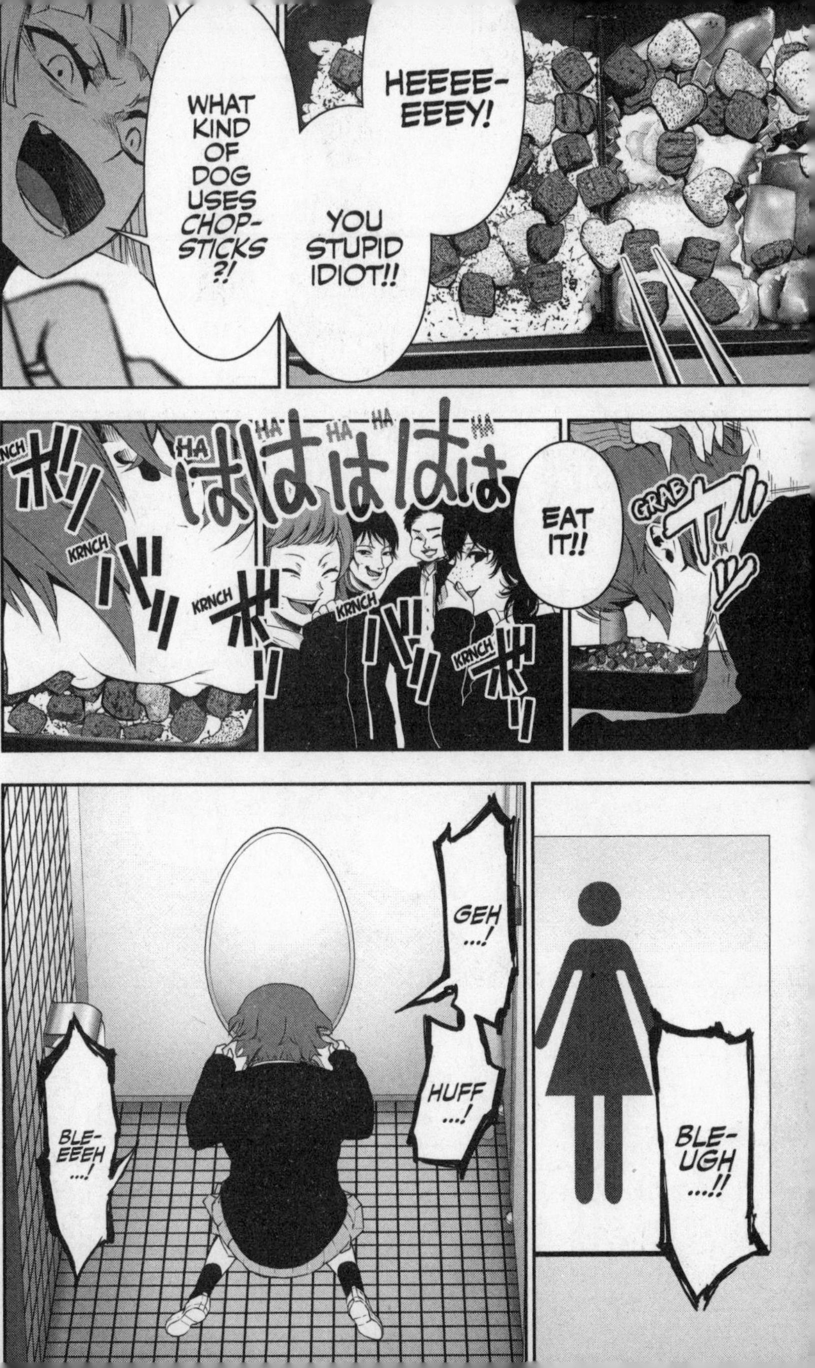
HEEEEE-EEEY!
YOU STUPID IDIOT!!
WHAT KIND OF DOG USES CHOP-STICKS ?!
GRAB
EAT IT!!
HA HA HA HA HA
ははははは
KRNCH
KRNCH
KRNCH
KRNCH
KRNCH
BLE-UGH ...!!
GEH ...!
HUFF ...!
BLE-EEEH ...!

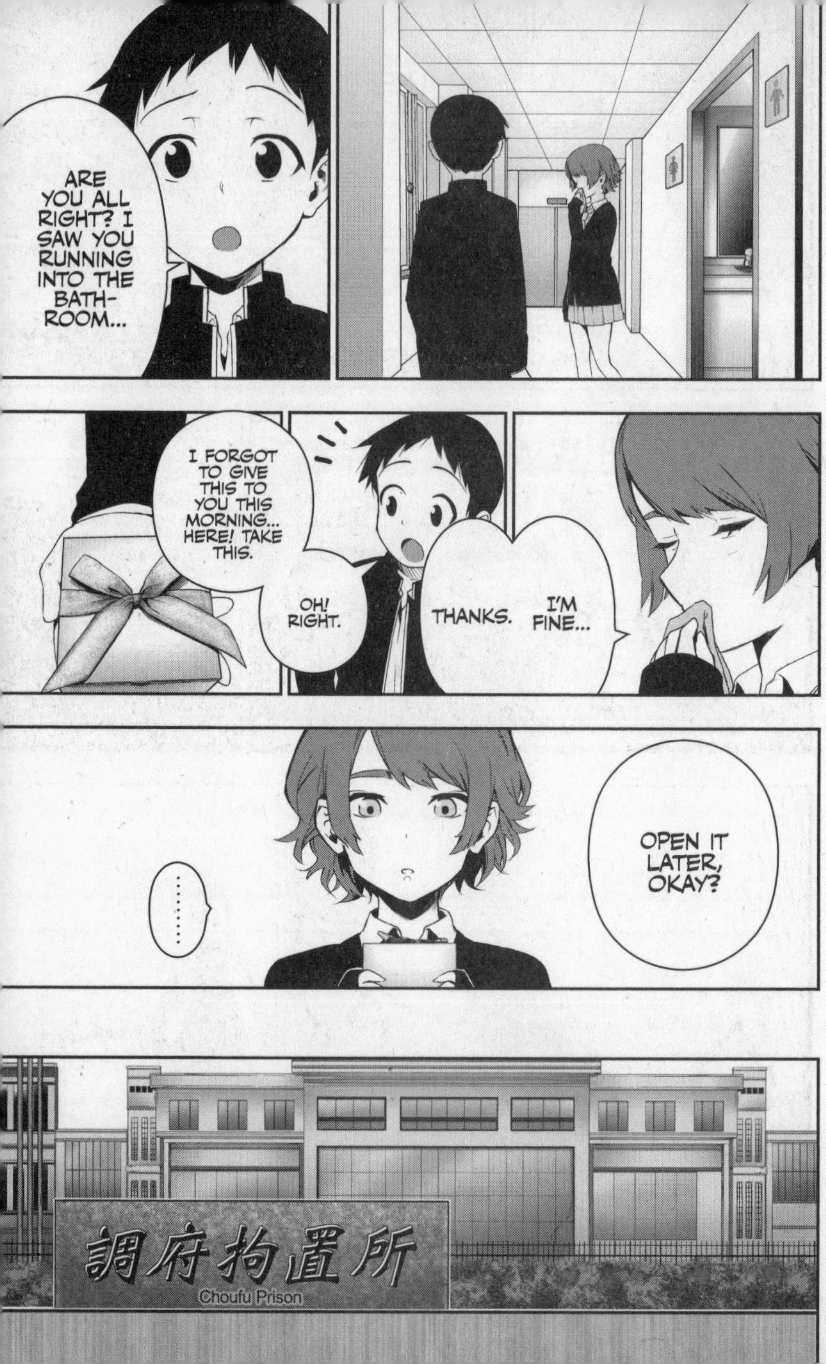
ARE YOU ALL RIGHT? I SAW YOU RUNNING INTO THE BATH-ROOM...
I'M FINE...
THANKS.
OH! RIGHT.
I FORGOT TO GIVE THIS TO YOU THIS MORNING... HERE! TAKE THIS.
OPEN IT LATER, OKAY?
......
調府拘置所
Choufu Prison

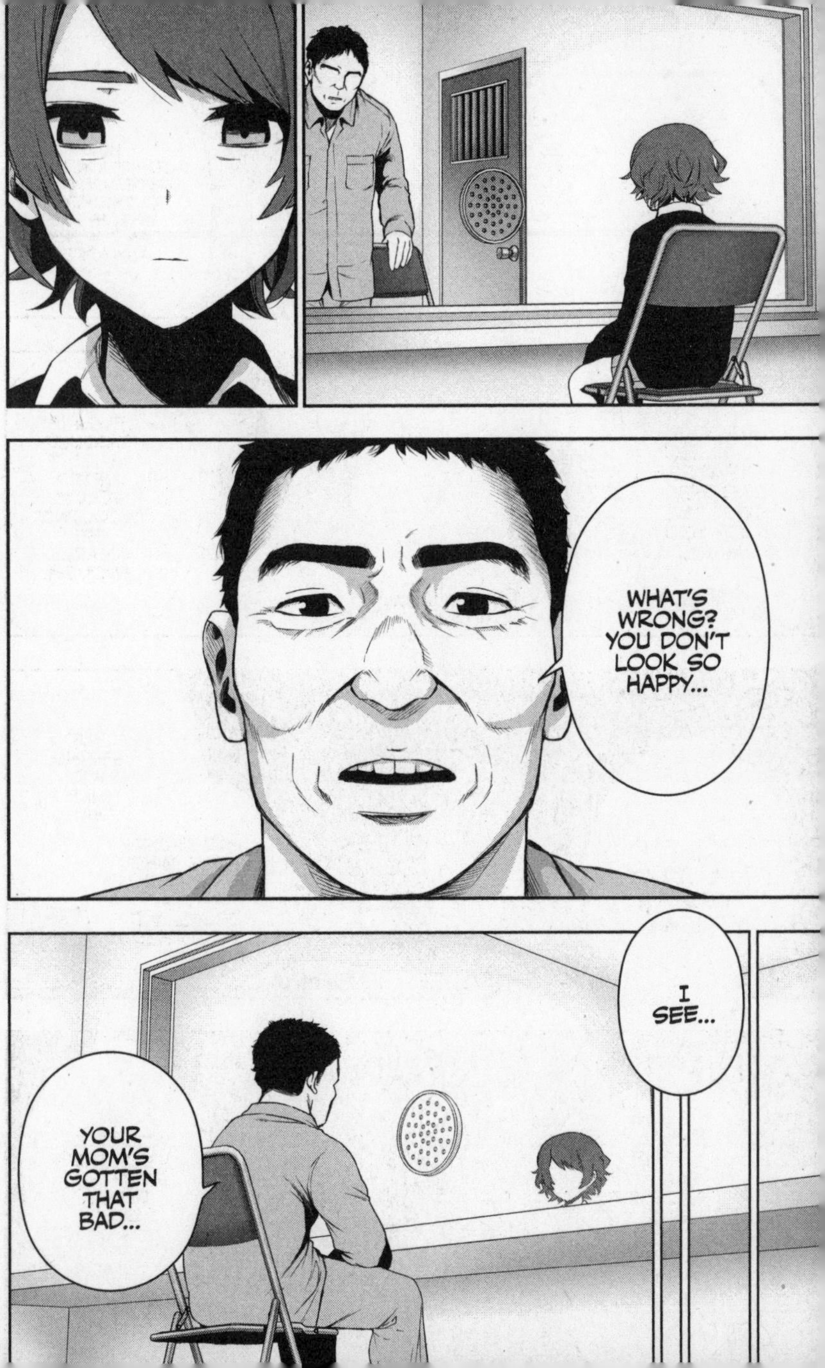
WHAT'S WRONG? YOU DON'T LOOK SO HAPPY...
I SEE...
YOUR MOM'S GOTTEN THAT BAD...

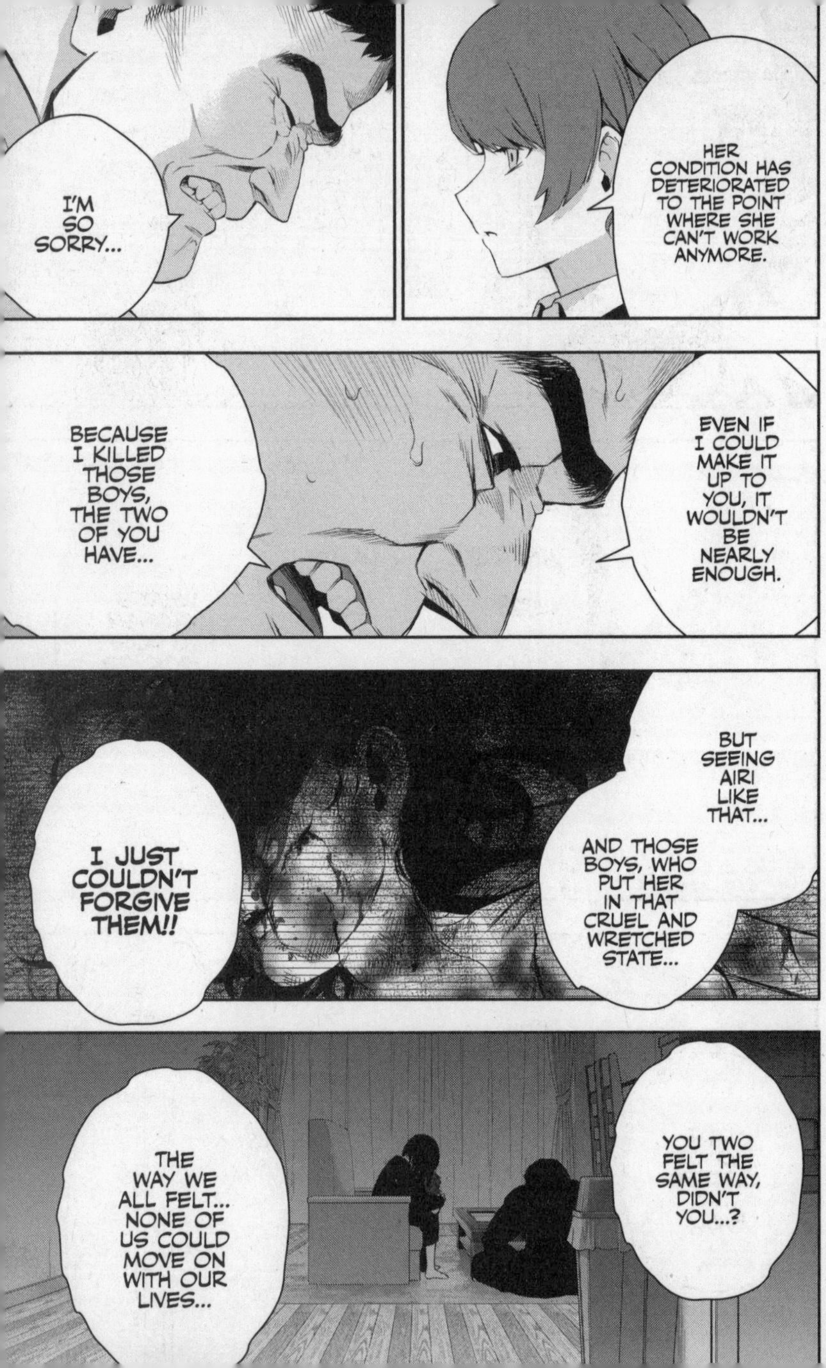
HER CONDITION HAS DETERIORATED TO THE POINT WHERE SHE CAN'T WORK ANYMORE.
I'M SO SORRY...
EVEN IF I COULD MAKE IT UP TO YOU, IT WOULDN'T BE NEARLY ENOUGH.
BECAUSE I KILLED THOSE BOYS, THE TWO OF YOU HAVE...
BUT SEEING AIRI LIKE THAT...
AND THOSE BOYS, WHO PUT HER IN THAT CRUEL AND WRETCHED STATE...
I JUST COULDN'T FORGIVE THEM!!
YOU TWO FELT THE SAME WAY, DIDN'T YOU...?
THE WAY WE ALL FELT... NONE OF US COULD MOVE ON WITH OUR LIVES...

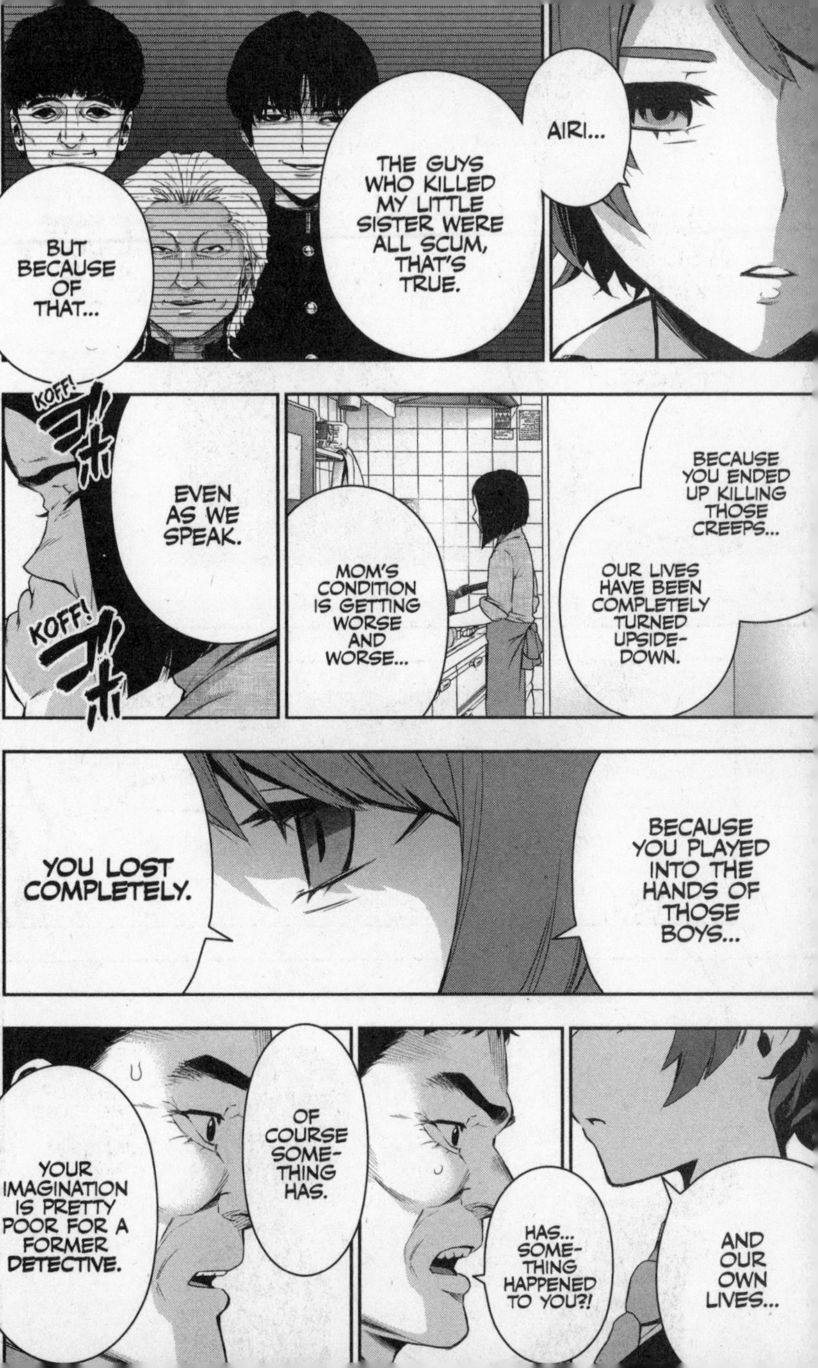
AIRI...
THE GUYS WHO KILLED MY LITTLE SISTER WERE ALL SCUM, THAT'S TRUE.
BUT BECAUSE OF THAT...
BECAUSE YOU ENDED UP KILLING THOSE CREEPS...
OUR LIVES HAVE BEEN COMPLETELY TURNED UPSIDE-DOWN.
MOM'S CONDITION IS GETTING WORSE AND WORSE...
EVEN AS WE SPEAK.
KOFF!
KOFF!
BECAUSE YOU PLAYED INTO THE HANDS OF THOSE BOYS...
YOU LOST COMPLETELY.
AND OUR OWN LIVES...
HAS... SOMETHING HAPPENED TO YOU?!
OF COURSE SOMETHING HAS.
YOUR IMAGINATION IS PRETTY POOR FOR A FORMER DETECTIVE.

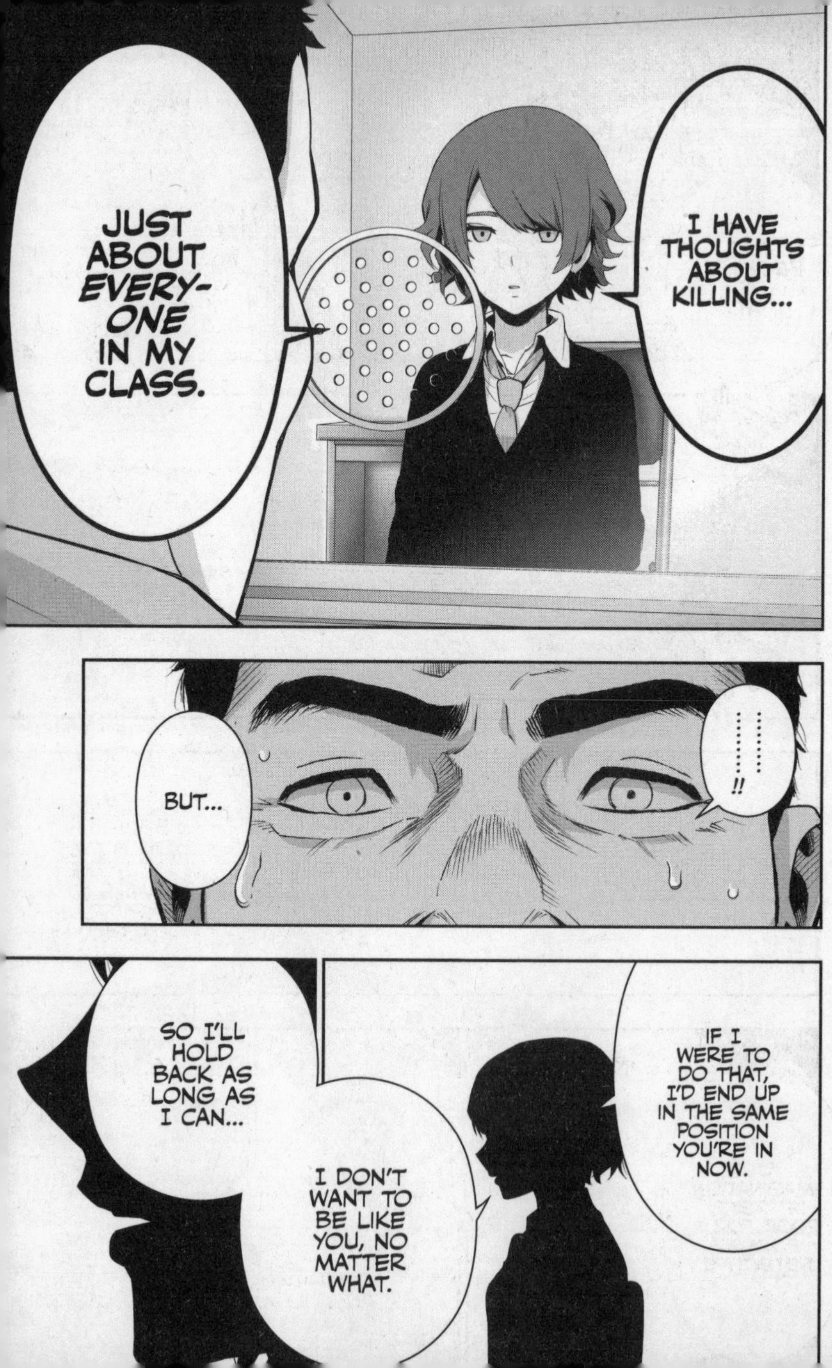
I HAVE THOUGHTS ABOUT KILLING...
JUST ABOUT EVERY-ONE IN MY CLASS.
......!!
BUT...
IF I WERE TO DO THAT, I'D END UP IN THE SAME POSITION YOU'RE IN NOW.
I DON'T WANT TO BE LIKE YOU, NO MATTER WHAT.
SO I'LL HOLD BACK AS LONG AS I CAN...

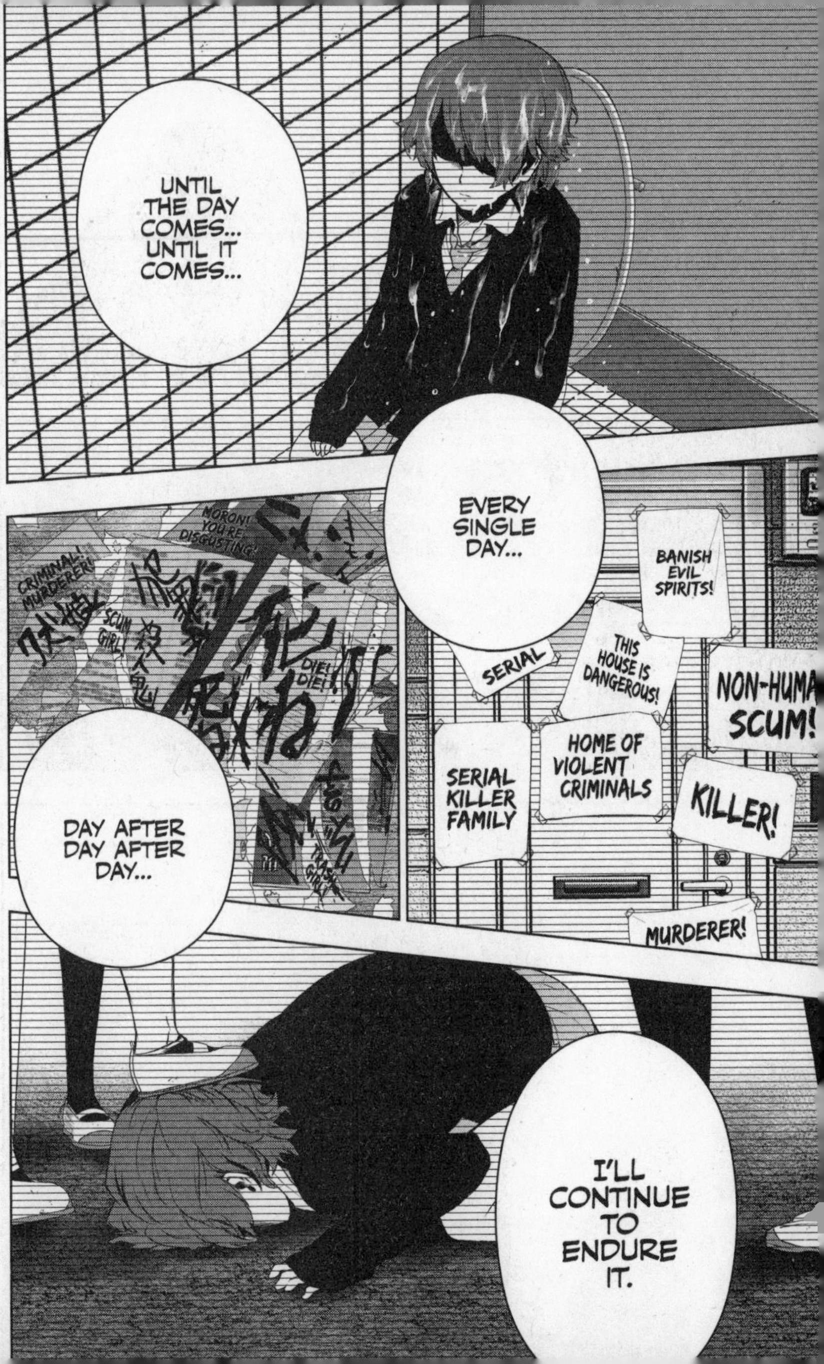
UNTIL THE DAY COMES... UNTIL IT COMES...
EVERY SINGLE DAY...
BANISH EVIL SPIRITS!
THIS HOUSE IS DANGEROUS!
NON-HUMA
SCUM!
SERIAL
HOME OF VIOLENT CRIMINALS
SERIAL KILLER FAMILY
KILLER!
MURDERER!
MORON! YOU'RE DISGUSTING!
CRIMINAL! MURDERER!
SCUM GIRL!
DIE! DIE!
TRASH GIRL
DAY AFTER DAY AFTER DAY...
I'LL CONTINUE TO ENDURE IT.

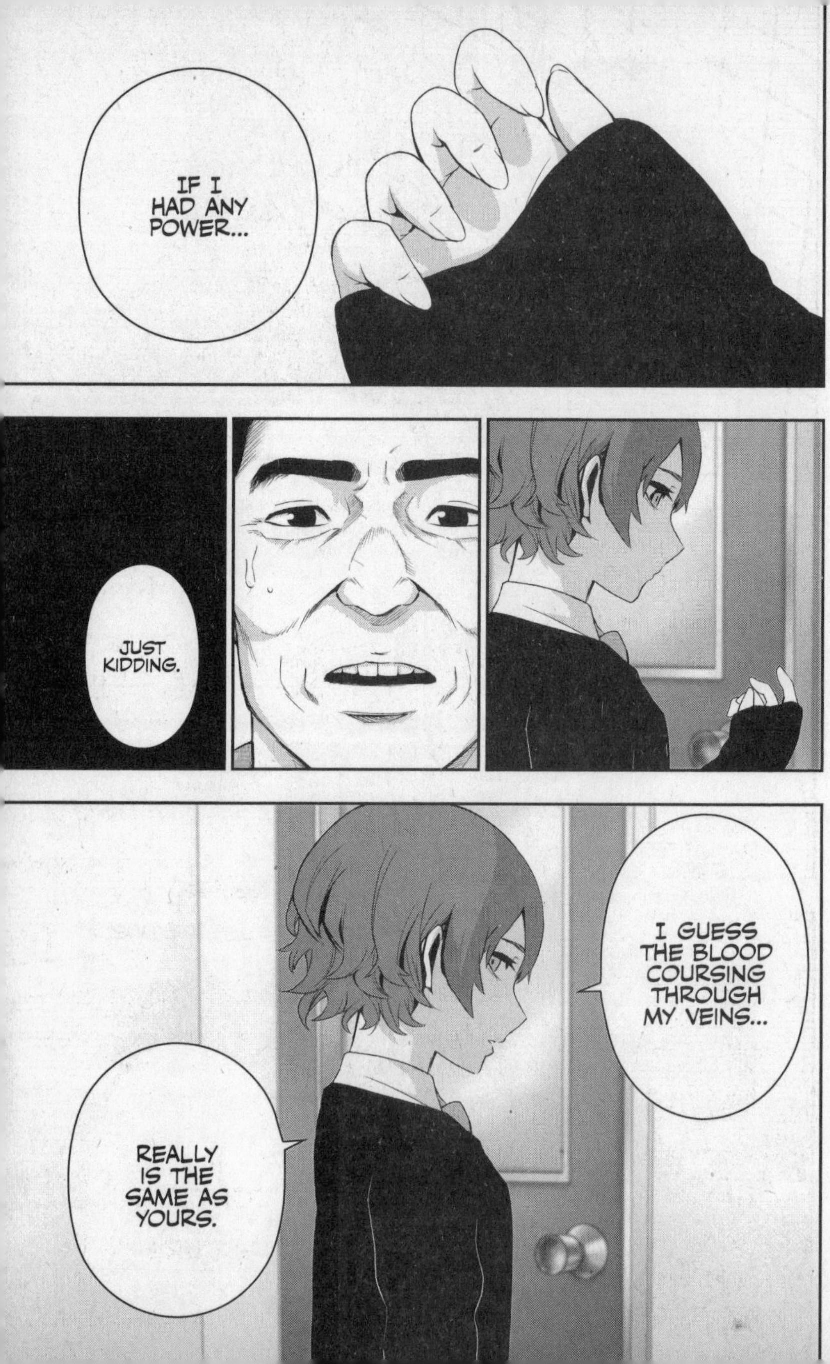
IF I HAD ANY POWER...
JUST KIDDING.
I GUESS THE BLOOD COURSING THROUGH MY VEINS...
REALLY IS THE SAME AS YOURS.

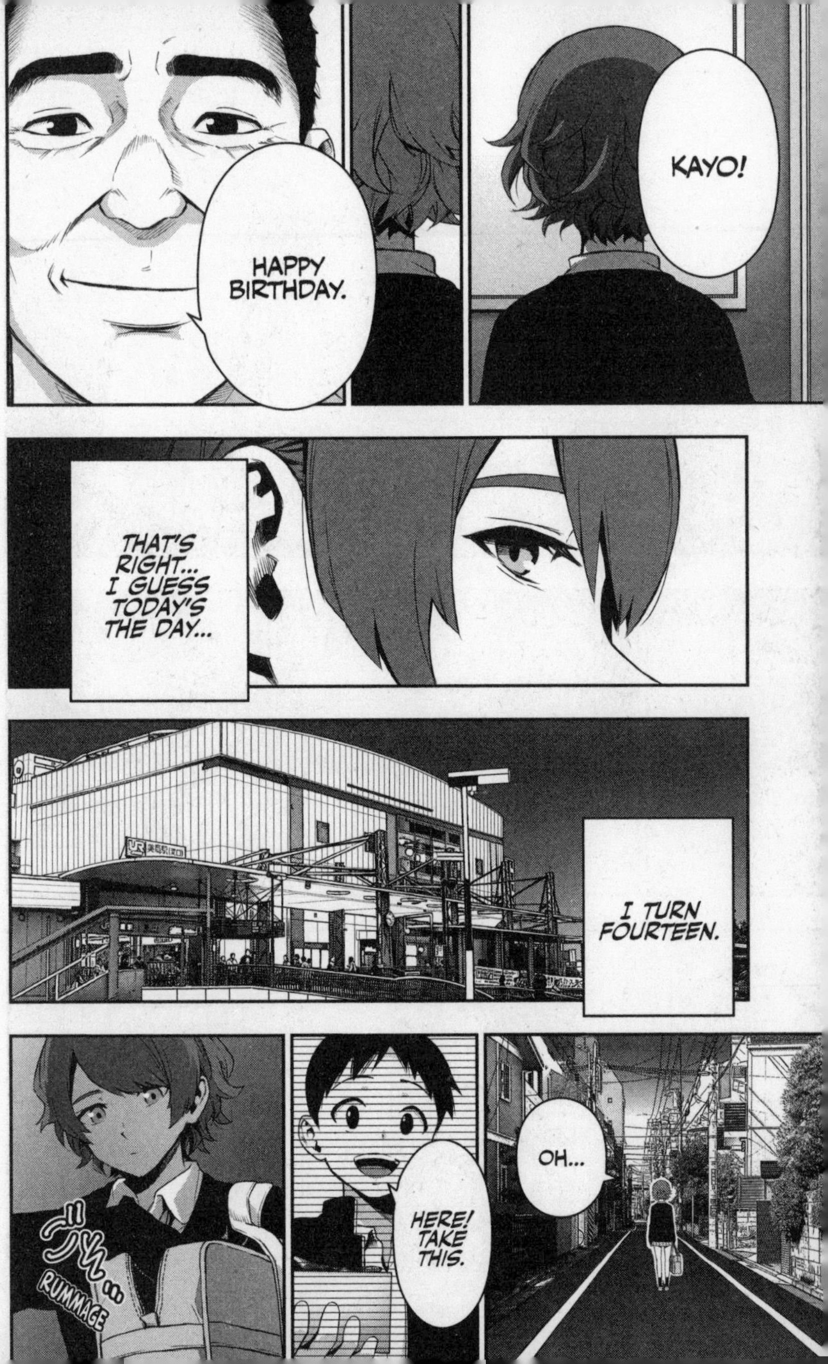
KAYO!
HAPPY BIRTHDAY.
THAT'S RIGHT... I GUESS TODAY'S THE DAY...
I TURN FOURTEEN.
OH...
HERE! TAKE THIS.
RUMMAGE

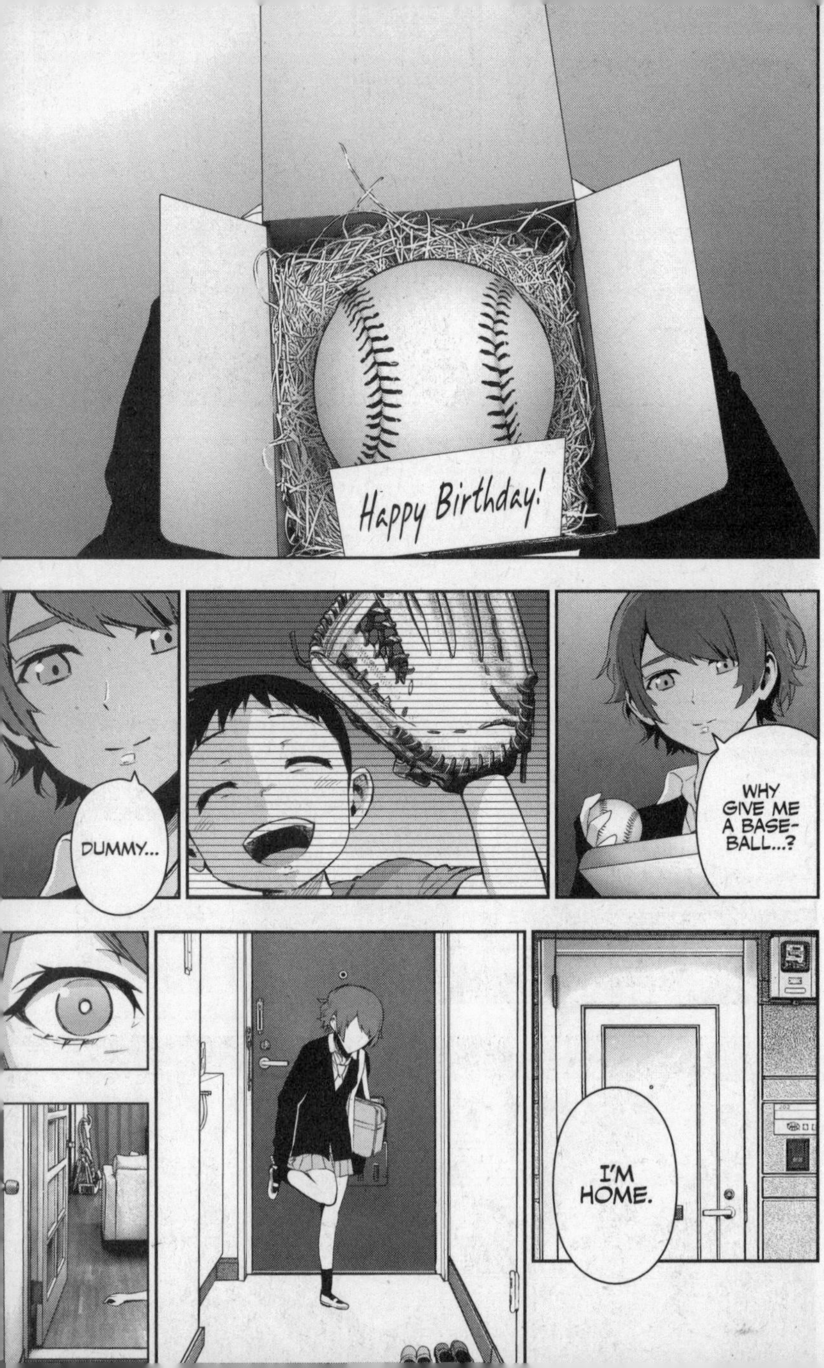
Happy Birthday!
WHY GIVE ME A BASE-BALL...?
DUMMY...
I'M HOME.

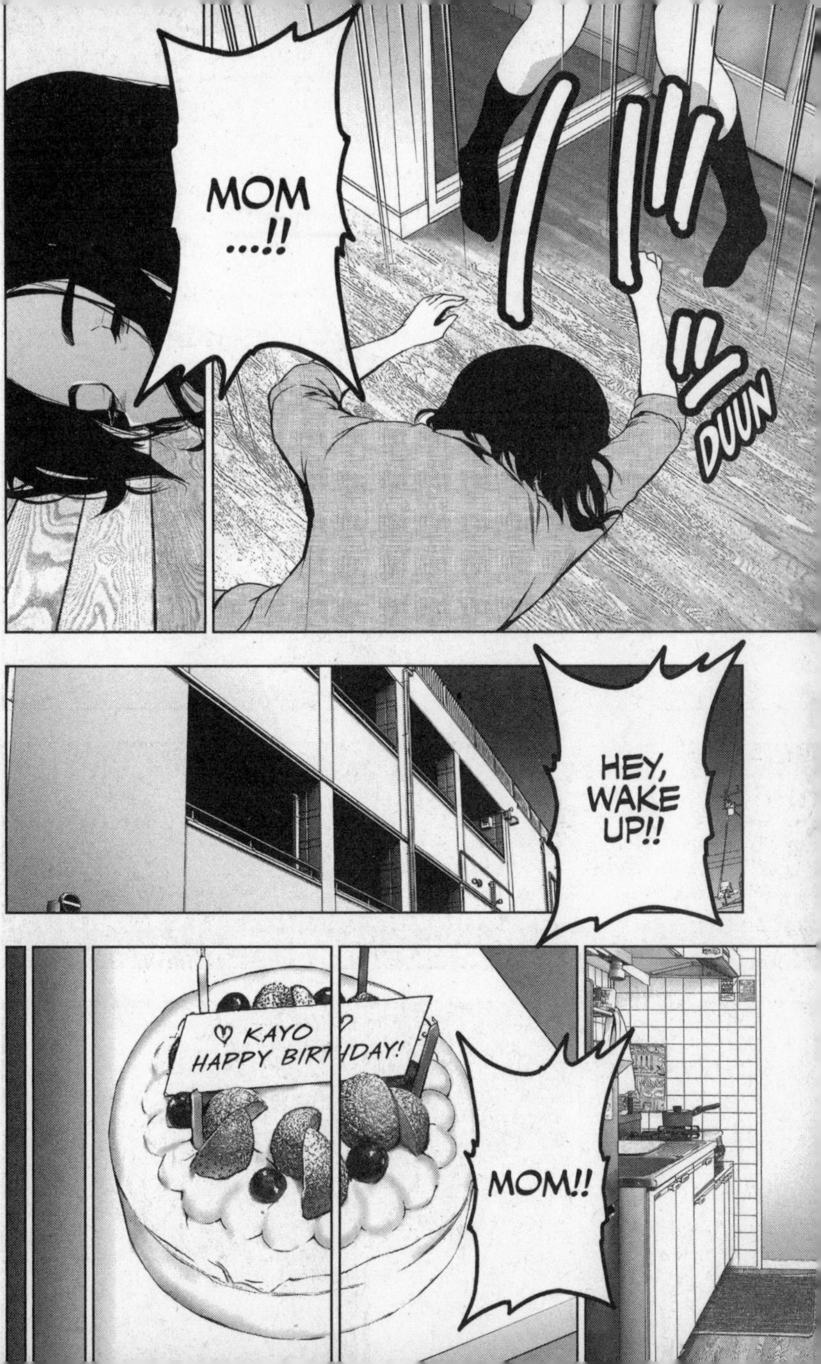
DUUN
MOM ...!!
HEY, WAKE UP!!
MOM!!
♡ KAYO ♡
HAPPY BIRTHDAY!

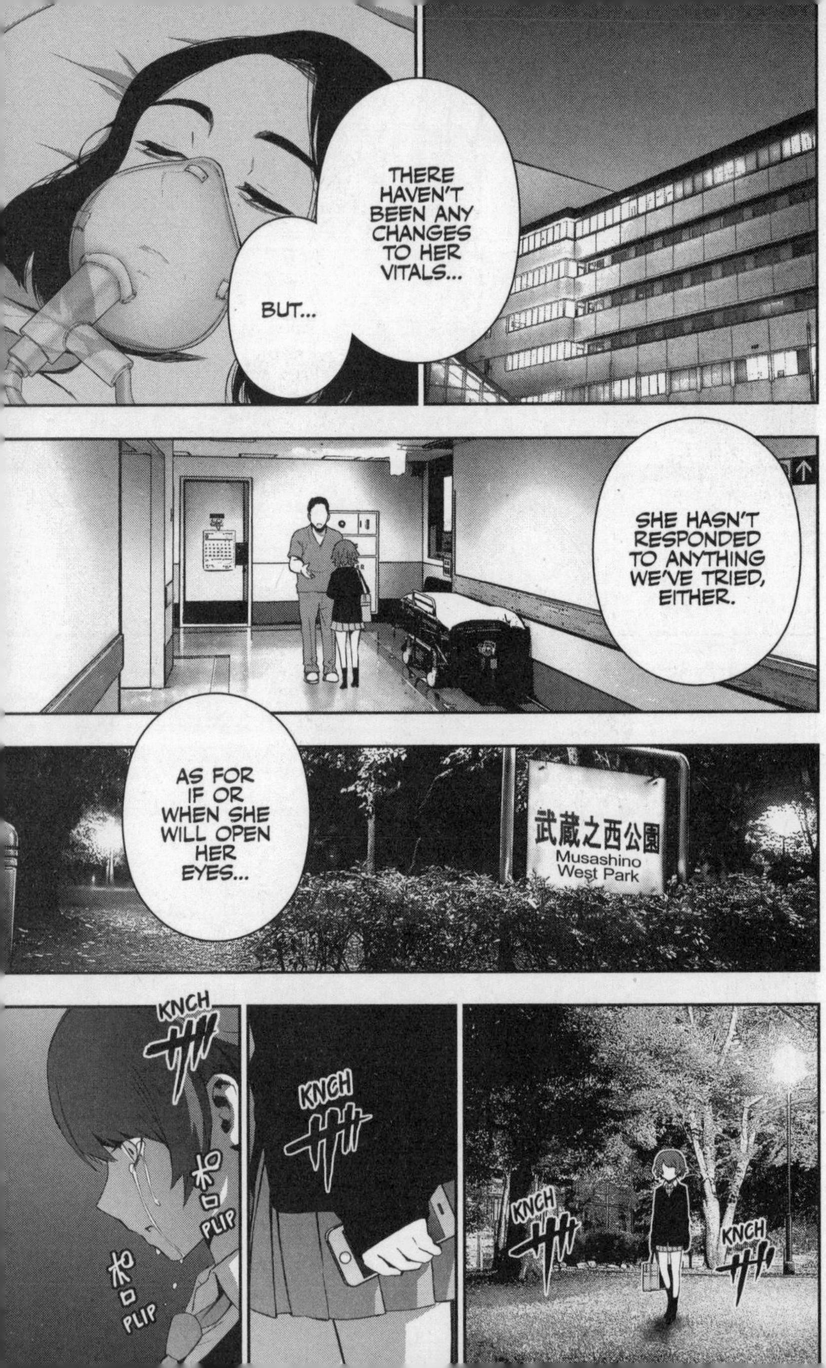
THERE HAVEN'T BEEN ANY CHANGES TO HER VITALS...
BUT...
SHE HASN'T RESPONDED TO ANYTHING WE'VE TRIED, EITHER.
武蔵之西公園
Musashino West Park
AS FOR IF OR WHEN SHE WILL OPEN HER EYES...
KNCH
KNCH
KNCH
KNCH
ポロ
PLIP
ポロ
PLIP

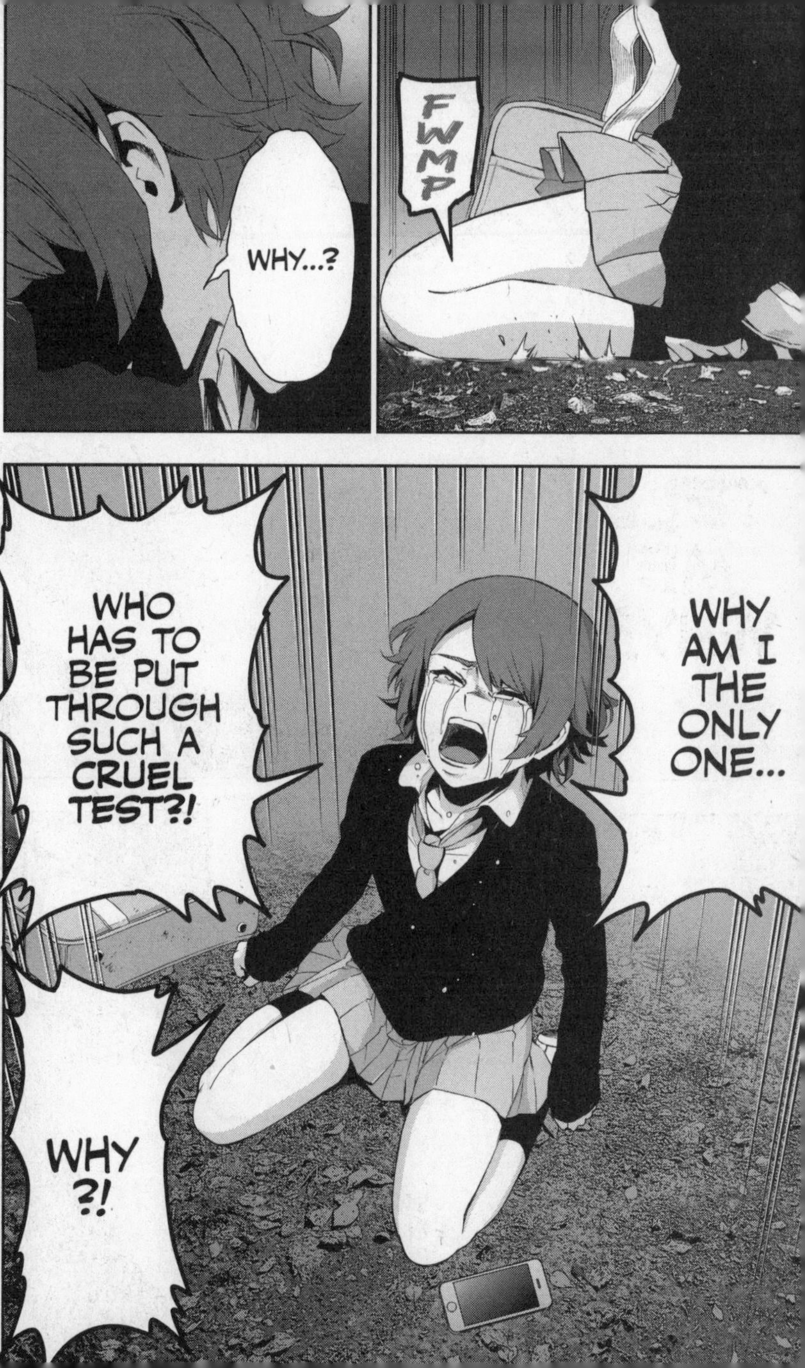
FWMP
WHY...?
WHY AM I THE ONLY ONE...
WHO HAS TO BE PUT THROUGH SUCH A CRUEL TEST?!
WHY?!

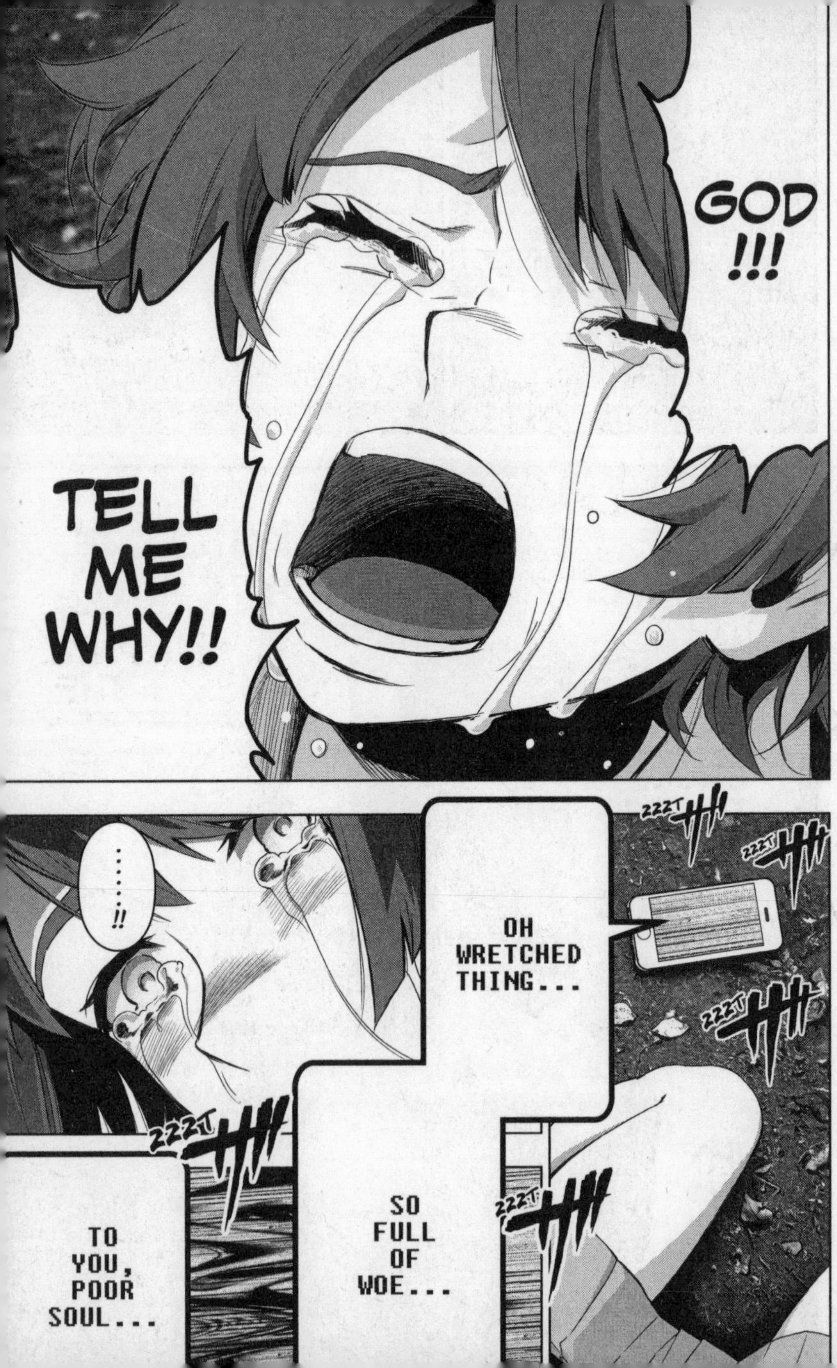
GOD!!!
TELL ME WHY!!
ZZZT
ZZZT
OH WRETCHED THING...
ZZZT
ZZZT
SO FULL OF WOE...
......!!
ZZZT
TO YOU, POOR SOUL...

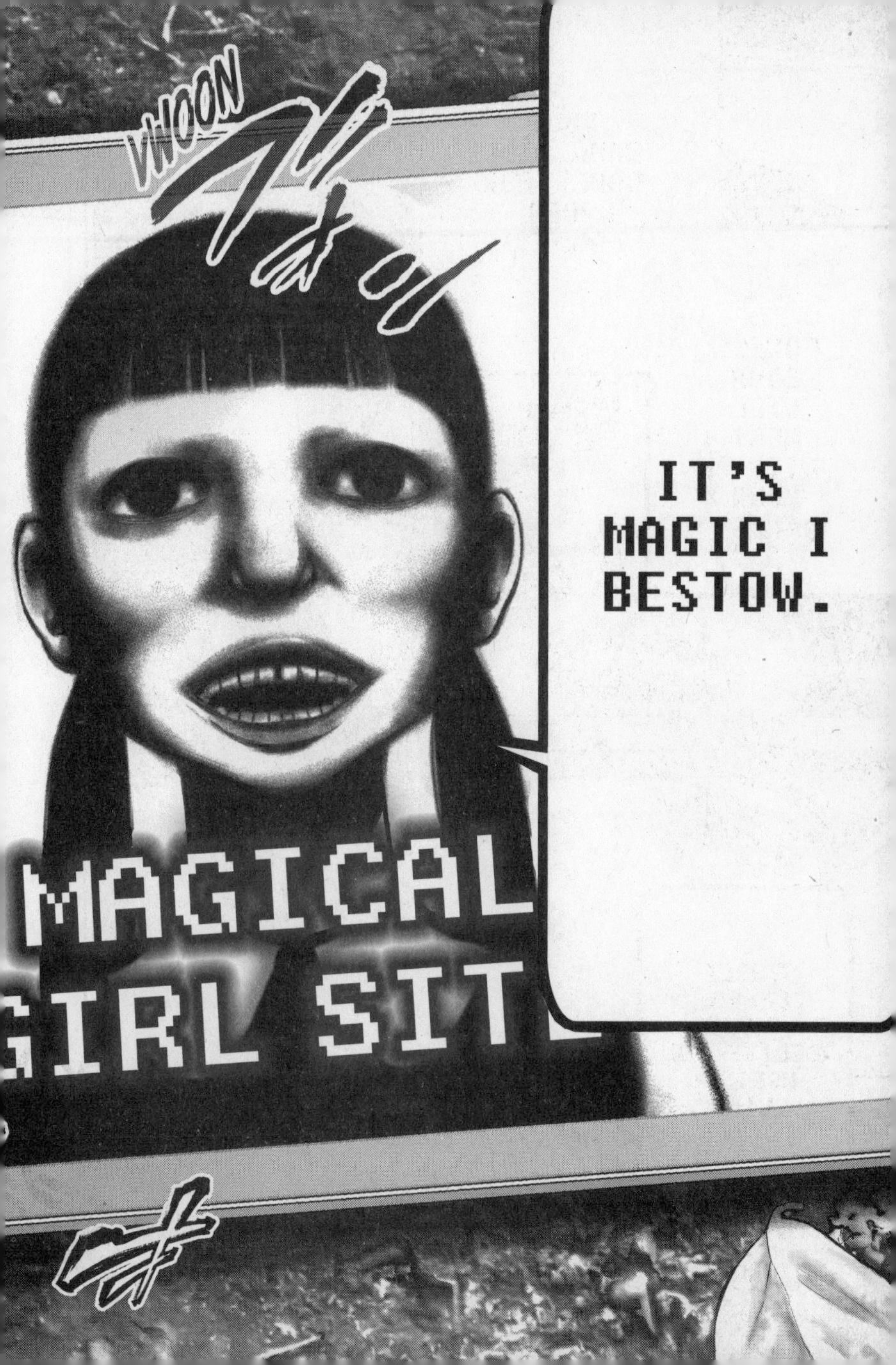
IT'S MAGIC I BESTOW.
VWOON
MAGICAL
GIRL SIT

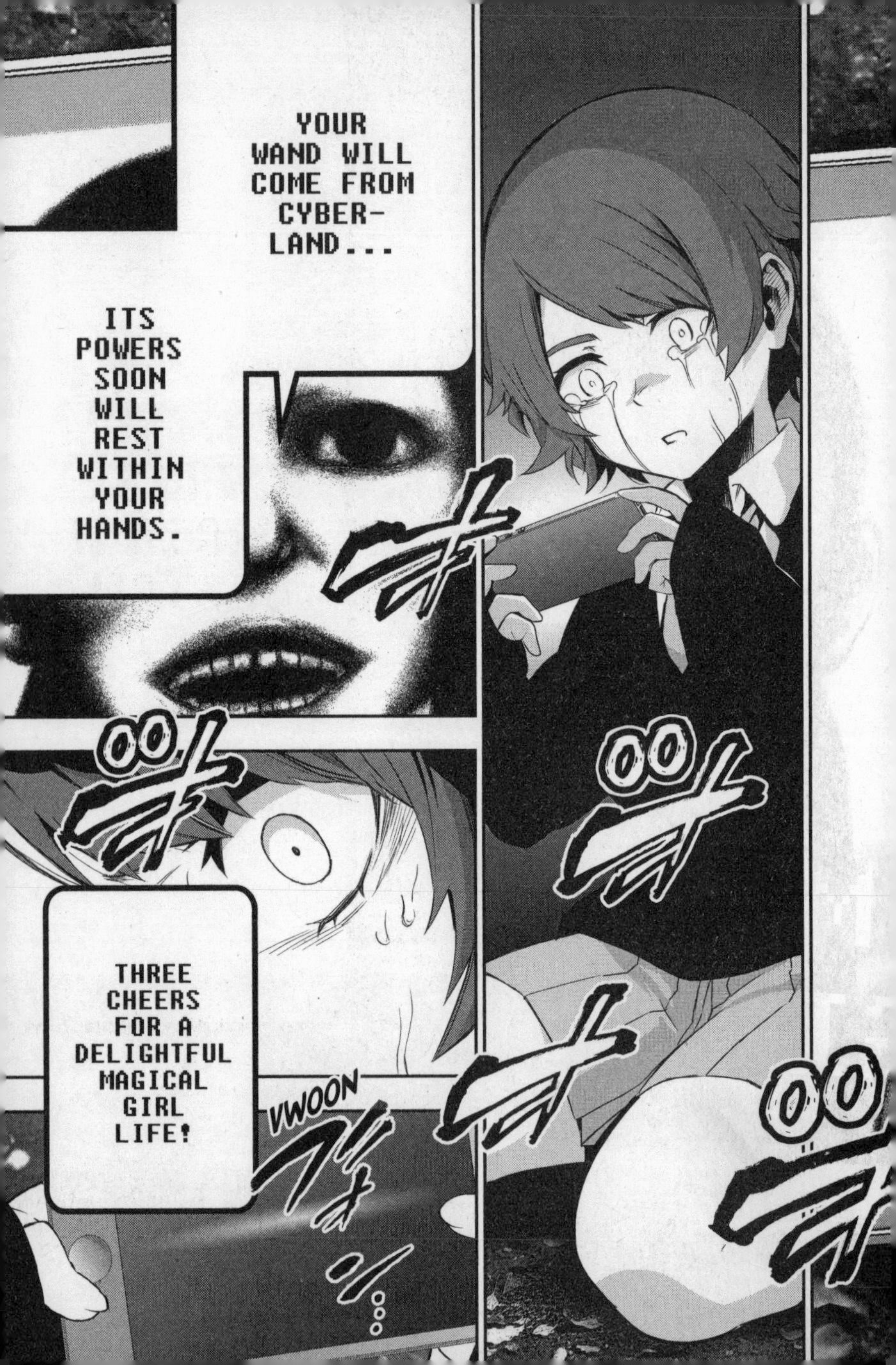
YOUR WAND WILL COME FROM CYBER-LAND...
ITS POWERS SOON WILL REST WITHIN YOUR HANDS.
THREE CHEERS FOR A DELIGHTFUL MAGICAL GIRL LIFE!
VWOON

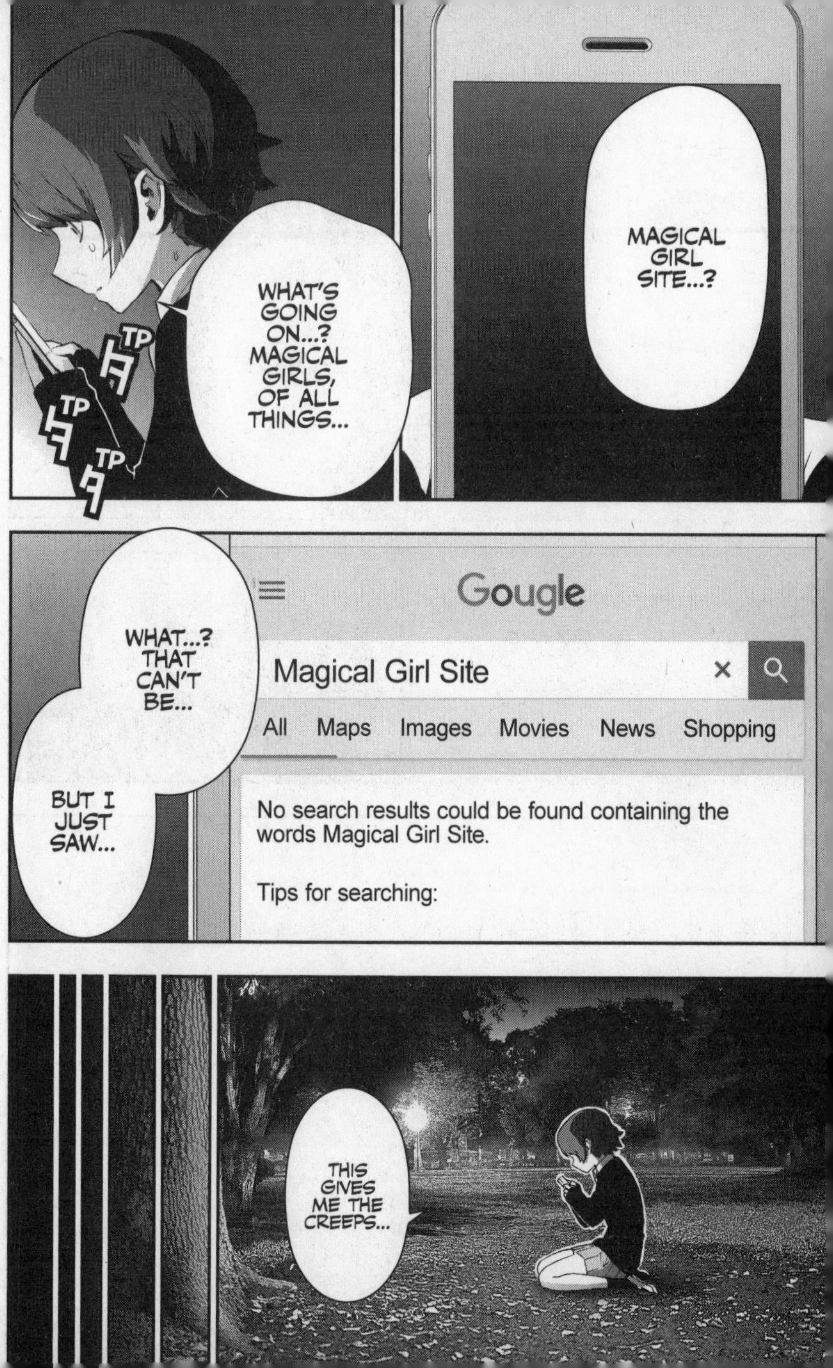
MAGICAL GIRL SITE...?
WHAT'S GOING ON...? MAGICAL GIRLS, OF ALL THINGS...
TP
TP
TP
Gougle
Magical Girl Site
All Maps Images Movies News Shopping
No search results could be found containing the words Magical Girl Site.
Tips for searching:
WHAT...? THAT CAN'T BE...
BUT I JUST SAW...
THIS GIVES ME THE CREEPS...

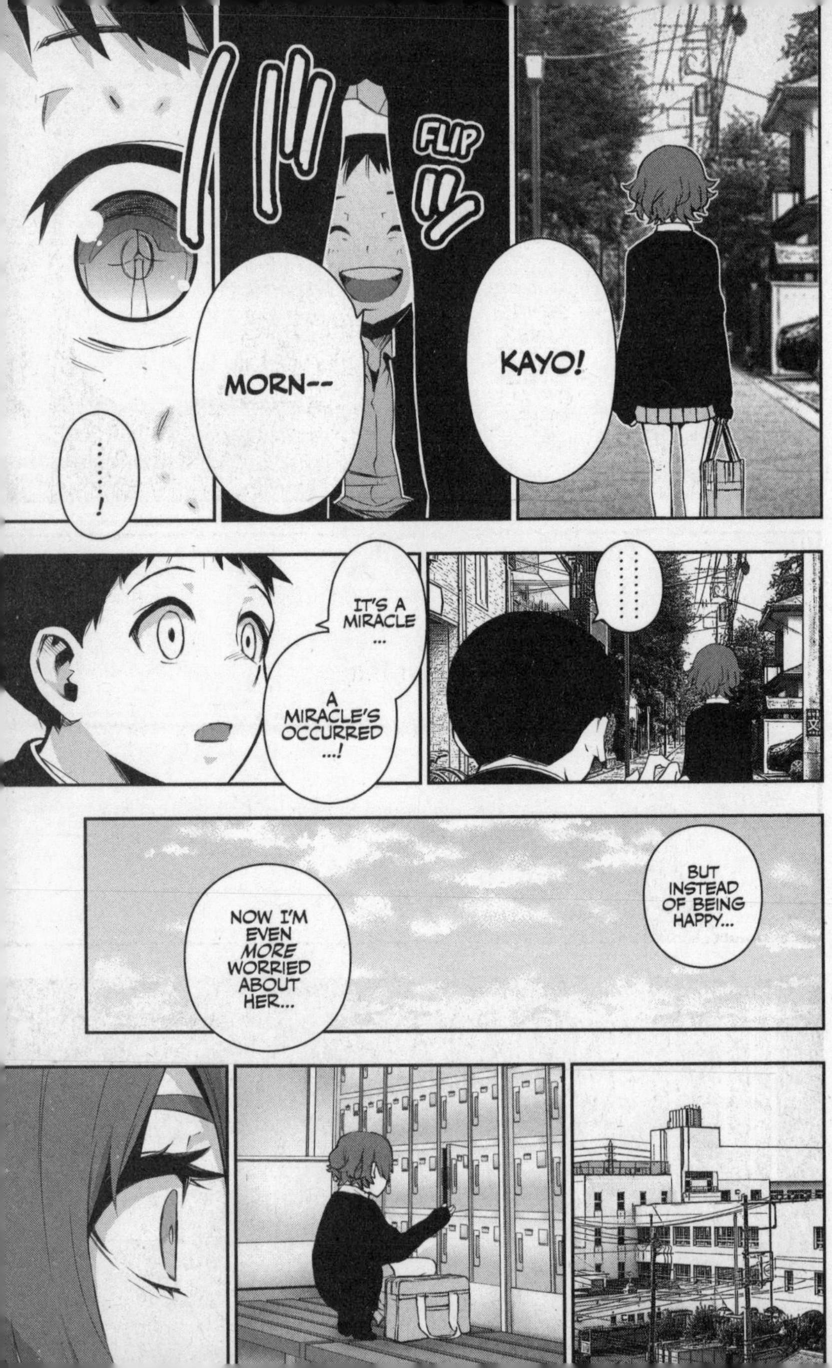
KAYO!
FLIP
MORN--
......!
......
IT'S A MIRACLE ...
A MIRACLE'S OCCURRED ...!
BUT INSTEAD OF BEING HAPPY...
NOW I'M EVEN *MORE* WORRIED ABOUT HER...

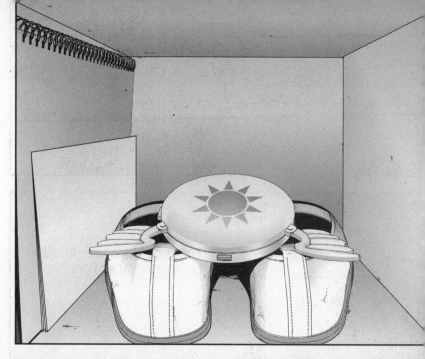

GLANCE
キョロ
GLANCE
キョロ
KRNKL
How to use your wand:
Touch a Magical Girl to copy her powers. That's it.
From now on, you're a Magical Girl.
Magical Girl SITE

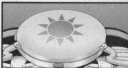

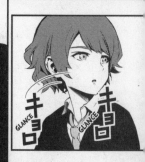

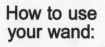

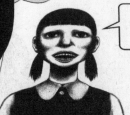

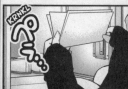

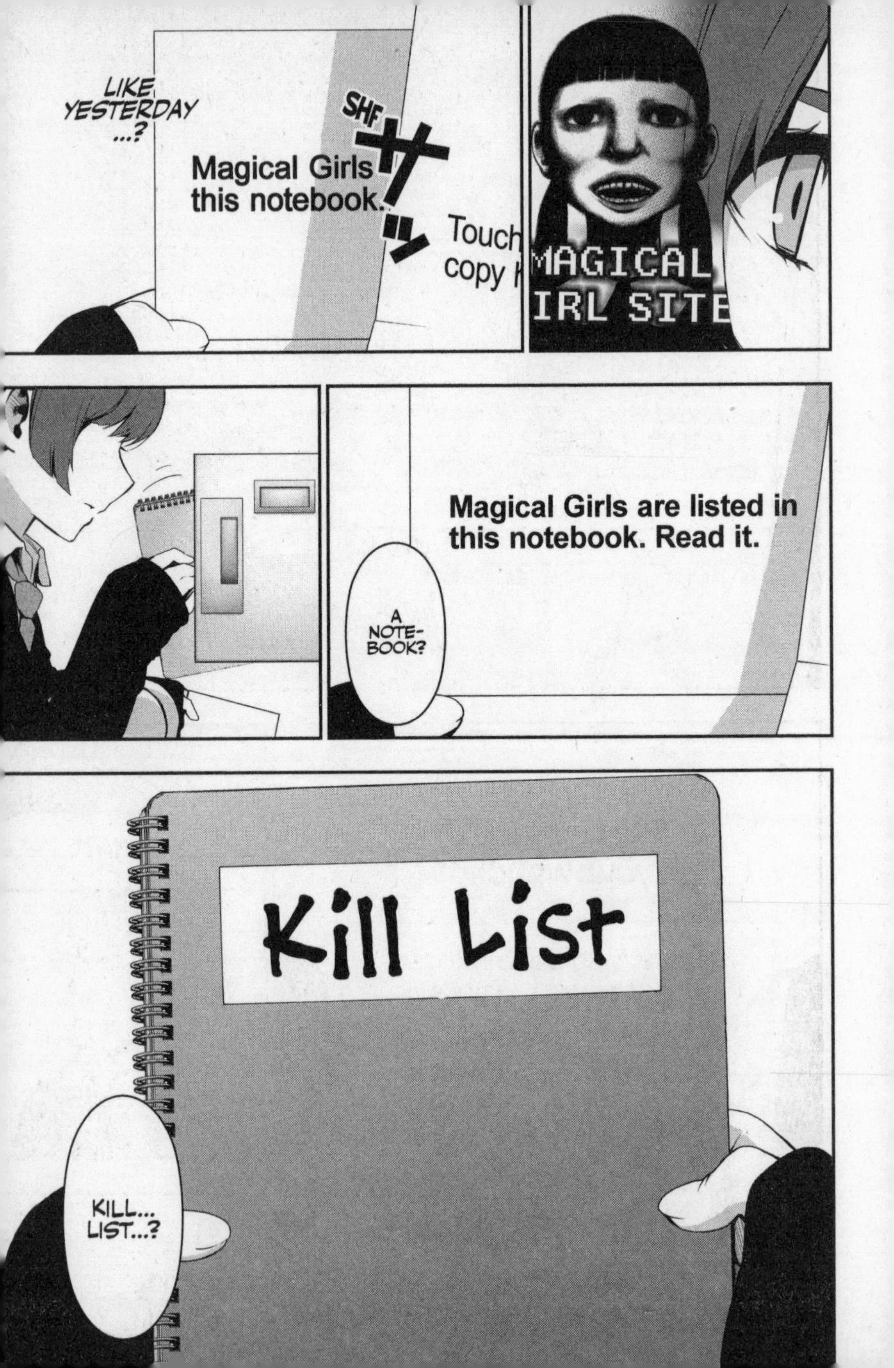
MAGICAL
IRL SITE
Touch
copy
LIKE YESTERDAY ...?
Magical Girls
this notebook.
SHF
Magical Girls are listed in this notebook. Read it.
A NOTE-BOOK?
Kill List
KILL... LIST...?

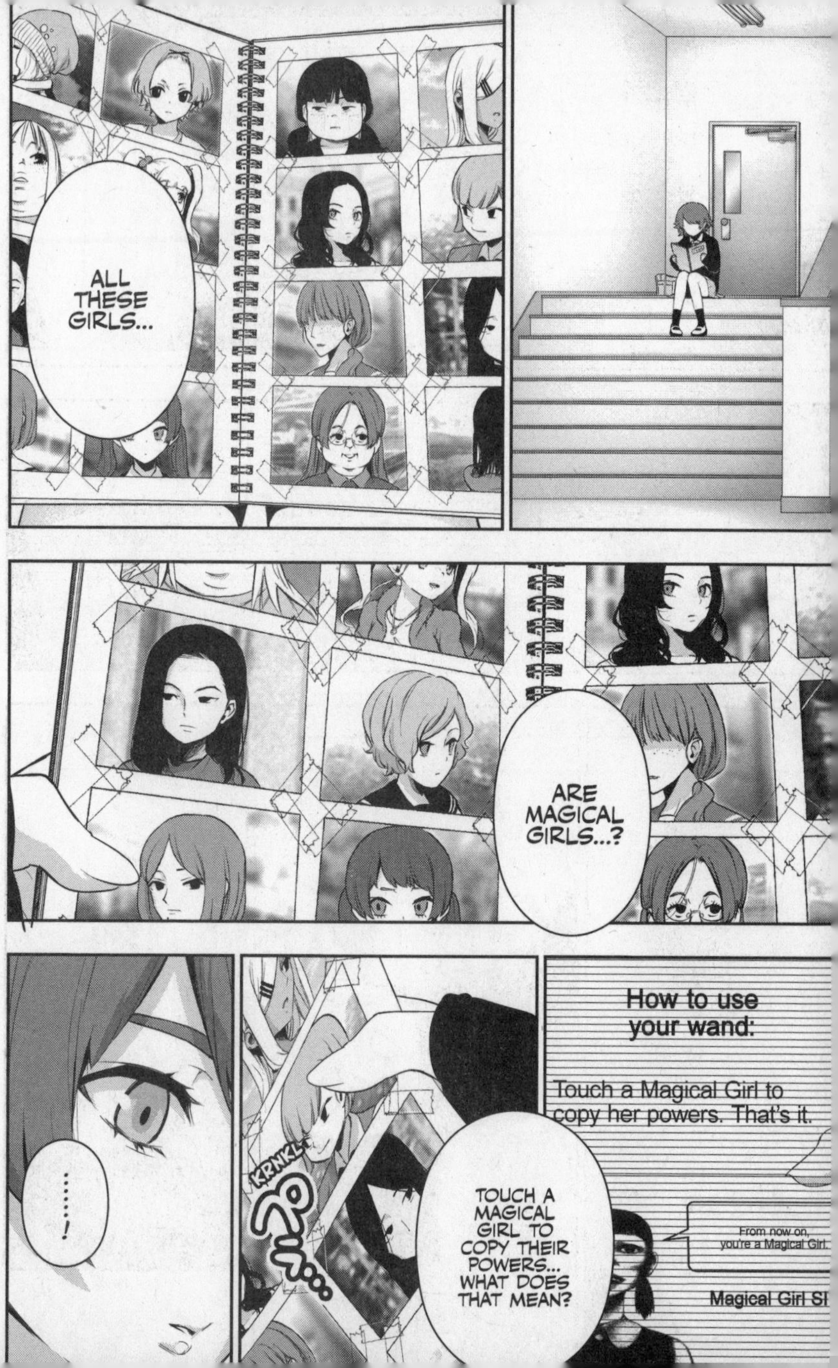
ALL THESE GIRLS...
ARE MAGICAL GIRLS...?
How to use your wand:
Touch a Magical Girl to copy her powers. That's it.
From now on, you're a Magical Girl.
Magical Girl Sl
KRNKL
TOUCH A MAGICAL GIRL TO COPY THEIR POWERS... WHAT DOES THAT MEAN?
......!

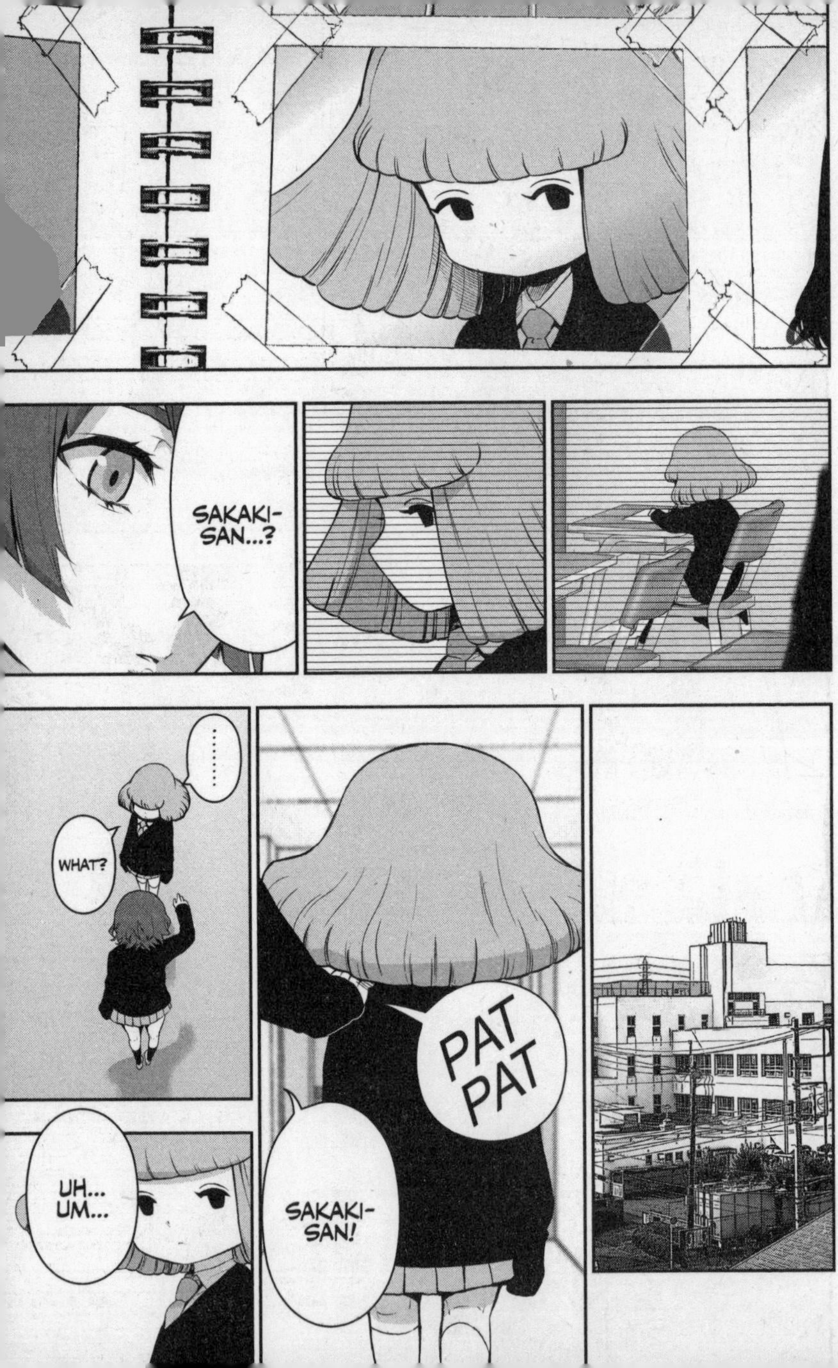
SAKAKI-SAN...?
PAT PAT
SAKAKI-SAN!
....
WHAT?
UH... UM...

HAD A THREAD ON YOU...

YOU...

STARE ----...

HMPH.

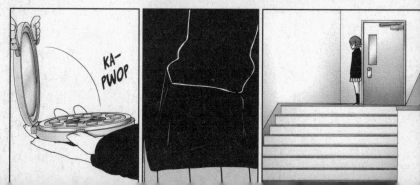

KA-PWOP

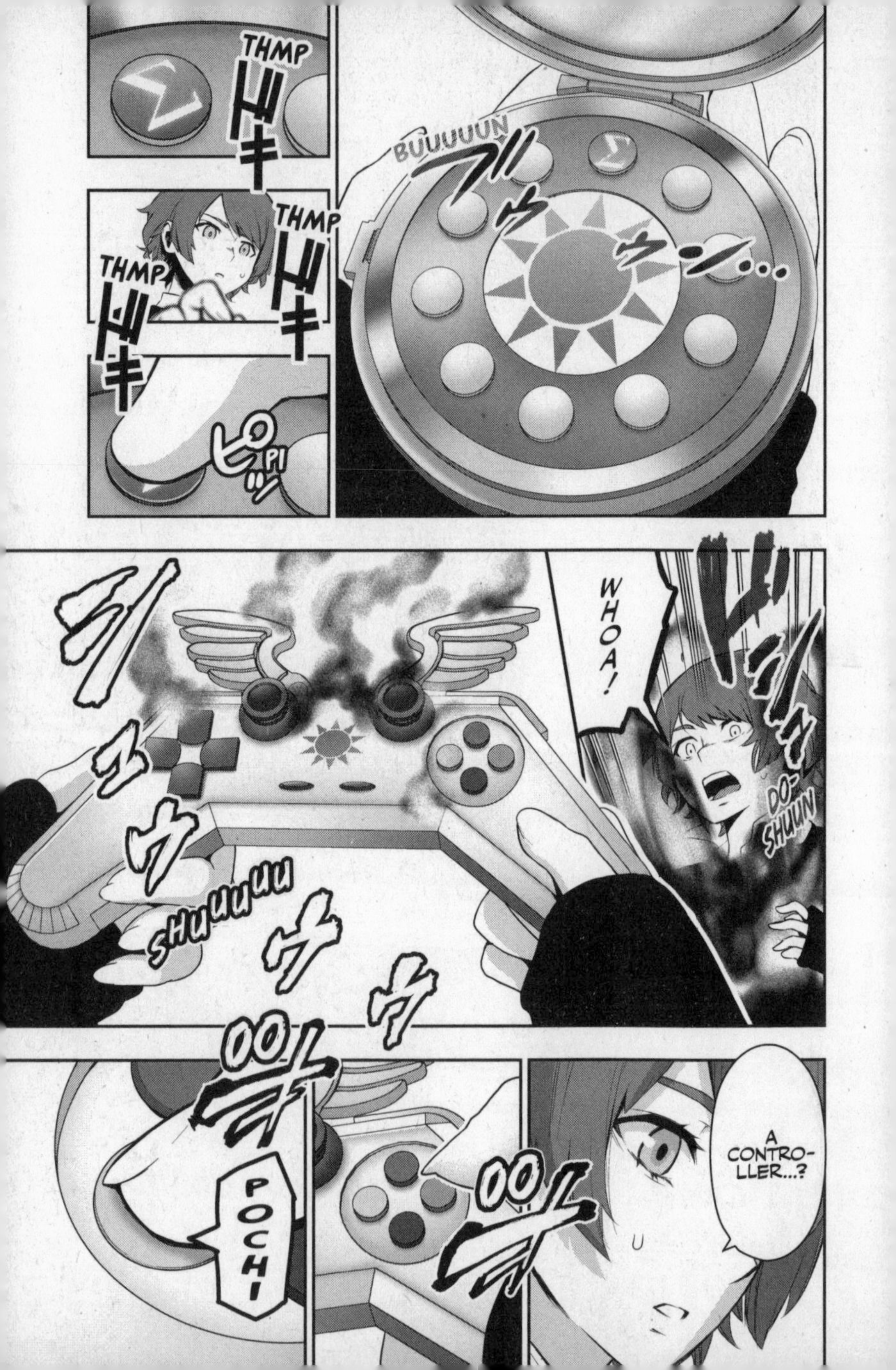
BUUUUUN
THMP
THMP
THMP
PI
WHOA!
DO-SHUUN
SHUUUUU
A CONTROLLER...?
OOH
POCHI
OOH

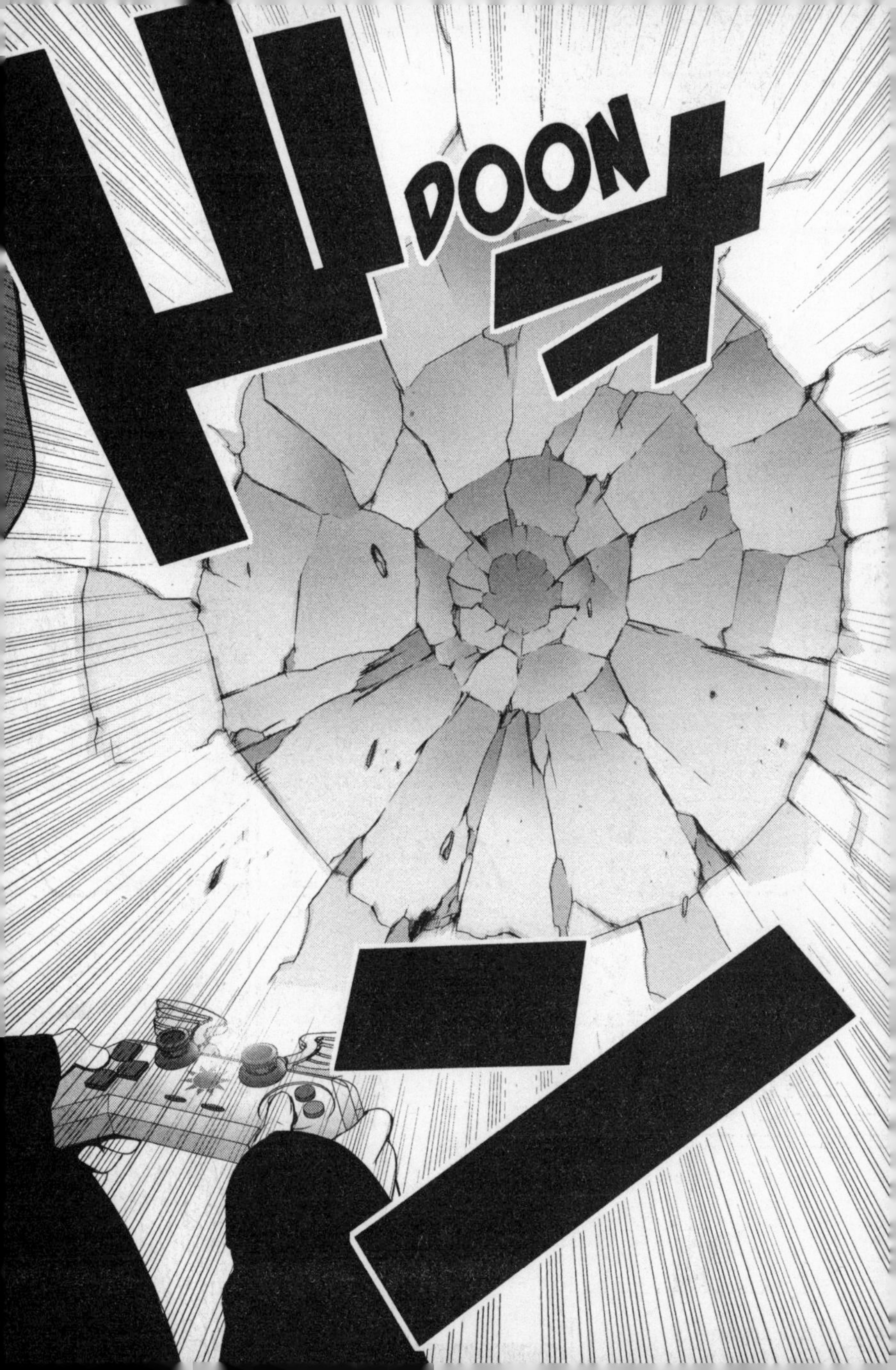
DOON

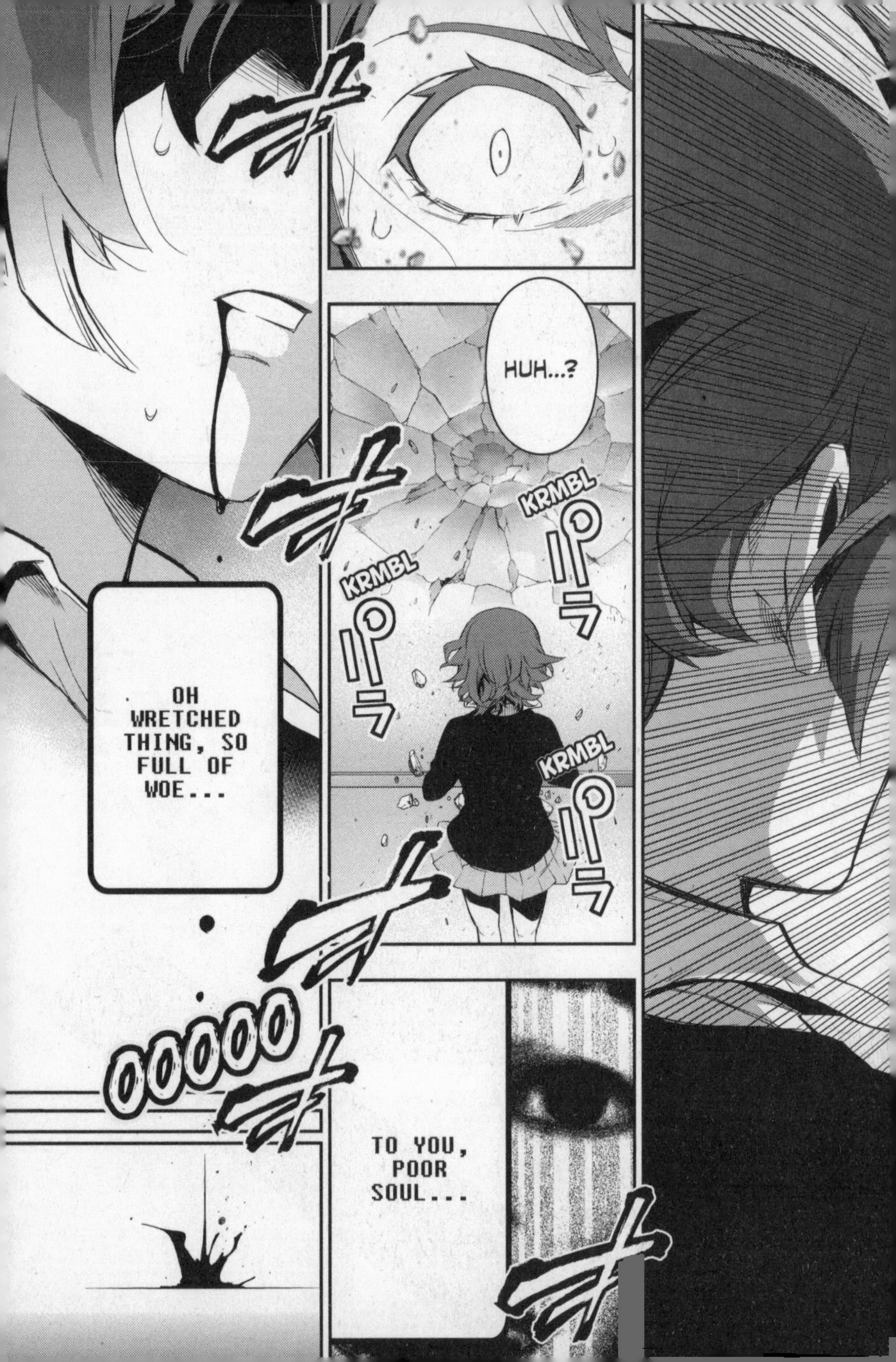

HUH...?
KRMBL
パラ
KRMBL
パラ
KRMBL
パラ
OH WRETCHED THING, SO FULL OF WOE...
OOOOO
TO YOU, POOR SOUL...

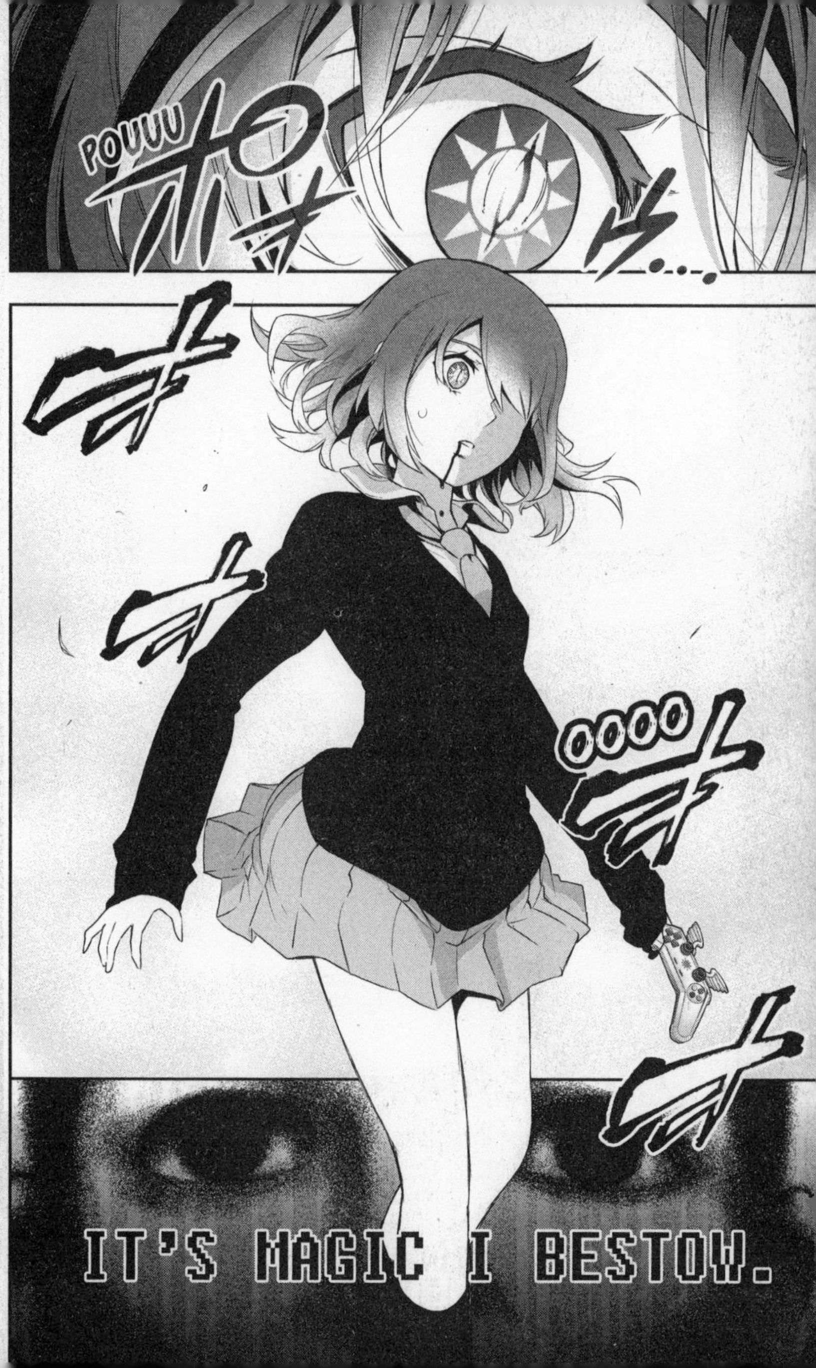
POUUU
OOOO
IT'S MAGIC I BESTOW.

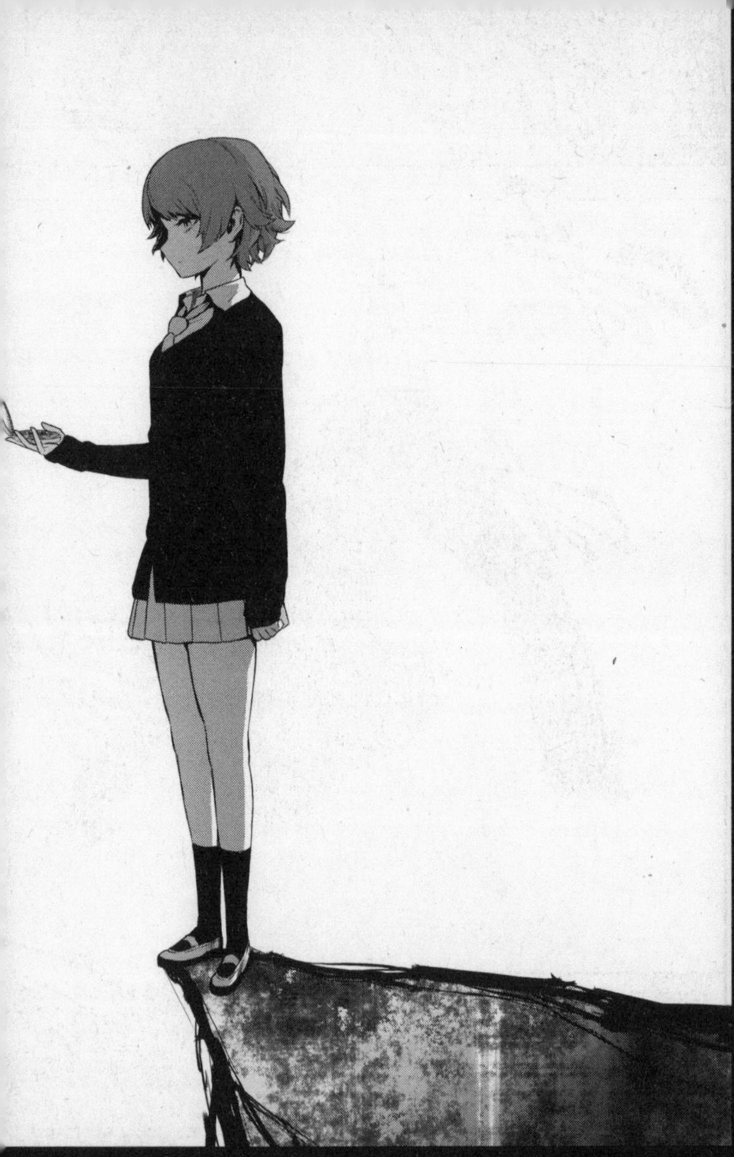

ENTER.57 MELISSA

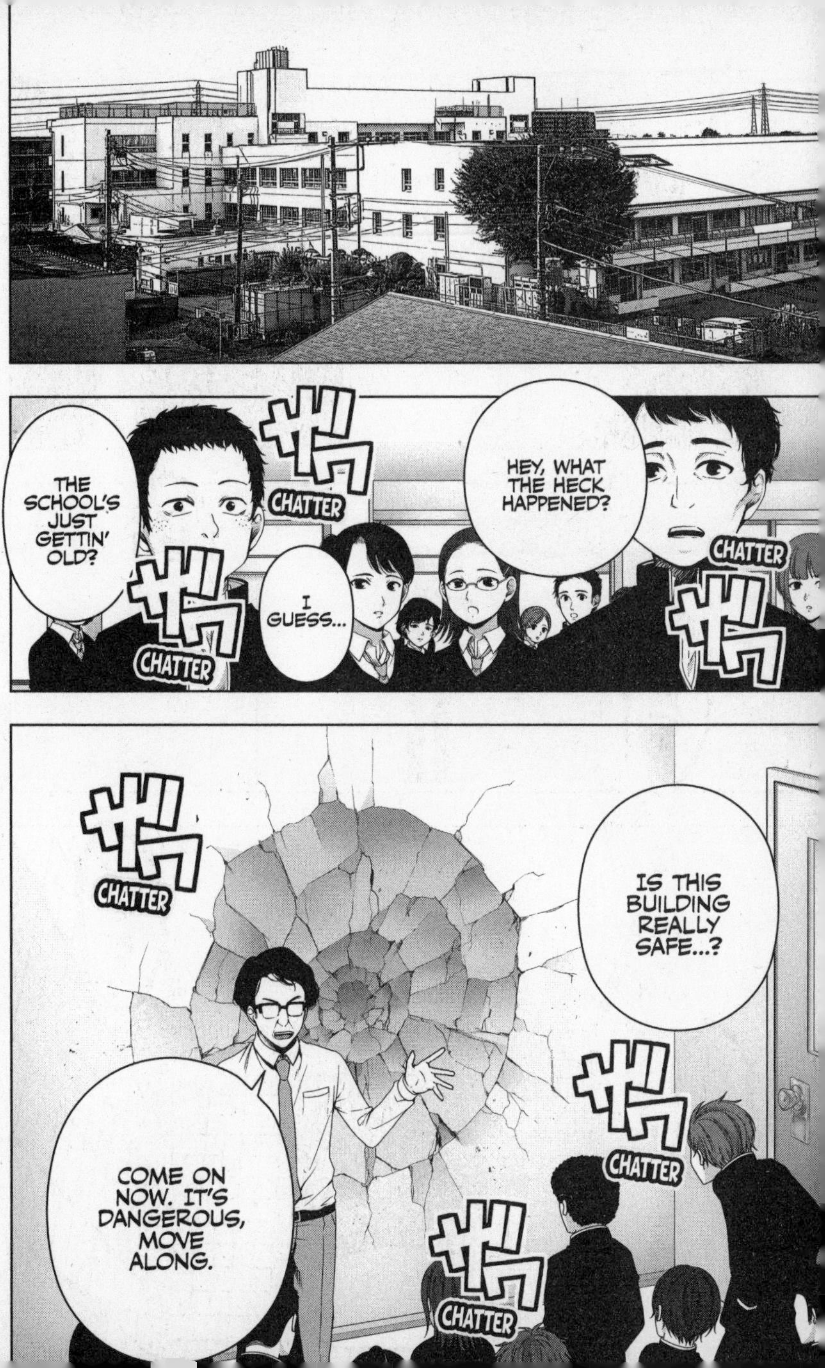
HEY, WHAT THE HECK HAPPENED?
ザワ
CHATTER
ザワ
CHATTER
THE SCHOOL'S JUST GETTIN' OLD?
I GUESS...
ザワ
CHATTER
IS THIS BUILDING REALLY SAFE...?
ザワ
CHATTER
ザワ
CHATTER
COME ON NOW. IT'S DANGEROUS, MOVE ALONG.
ザワ
CHATTER

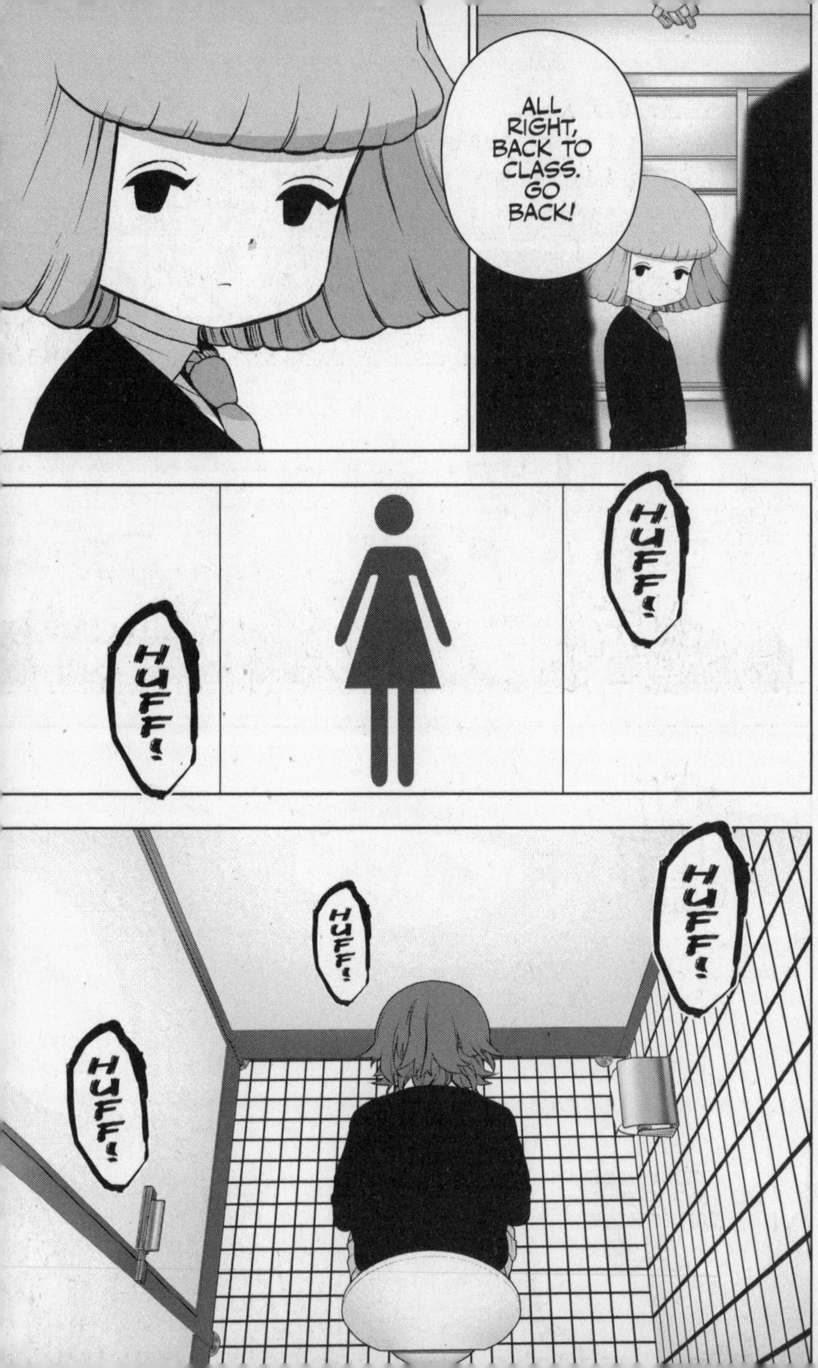
ALL RIGHT, BACK TO CLASS. GO BACK!
HUFF!
HUFF!
HUFF!
HUFF!
HUFF!

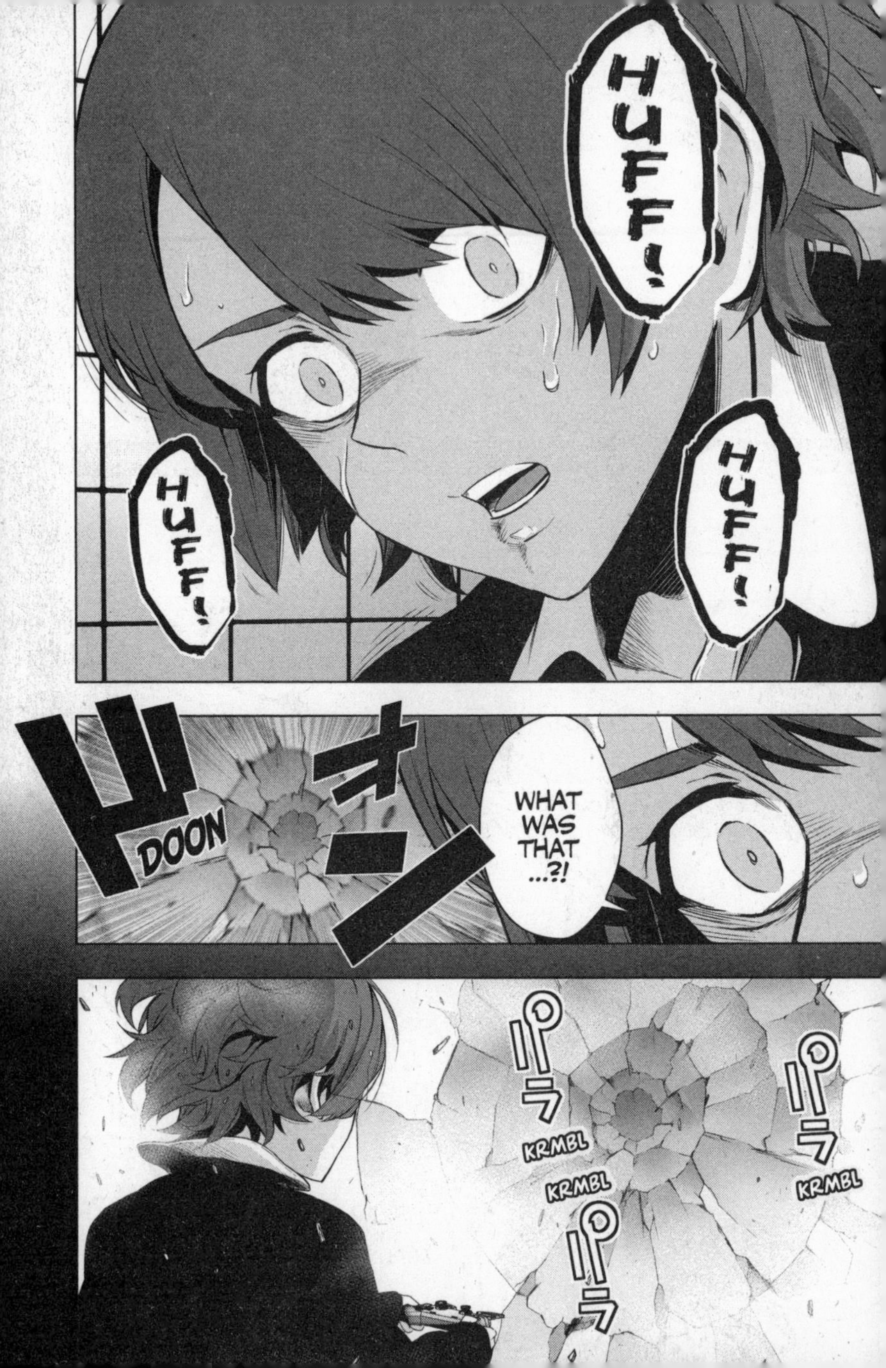
HUFF!
HUFF!
HUFF!
WHAT WAS THAT ...?!
DOON
KRMBL
KRMBL
KRMBL

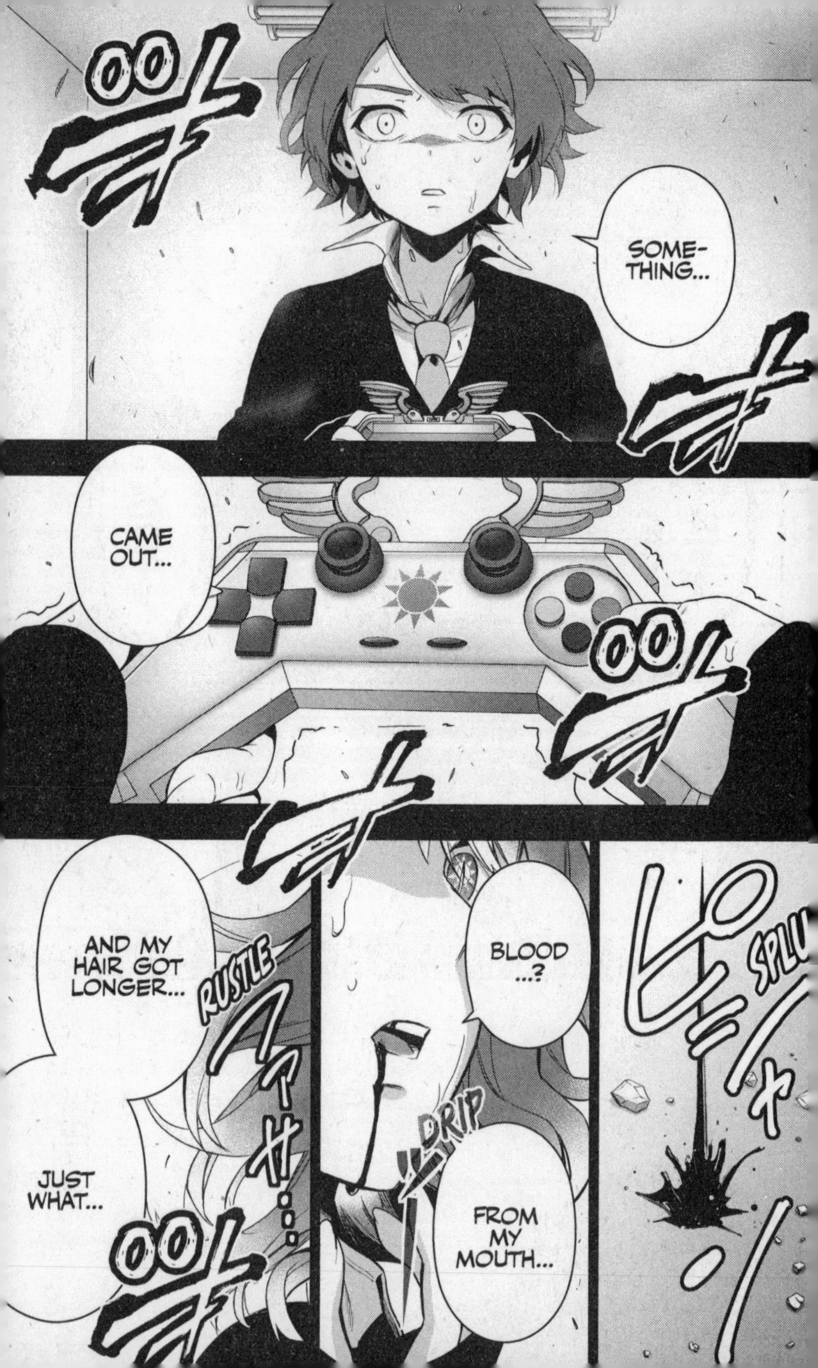

SOME-THING...
CAME OUT...
SPLU
BLOOD ...?
DRIP
FROM MY MOUTH...
AND MY HAIR GOT LONGER...
RUSTLE
JUST WHAT...

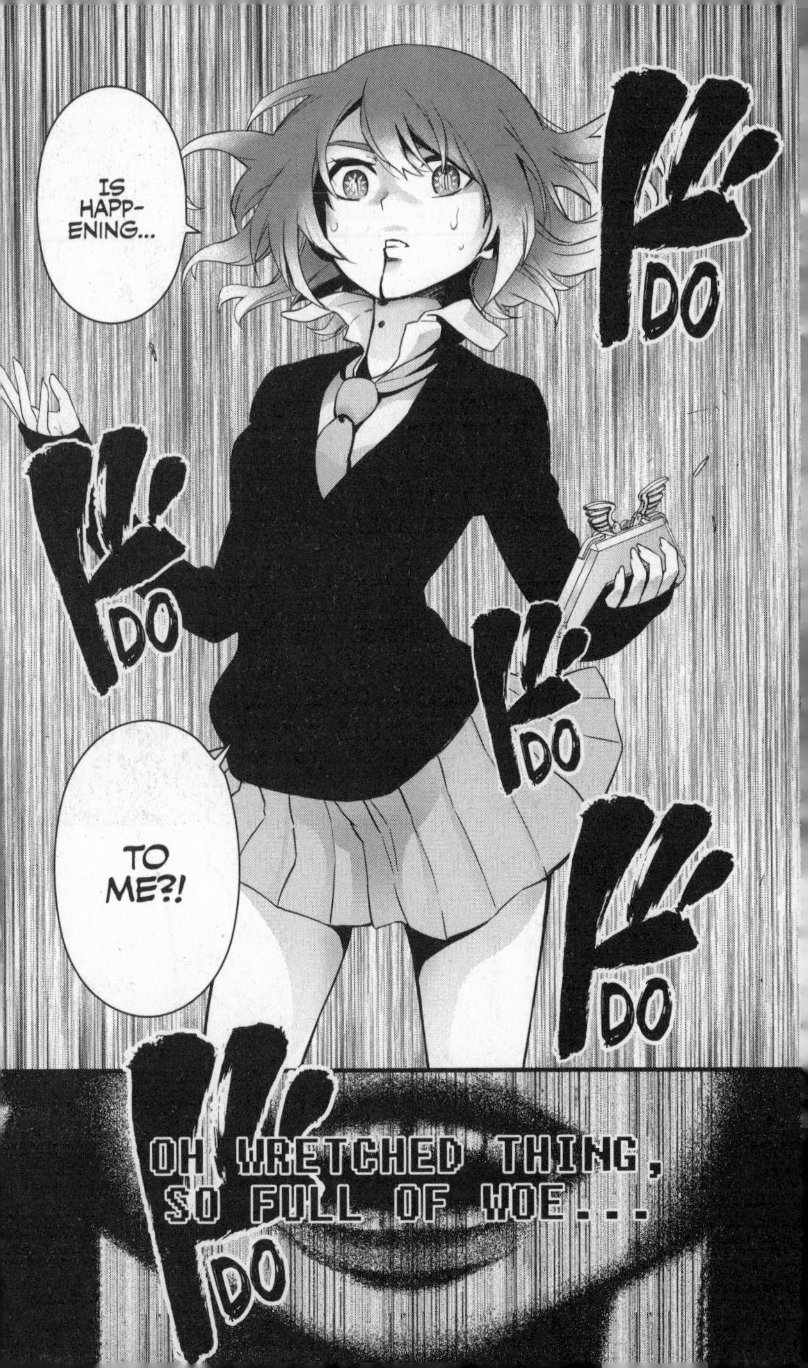
DO
IS HAPP-ENING...
DO
DO
DO
TO ME?!
DO
OH WRETCHED THING, SO FULL OF WOE...

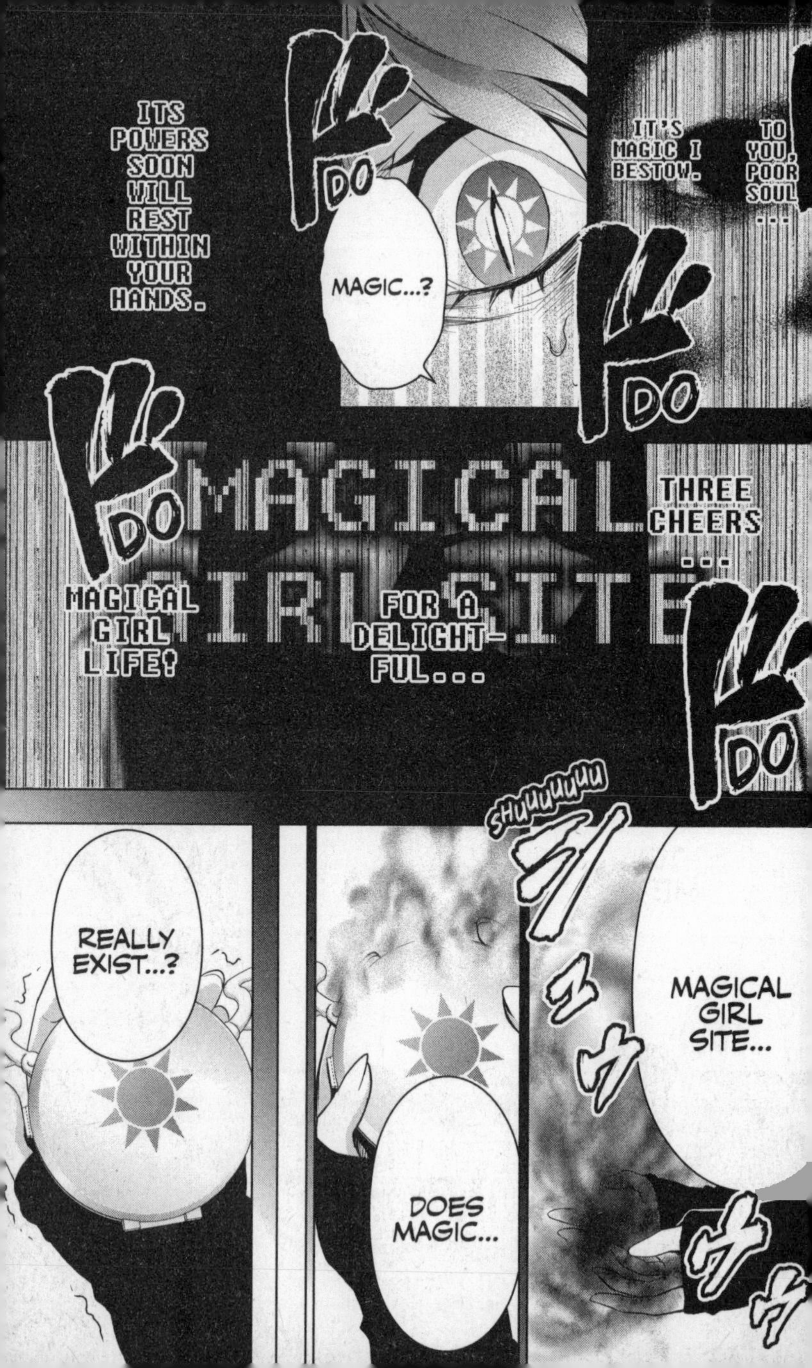
DO
TO YOU, POOR SOUL...
IT'S MAGIC I BESTOW.
DO
MAGIC...?
ITS POWERS SOON WILL REST WITHIN YOUR HANDS.
DO
THREE CHEERS...
MAGICAL GIRL SITE
FOR A DELIGHT-FUL...
MAGICAL GIRL LIFE!
DO
SHUUUUUUU
MAGICAL GIRL SITE...
DOES MAGIC...
REALLY EXIST...?

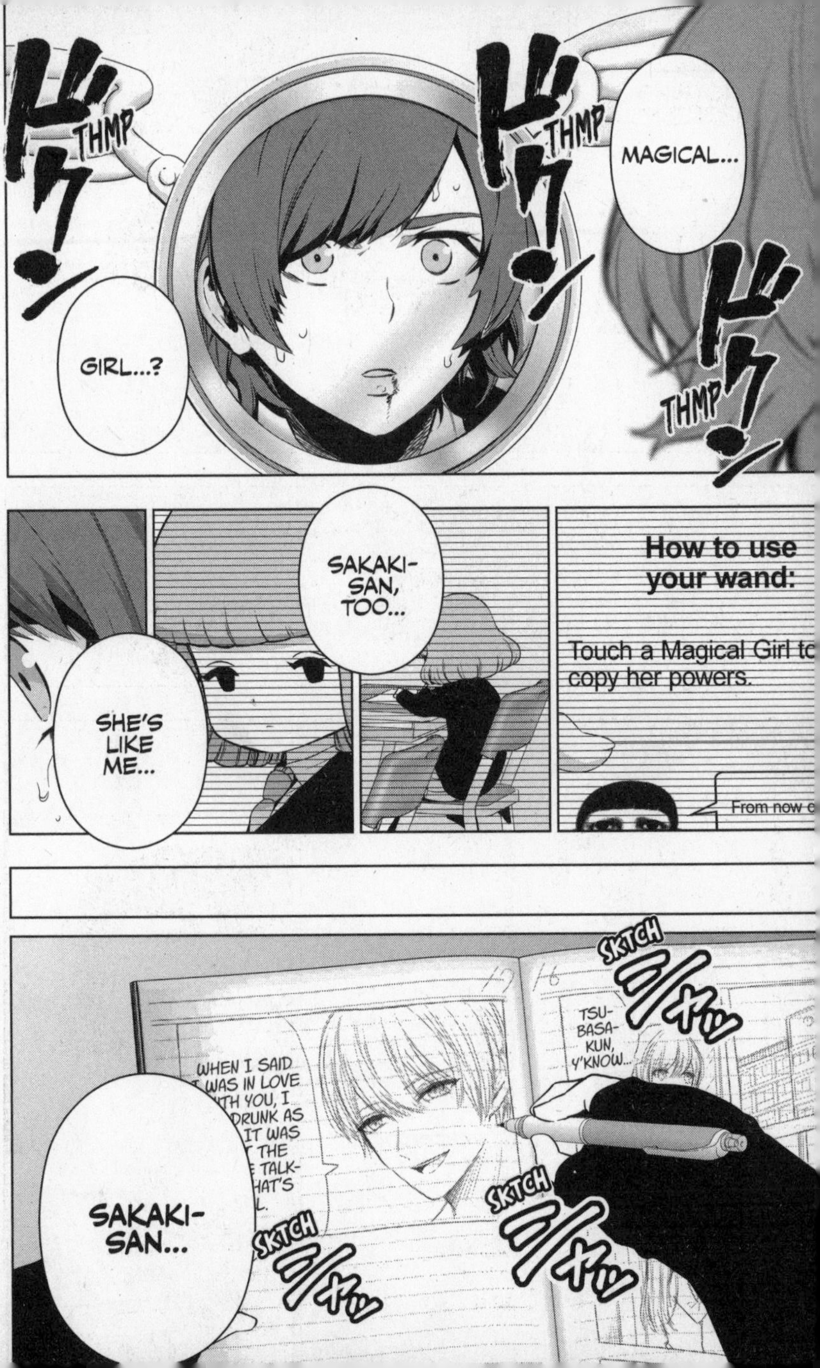
MAGICAL...
THMP
THMP
THMP
GIRL...?
How to use your wand:
Touch a Magical Girl to copy her powers.
From now o
SAKAKI-SAN, TOO...
SHE'S LIKE ME...
SKTCH
TSU-BASA-KUN, Y'KNOW...
WHEN I SAID I WAS IN LOVE WITH YOU, I
SKTCH
SKTCH
SAKAKI-SAN...

SORRY. IT'S NOTHING IMPORTANT...

WHAT?

....

UMM...

ER...

.......!

SO THAT'S IT.

I FIGURED...

TCH...

DISGUSTING OLD MAN...!

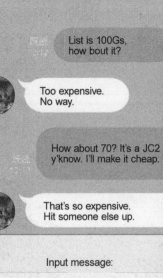

List is 100Gs, how bout it?

Too expensive. No way.

How about 70? It's a JC2 y'know. I'll make it cheap.

That's so expensive. Hit someone else up.

Input message:

but   and   so   for

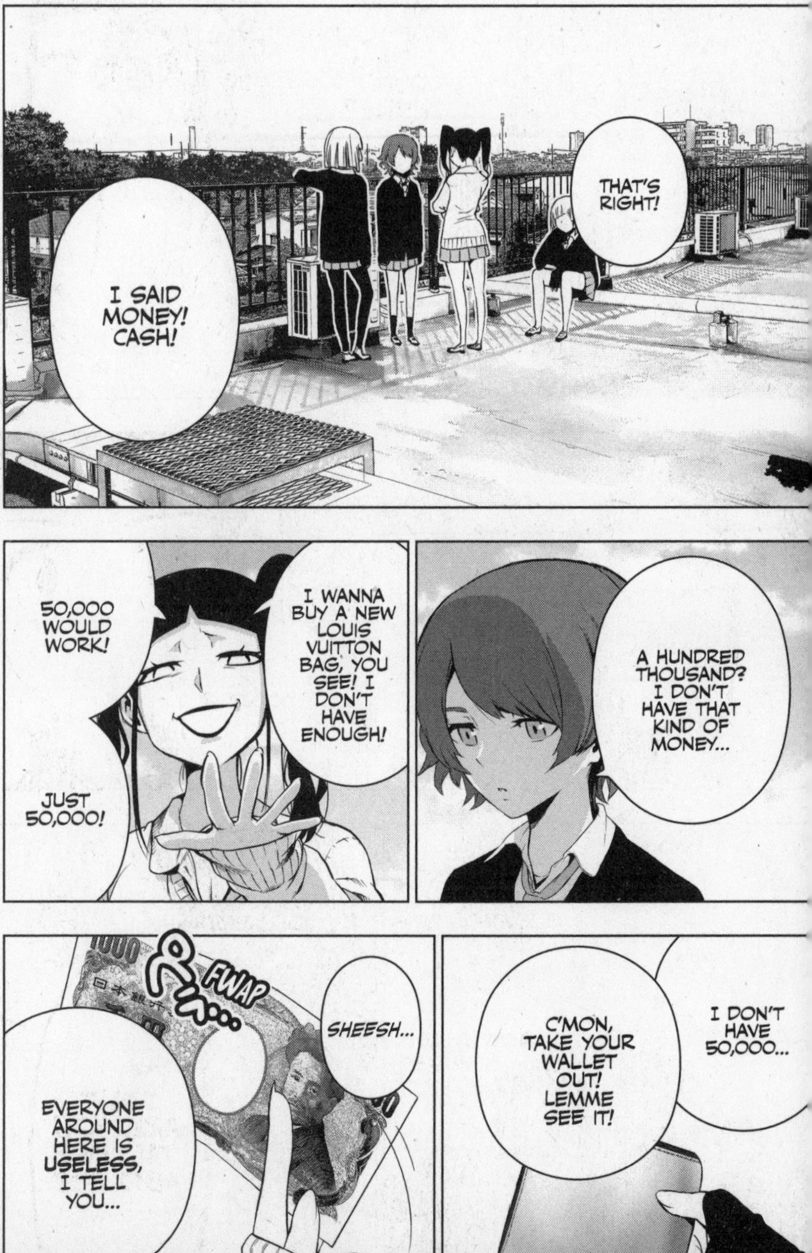
THAT'S RIGHT!
I SAID MONEY! CASH!
A HUNDRED THOUSAND? I DON'T HAVE THAT KIND OF MONEY...
I WANNA BUY A NEW LOUIS VUITTON BAG, YOU SEE! I DON'T HAVE ENOUGH!
50,000 WOULD WORK!
JUST 50,000!
I DON'T HAVE 50,000...
C'MON, TAKE YOUR WALLET OUT! LEMME SEE IT!
FWAP
SHEESH...
EVERYONE AROUND HERE IS USELESS, I TELL YOU...

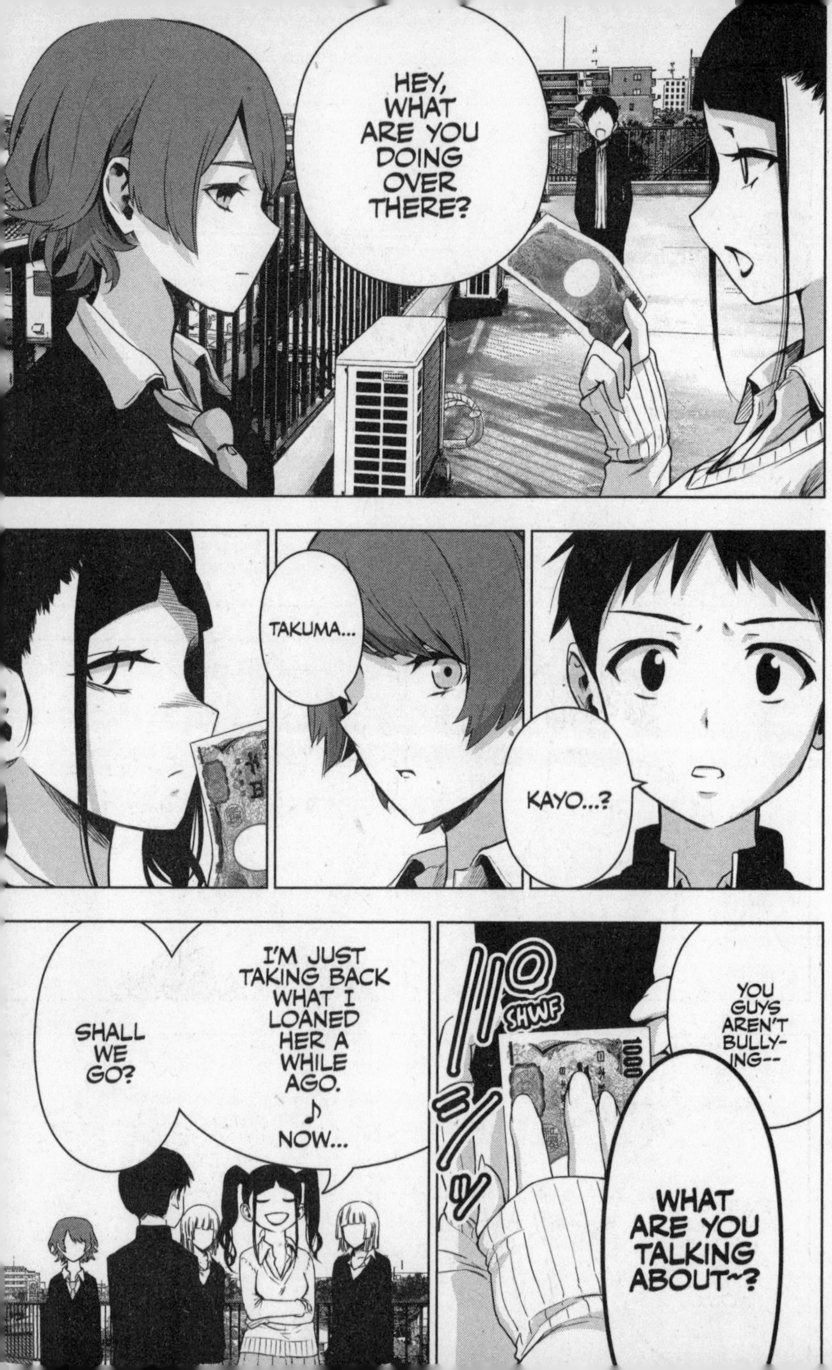
HEY, WHAT ARE YOU DOING OVER THERE?
KAYO...?
TAKUMA...
YOU GUYS AREN'T BULLY-ING--
SHWF
WHAT ARE YOU TALKING ABOUT~?
I'M JUST TAKING BACK WHAT I LOANED HER A WHILE AGO. ♪ NOW...
SHALL WE GO?

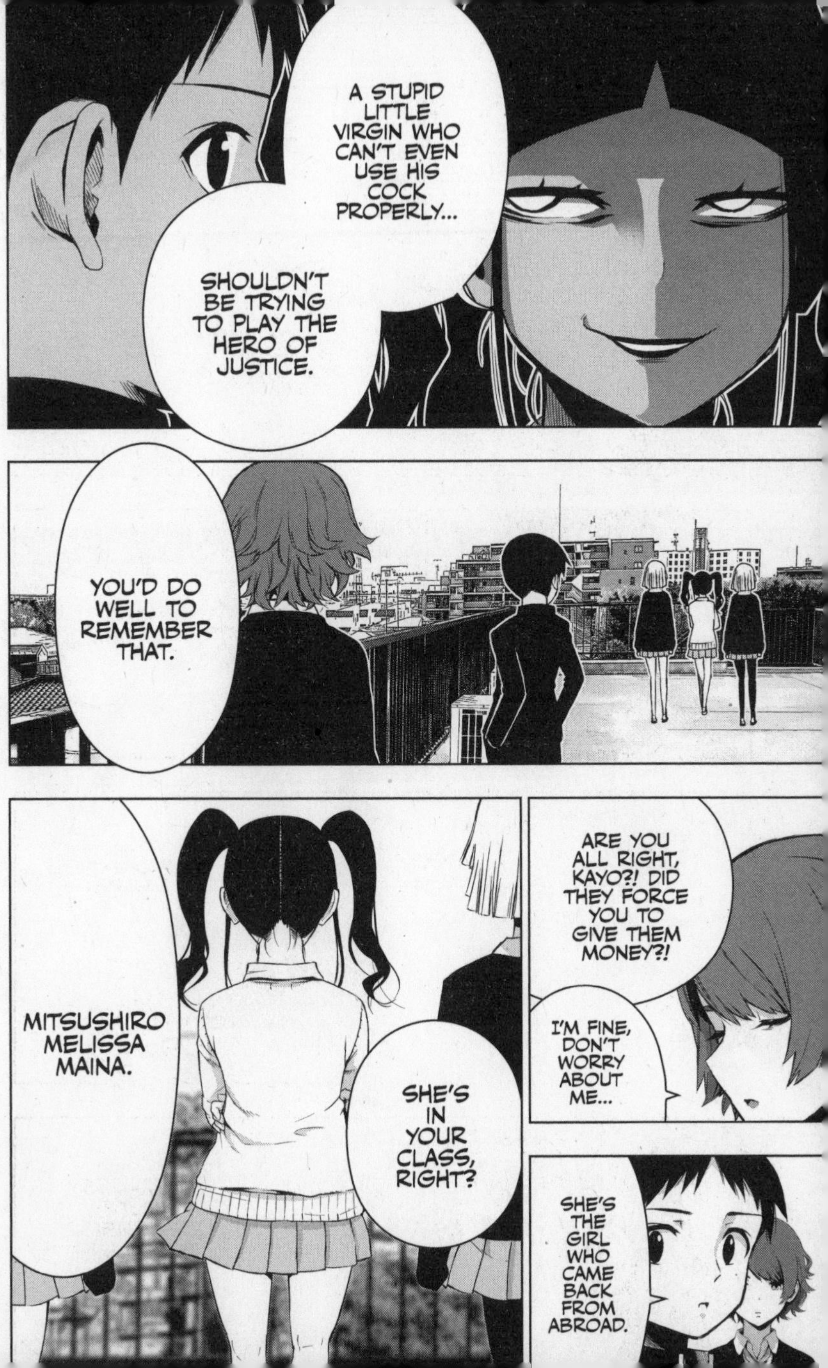
A STUPID LITTLE VIRGIN WHO CAN'T EVEN USE HIS COCK PROPERLY...
SHOULDN'T BE TRYING TO PLAY THE HERO OF JUSTICE.
YOU'D DO WELL TO REMEMBER THAT.
ARE YOU ALL RIGHT, KAYO?! DID THEY FORCE YOU TO GIVE THEM MONEY?!
I'M FINE, DON'T WORRY ABOUT ME...
SHE'S THE GIRL WHO CAME BACK FROM ABROAD.
SHE'S IN YOUR CLASS, RIGHT?
MITSUSHIRO MELISSA MAINA.

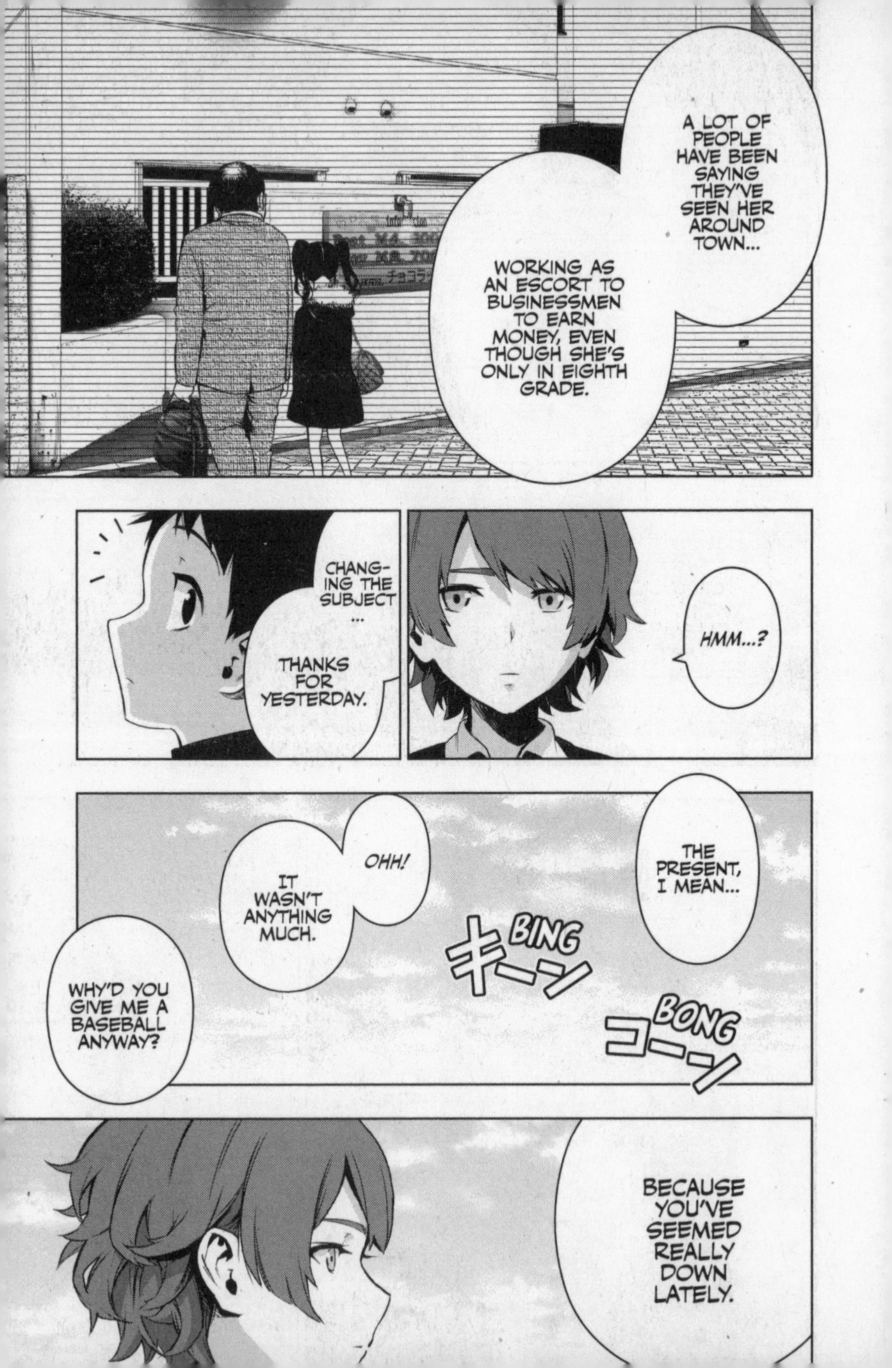
A LOT OF PEOPLE HAVE BEEN SAYING THEY'VE SEEN HER AROUND TOWN...
WORKING AS AN ESCORT TO BUSINESSMEN TO EARN MONEY, EVEN THOUGH SHE'S ONLY IN EIGHTH GRADE.
HMM...?
CHANG-ING THE SUBJECT...
THANKS FOR YESTERDAY.
THE PRESENT, I MEAN...
BING
キーン
BONG
コーン
OHH!
IT WASN'T ANYTHING MUCH.
WHY'D YOU GIVE ME A BASEBALL ANYWAY?
BECAUSE YOU'VE SEEMED REALLY DOWN LATELY.

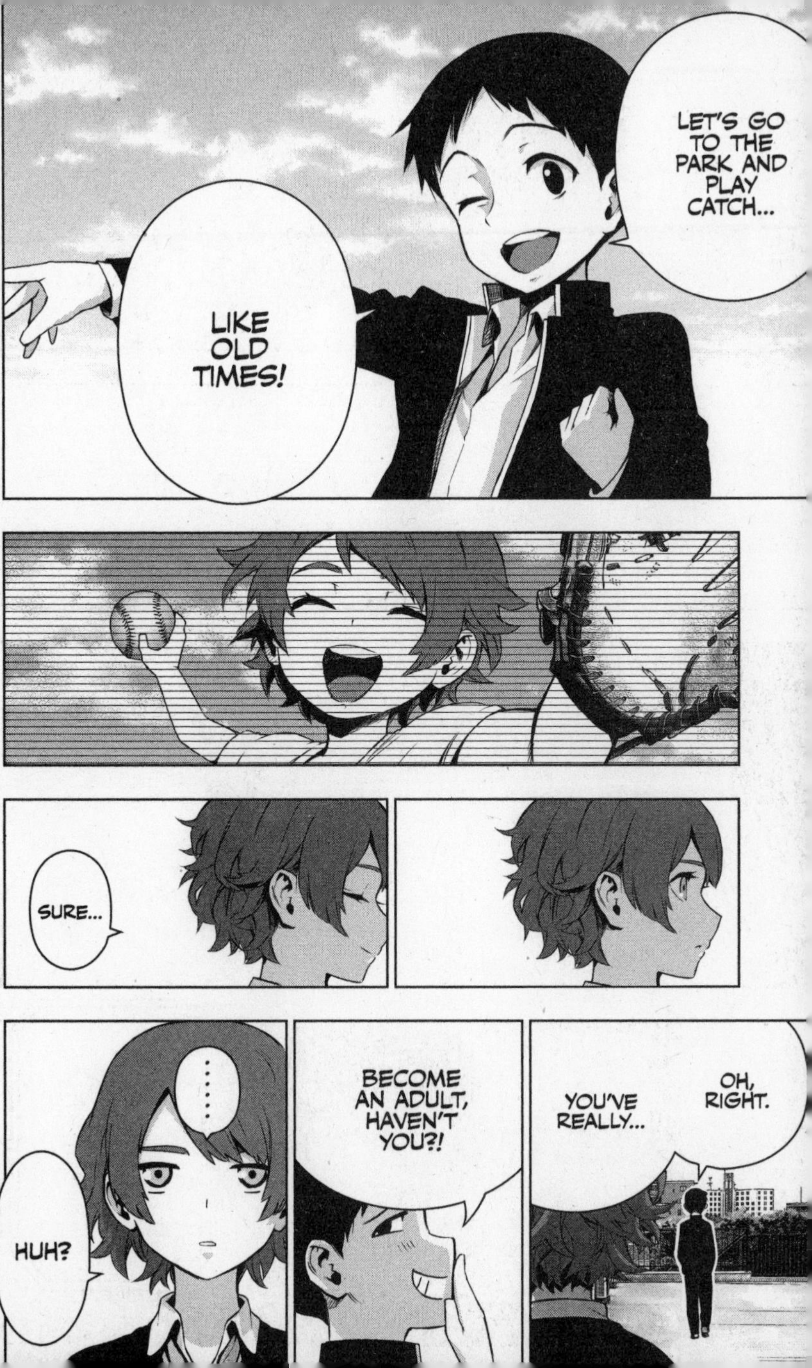
LET'S GO TO THE PARK AND PLAY CATCH...
LIKE OLD TIMES!
SURE...
OH, RIGHT.
YOU'VE REALLY...
BECOME AN ADULT, HAVEN'T YOU?!
......
HUH?

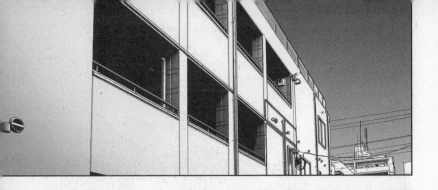

202

KOMURA SACHIKO
KAYO

I CAN LOVE NO ONE ELSE BUT YOU~! ♪

♡ KAYO ♡
HAPPY BIRTHDAY!

NO ONE ELSE~! NO ONE ELSE~! ♪

愛せない 愛せない 愛せない
中島タカマサ
No one else! No one else! No one else!
Nakajima Takamasa

TV初放映
TV Debut

I CAN LOVE NO ONE ELSE, NO ONE ELSE, NO ONE ELSE BUT YOU
もう君以外は愛せない 愛せない 愛せない

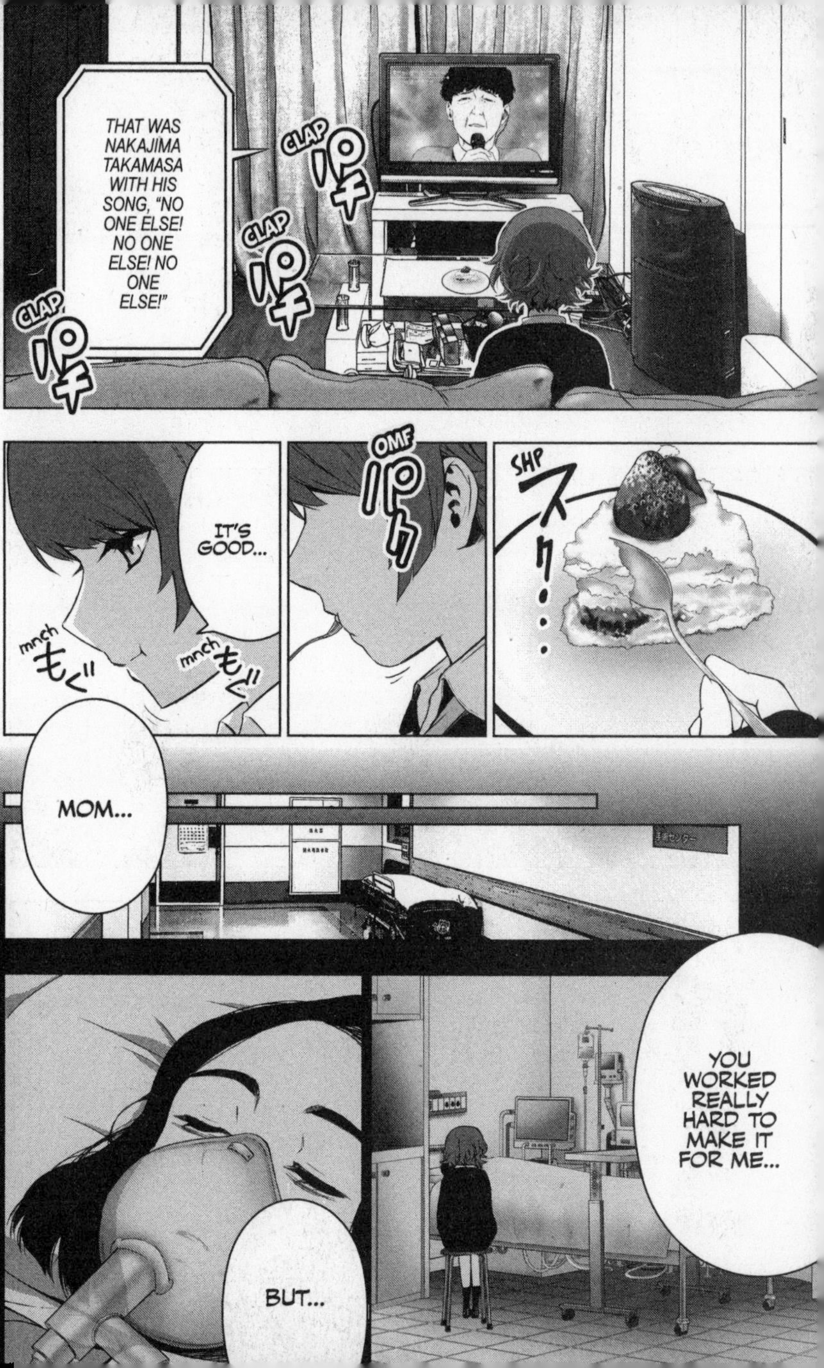
CLAP パチ
THAT WAS NAKAJIMA TAKAMASA WITH HIS SONG, "NO ONE ELSE! NO ONE ELSE! NO ONE ELSE!"
CLAP パチ
CLAP パチ
SHP スク…
OMF パク
mnch もぐ
IT'S GOOD...
mnch もぐ
MOM...
YOU WORKED REALLY HARD TO MAKE IT FOR ME...
BUT...

WITHOUT YOU HERE WITH ME...

I CAN'T EAT IT ALL.

OUR NEXT GUEST IS...

THE GIRLS FROM THE HIT IDOL GROUP "PUPPY PLAY"!

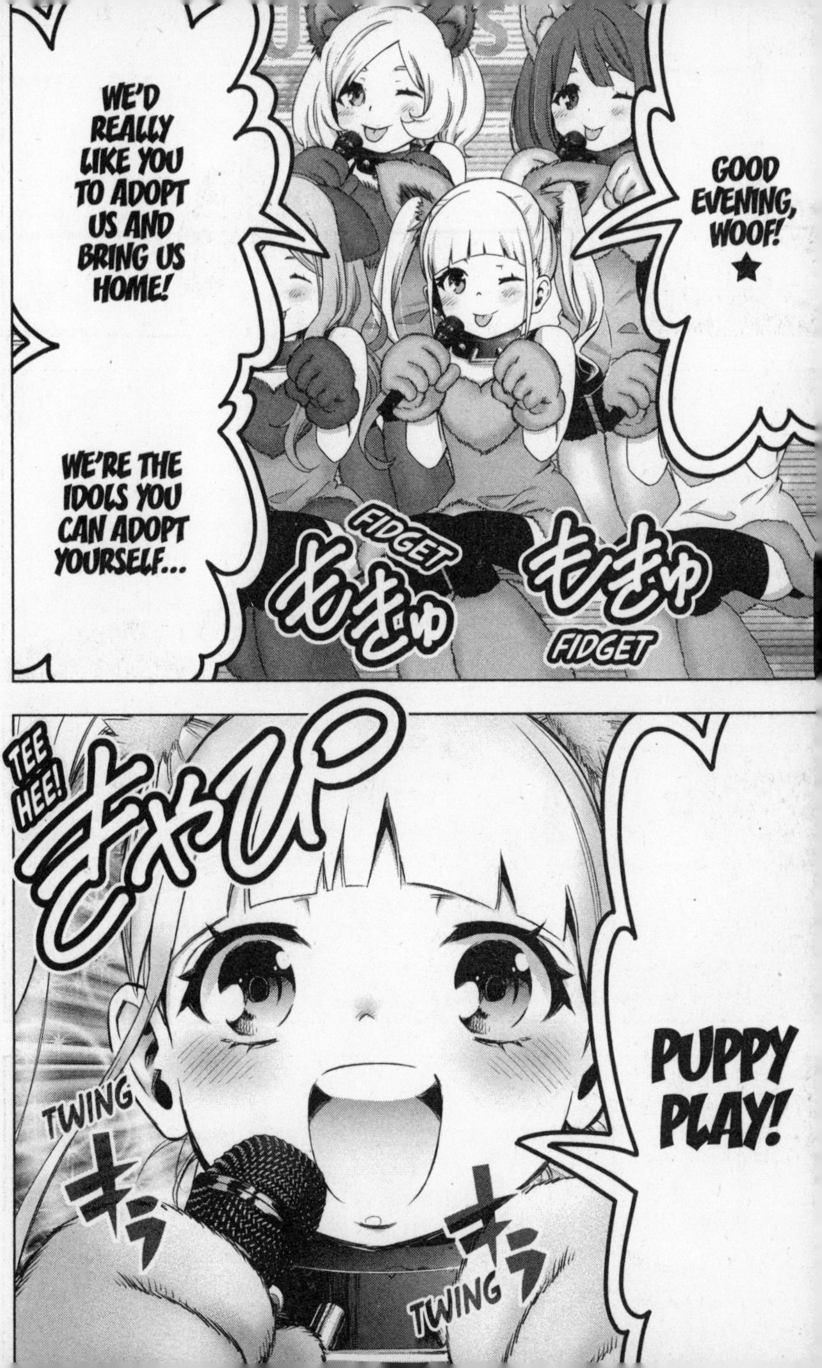
GOOD EVENING, WOOF! ★
WE'D REALLY LIKE YOU TO ADOPT US AND BRING US HOME!
WE'RE THE IDOLS YOU CAN ADOPT YOURSELF...
FIDGET
もきゅ
もきゅ
FIDGET
TEE HEE!
きゃぴ
PUPPY PLAY!
TWING
キラ
キラ
TWING

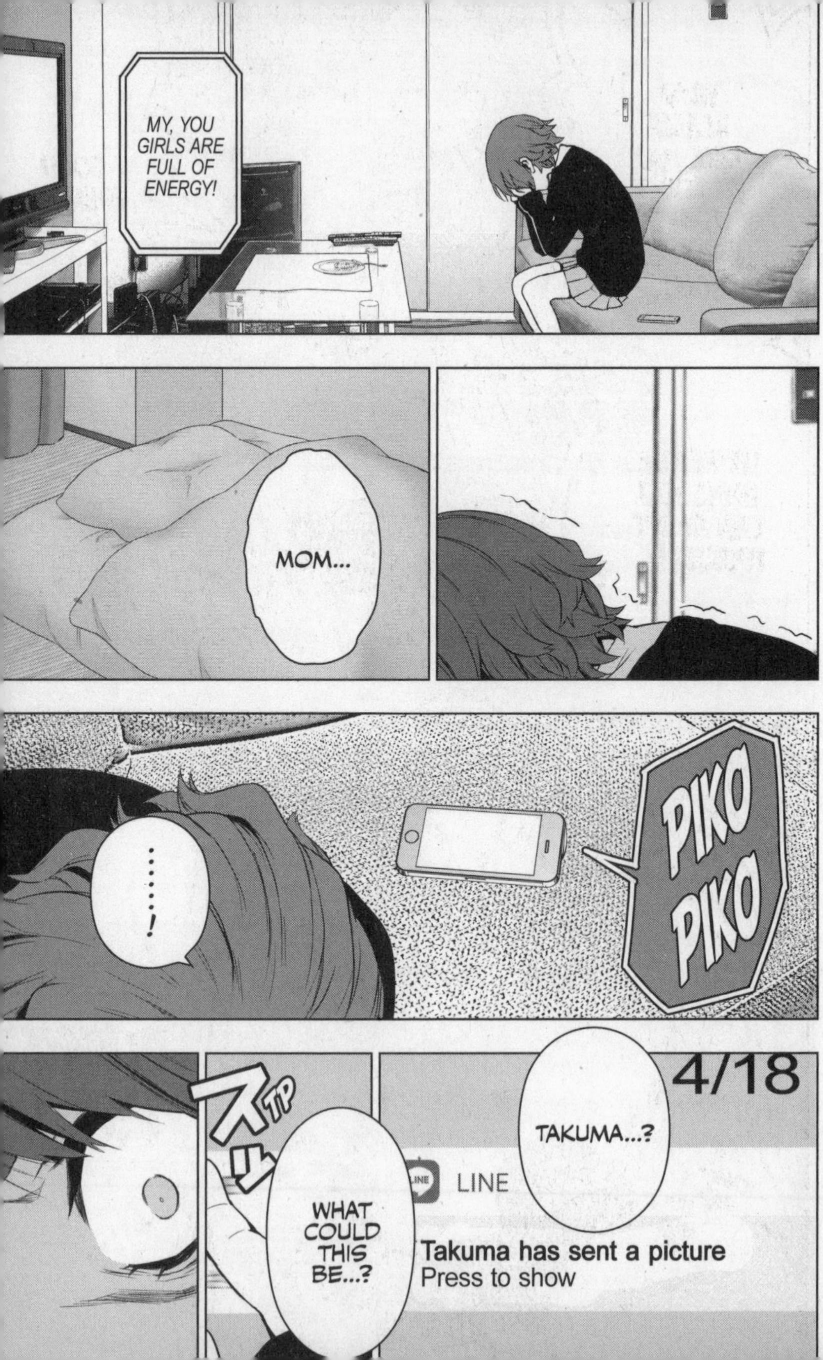
MY, YOU GIRLS ARE FULL OF ENERGY!
MOM...
PIKO PIKO
......!
4/18
TAKUMA...?
LINE
Takuma has sent a picture
Press to show
WHAT COULD THIS BE...?
TIP
スッ

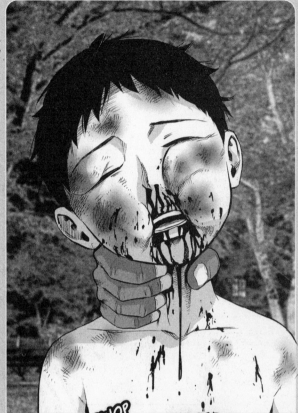

PWOP スポッ

oo ✗

TAKUMA ...!!

If you don't bring 100,000 right now, far worse things might happen to him.

 Enter message:

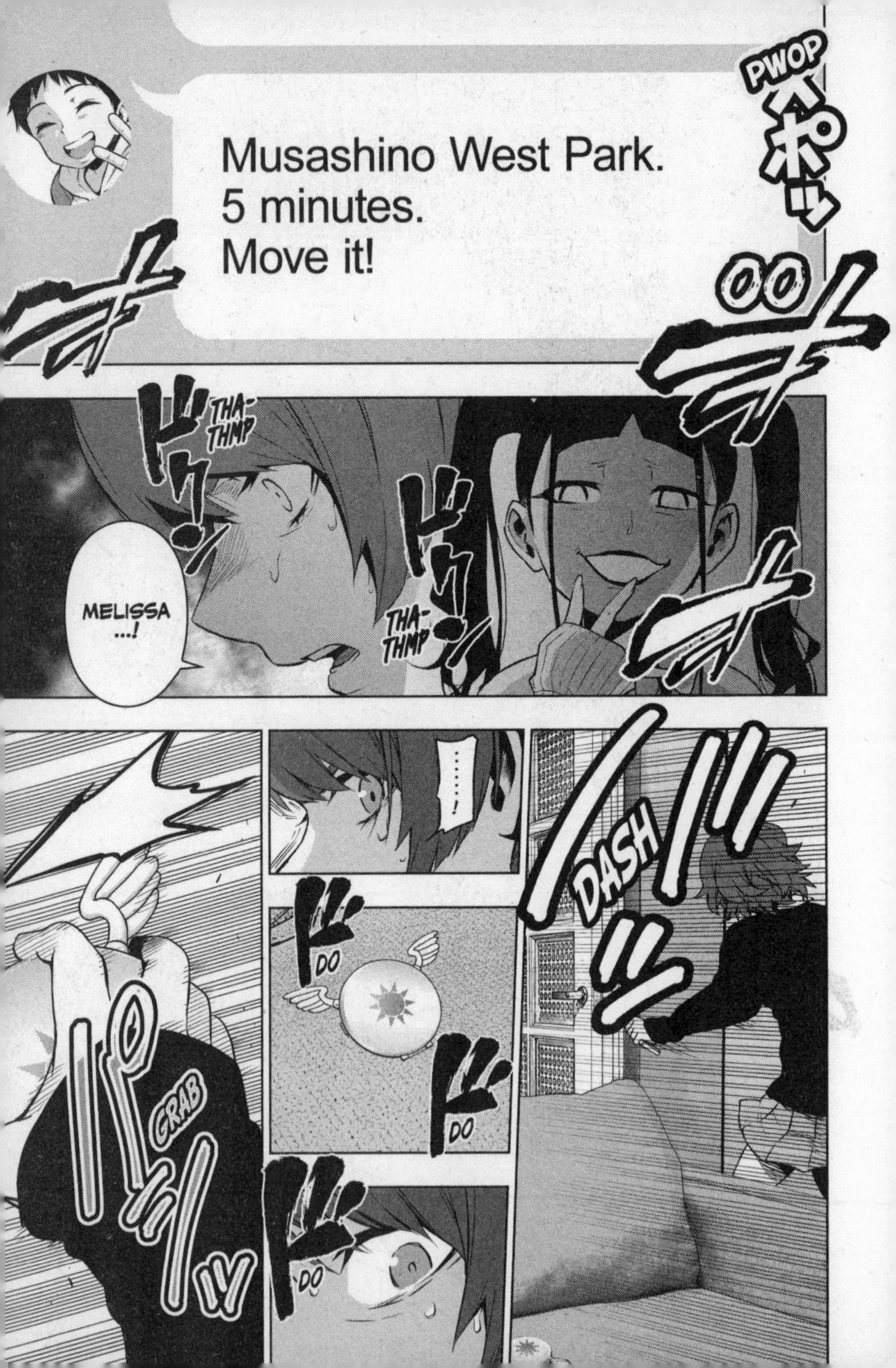
PWOP
Musashino West Park.
5 minutes.
Move it!
THA-THMP
THA-THMP
MELISSA ...!
DASH
......!
DO
DO
DO
GRAB

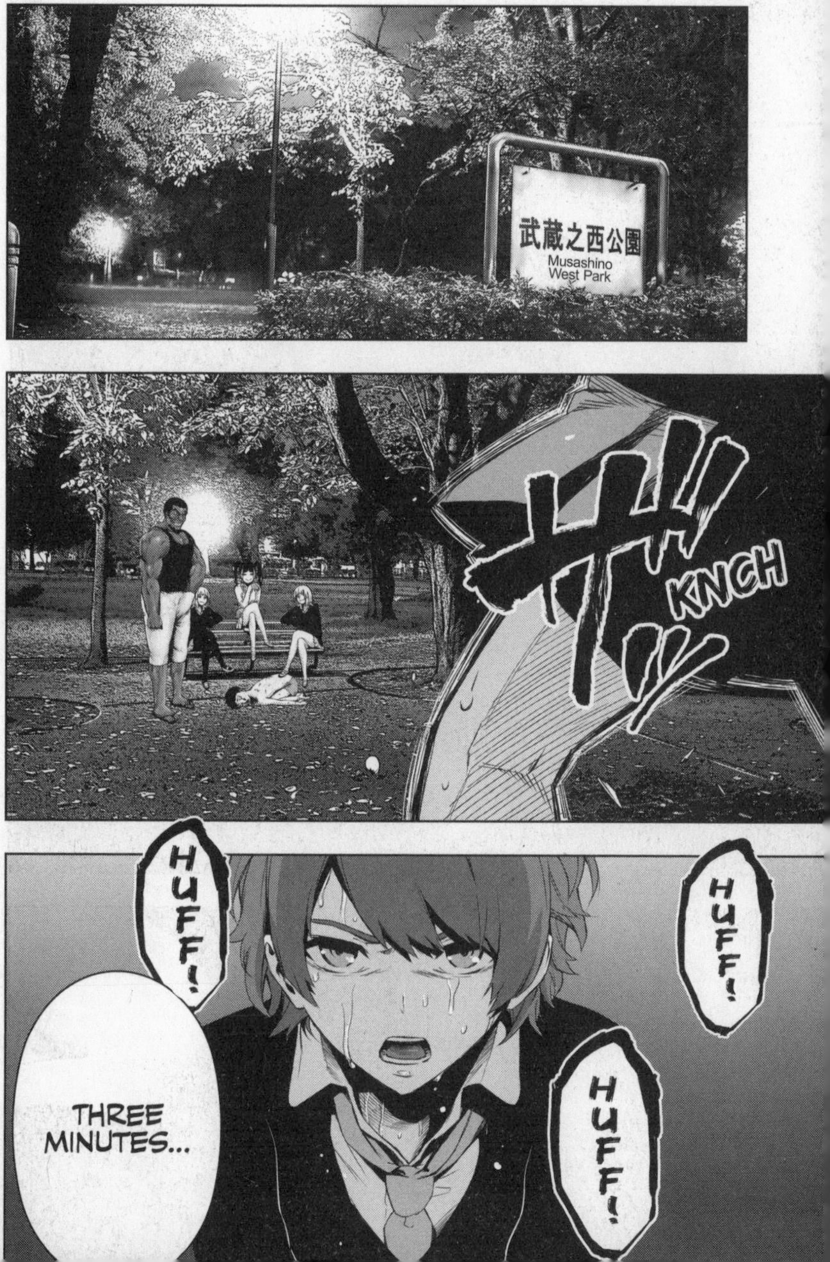
武蔵之西公園
Musashino
West Park
KNCH
HUFF!
HUFF!
HUFF!
THREE MINUTES...

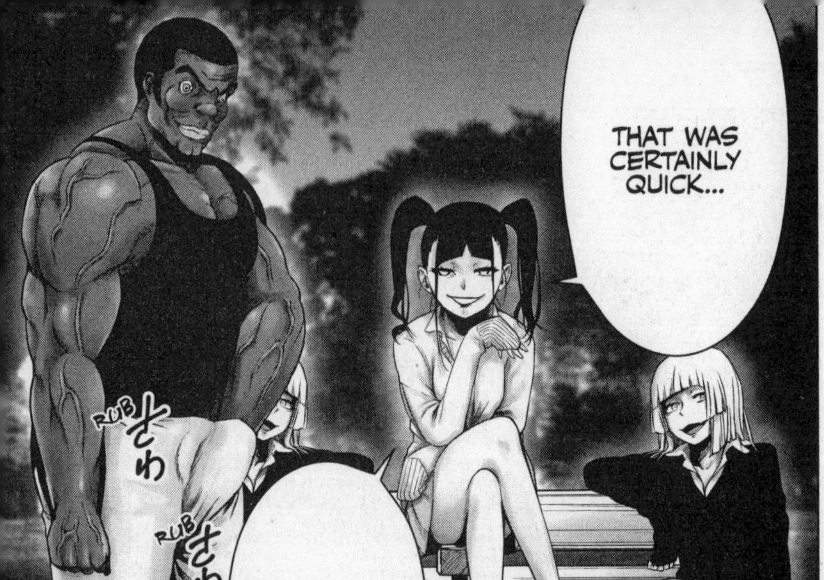
THAT WAS CERTAINLY QUICK...
MURDERER'S DAUGHTER!
RUB さわ
RUB さわ
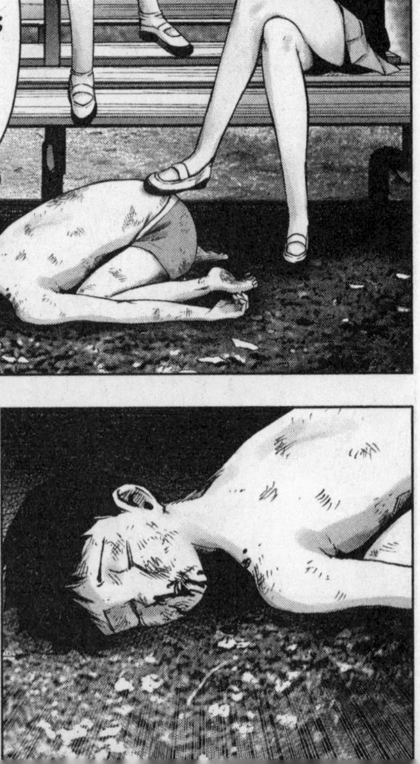
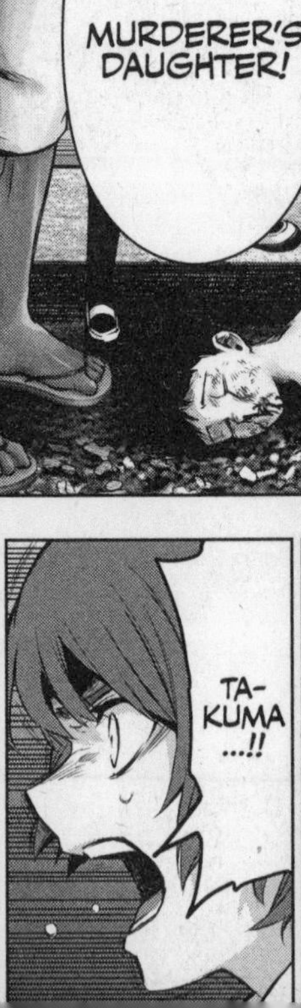
TA-KUMA ...!!
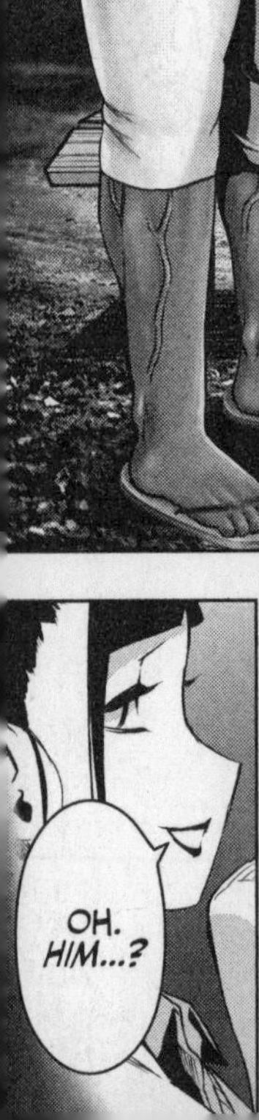
OH. HIM...?

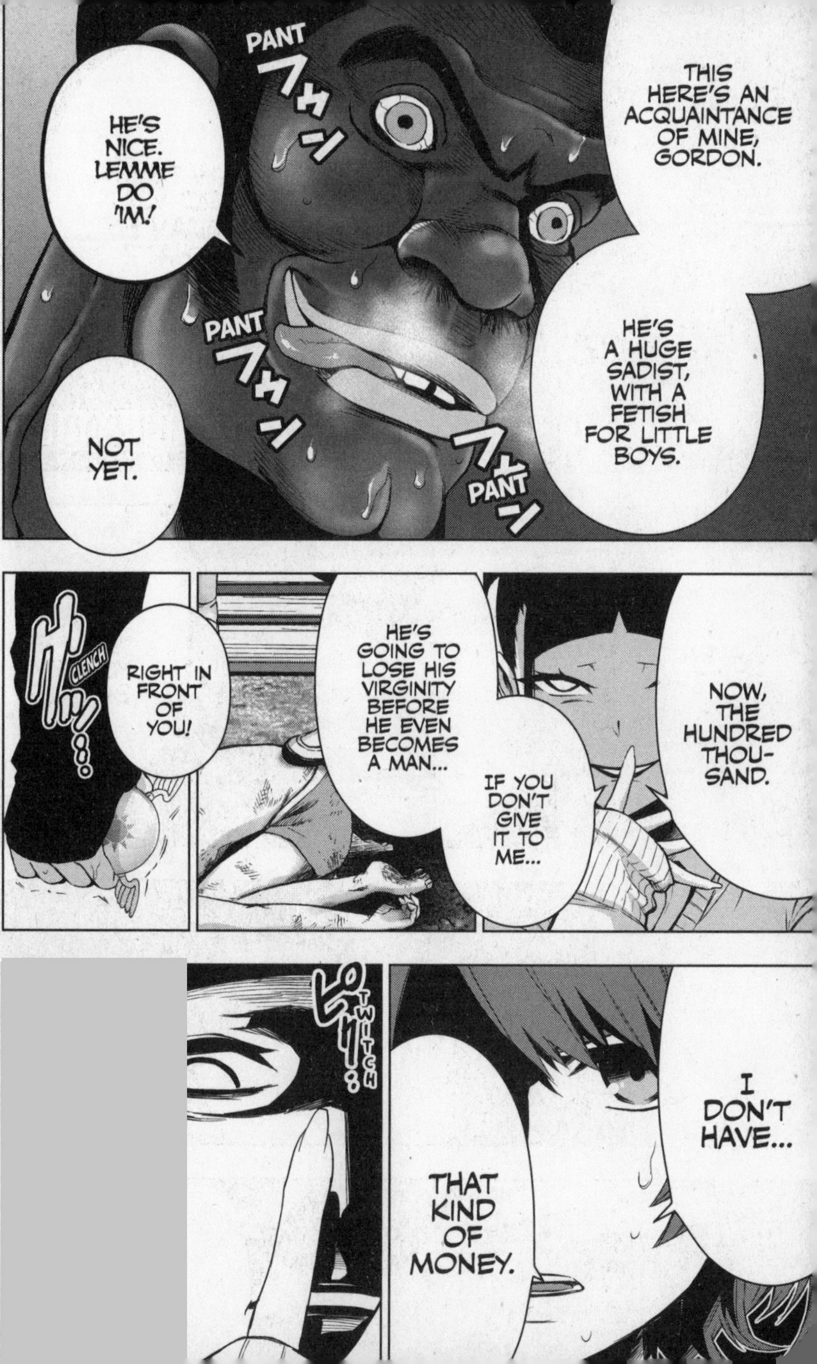
THIS HERE'S AN ACQUAINTANCE OF MINE, GORDON.
HE'S A HUGE SADIST, WITH A FETISH FOR LITTLE BOYS.
PANT
PANT
PANT
HE'S NICE. LEMME DO 'IM!
NOT YET.
NOW, THE HUNDRED THOU-SAND.
IF YOU DON'T GIVE IT TO ME...
HE'S GOING TO LOSE HIS VIRGINITY BEFORE HE EVEN BECOMES A MAN...
RIGHT IN FRONT OF YOU!
CLENCH
I DON'T HAVE...
THAT KIND OF MONEY.
TWITCH

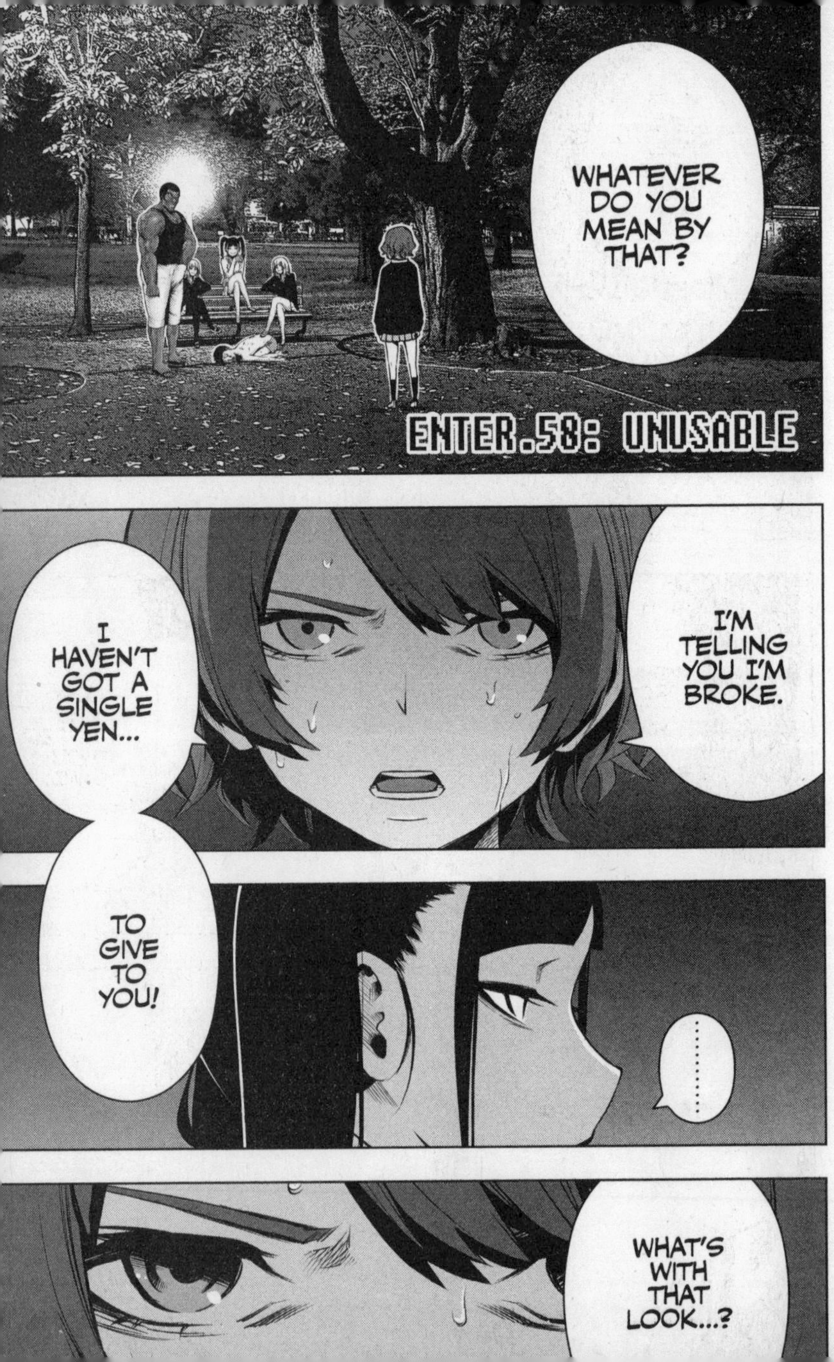
WHATEVER DO YOU MEAN BY THAT?
ENTER.58: UNUSABLE
I'M TELLING YOU I'M BROKE.
I HAVEN'T GOT A SINGLE YEN...
TO GIVE TO YOU!
......
WHAT'S WITH THAT LOOK...?

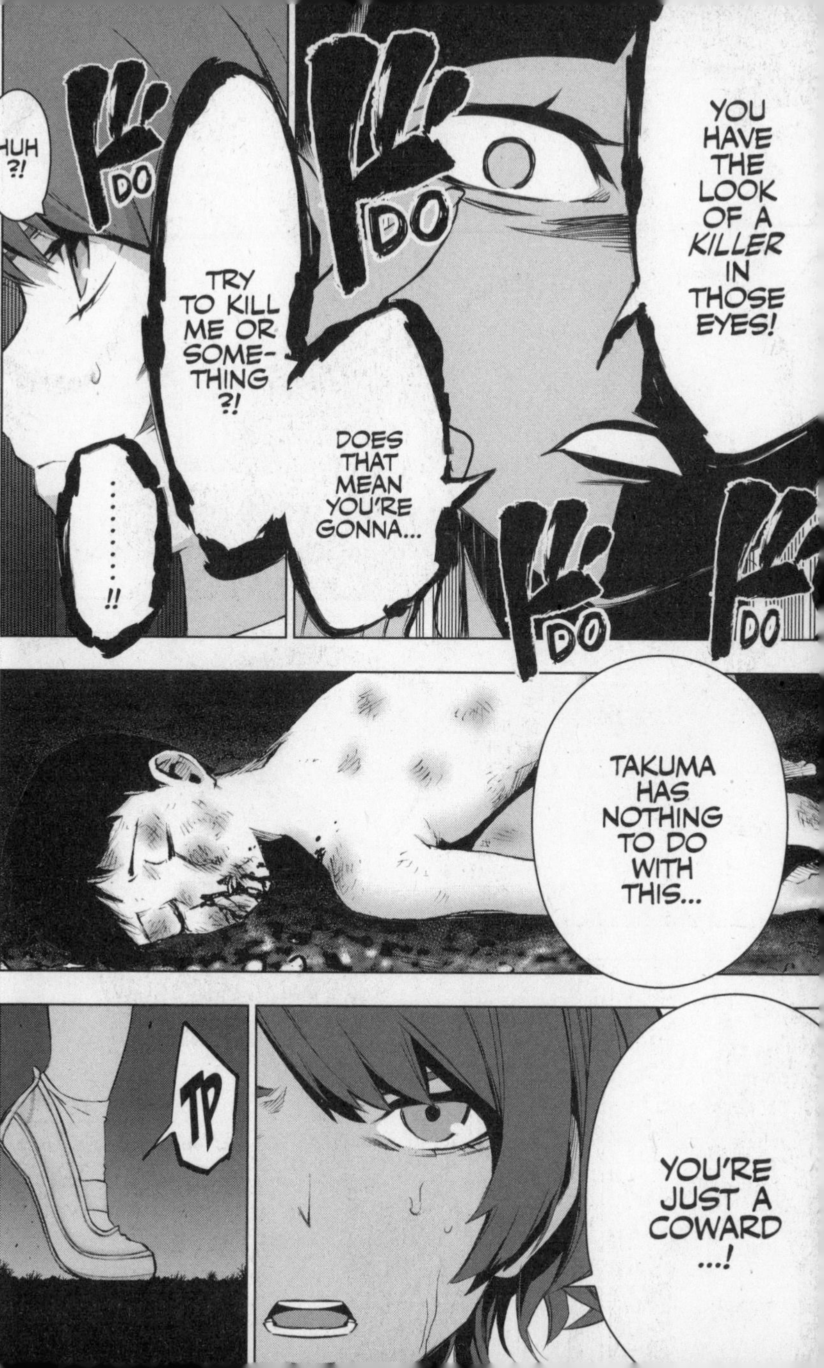
YOU HAVE THE LOOK OF A *KILLER* IN THOSE EYES!
DO
DO
DO
DO
DOES THAT MEAN YOU'RE GONNA...
TRY TO KILL ME OR SOME-THING ?!
HUH ?!
......!!
TAKUMA HAS NOTHING TO DO WITH THIS...
YOU'RE JUST A COWARD ...!
TP

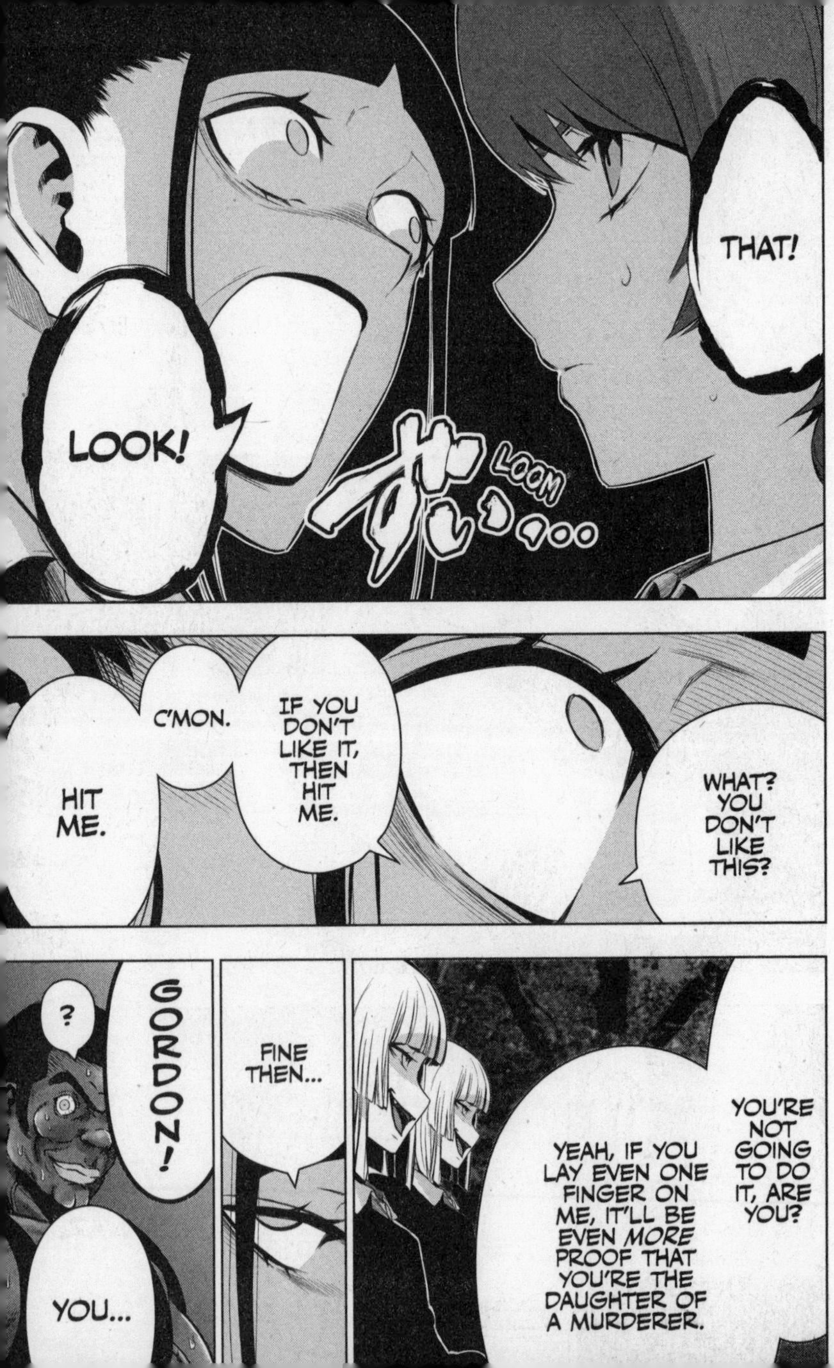
THAT!
LOOM
LOOK!
WHAT? YOU DON'T LIKE THIS?
IF YOU DON'T LIKE IT, THEN HIT ME.
C'MON.
HIT ME.
YOU'RE NOT GOING TO DO IT, ARE YOU?
YEAH, IF YOU LAY EVEN ONE FINGER ON ME, IT'LL BE EVEN *MORE* PROOF THAT YOU'RE THE DAUGHTER OF A MURDERER.
FINE THEN...
GORDON!
?
YOU...

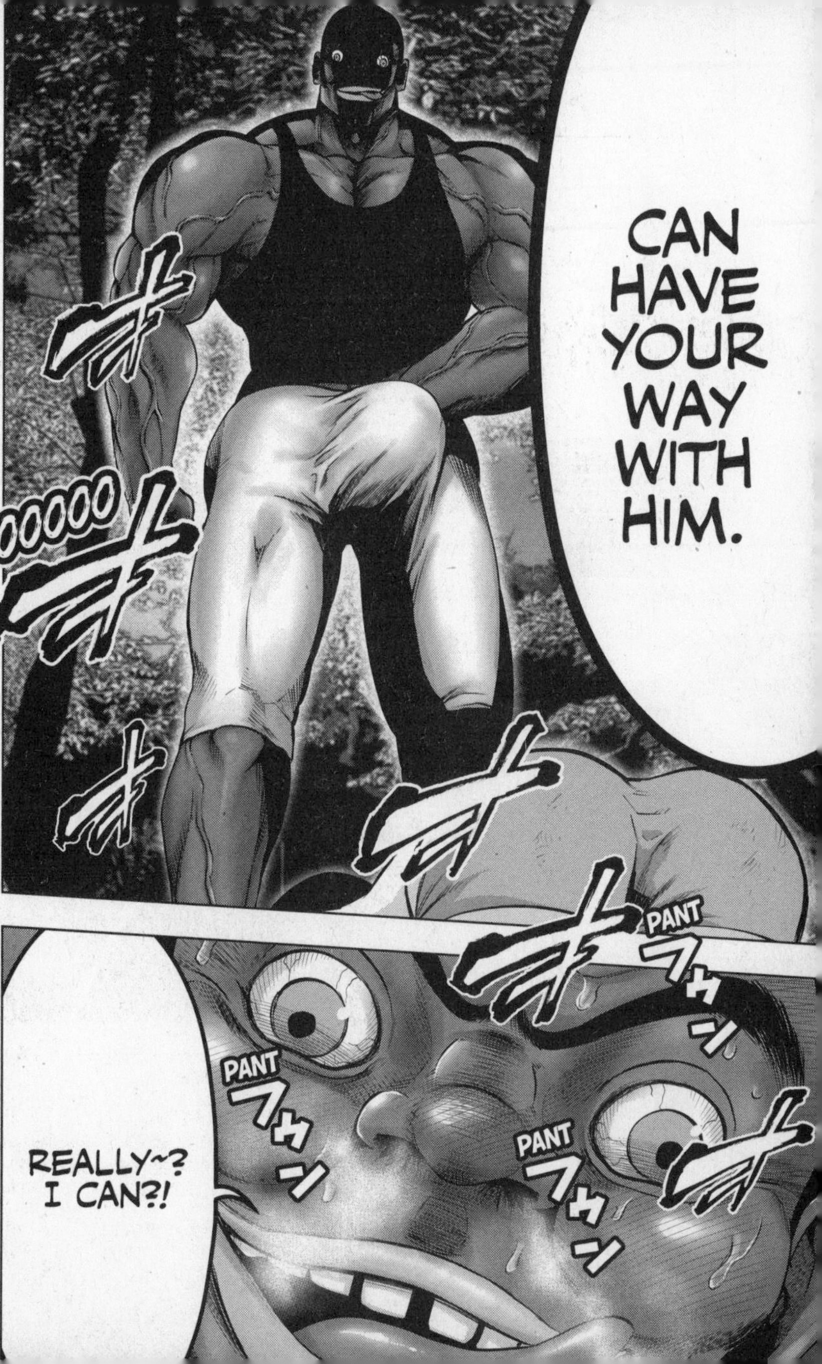
CAN HAVE YOUR WAY WITH HIM.
OOOOOO
PANT
PANT
PANT
REALLY~? I CAN?!

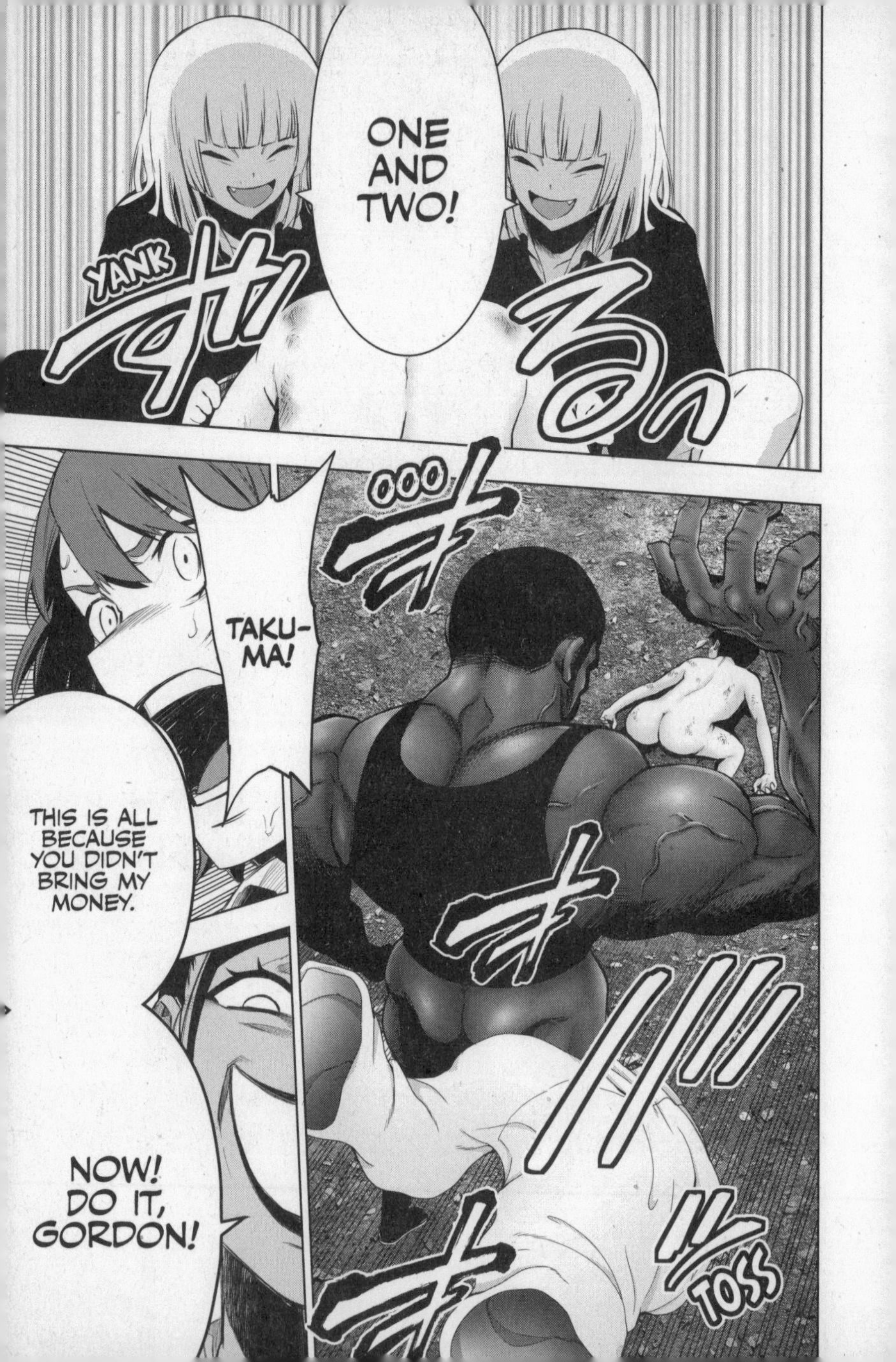
ONE AND TWO!
YANK
OOO
TOSS
TAKUMA!
THIS IS ALL BECAUSE YOU DIDN'T BRING MY MONEY.
NOW! DO IT, GORDON!

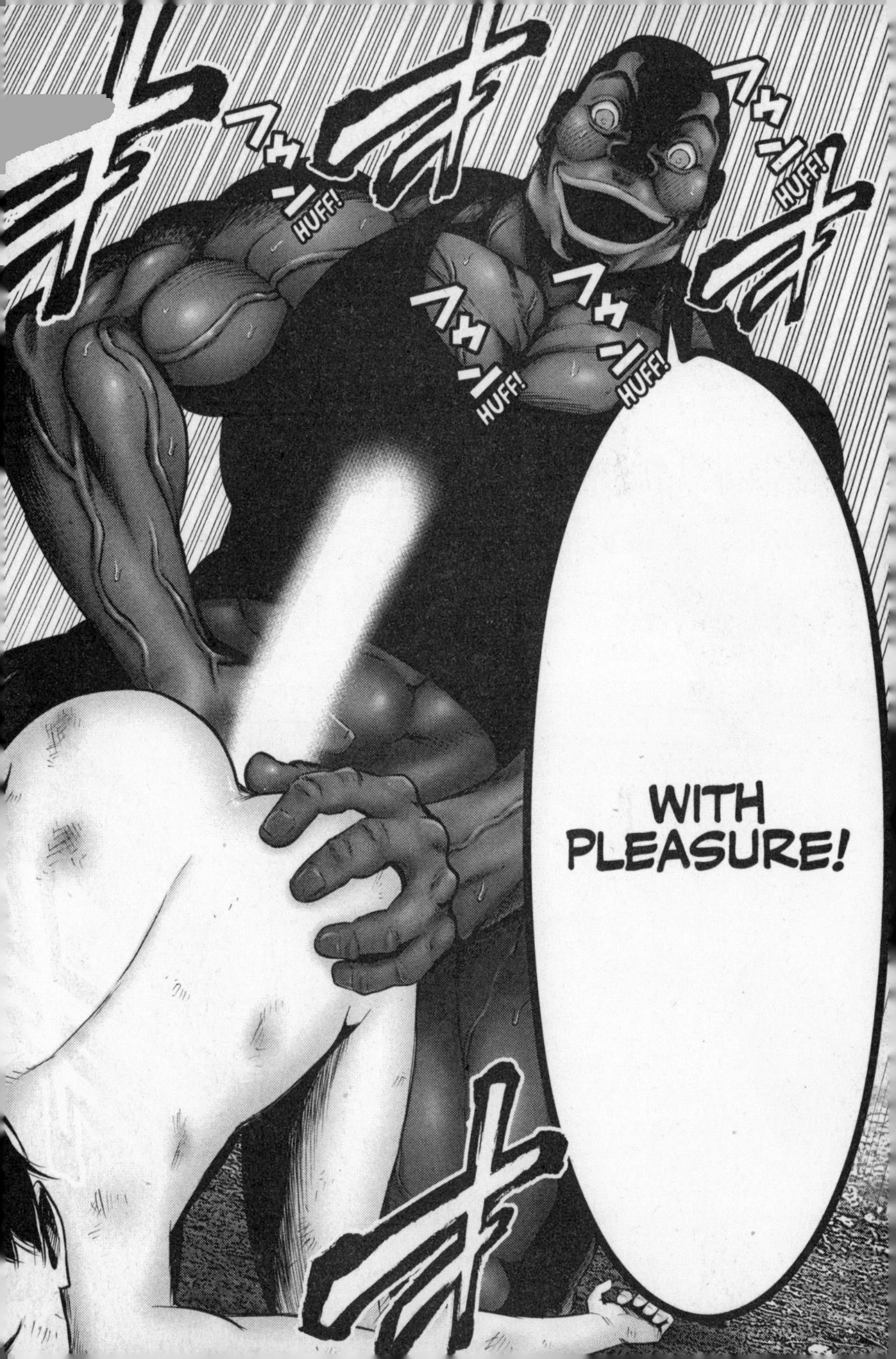

フゥン
HUFF!
フゥン
HUFF!
フゥン
HUFF!
フゥン
HUFF!
WITH PLEASURE!

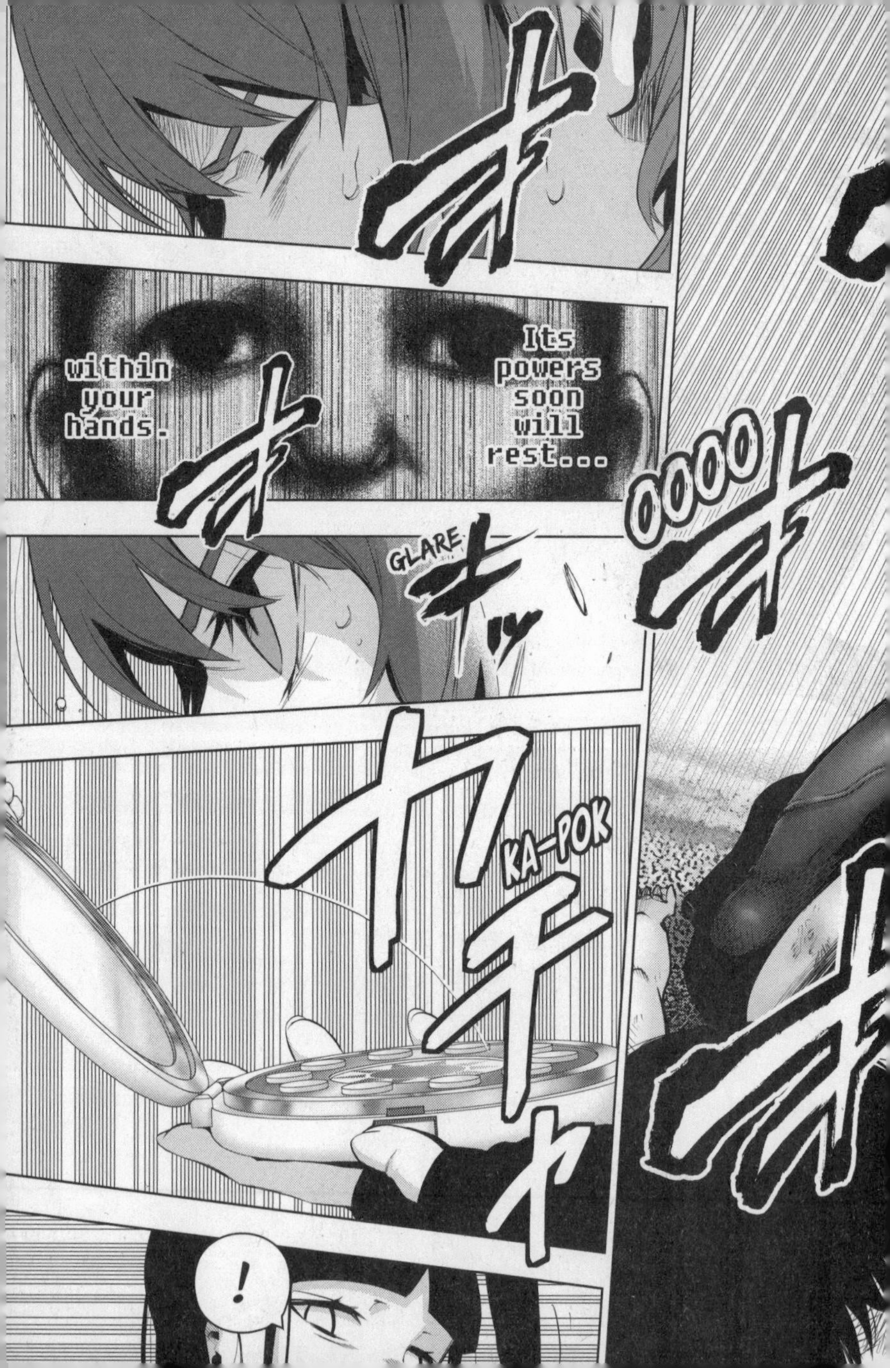
OOOO
Its powers soon will rest...
within your hands.
GLARE
KA-POK
!

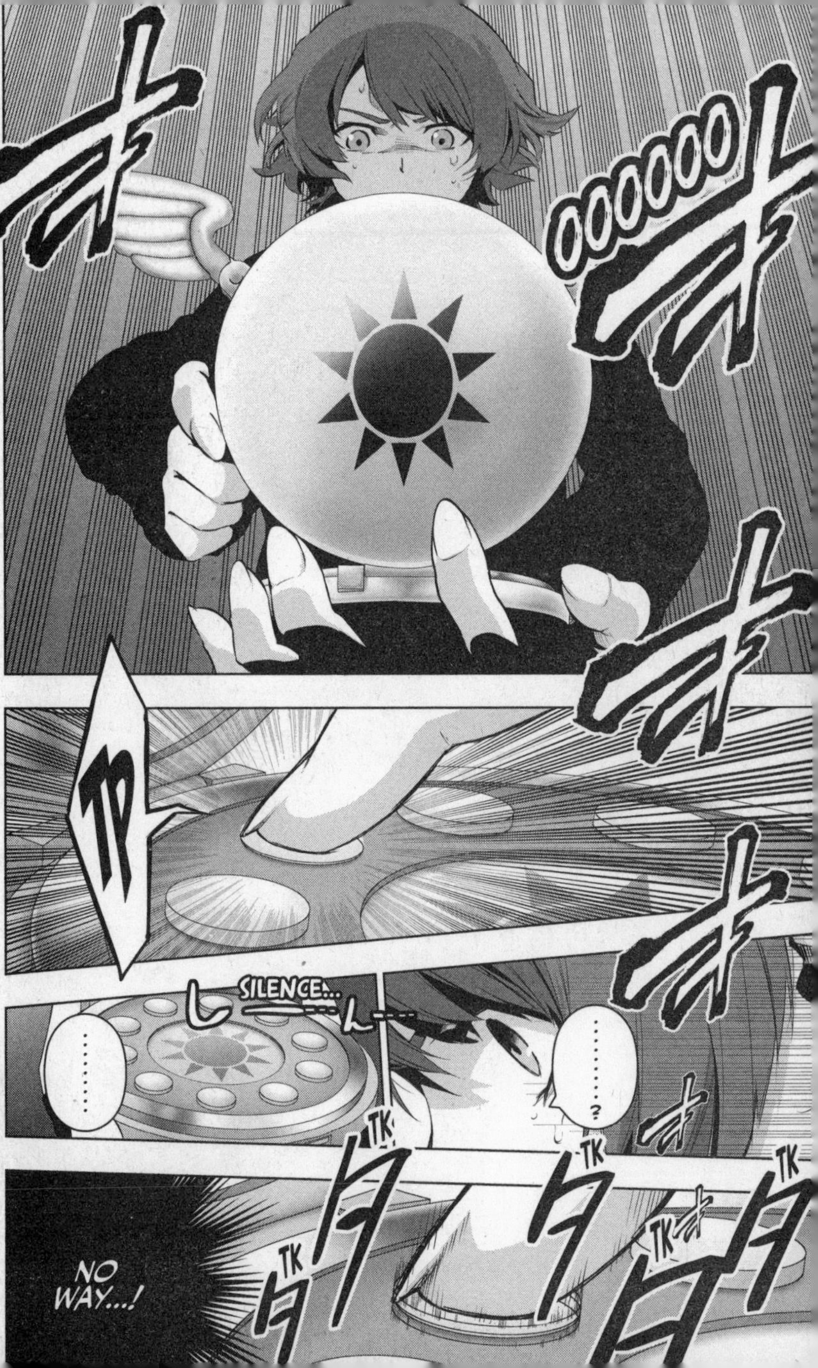

OOOOOO
TP
SILENCE...
.......?
....
TK TK TK TK TK
NO WAY...!

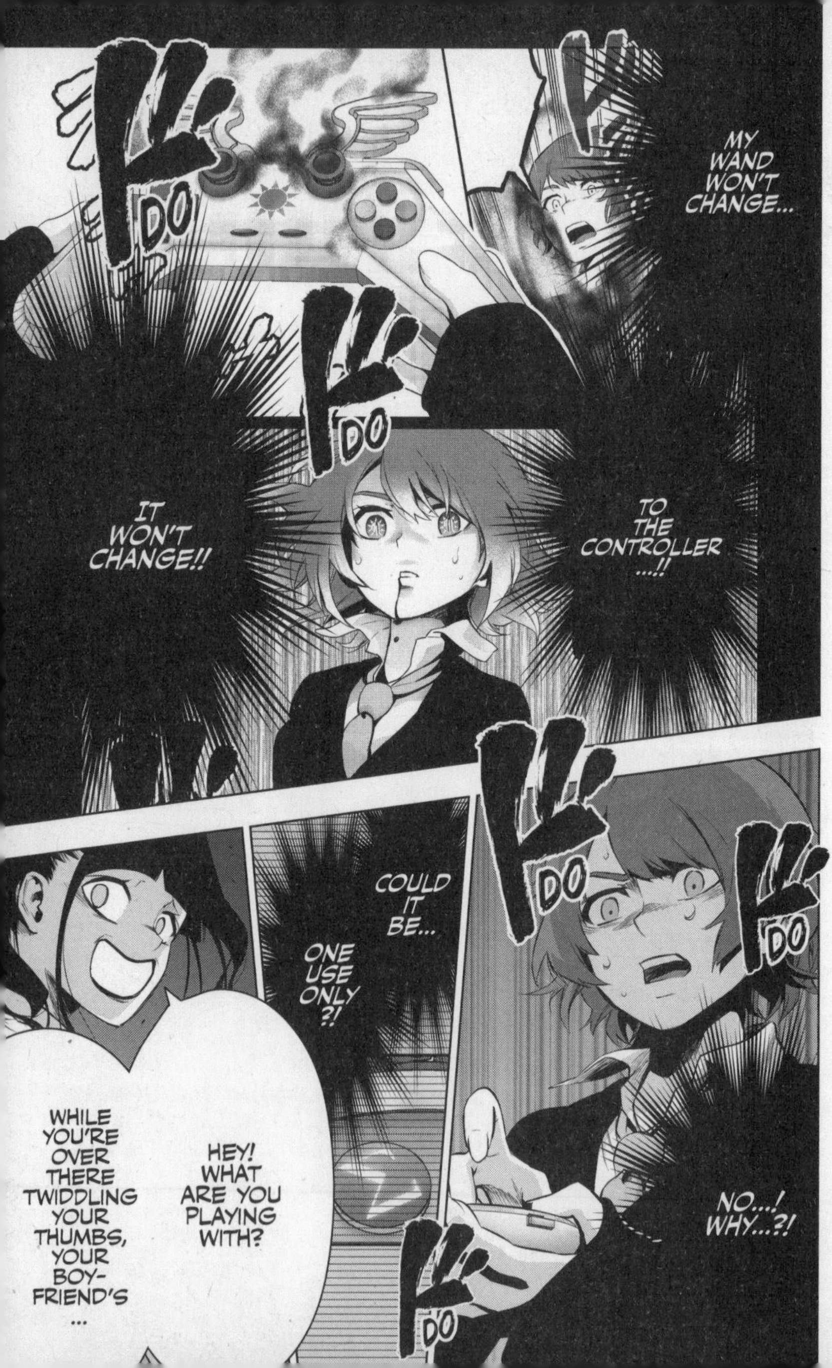
MY WAND WON'T CHANGE...
DO
DO
DO
TO THE CONTROLLER ...!!
IT WON'T CHANGE!!
DO
DO
NO...! WHY...?!
DO
COULD IT BE...
ONE USE ONLY?!
HEY! WHAT ARE YOU PLAYING WITH?
WHILE YOU'RE OVER THERE TWIDDLING YOUR THUMBS, YOUR BOY-FRIEND'S ...

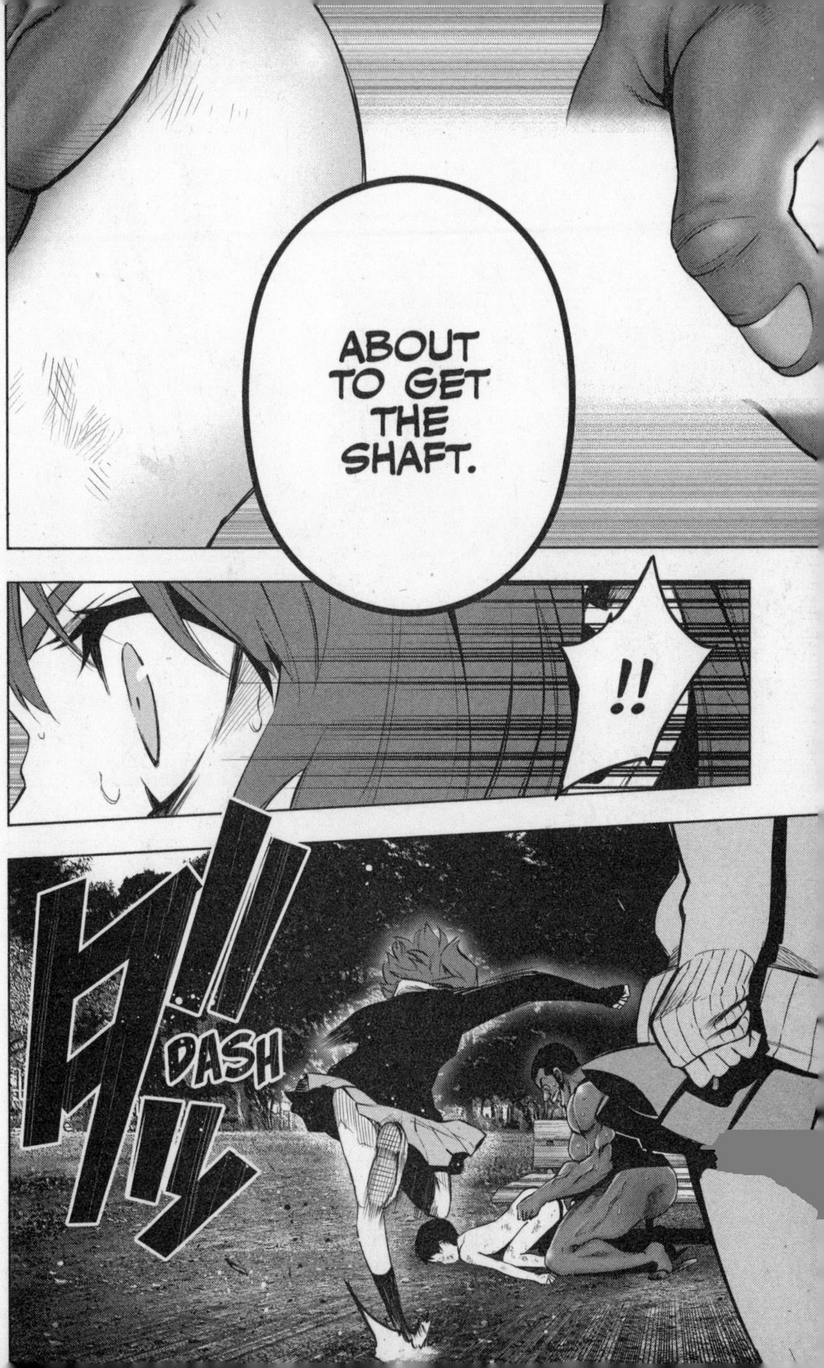
ABOUT TO GET THE SHAFT.
!!
DASH

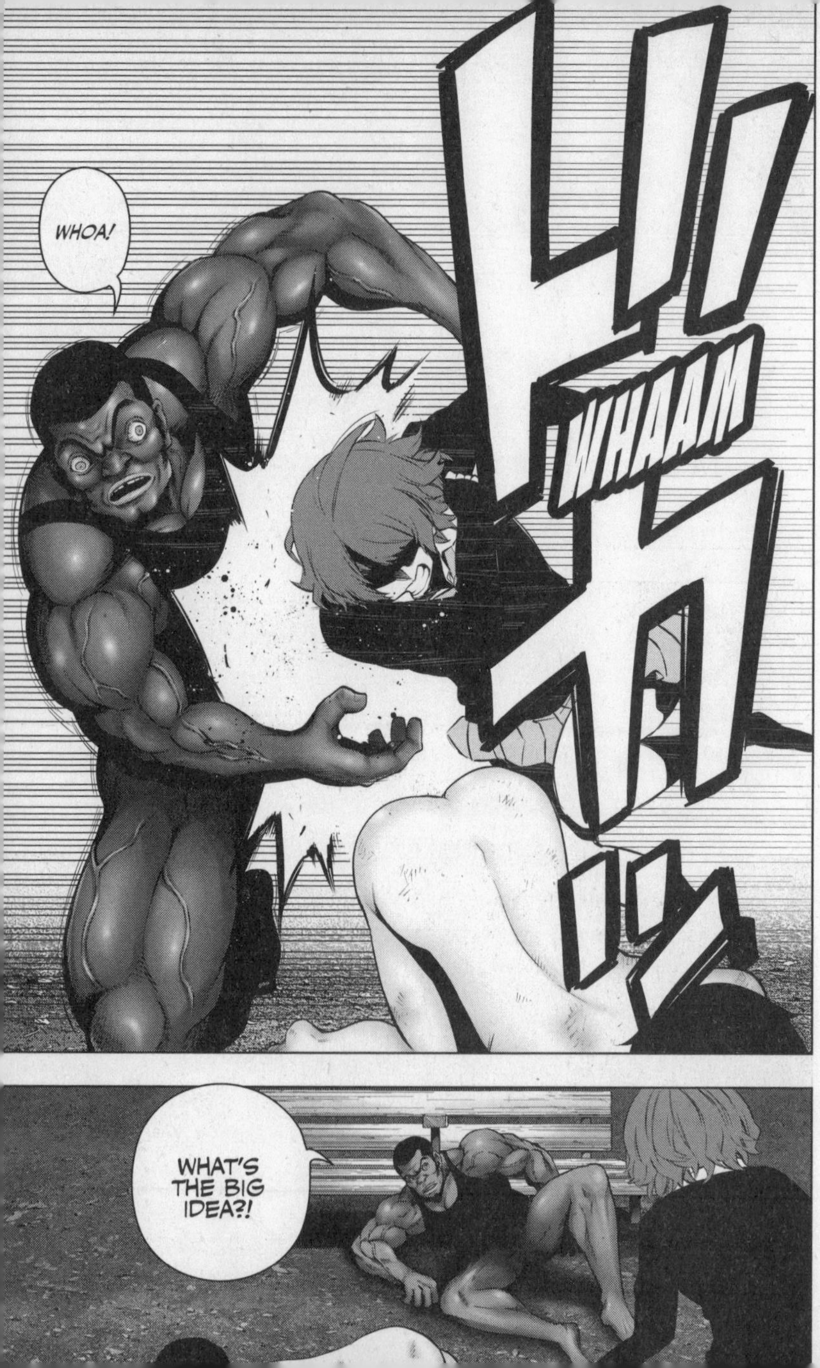
WHOA!
WHAAM
WHAT'S THE BIG IDEA?!

TAKUMA HAS NOTHING TO DO WITH ANY OF THIS!

IF YOU'RE GOING TO HURT SOME- ONE, HURT ME!!

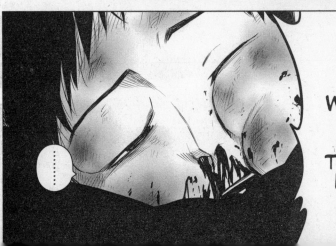

I WON'T LET YOU TOUCH HIM!!

......

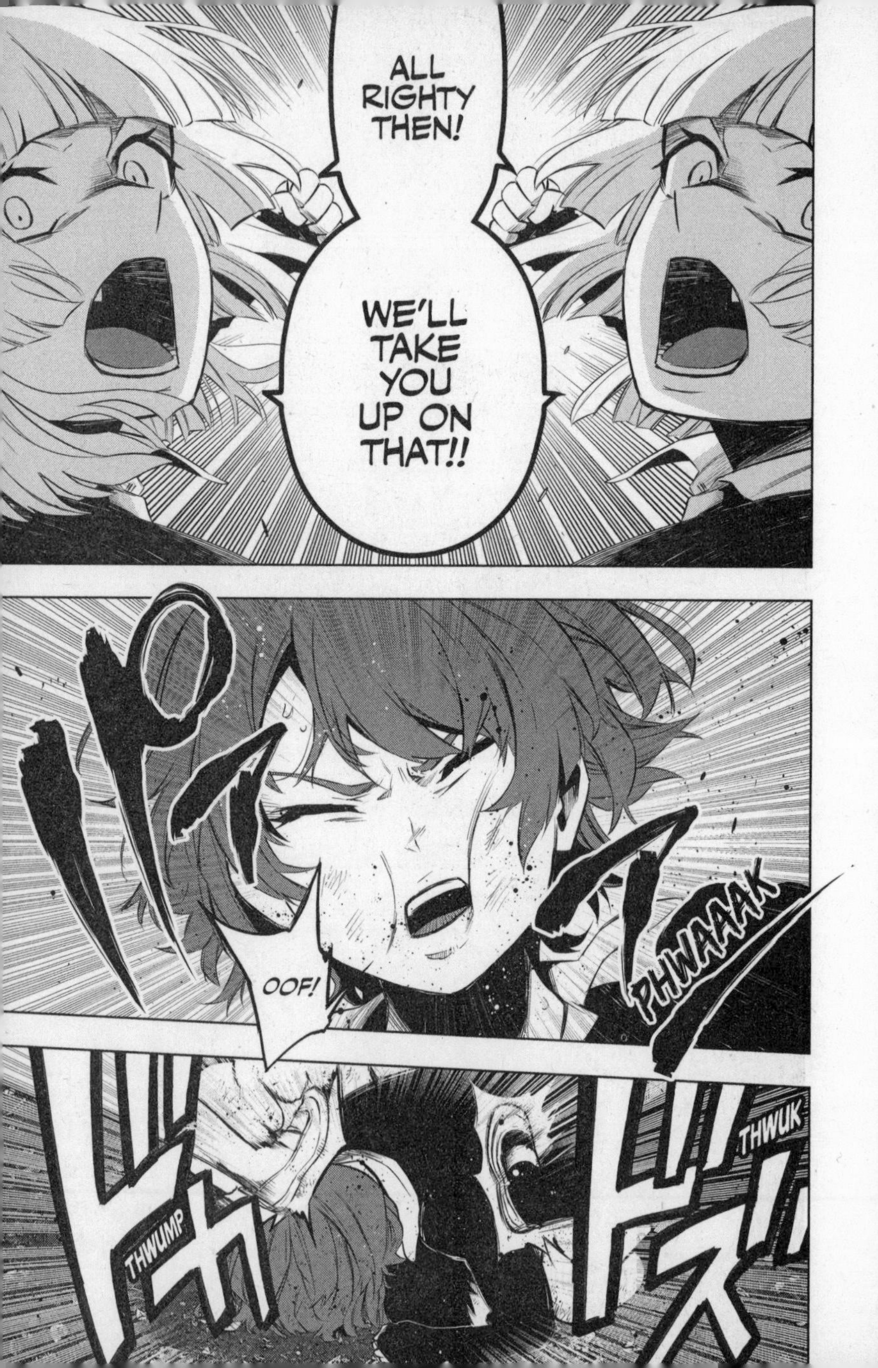
ALL RIGHTY THEN!
WE'LL TAKE YOU UP ON THAT!!
PHWAAAK
OOF!
THWUK
THWUMP

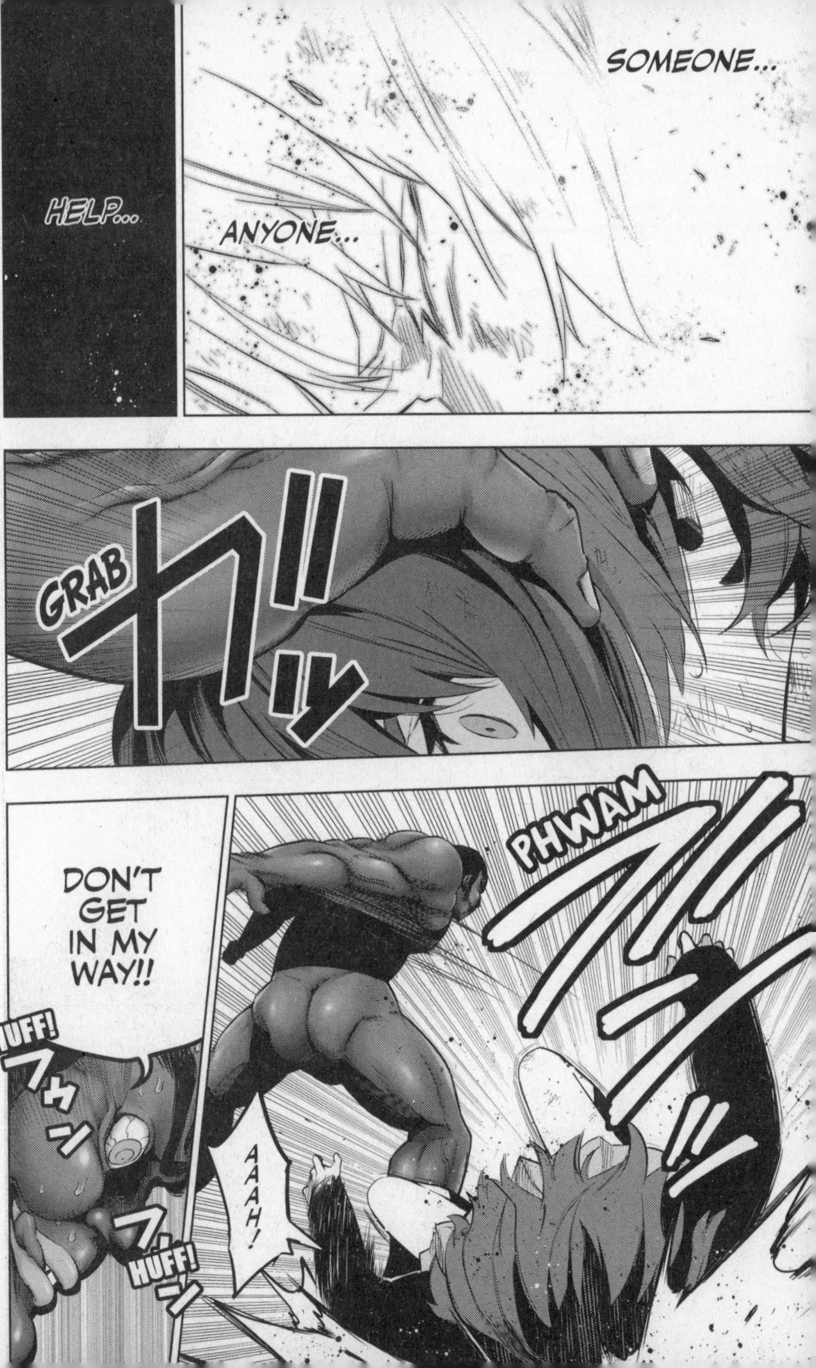
SOMEONE...
ANYONE...
HELP...
GRAB
PHWAM
AAAH!
DON'T GET IN MY WAY!!
HUFF!
HUFF!

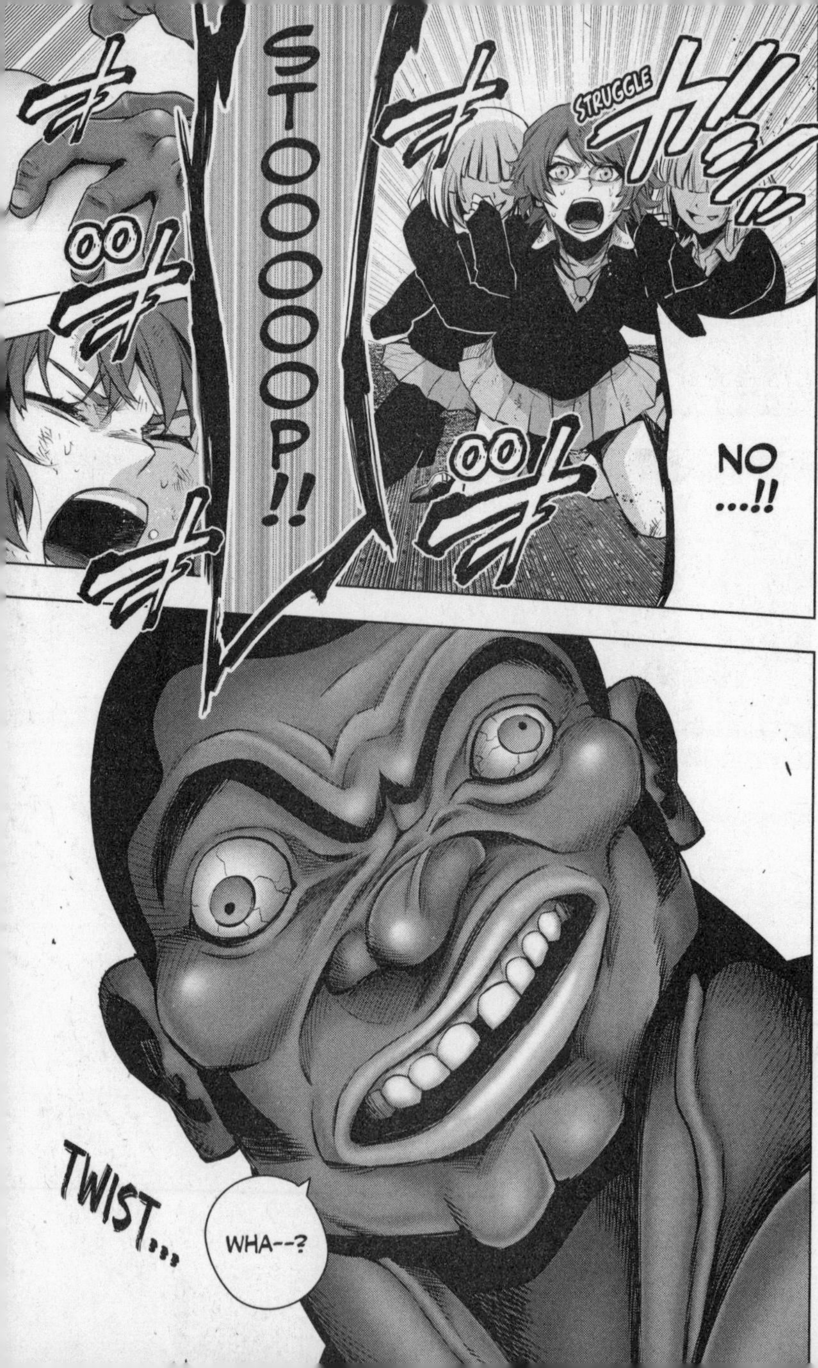
STRUGGLE
NO ...!!
OO
STOOOOOP!!
OO
WHA--?
TWIST...

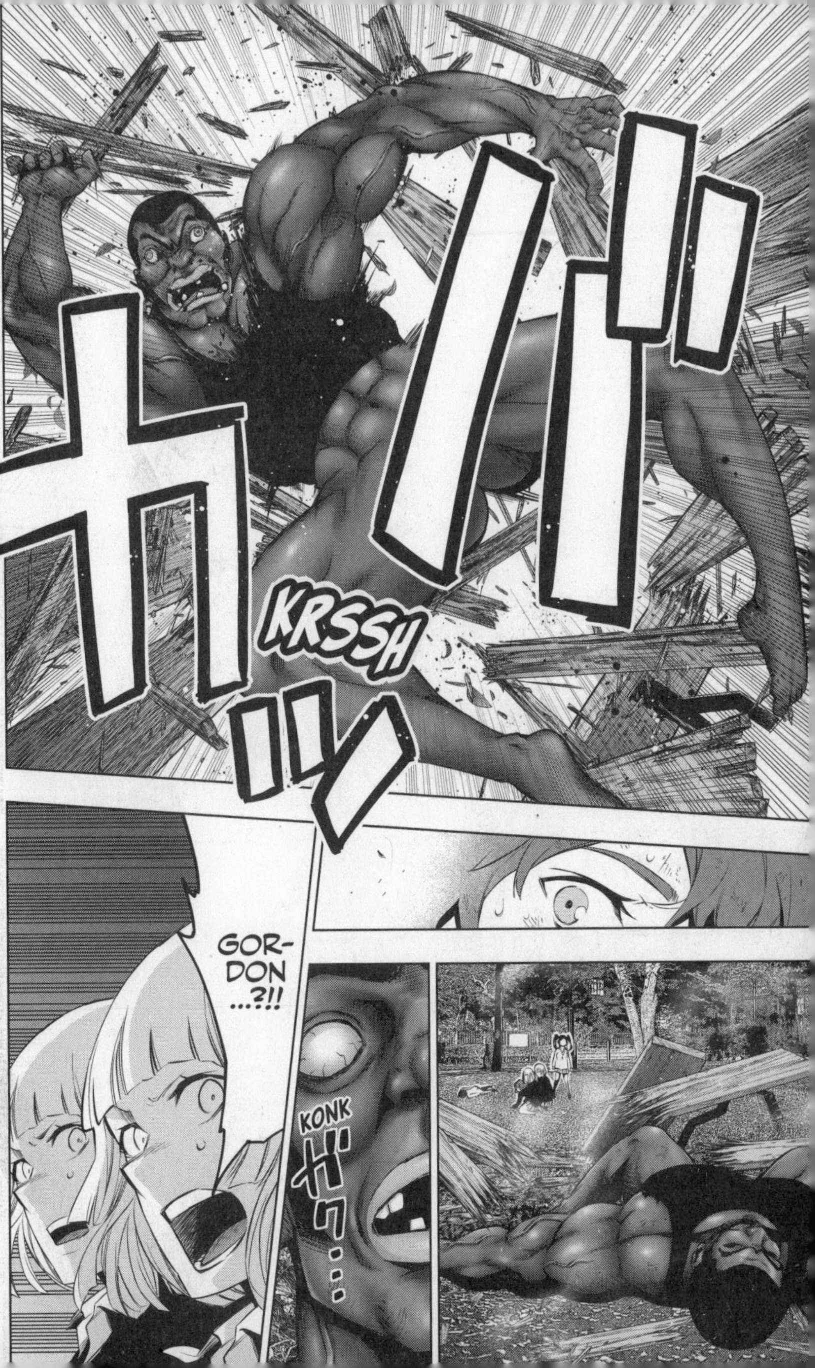
KRSSH
KONK
GOR-DON ...?!!

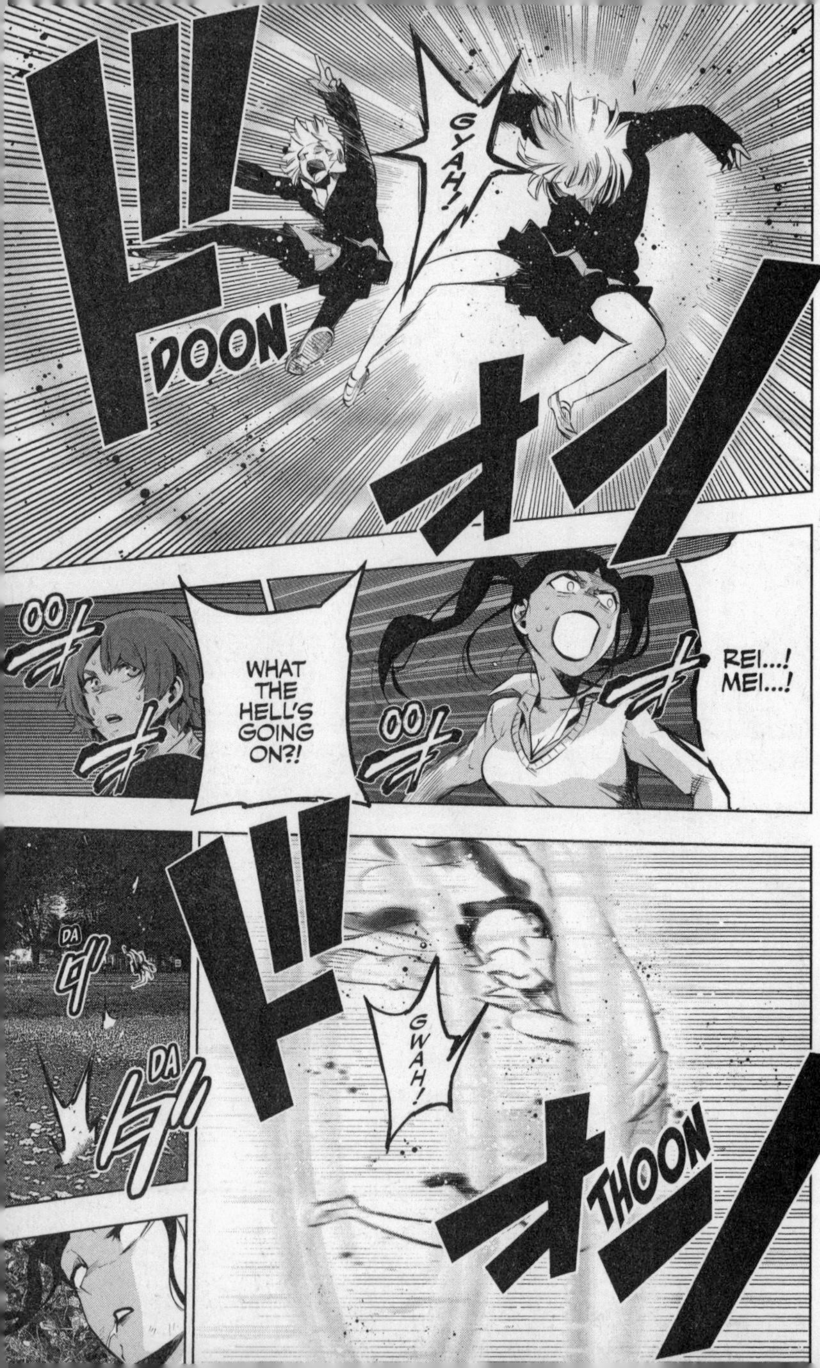
GYAH!
DOON
REI...! MEI...!
OO
WHAT THE HELL'S GOING ON?!
OO
GWAH!
THOON
DA
DA

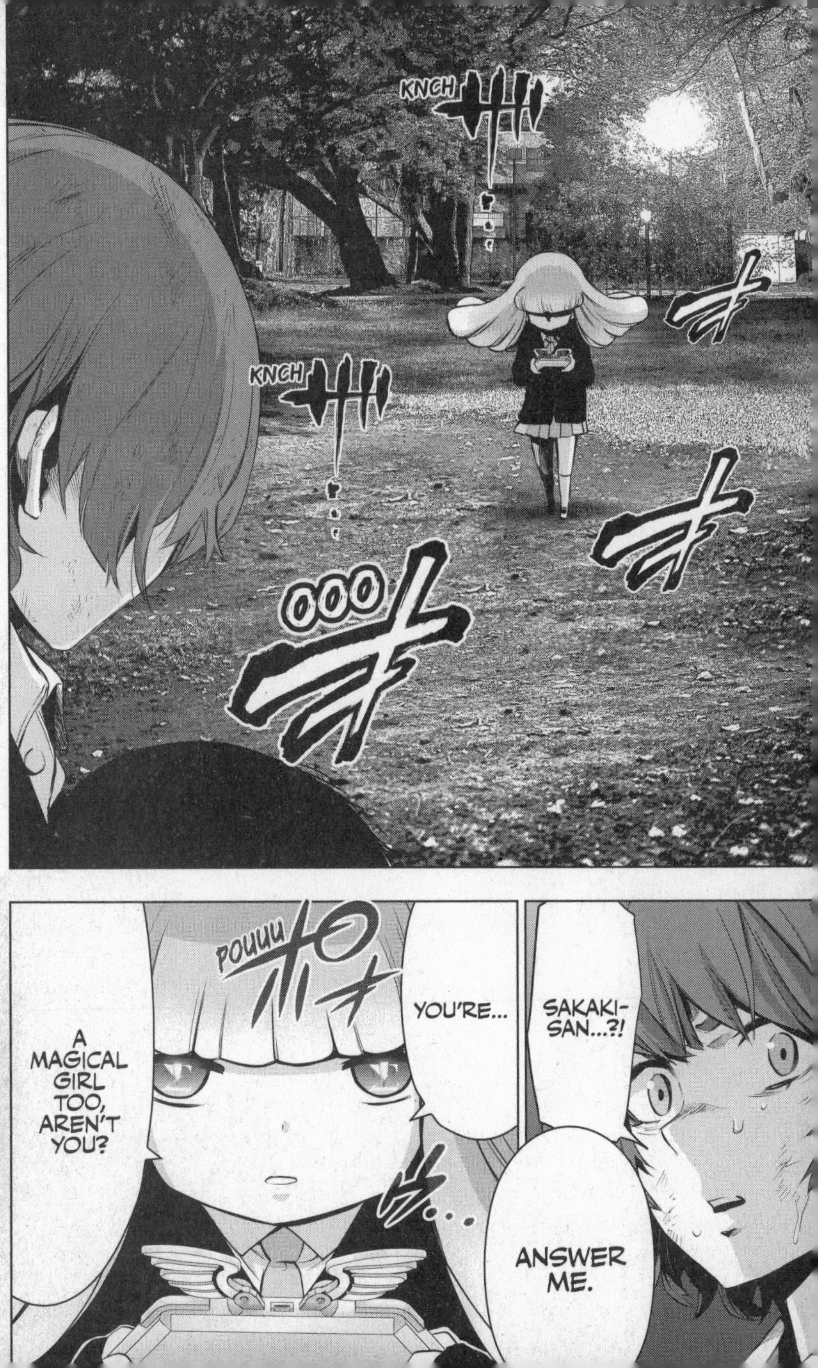
KNCH
KNCH
OOO
SAKAKI-SAN...?!
POUUU
YOU'RE...
A MAGICAL GIRL TOO, AREN'T YOU?
ANSWER ME.

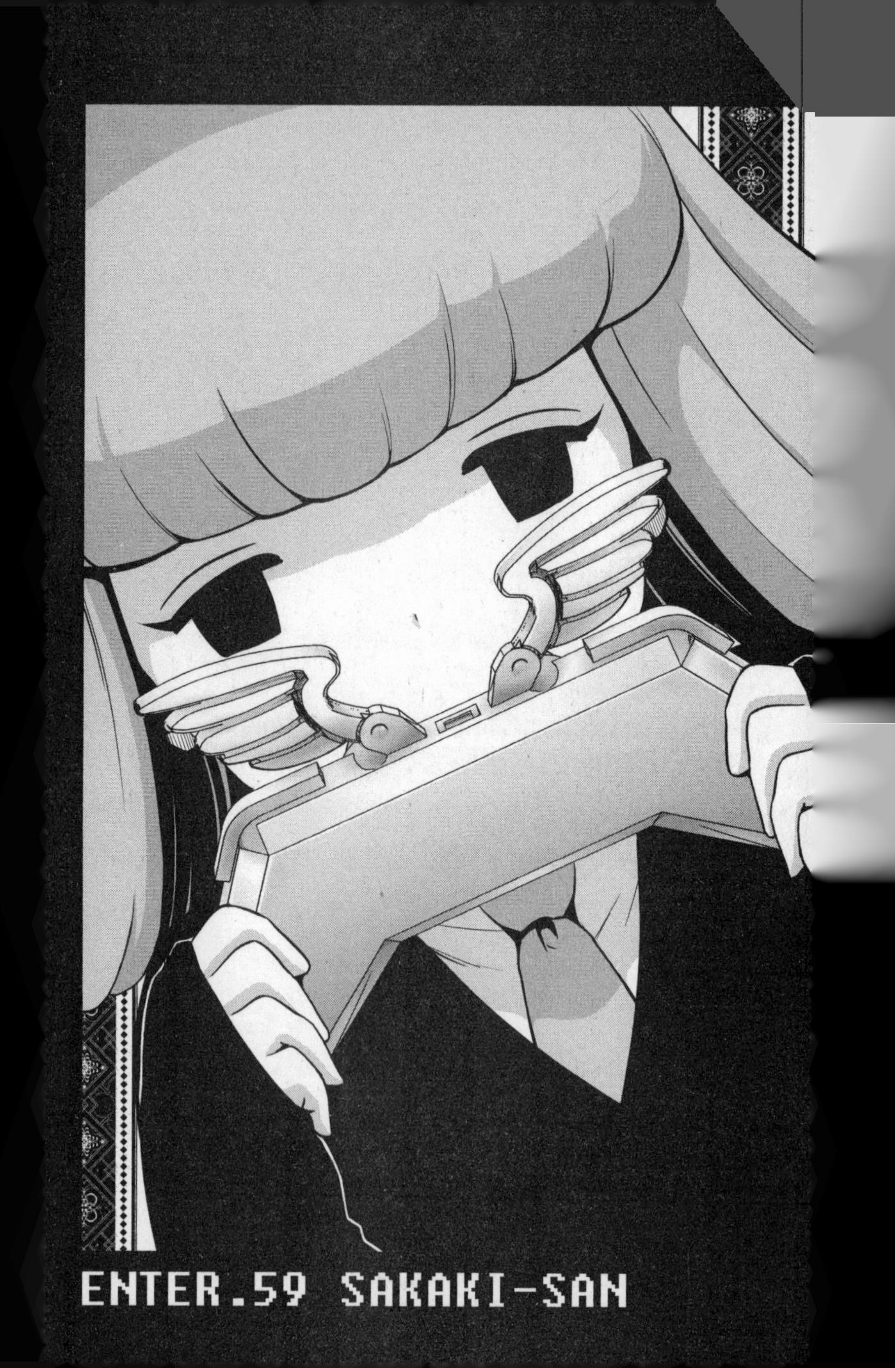

ENTER.59 SAKAKI-SAN

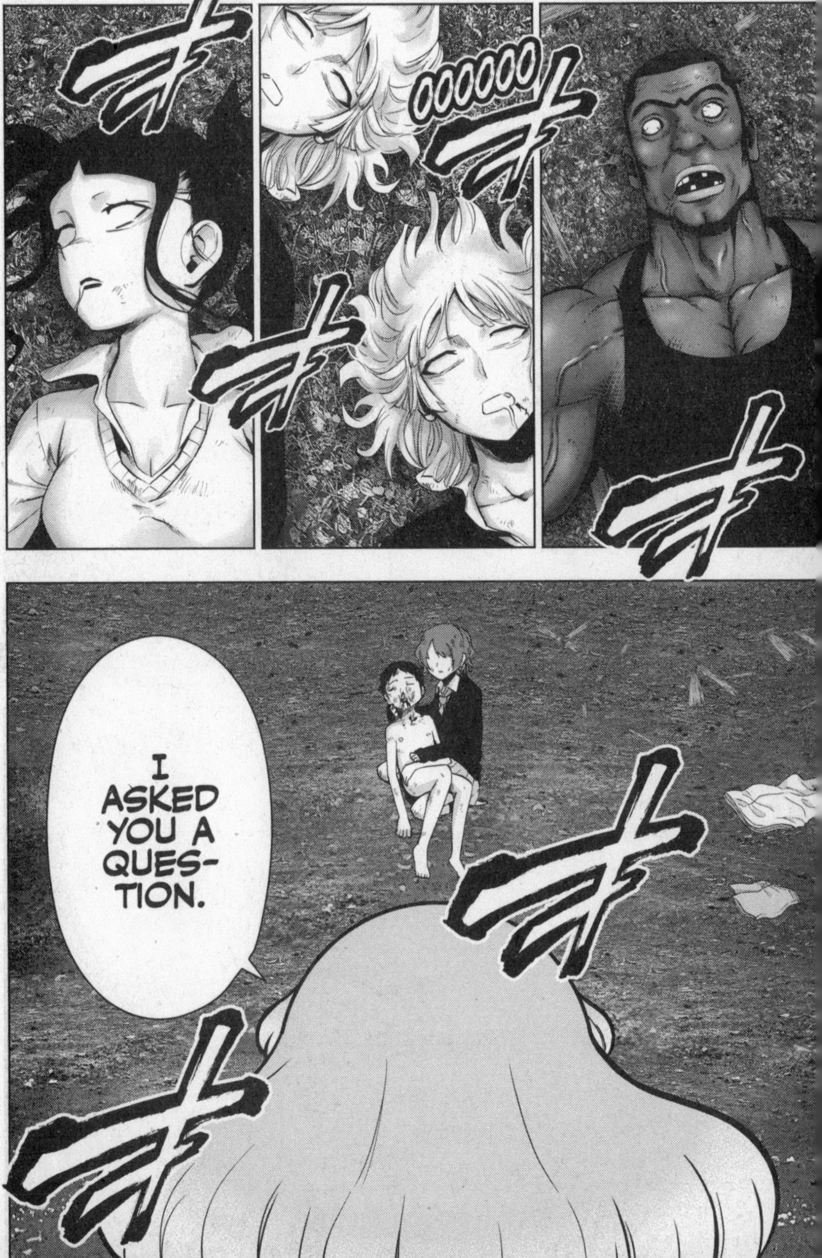
OOOOOO
I ASKED YOU A QUES-TION.

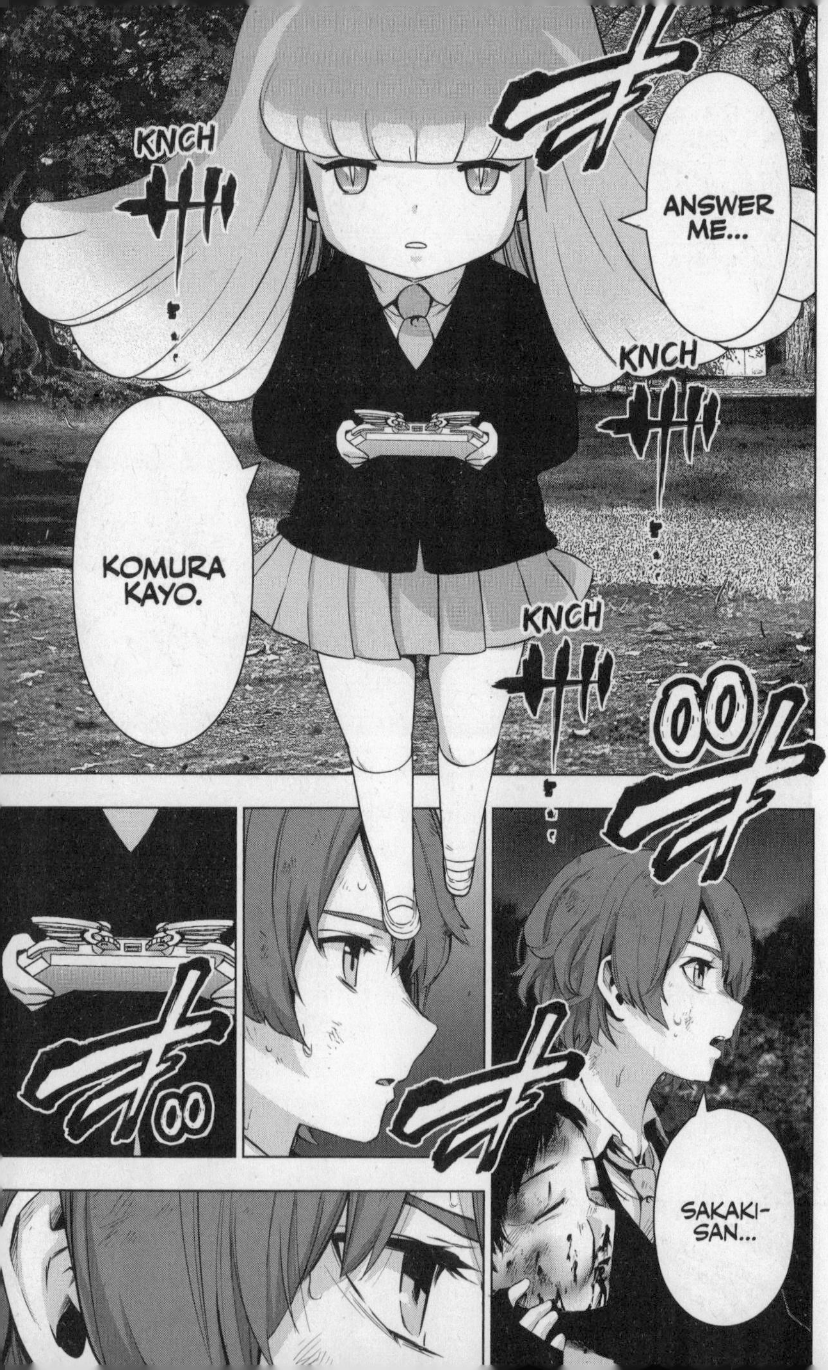
ANSWER ME...
KNCH
KNCH
KNCH
KOMURA KAYO.
SAKAKI-SAN...

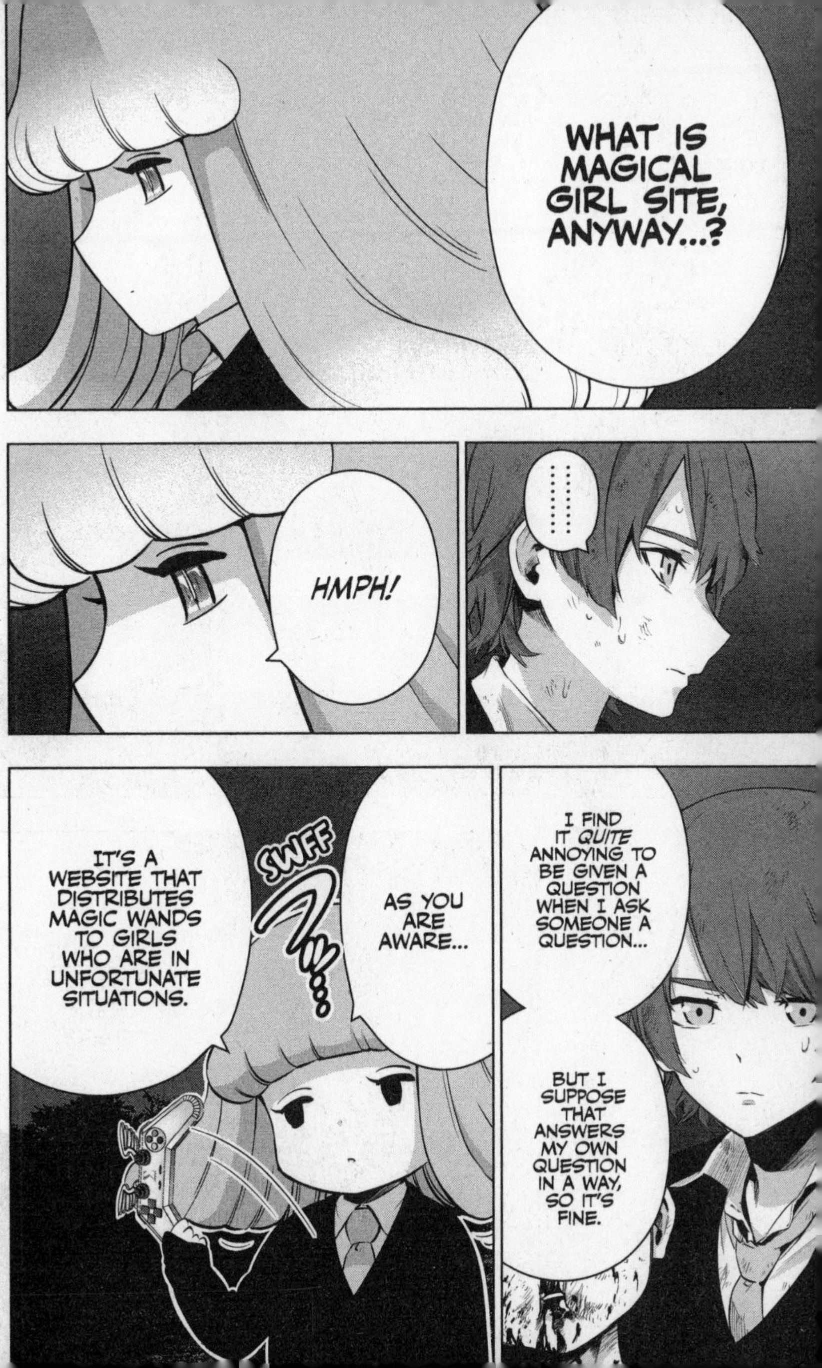
WHAT IS MAGICAL GIRL SITE, ANYWAY...?
......
HMPH!
I FIND IT *QUITE* ANNOYING TO BE GIVEN A QUESTION WHEN I ASK SOMEONE A QUESTION...
BUT I SUPPOSE THAT ANSWERS MY OWN QUESTION IN A WAY, SO IT'S FINE.
AS YOU ARE AWARE...
SWFF
IT'S A WEBSITE THAT DISTRIBUTES MAGIC WANDS TO GIRLS WHO ARE IN UNFORTUNATE SITUATIONS.

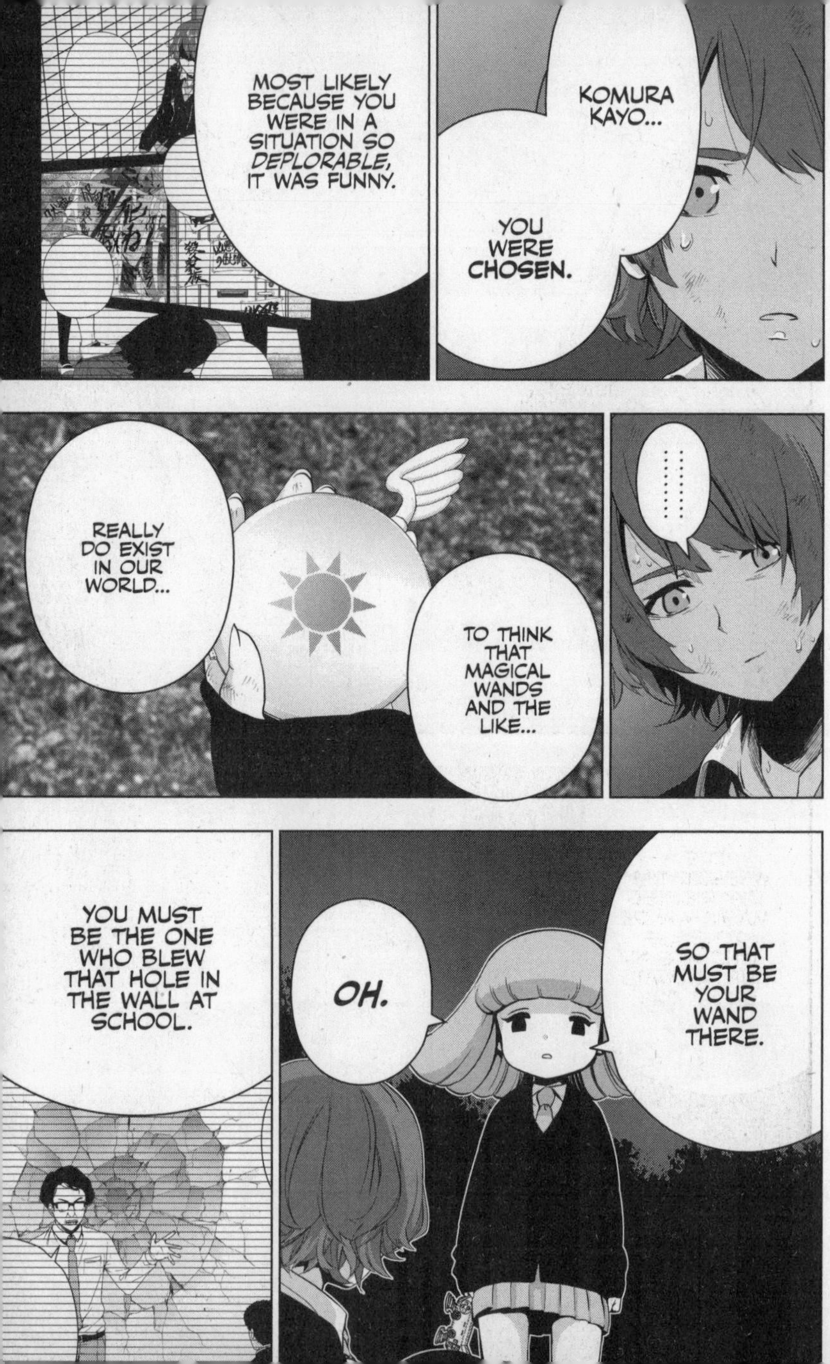
KOMURA KAYO...
YOU WERE CHOSEN.
MOST LIKELY BECAUSE YOU WERE IN A SITUATION SO *DEPLORABLE*, IT WAS FUNNY.
......
TO THINK THAT MAGICAL WANDS AND THE LIKE...
REALLY DO EXIST IN OUR WORLD...
SO THAT MUST BE YOUR WAND THERE.
OH.
YOU MUST BE THE ONE WHO BLEW THAT HOLE IN THE WALL AT SCHOOL.

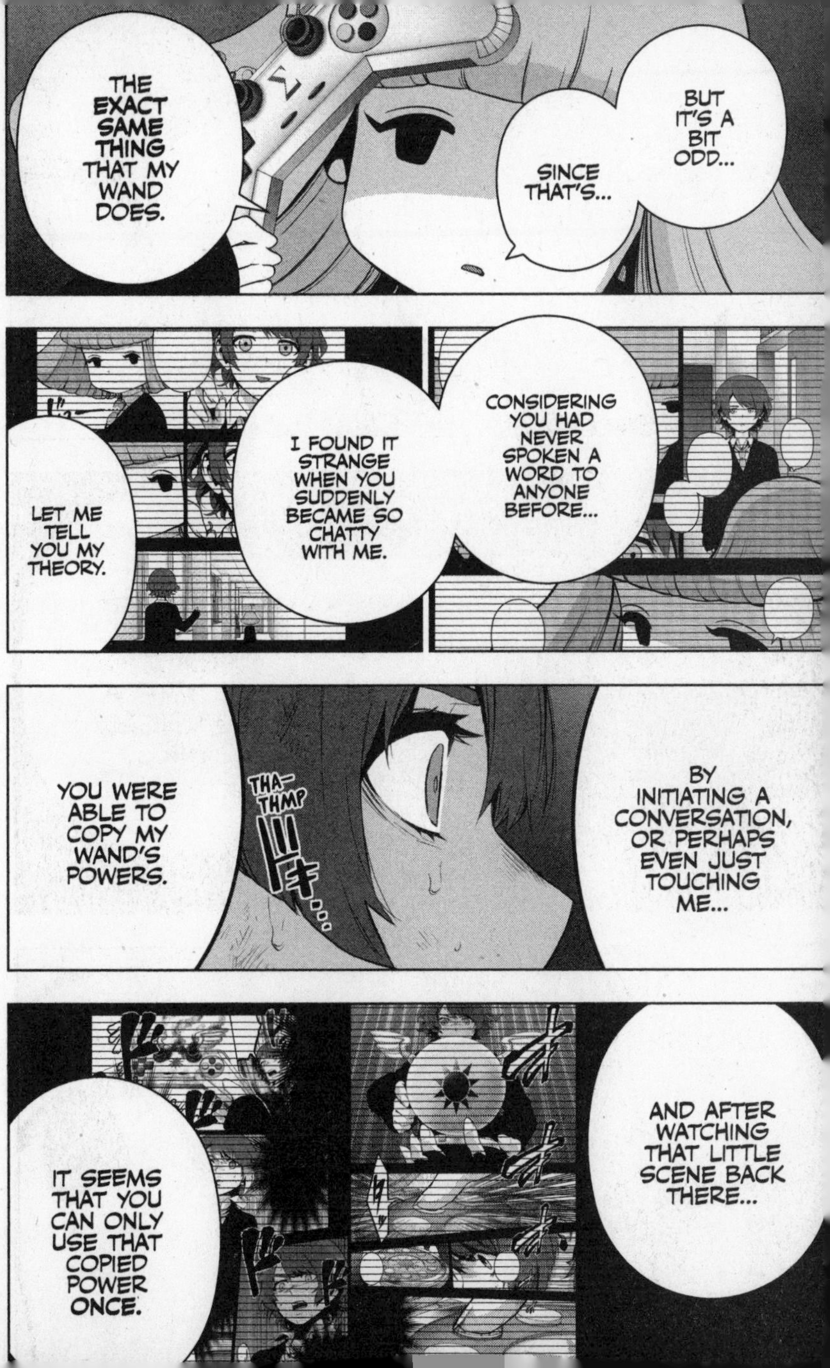
BUT IT'S A BIT ODD...
SINCE THAT'S...
THE EXACT SAME THING THAT MY WAND DOES.
CONSIDERING YOU HAD NEVER SPOKEN A WORD TO ANYONE BEFORE...
I FOUND IT STRANGE WHEN YOU SUDDENLY BECAME SO CHATTY WITH ME.
LET ME TELL YOU MY THEORY.
BY INITIATING A CONVERSATION, OR PERHAPS EVEN JUST TOUCHING ME...
THA-THMP
YOU WERE ABLE TO COPY MY WAND'S POWERS.
AND AFTER WATCHING THAT LITTLE SCENE BACK THERE...
IT SEEMS THAT YOU CAN ONLY USE THAT COPIED POWER ONCE.

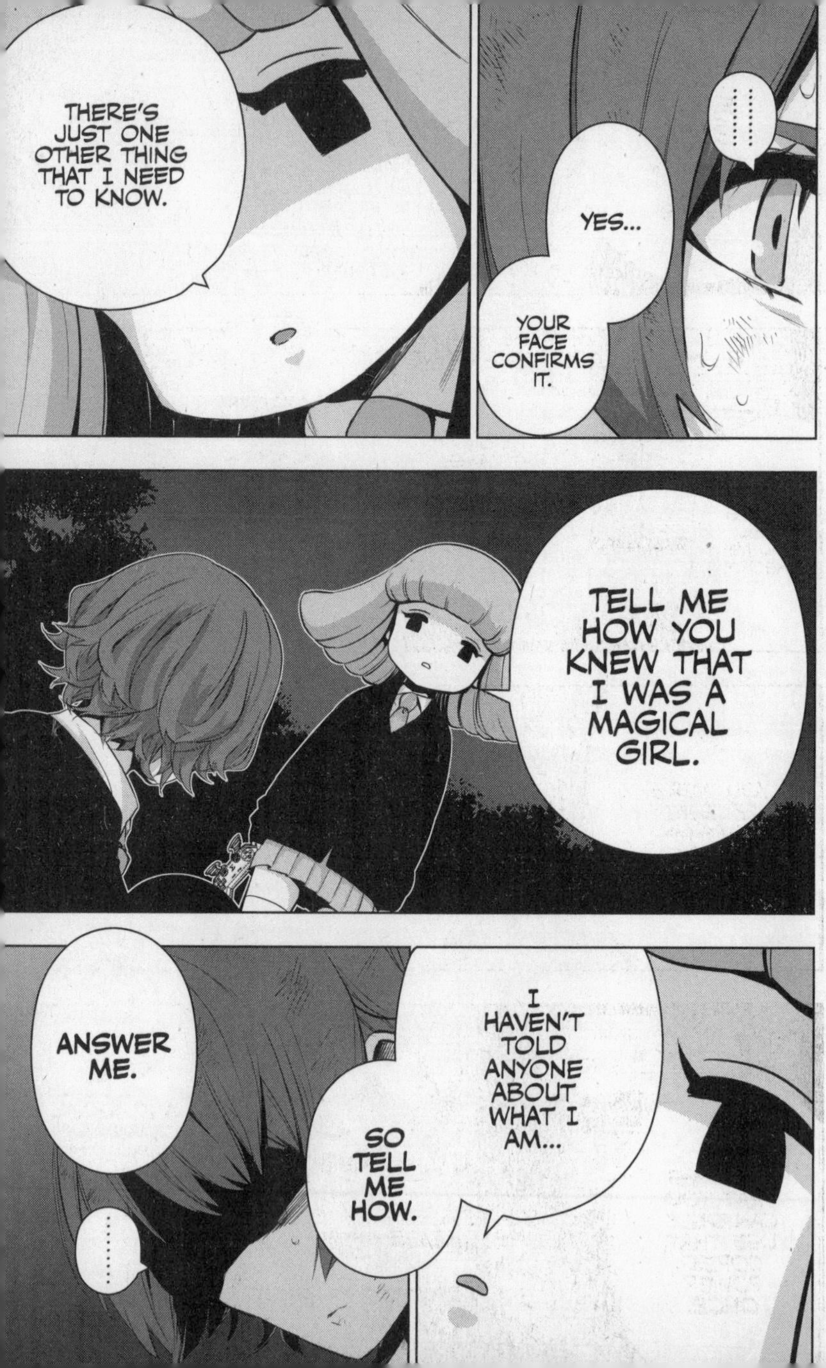
......
YES...
YOUR FACE CONFIRMS IT.
THERE'S JUST ONE OTHER THING THAT I NEED TO KNOW.
TELL ME HOW YOU KNEW THAT I WAS A MAGICAL GIRL.
I HAVEN'T TOLD ANYONE ABOUT WHAT I AM...
SO TELL ME HOW.
ANSWER ME.
......

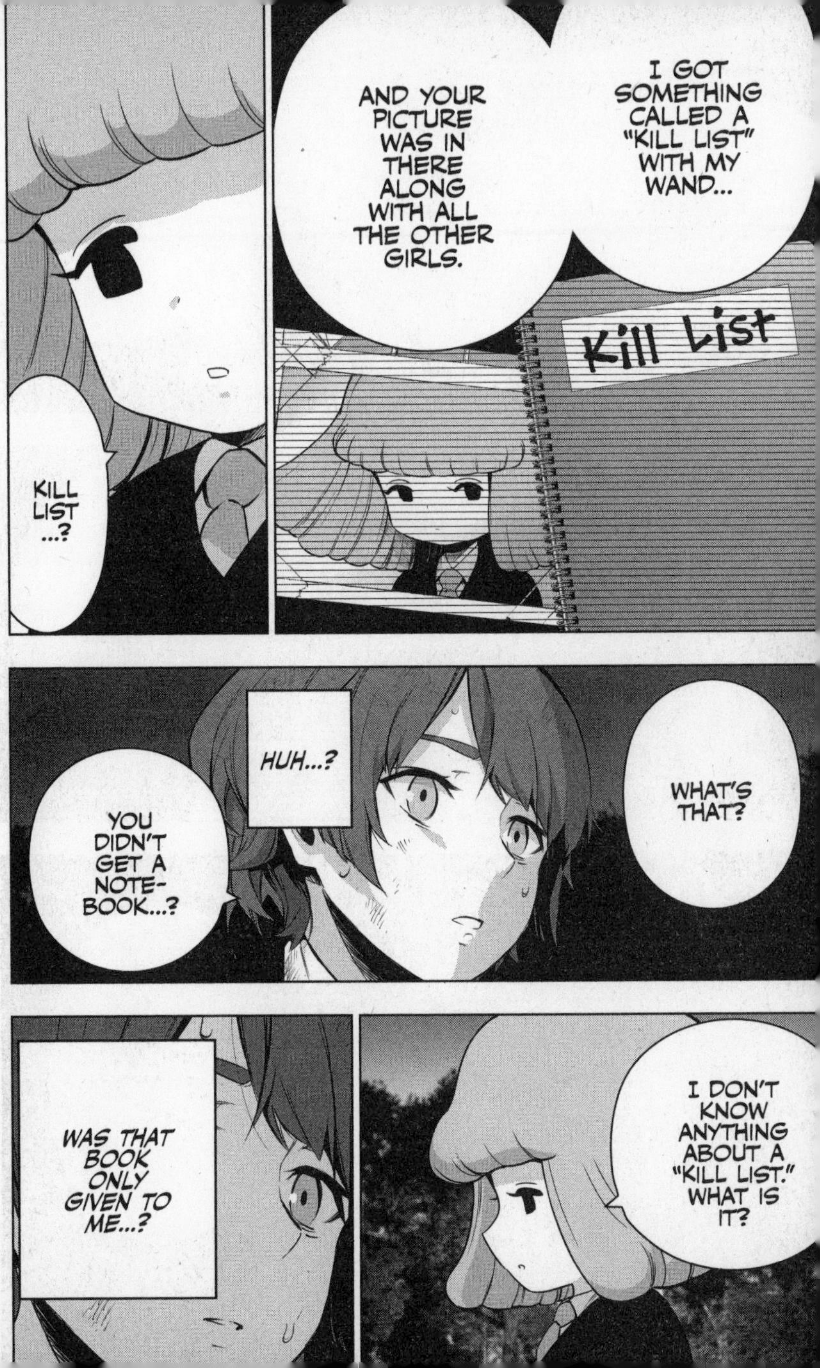
I GOT SOMETHING CALLED A "KILL LIST" WITH MY WAND...
AND YOUR PICTURE WAS IN THERE ALONG WITH ALL THE OTHER GIRLS.
Kill List
KILL LIST ...?
WHAT'S THAT?
HUH...?
YOU DIDN'T GET A NOTE-BOOK...?
I DON'T KNOW ANYTHING ABOUT A "KILL LIST." WHAT IS IT?
WAS THAT BOOK ONLY GIVEN TO ME...?

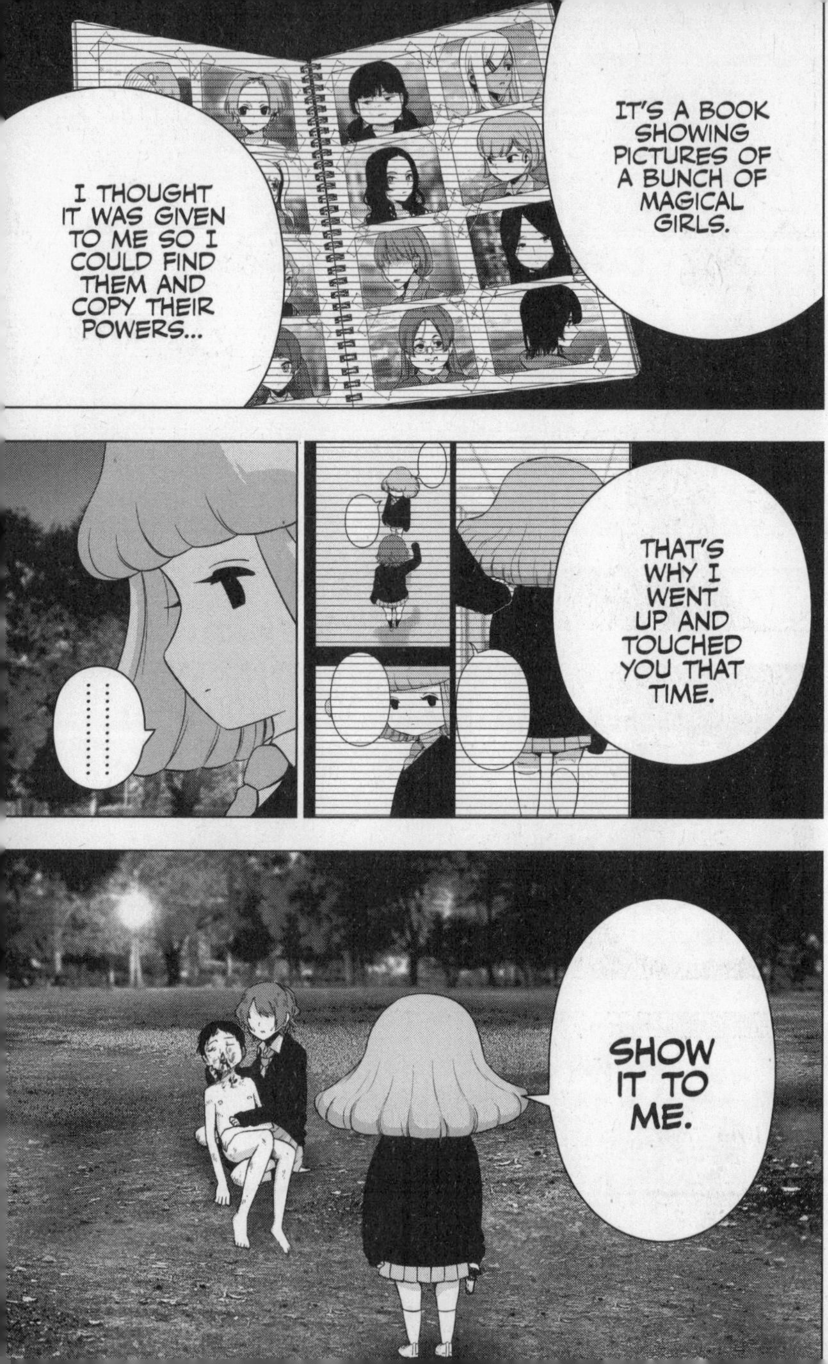
IT'S A BOOK SHOWING PICTURES OF A BUNCH OF MAGICAL GIRLS.
I THOUGHT IT WAS GIVEN TO ME SO I COULD FIND THEM AND COPY THEIR POWERS...
THAT'S WHY I WENT UP AND TOUCHED YOU THAT TIME.
......
SHOW IT TO ME.

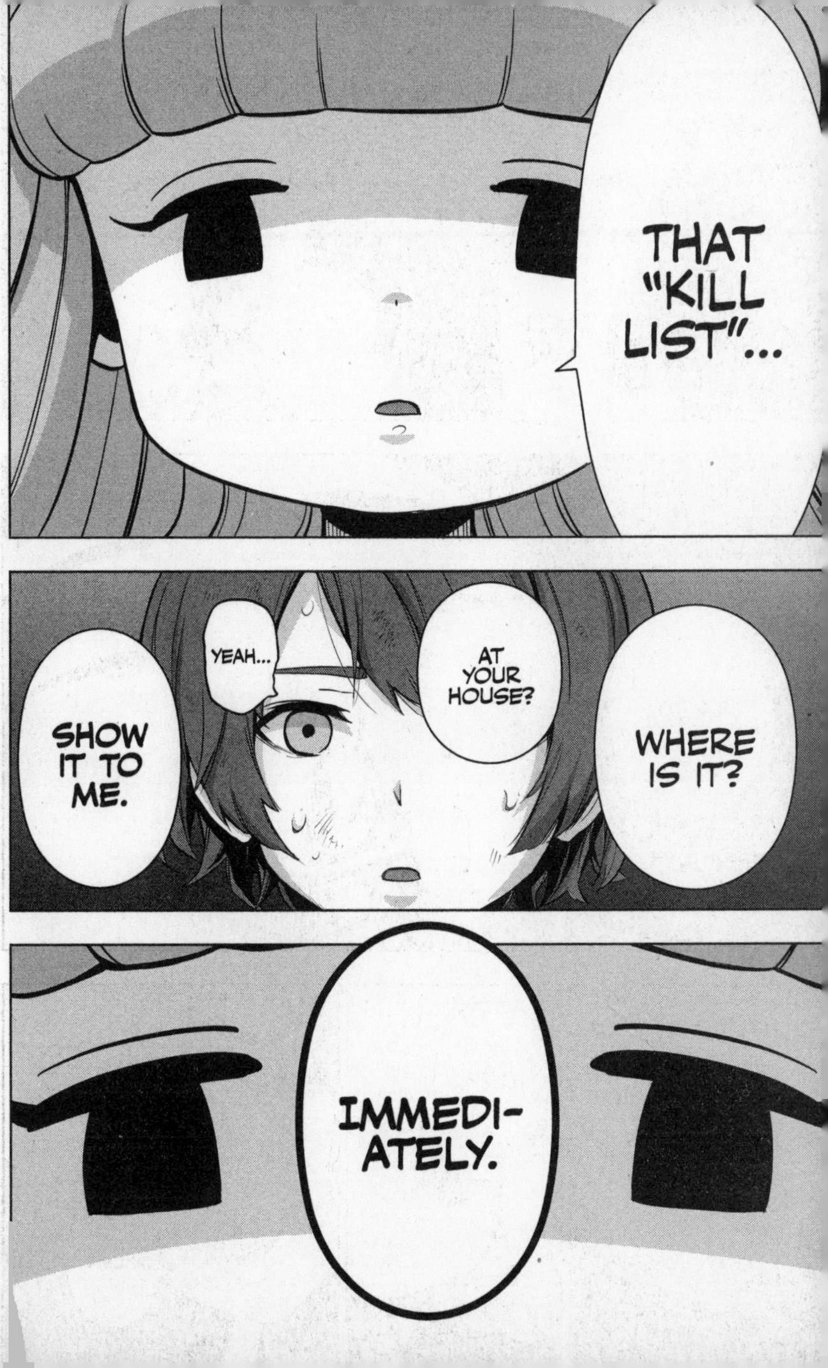
THAT "KILL LIST"...
WHERE IS IT?
AT YOUR HOUSE?
YEAH...
SHOW IT TO ME.
IMMEDI-ATELY.

TAKU-MA!

TWITCH

UGH...

KAYO...

LET'S GET HIM TO THE HOSPITAL FIRST.

HMPH.

I CAN'T OPEN MY EYES...

TAKUMA...

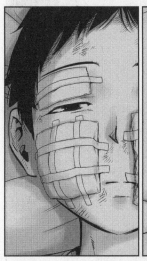
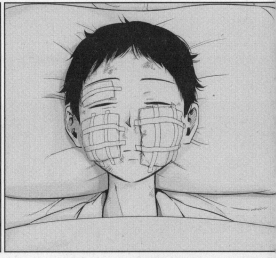

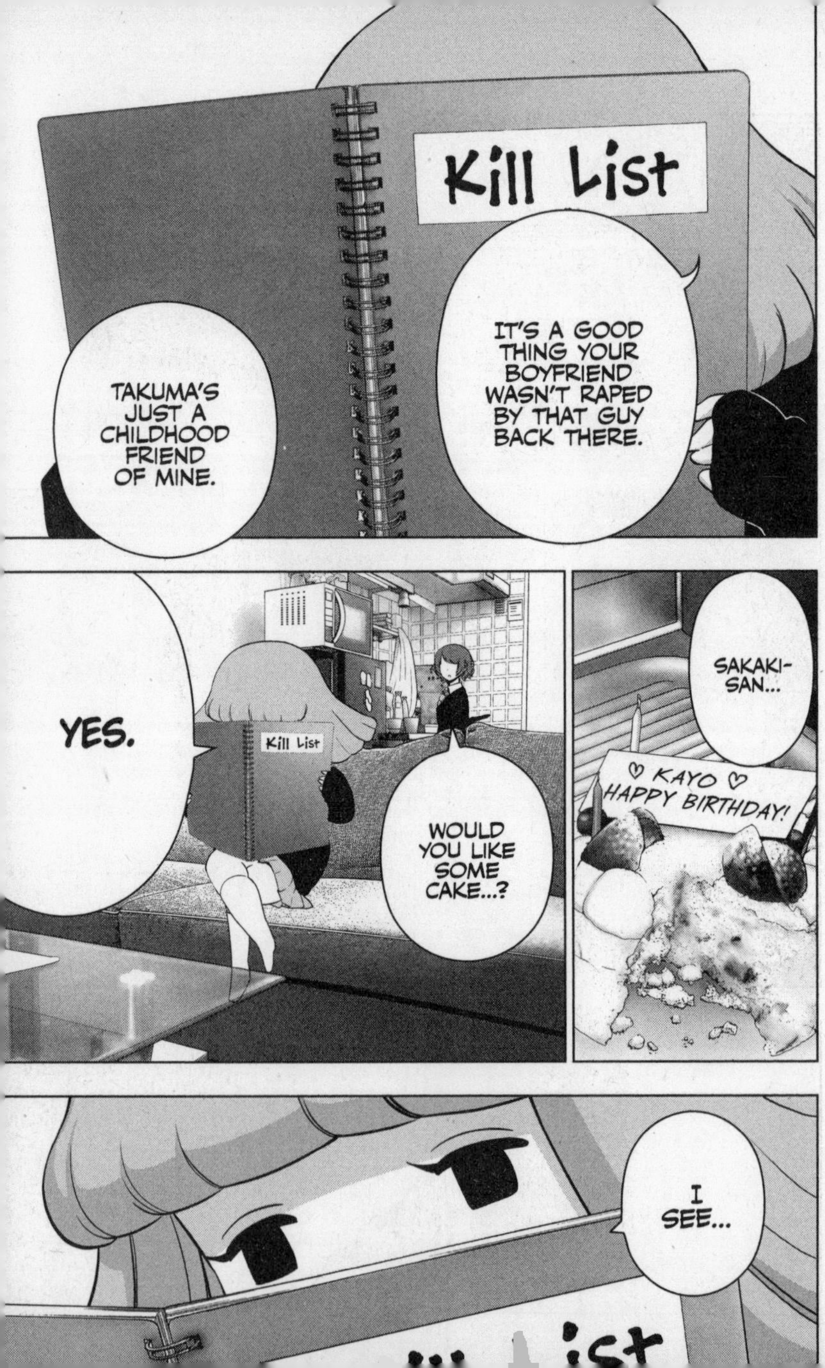
Kill List
IT'S A GOOD THING YOUR BOYFRIEND WASN'T RAPED BY THAT GUY BACK THERE.
TAKUMA'S JUST A CHILDHOOD FRIEND OF MINE.
SAKAKI-SAN...
♡ KAYO ♡ HAPPY BIRTHDAY!
Kill List
WOULD YOU LIKE SOME CAKE...?
YES.
I SEE...

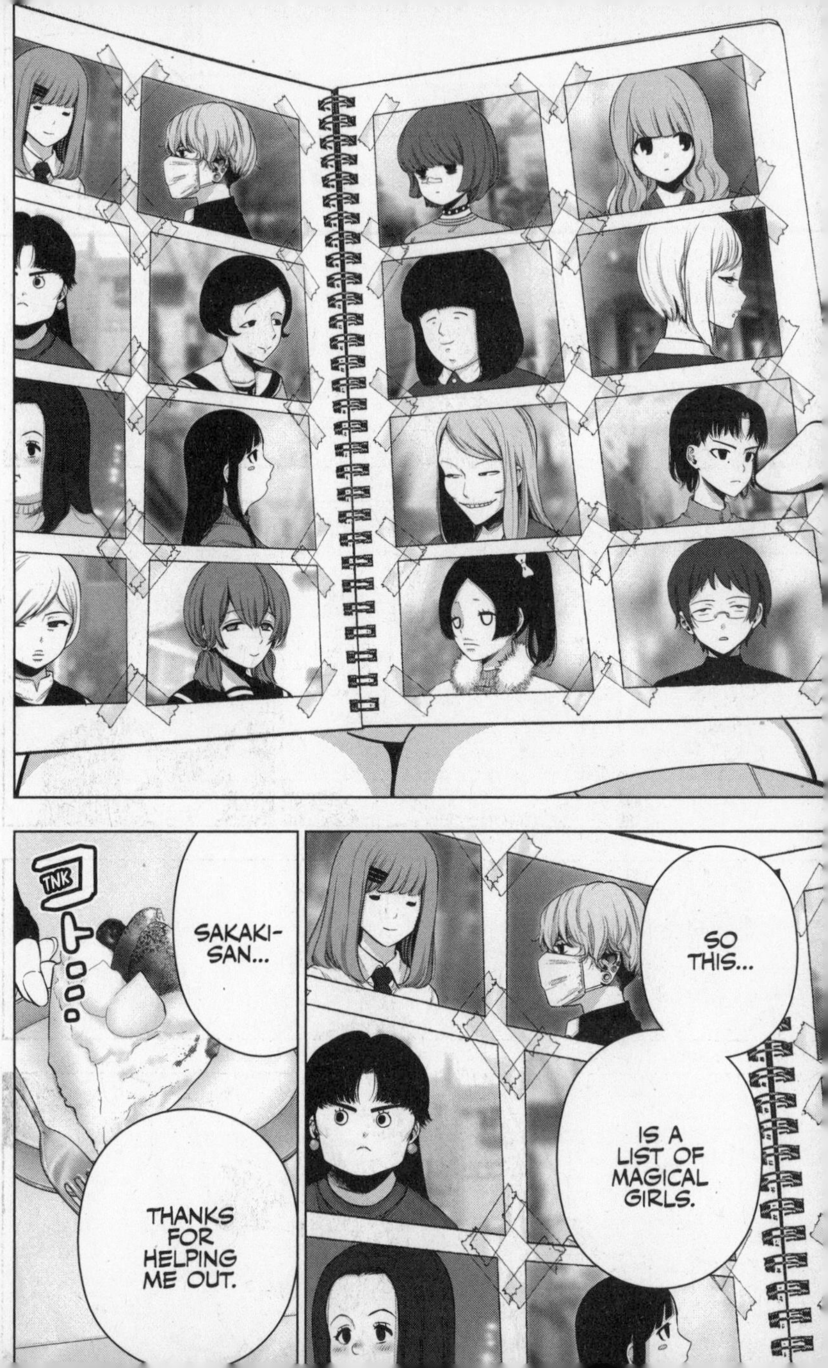
SO THIS...
IS A LIST OF MAGICAL GIRLS.
SAKAKI-SAN...
THANKS FOR HELPING ME OUT.
TNK

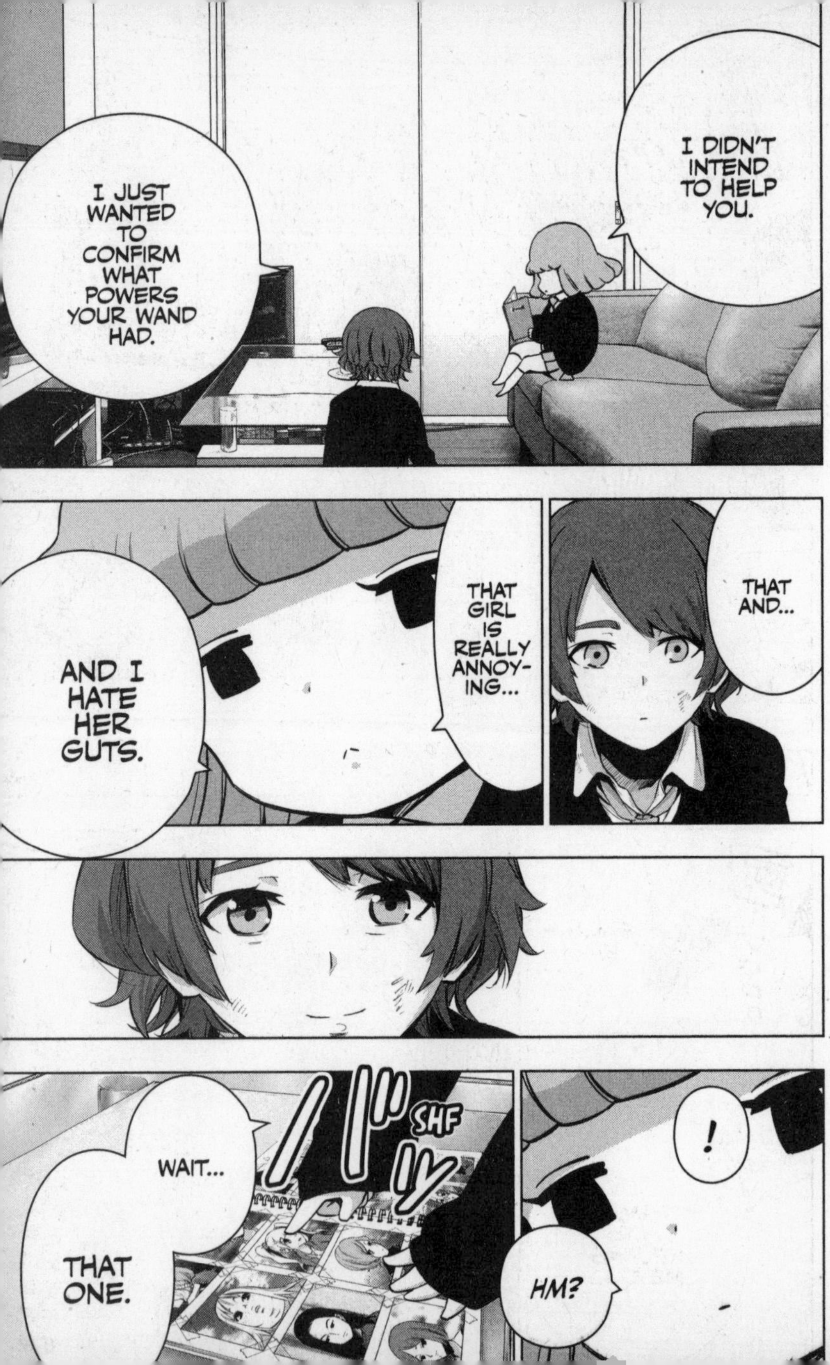
I DIDN'T INTEND TO HELP YOU.
I JUST WANTED TO CONFIRM WHAT POWERS YOUR WAND HAD.
THAT AND...
THAT GIRL IS REALLY ANNOYING...
AND I HATE HER GUTS.
!
HM?
SHF
WAIT...
THAT ONE.

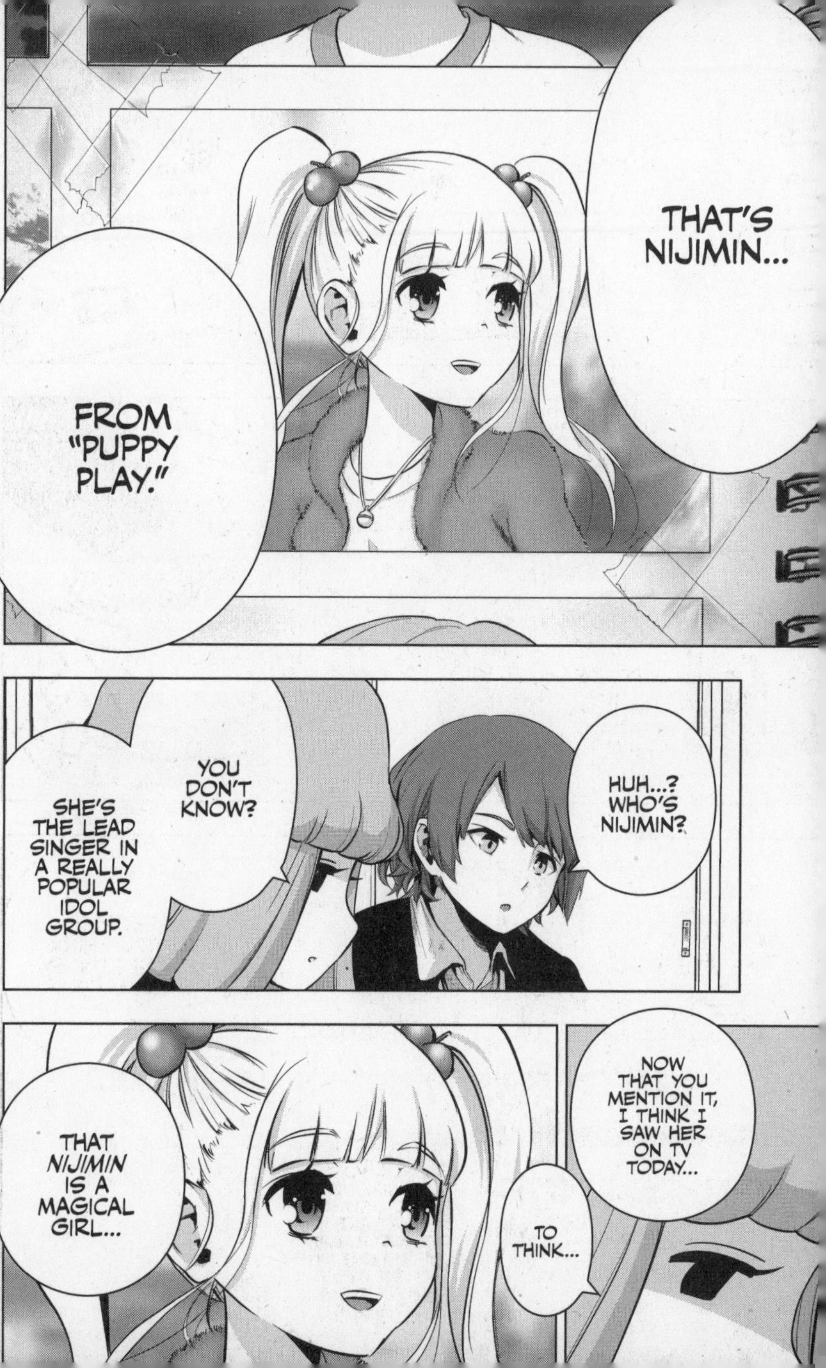
THAT'S NIJIMIN...
FROM "PUPPY PLAY."
HUH...? WHO'S NIJIMIN?
YOU DON'T KNOW?
SHE'S THE LEAD SINGER IN A REALLY POPULAR IDOL GROUP.
NOW THAT YOU MENTION IT, I THINK I SAW HER ON TV TODAY...
TO THINK...
THAT *NIJIMIN* IS A MAGICAL GIRL...

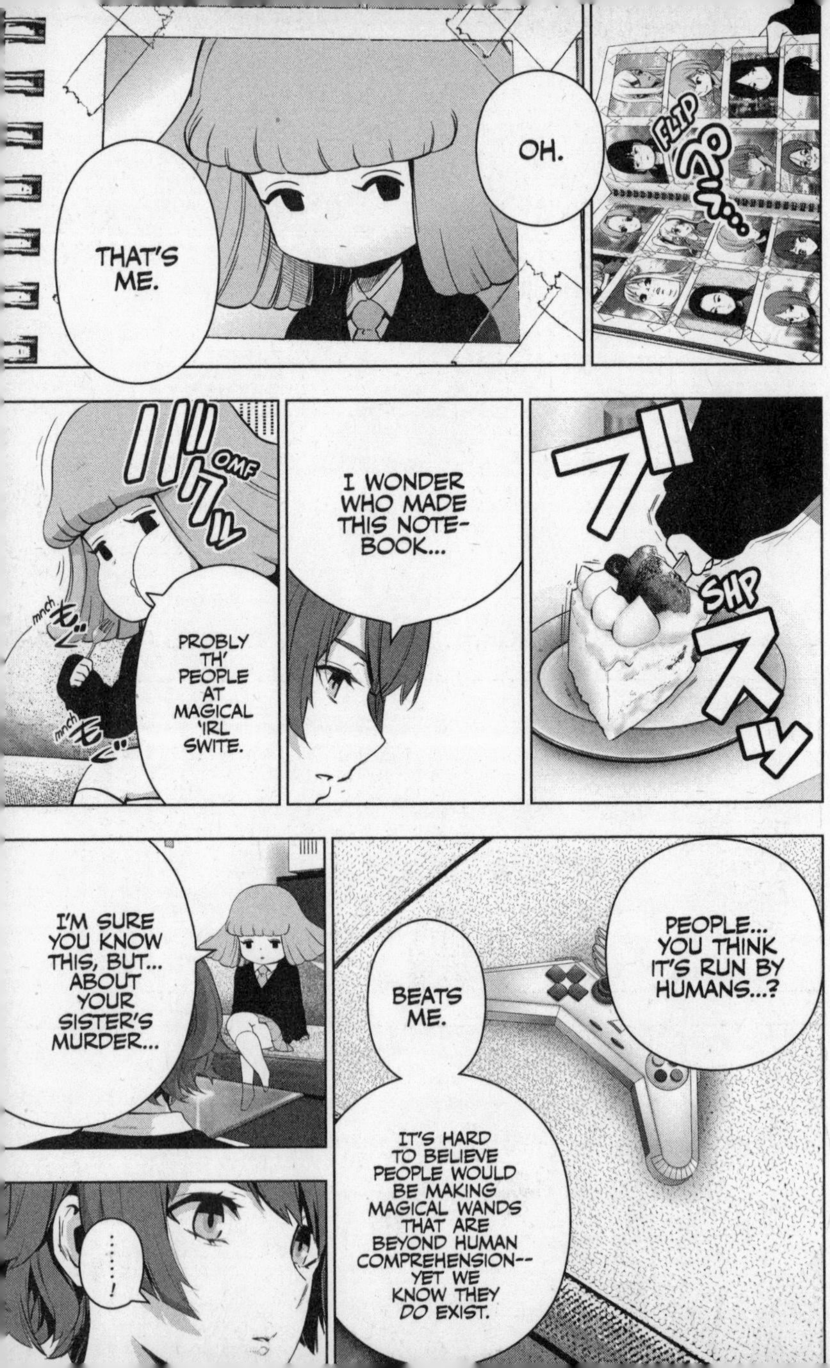
FLIP
ペラ…
OH.
THAT'S ME.
ブ
SHP
スッ
I WONDER WHO MADE THIS NOTE-BOOK...
バクッ
OMF
mnch もぐ
mnch もぐ
PROBLY TH' PEOPLE AT MAGICAL 'IRL SWITE.
PEOPLE... YOU THINK IT'S RUN BY HUMANS...?
BEATS ME.
IT'S HARD TO BELIEVE PEOPLE WOULD BE MAKING MAGICAL WANDS THAT ARE BEYOND HUMAN COMPREHENSION-- YET WE KNOW THEY *DO* EXIST.
I'M SURE YOU KNOW THIS, BUT... ABOUT YOUR SISTER'S MURDER...
......!

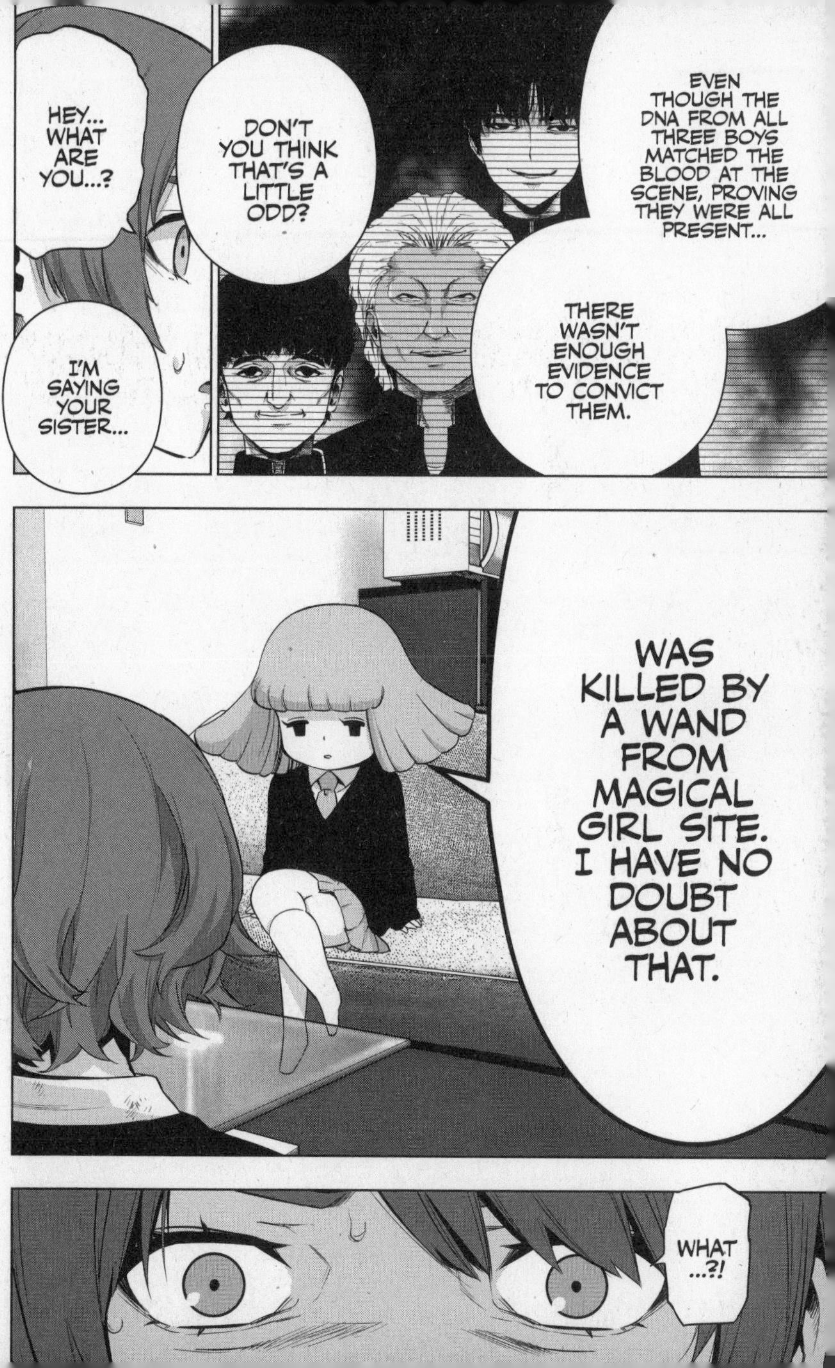
EVEN THOUGH THE DNA FROM ALL THREE BOYS MATCHED THE BLOOD AT THE SCENE, PROVING THEY WERE ALL PRESENT...
THERE WASN'T ENOUGH EVIDENCE TO CONVICT THEM.
DON'T YOU THINK THAT'S A LITTLE ODD?
HEY... WHAT ARE YOU...?
I'M SAYING YOUR SISTER...
WAS KILLED BY A WAND FROM MAGICAL GIRL SITE. I HAVE NO DOUBT ABOUT THAT.
WHAT ...?!

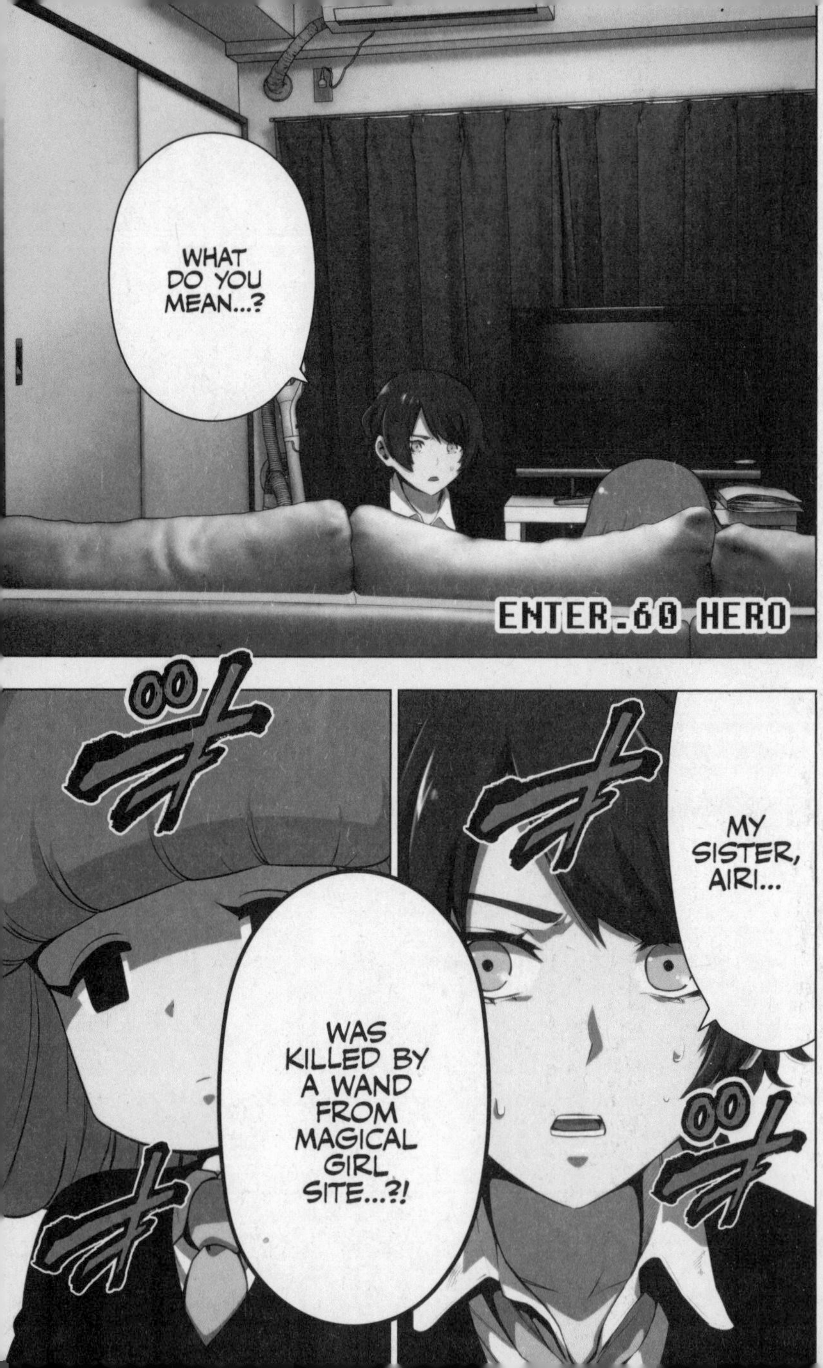
WHAT DO YOU MEAN...?
ENTER.60 HERO
MY SISTER, AIRI...
WAS KILLED BY A WAND FROM MAGICAL GIRL SITE...?!

ENTER.60 HERO

Koganei City Lynching Case

Three cheers for a delightful magical girl life!

If only I had some power...

Day after day after day, I'll continue to endure it.

Oh wretched thing.

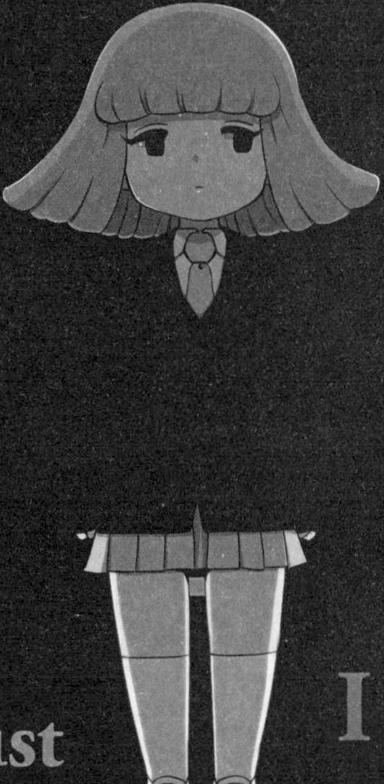

Just kidding.

Why am I the only one who has to be put through such a cruel test?!

What do you mean... magical girl?

You're a magical girl too, aren't you?!

It's magic I bestow..

My angels... I did it!

I guess the blood coursing through my veins really is the same as yours.

Its powers soon will rest within your hands.

I have thoughts about killing just about everyone in my class.

Komura Kayo

Sex: Female
Age: 14
Date of Birth: April 17 (Aries)
Height: 151cm
Weight: 44kg
Blood Type: A
Birthplace: Tokyo

Interests/Hobbies: Household chores (all), softball

Strengths: Very patient; quick reflexes

Dislikes/Weakness: Singing, dancing

Likes: Her mother's cooking, sweets

• Though she seems fretful and not very emotionally expressive, before her little sister's death, she was a happy, smiling girl.

• After living alone with her mother, she became quite adept at household chores by helping her out and eventually had to take over most of them.

• She has strong nerves and resilience.

• Her hair can grow quite curly, so she cuts it short.

• She has never once had rough skin.

The Koganei City Lynching Case

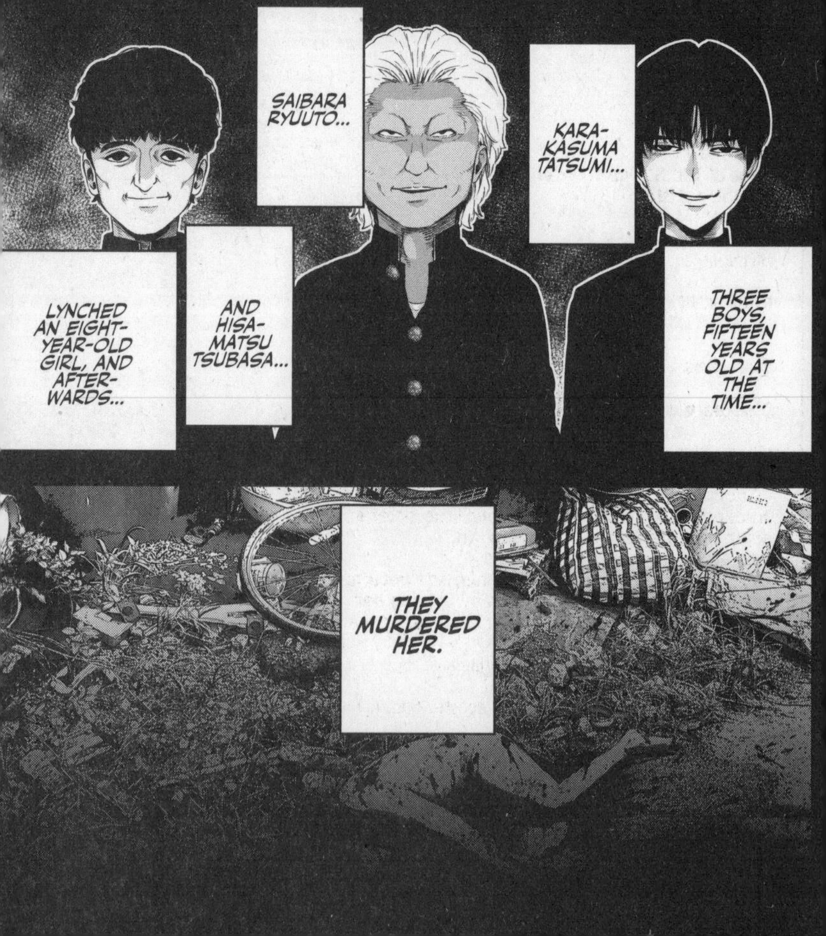
THREE BOYS, FIFTEEN YEARS OLD AT THE TIME...
KARA-KASUMA TATSUMI...
SAIBARA RYUUTO...
AND HISA-MATSU TSUBASA...
LYNCHED AN EIGHT-YEAR-OLD GIRL, AND AFTER-WARDS...
THEY MURDERED HER.

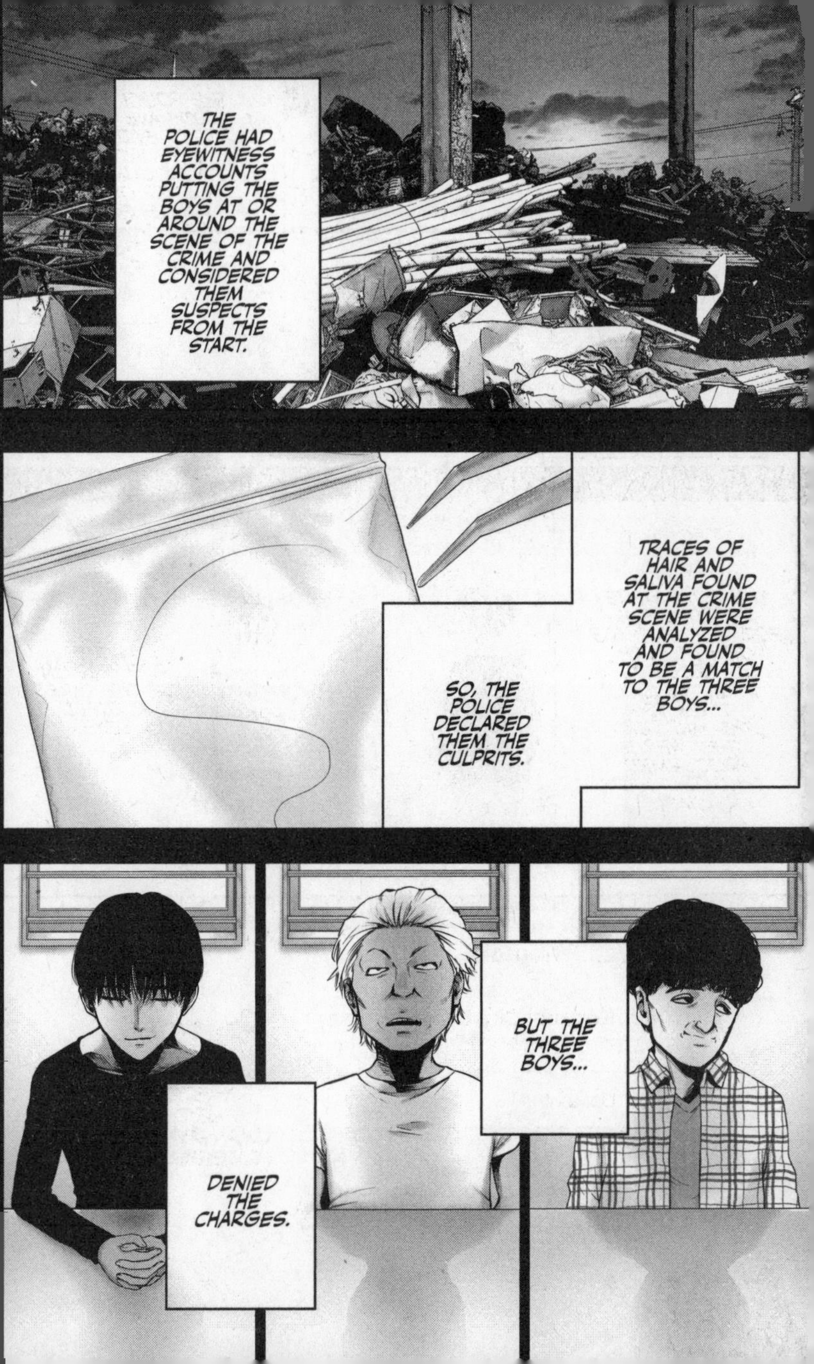
THE POLICE HAD EYEWITNESS ACCOUNTS PUTTING THE BOYS AT OR AROUND THE SCENE OF THE CRIME AND CONSIDERED THEM SUSPECTS FROM THE START.
TRACES OF HAIR AND SALIVA FOUND AT THE CRIME SCENE WERE ANALYZED AND FOUND TO BE A MATCH TO THE THREE BOYS...
SO, THE POLICE DECLARED THEM THE CULPRITS.
BUT THE THREE BOYS...
DENIED THE CHARGES.

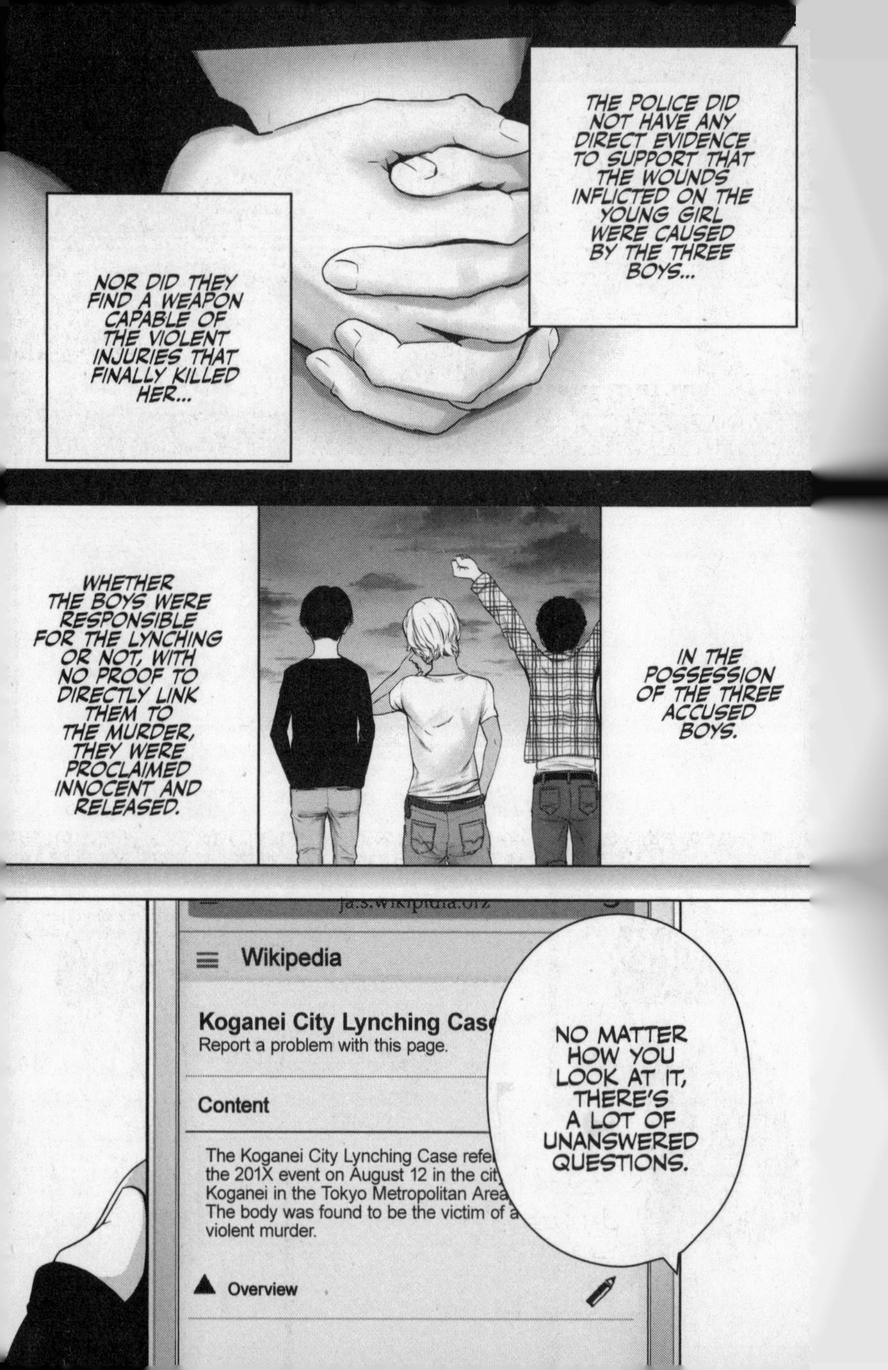
THE POLICE DID NOT HAVE ANY DIRECT EVIDENCE TO SUPPORT THAT THE WOUNDS INFLICTED ON THE YOUNG GIRL WERE CAUSED BY THE THREE BOYS...
NOR DID THEY FIND A WEAPON CAPABLE OF THE VIOLENT INJURIES THAT FINALLY KILLED HER...
IN THE POSSESSION OF THE THREE ACCUSED BOYS.
WHETHER THE BOYS WERE RESPONSIBLE FOR THE LYNCHING OR NOT, WITH NO PROOF TO DIRECTLY LINK THEM TO THE MURDER, THEY WERE PROCLAIMED INNOCENT AND RELEASED.
Wikipedia
Koganei City Lynching
Report a problem with this page.
Content
The Koganei City Lynching Case
the 201X event on August 12 in the
Koganei in the Tokyo Metropolitan
The body was found to be the victim of
violent murder.
Overview
NO MATTER HOW YOU LOOK AT IT, THERE'S A LOT OF UNANSWERED QUESTIONS.

TO THINK THAT SOME BOYS COULD KILL A YOUNG GIRL WITHOUT LEAVING A SINGLE TRACE OF EVIDENCE...

I CAN'T THINK OF ANYTHING BESIDES A MAGICAL GIRL SITE WAND THAT COULD DO THAT.

THEN THOSE BOYS GOT A WAND FROM MAGICAL GIRL SITE, TOO...?!

THAT OR...

NO WAY!

THEY GOT THEIR HANDS ON SOMEONE *ELSE'S* WAND.

SOME-ONE ELSE...?

THERE WERE SOME STRANGE THINGS ABOUT MY SISTER'S BODY.

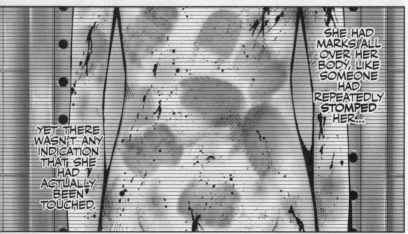

SHE HAD MARKS ALL OVER HER BODY, LIKE SOMEONE HAD REPEATEDLY STOMPED HER...

YET THERE WASN'T ANY INDICATION THAT SHE HAD ACTUALLY BEEN TOUCHED.

HUFF!

HUFF!

HUFF!

EVERY TIME I REMEMBER...

S-SORRY...

BLERGH!!

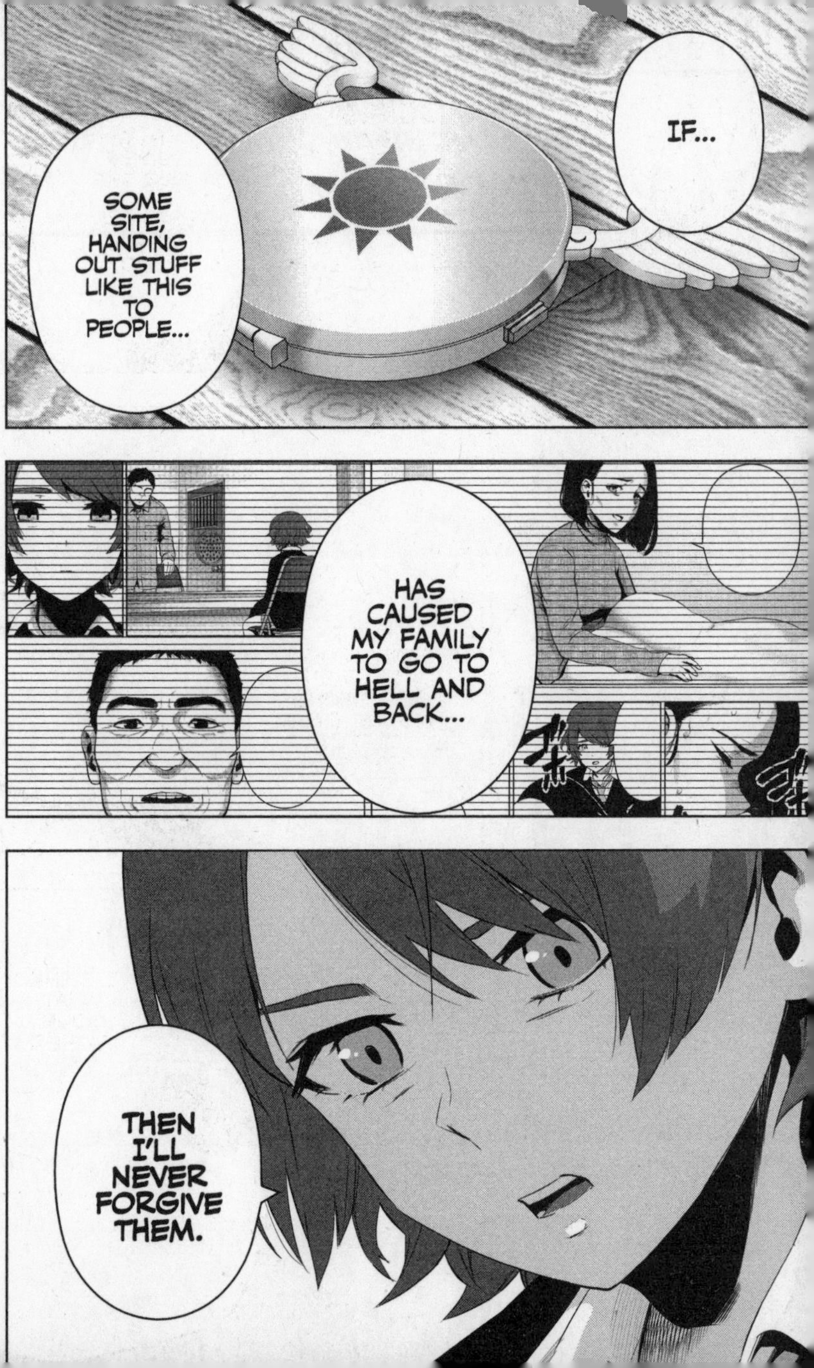
IF...
SOME SITE, HANDING OUT STUFF LIKE THIS TO PEOPLE...
HAS CAUSED MY FAMILY TO GO TO HELL AND BACK...
THEN I'LL NEVER FORGIVE THEM.

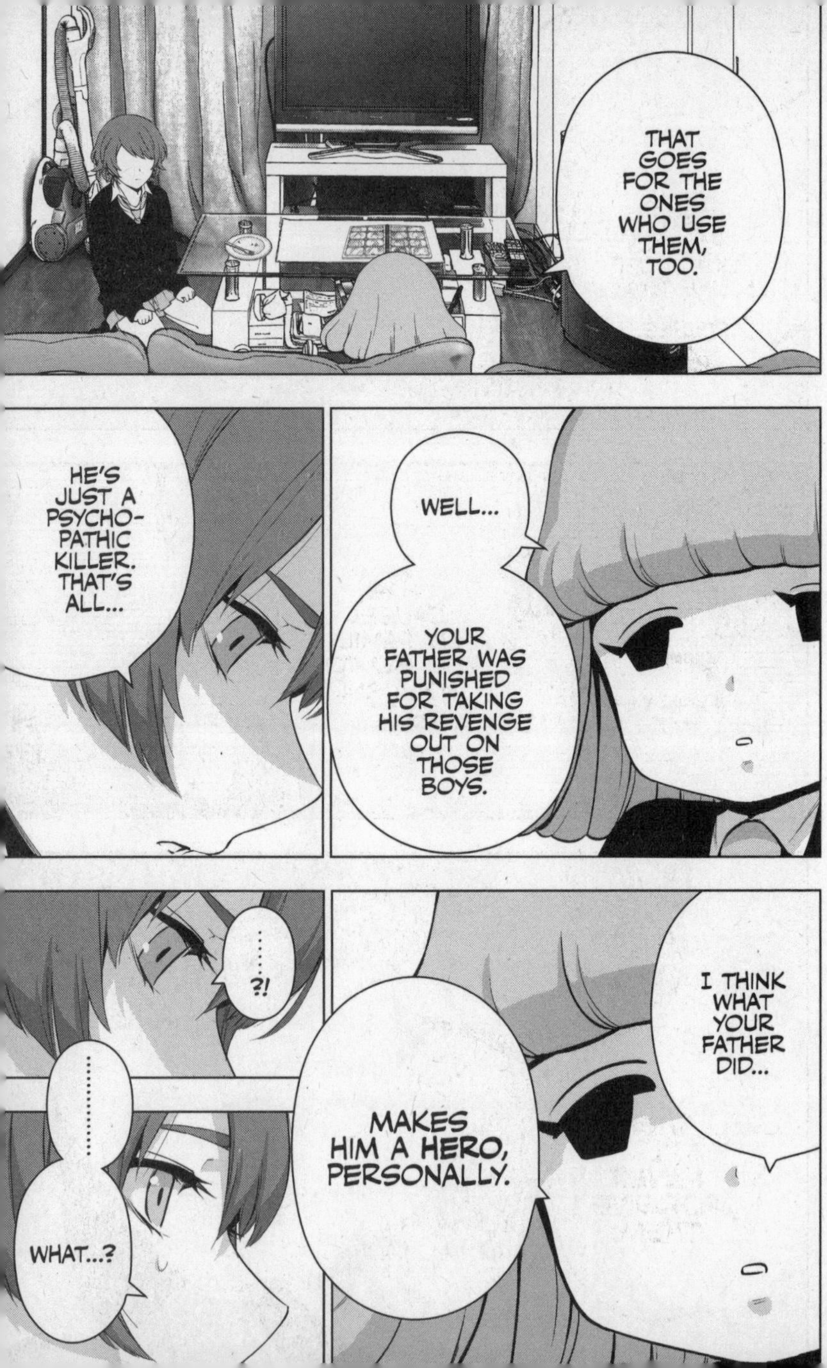
THAT GOES FOR THE ONES WHO USE THEM, TOO.
WELL...
YOUR FATHER WAS PUNISHED FOR TAKING HIS REVENGE OUT ON THOSE BOYS.
HE'S JUST A PSYCHO-PATHIC KILLER. THAT'S ALL...
I THINK WHAT YOUR FATHER DID...
MAKES HIM A HERO, PERSONALLY.
......?!
....
WHAT...?

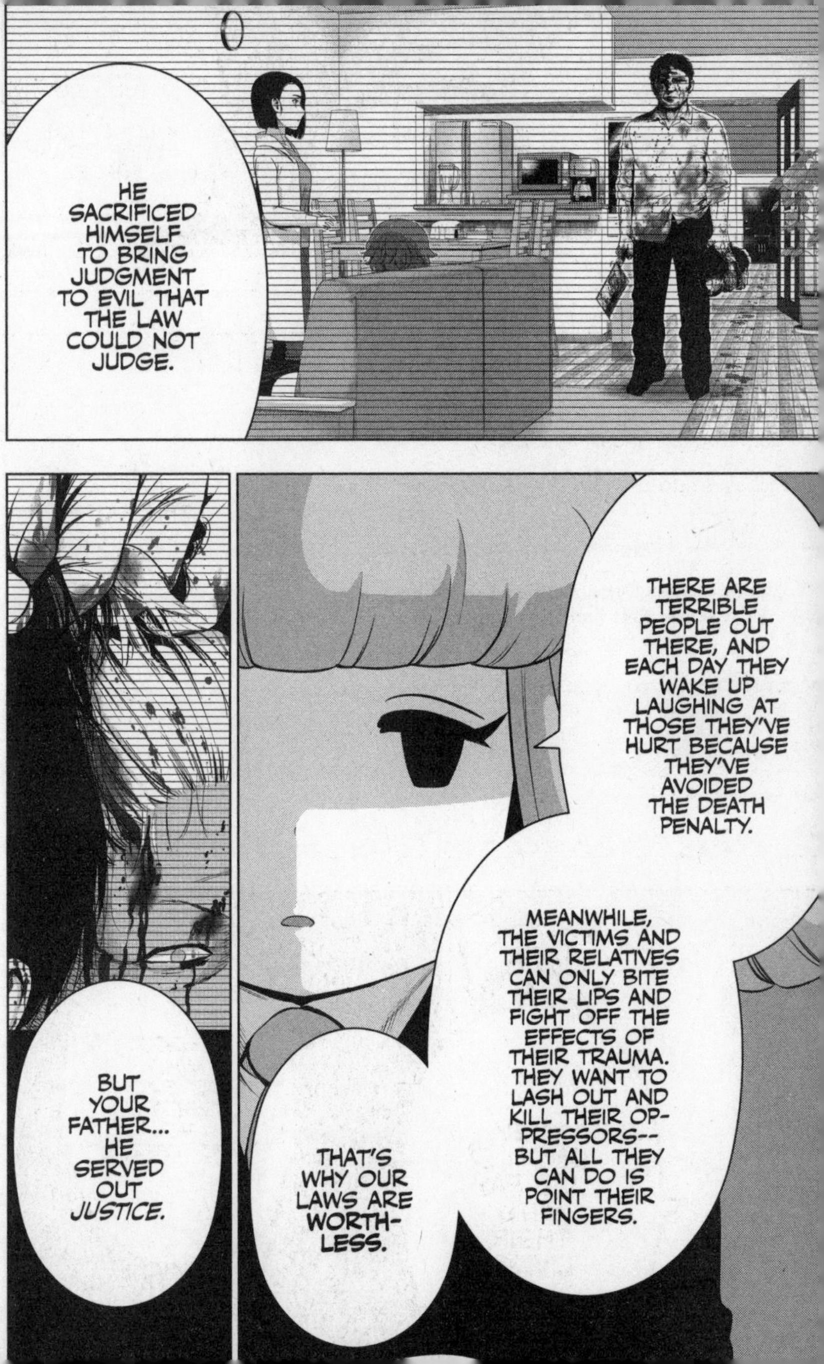
HE SACRIFICED HIMSELF TO BRING JUDGMENT TO EVIL THAT THE LAW COULD NOT JUDGE.
THERE ARE TERRIBLE PEOPLE OUT THERE, AND EACH DAY THEY WAKE UP LAUGHING AT THOSE THEY'VE HURT BECAUSE THEY'VE AVOIDED THE DEATH PENALTY.
MEANWHILE, THE VICTIMS AND THEIR RELATIVES CAN ONLY BITE THEIR LIPS AND FIGHT OFF THE EFFECTS OF THEIR TRAUMA. THEY WANT TO LASH OUT AND KILL THEIR OP-PRESSORS-- BUT ALL THEY CAN DO IS POINT THEIR FINGERS.
THAT'S WHY OUR LAWS ARE WORTH-LESS.
BUT YOUR FATHER... HE SERVED OUT *JUSTICE*.

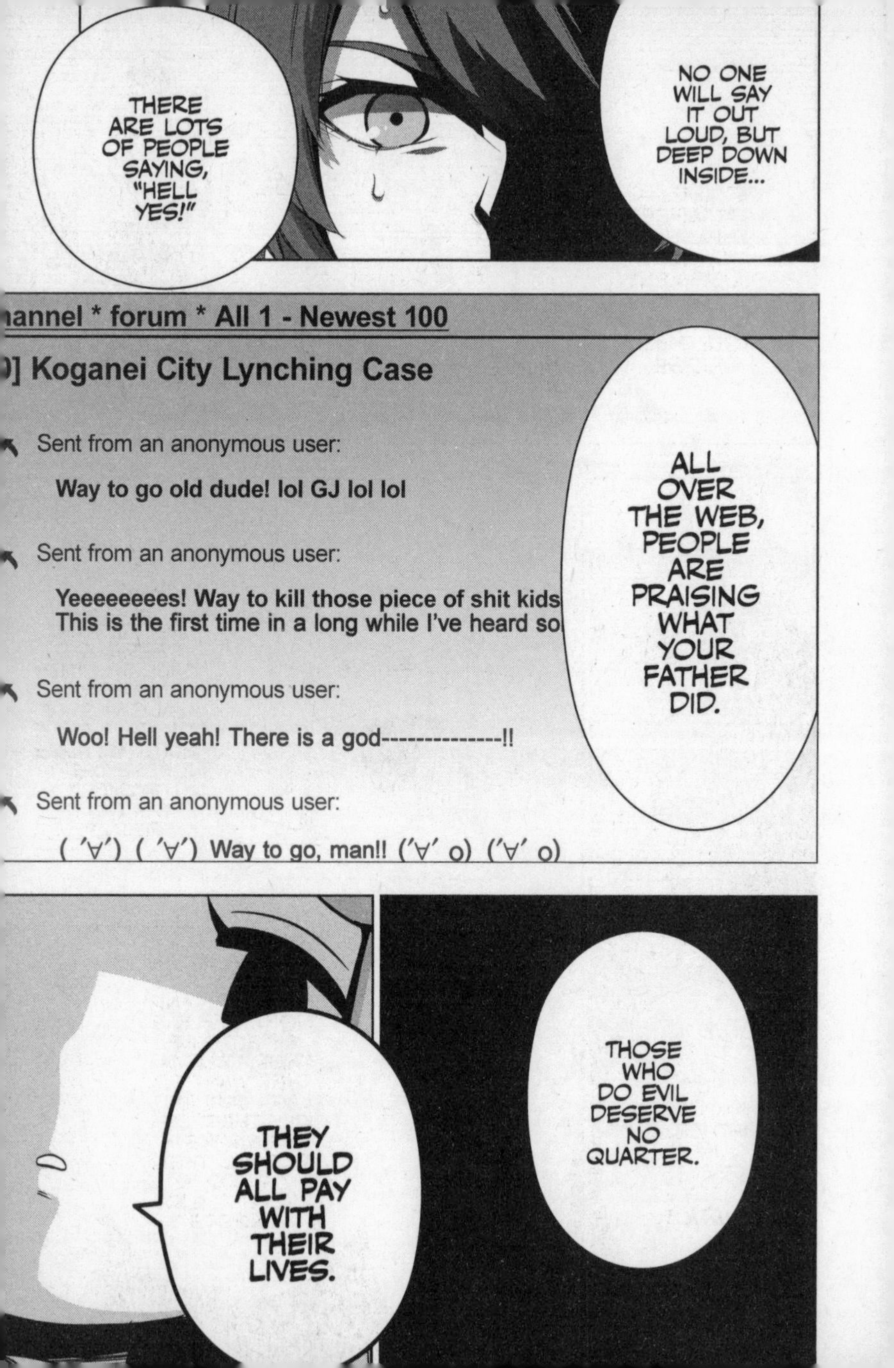
NO ONE WILL SAY IT OUT LOUD, BUT DEEP DOWN INSIDE...
THERE ARE LOTS OF PEOPLE SAYING, "HELL YES!"
annel * forum * All 1 - Newest 100
]] Koganei City Lynching Case
Sent from an anonymous user:
Way to go old dude! lol GJ lol lol
Sent from an anonymous user:
Yeeeeeeees! Way to kill those piece of shit kids
This is the first time in a long while I've heard so
Sent from an anonymous user:
Woo! Hell yeah! There is a god-------------!!
Sent from an anonymous user:
(’∀’) (’∀’) Way to go, man!! (’∀’ o) (’∀’ o)
ALL OVER THE WEB, PEOPLE ARE PRAISING WHAT YOUR FATHER DID.
THOSE WHO DO EVIL DESERVE NO QUARTER.
THEY SHOULD ALL PAY WITH THEIR LIVES.

HMPH.

SAKAKI-SAN...

ALL CHANGED BECAUSE OF HIM.

BUT...

MY LIFE AND MOM'S...

I DON'T REALLY THINK...

HE SAVED ME IN THE SLIGHTEST.

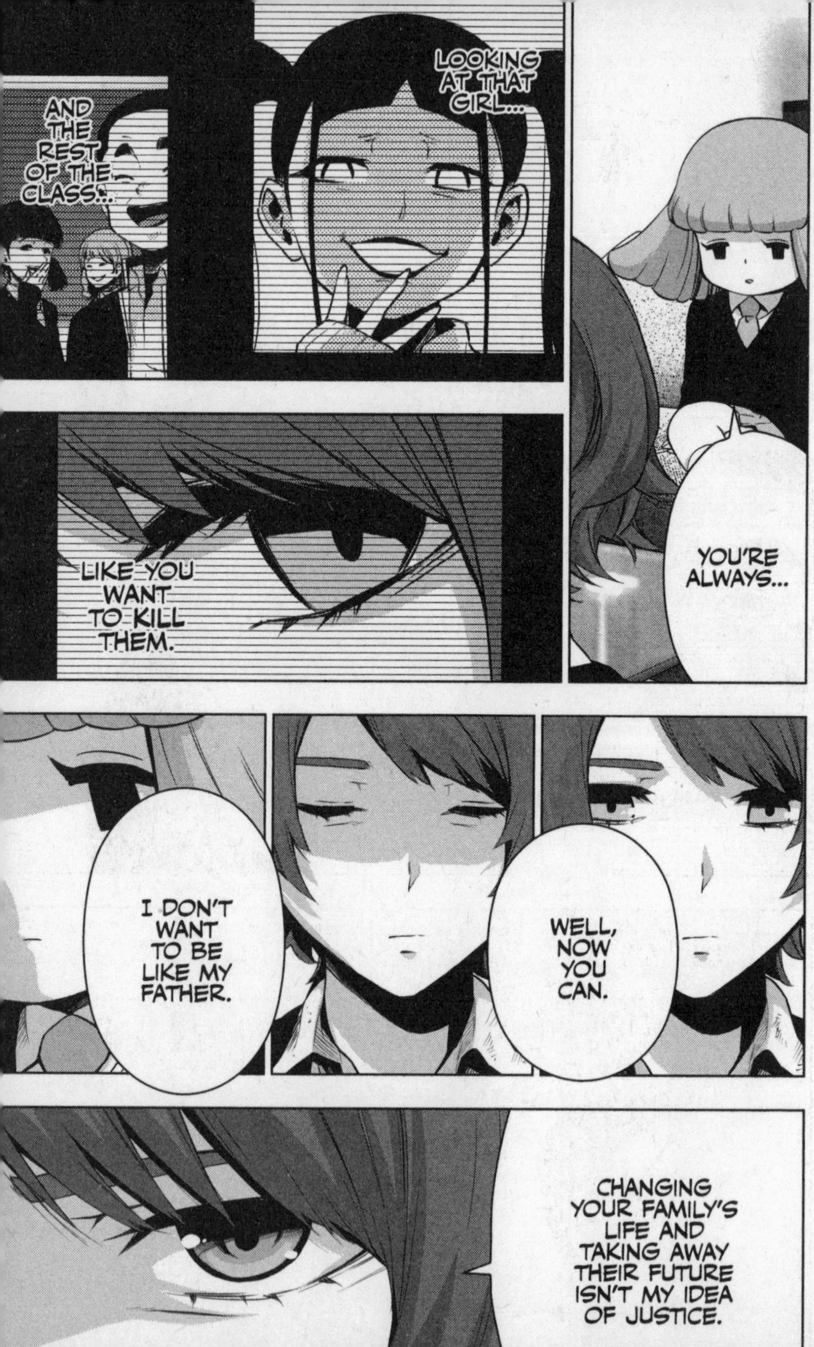
YOU'RE ALWAYS...
LOOKING AT THAT GIRL...
AND THE REST OF THE CLASS...
LIKE YOU WANT TO KILL THEM.
WELL, NOW YOU CAN.
I DON'T WANT TO BE LIKE MY FATHER.
CHANGING YOUR FAMILY'S LIFE AND TAKING AWAY THEIR FUTURE ISN'T MY IDEA OF JUSTICE.

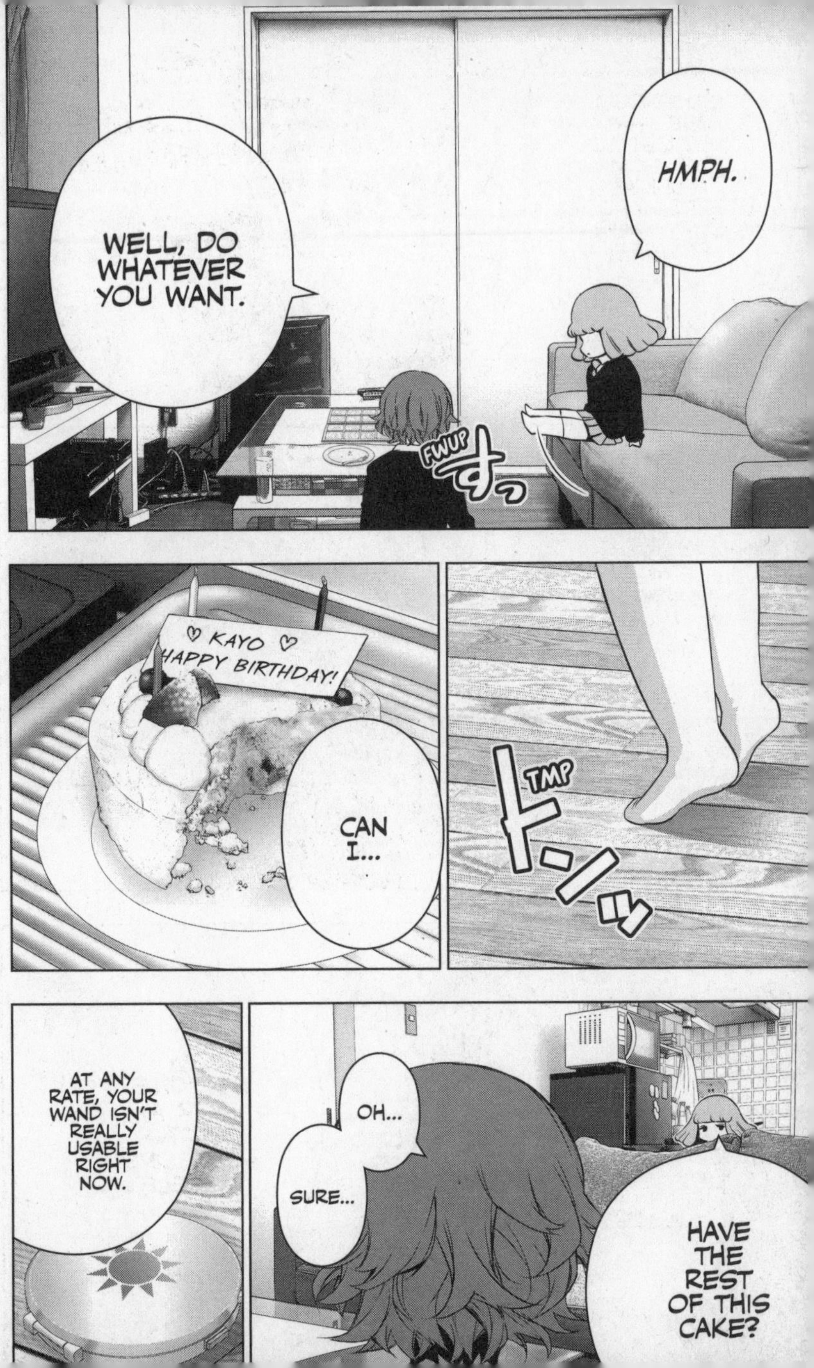
HMPH.
WELL, DO WHATEVER YOU WANT.
FWUP
TMP
♡ KAYO ♡
HAPPY BIRTHDAY!
CAN I...
HAVE THE REST OF THIS CAKE?
OH...
SURE...
AT ANY RATE, YOUR WAND ISN'T REALLY USABLE RIGHT NOW.

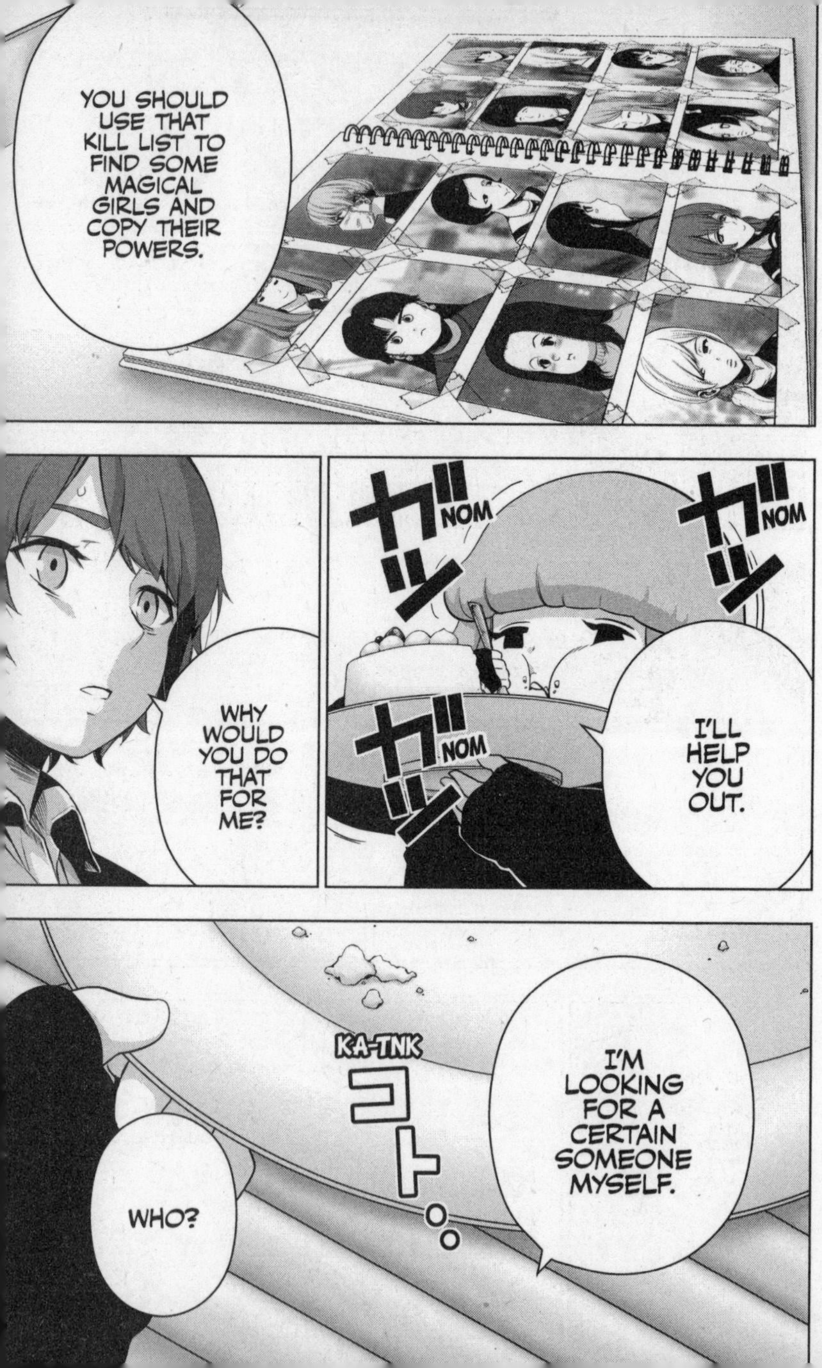
YOU SHOULD USE THAT KILL LIST TO FIND SOME MAGICAL GIRLS AND COPY THEIR POWERS.
NOM
NOM
NOM
I'LL HELP YOU OUT.
WHY WOULD YOU DO THAT FOR ME?
I'M LOOKING FOR A CERTAIN SOMEONE MYSELF.
KA-TNK
WHO?

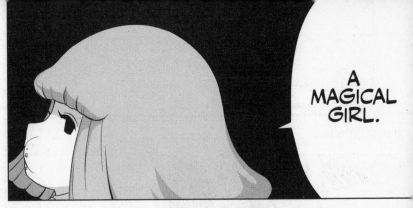

A MAGICAL GIRL.

SHE'S NOT ON THAT KILL LIST. THOUGH...

HUH...?

I DON'T KNOW HER NAME OR WHAT SHE LOOKS LIKE.

YOU DON'T KNOW, AND YET YOU'RE LOOKING FOR HER... WHY?

GULP!

MNCH

もぐ

MNCH

もぐ

MNCH

もぐ

もぐ

MNCH

もぐ

MNCH

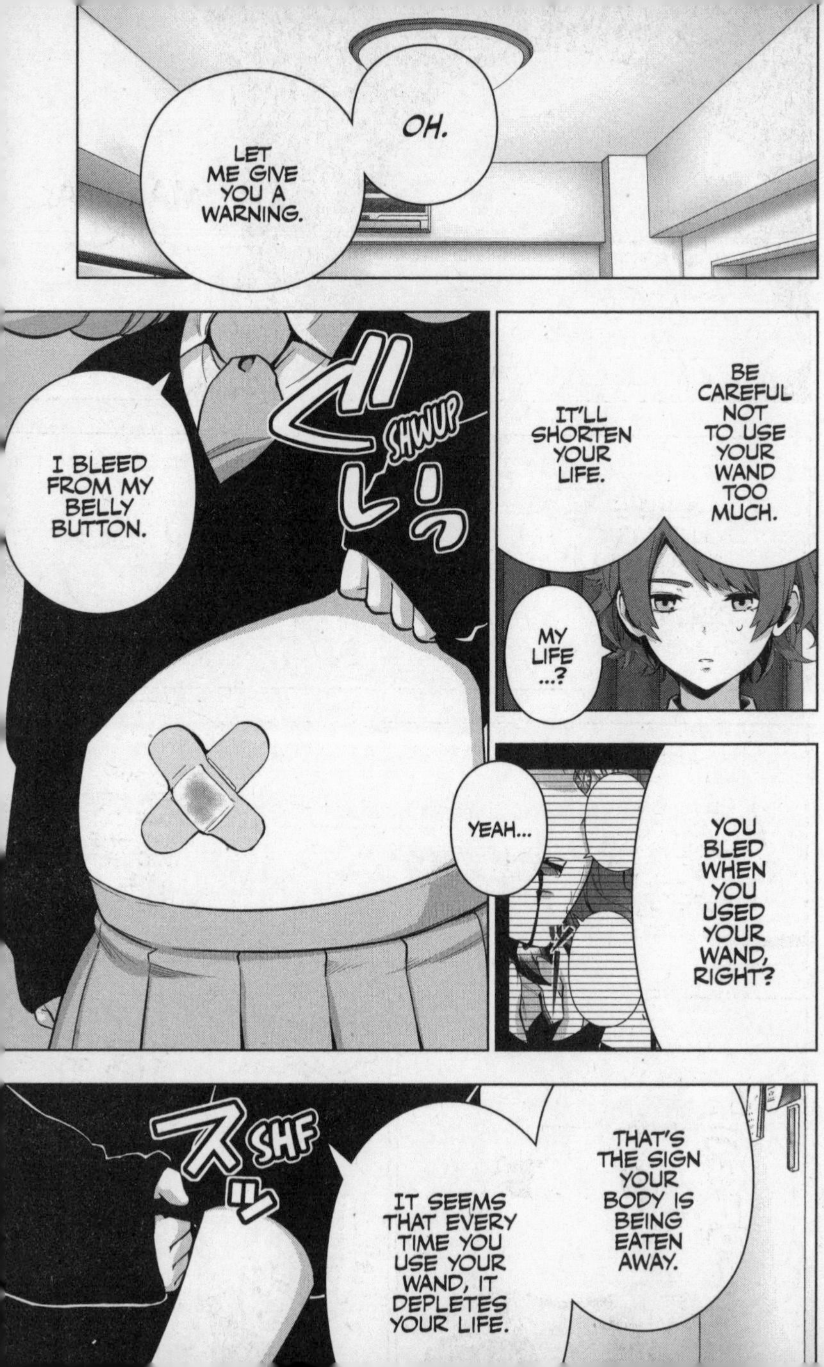
OH.
LET ME GIVE YOU A WARNING.
BE CAREFUL NOT TO USE YOUR WAND TOO MUCH.
IT'LL SHORTEN YOUR LIFE.
MY LIFE ...?
YOU BLED WHEN YOU USED YOUR WAND, RIGHT?
YEAH...
ぐいっ
SHWUP
I BLEED FROM MY BELLY BUTTON.
THAT'S THE SIGN YOUR BODY IS BEING EATEN AWAY.
IT SEEMS THAT EVERY TIME YOU USE YOUR WAND, IT DEPLETES YOUR LIFE.
スッ
SHF

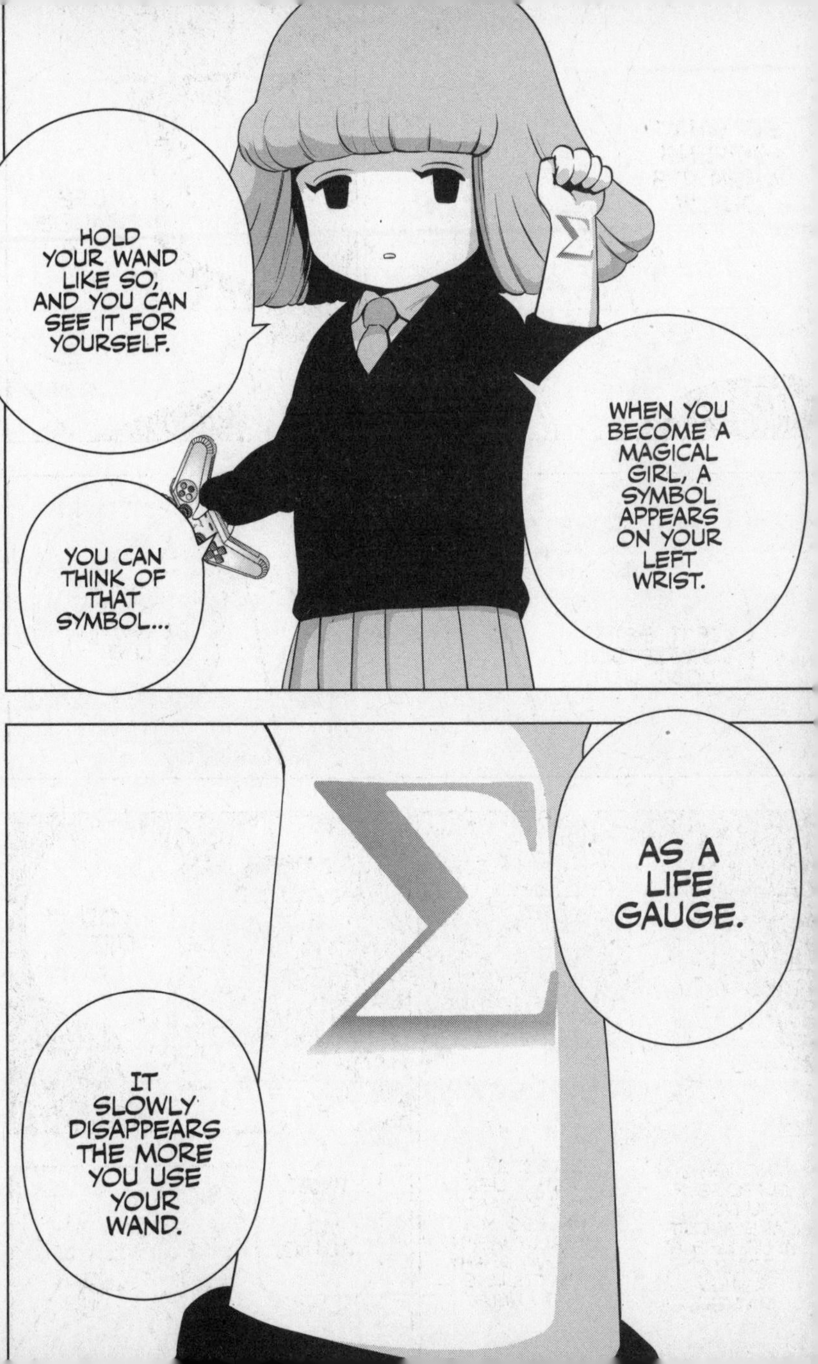
WHEN YOU BECOME A MAGICAL GIRL, A SYMBOL APPEARS ON YOUR LEFT WRIST.
HOLD YOUR WAND LIKE SO, AND YOU CAN SEE IT FOR YOURSELF.
YOU CAN THINK OF THAT SYMBOL...
AS A LIFE GAUGE.
IT SLOWLY DISAPPEARS THE MORE YOU USE YOUR WAND.

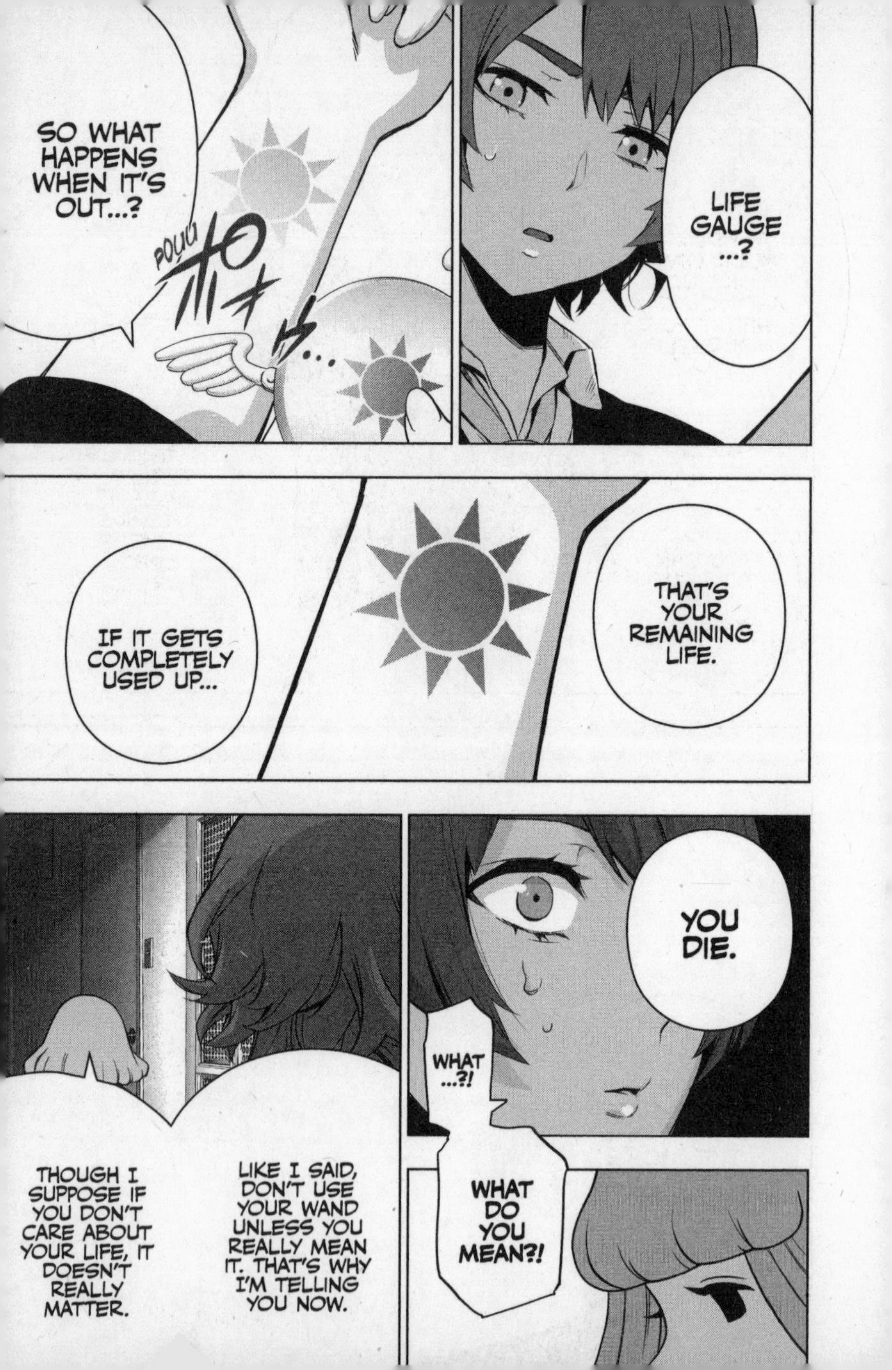
LIFE GAUGE ...?
SO WHAT HAPPENS WHEN IT'S OUT...?
POYUU
THAT'S YOUR REMAINING LIFE.
IF IT GETS COMPLETELY USED UP...
YOU DIE.
WHAT ...?!
WHAT DO YOU MEAN?!
LIKE I SAID, DON'T USE YOUR WAND UNLESS YOU REALLY MEAN IT. THAT'S WHY I'M TELLING YOU NOW.
THOUGH I SUPPOSE IF YOU DON'T CARE ABOUT YOUR LIFE, IT DOESN'T REALLY MATTER.

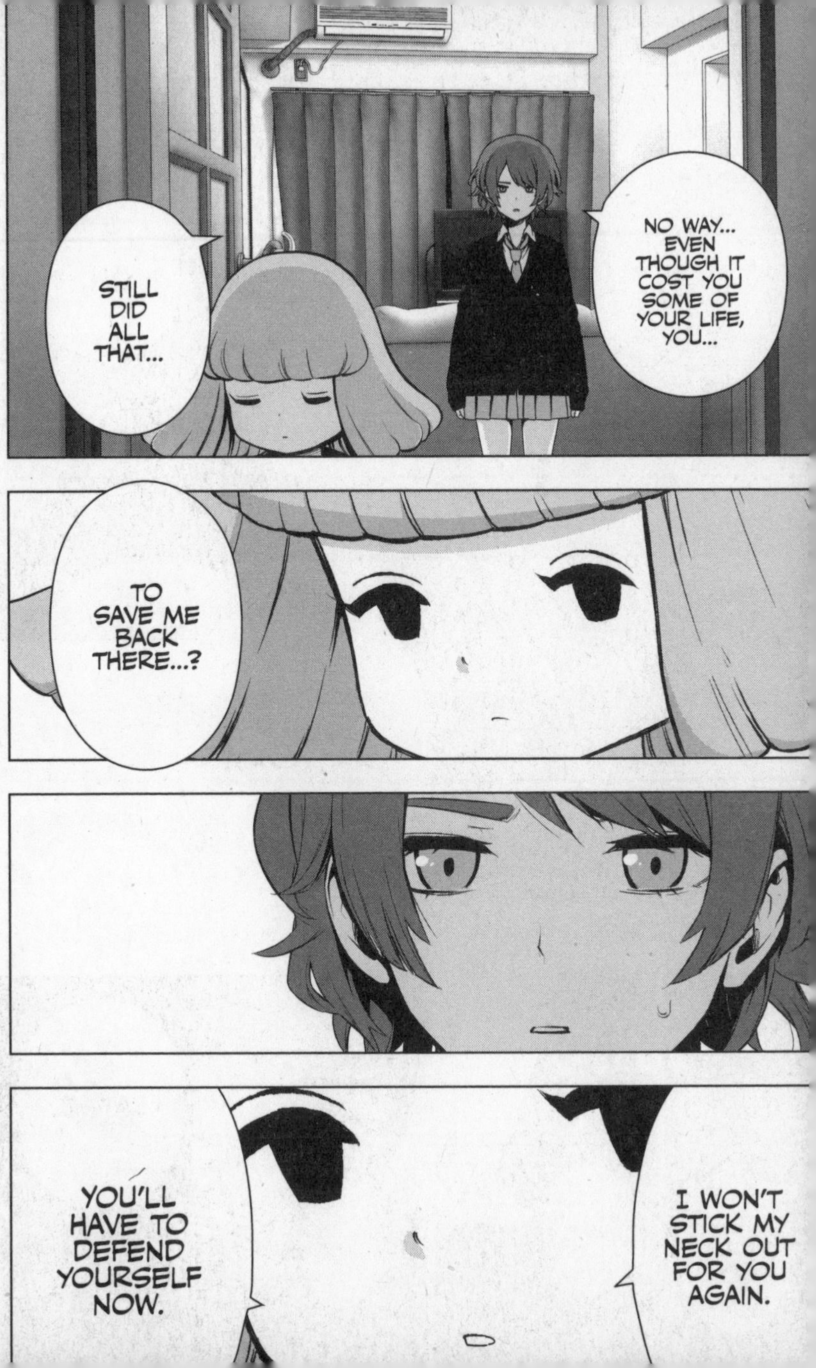
NO WAY... EVEN THOUGH IT COST YOU SOME OF YOUR LIFE, YOU...
STILL DID ALL THAT...
TO SAVE ME BACK THERE...?
I WON'T STICK MY NECK OUT FOR YOU AGAIN.
YOU'LL HAVE TO DEFEND YOURSELF NOW.

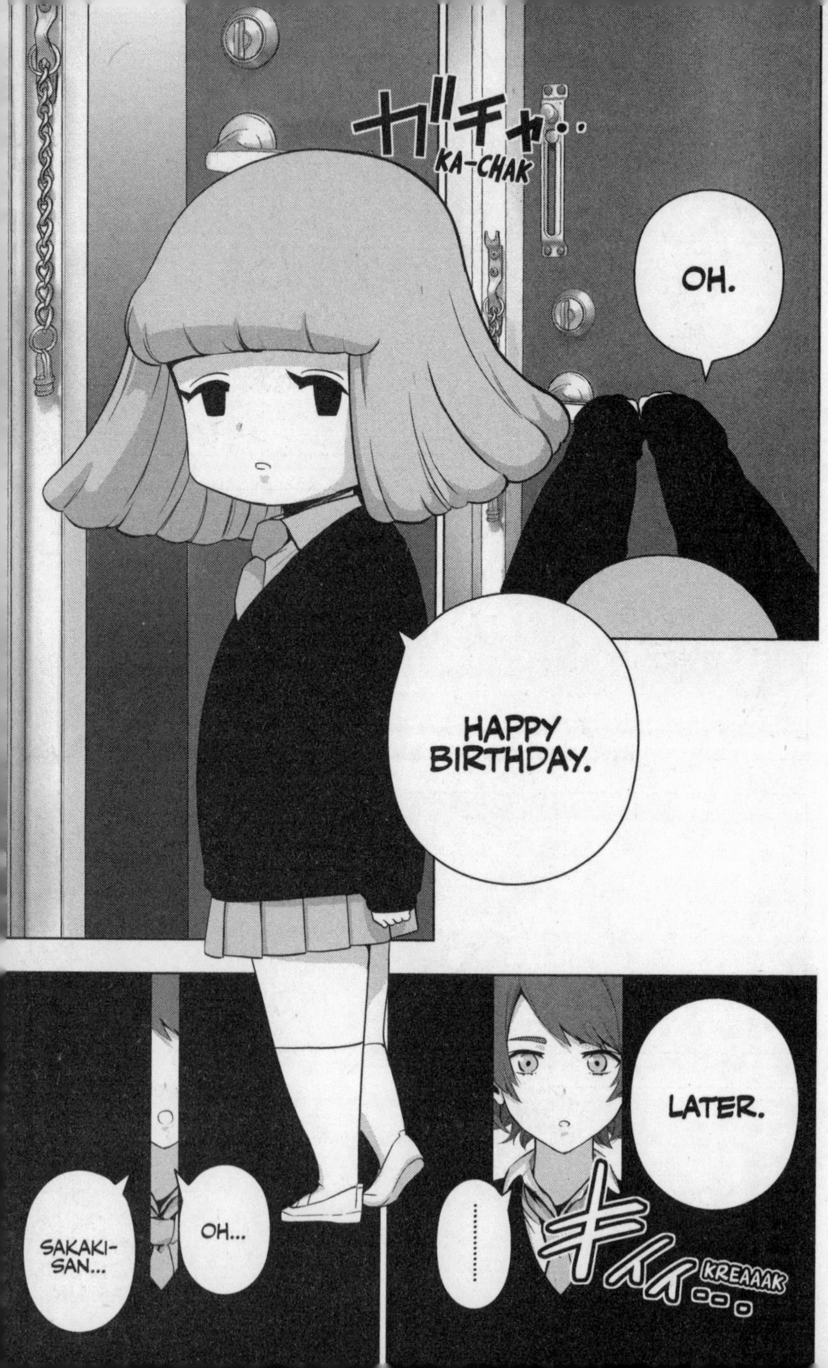
OH.
ガチャ
KA-CHAK
HAPPY BIRTHDAY.
LATER.
......
キィィ...
KREAAAK
OH...
SAKAKI-SAN...

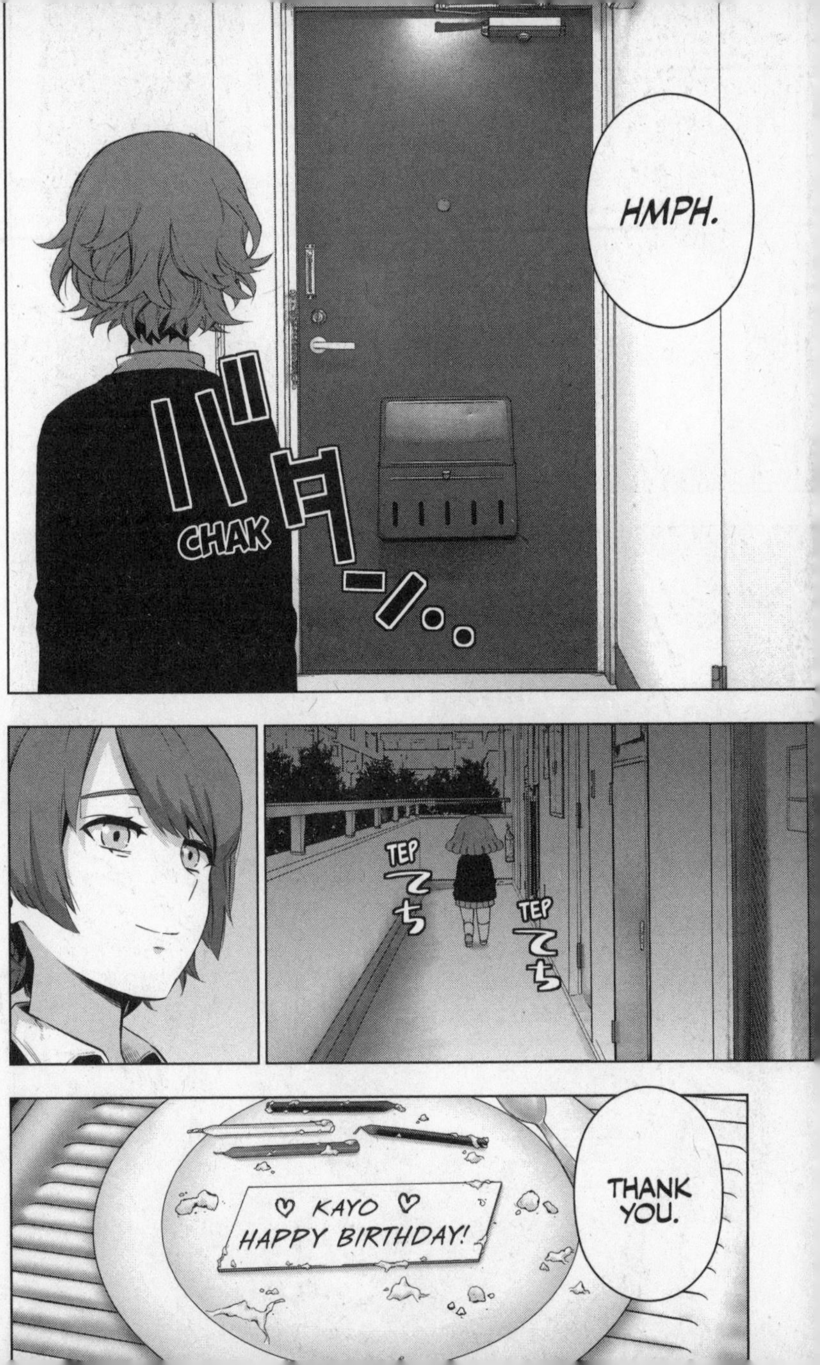
HMPH.
バターン。。
CHAK
TEP
てち
TEP
てち
THANK YOU.
KAYO
HAPPY BIRTHDAY!

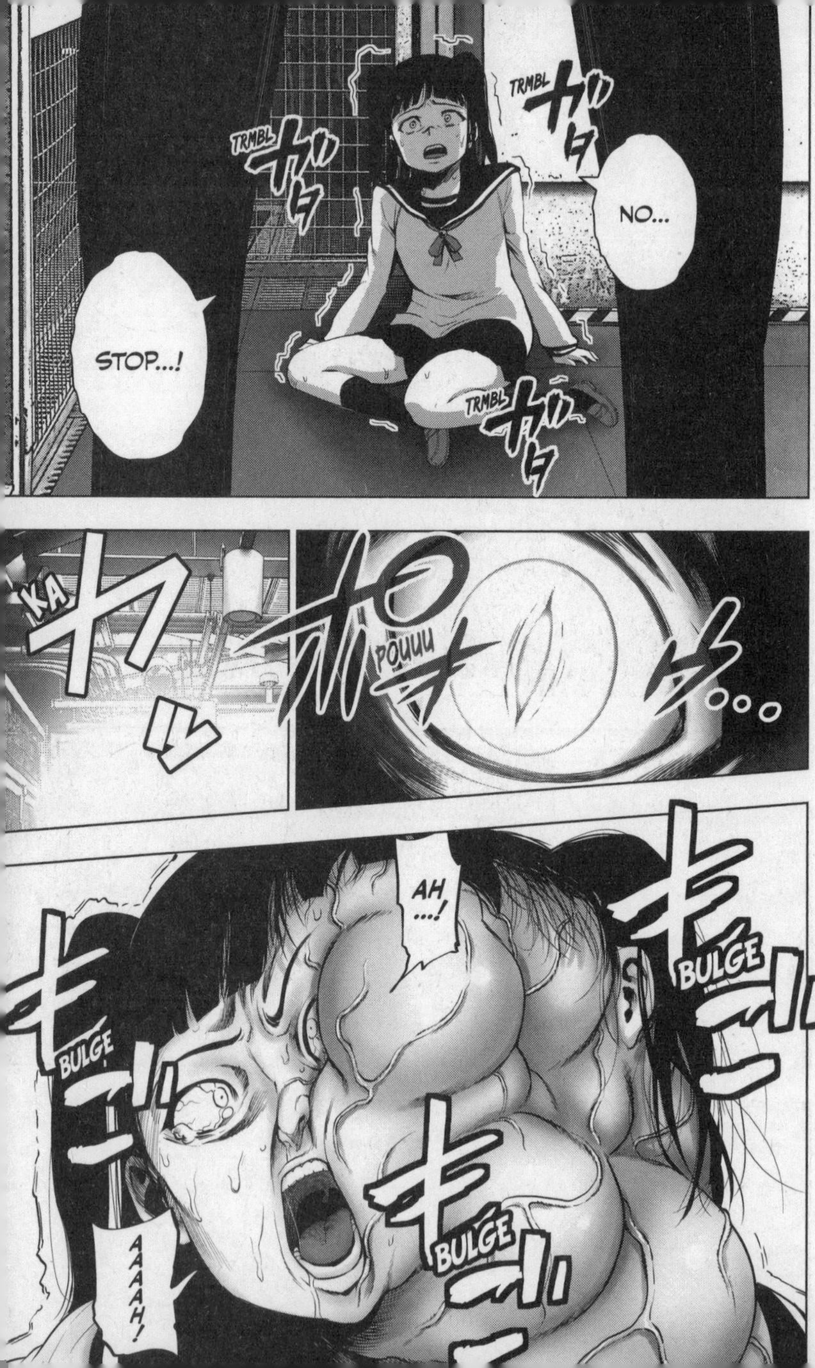
TRMBL
NO...
TRMBL
STOP...!
TRMBL
POUUU
KA
BULGE
AH ...!
BULGE
BULGE
AAAAH!

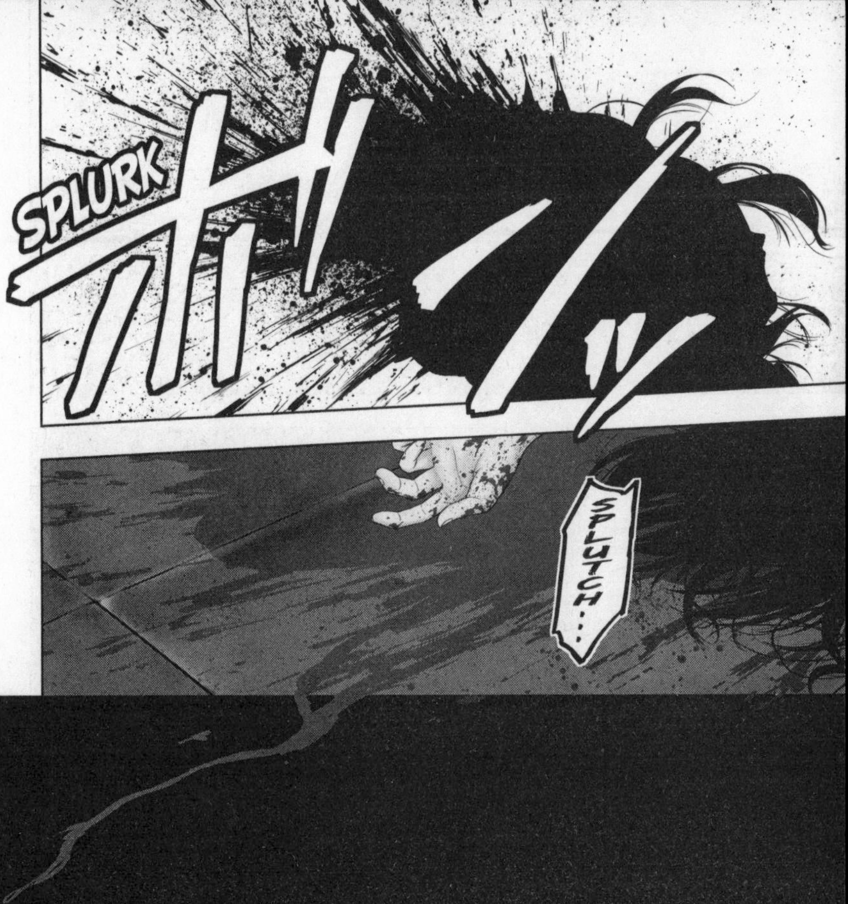
SPLURK
SPLUTCH...

ENTER.61 "A"

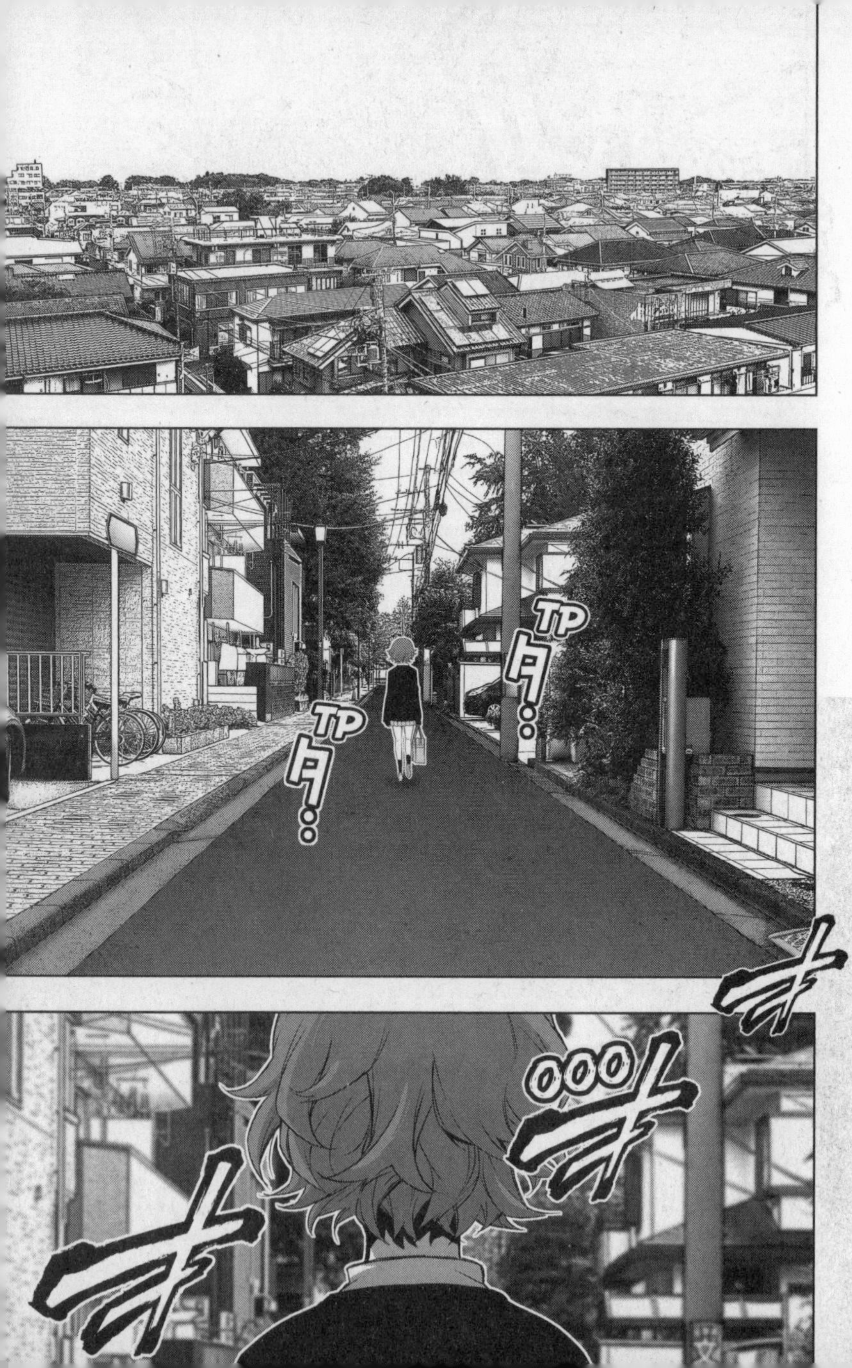
TP
TP

MORNING!

PAT

TAKUMA, ARE YOU ALL RIGHT NOW?

THANKS TO YOU, AS YOU CAN SEE!

DUUN

SURE AM!

BECAUSE OF ME, YOU...

WH-WHAT ARE YOU TALKING ABOUT...?!

BA-THMP

I'M SORRY, TAKUMA.

BA-THMP

SHF

BA-THMP

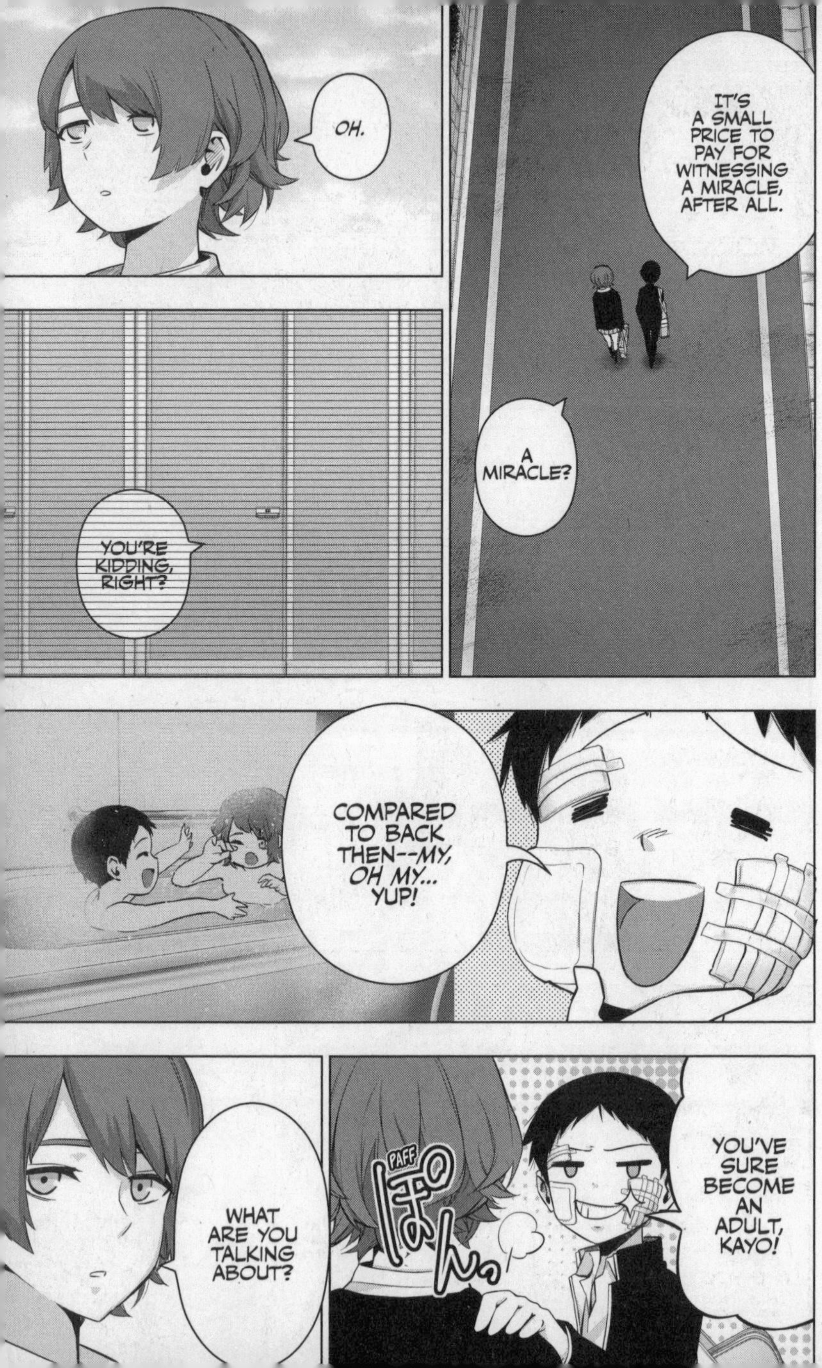
IT'S A SMALL PRICE TO PAY FOR WITNESSING A MIRACLE, AFTER ALL.
A MIRACLE?
OH.
YOU'RE KIDDING, RIGHT?
COMPARED TO BACK THEN--*MY, OH MY*... YUP!
YOU'VE SURE BECOME AN ADULT, KAYO!
PAFF
WHAT ARE YOU TALKING ABOUT?

YOU'VE BECOME AN ADULT TOO, YOU KNOW.

BLUUUUSH

WHADDYA MEAN YOU DIDN'T WANT TO SEE IT?!

I'D RATHER NOT HAVE...

YOU... YOU *SAW*, DIDN'T YOU?!

RIGHT...

WHAT ARE YOU DOING? WE'RE GOING TO BE LATE.

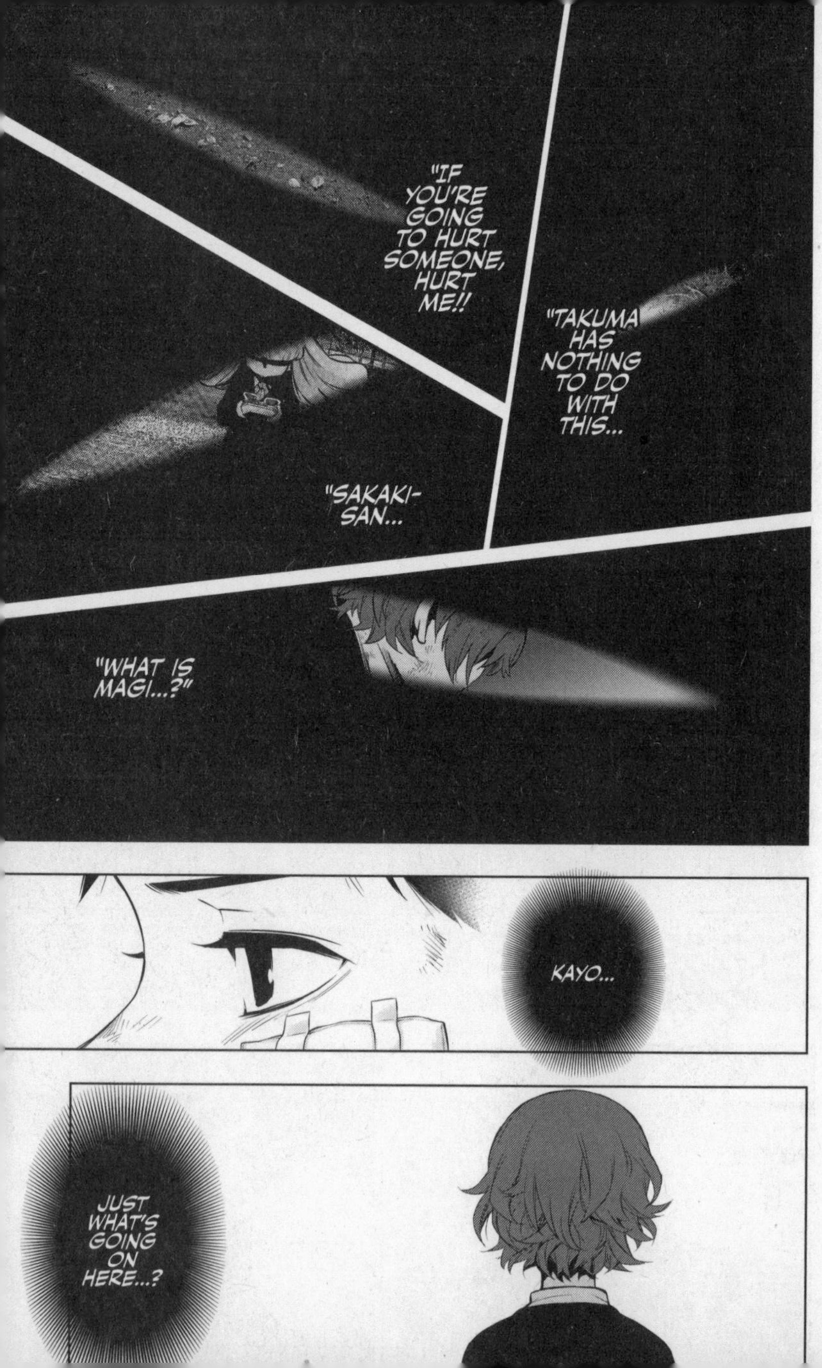
"TAKUMA HAS NOTHING TO DO WITH THIS...
"IF YOU'RE GOING TO HURT SOMEONE, HURT ME!!
"SAKAKI-SAN...
"WHAT IS MAGI...?"
KAYO...
JUST WHAT'S GOING ON HERE...?

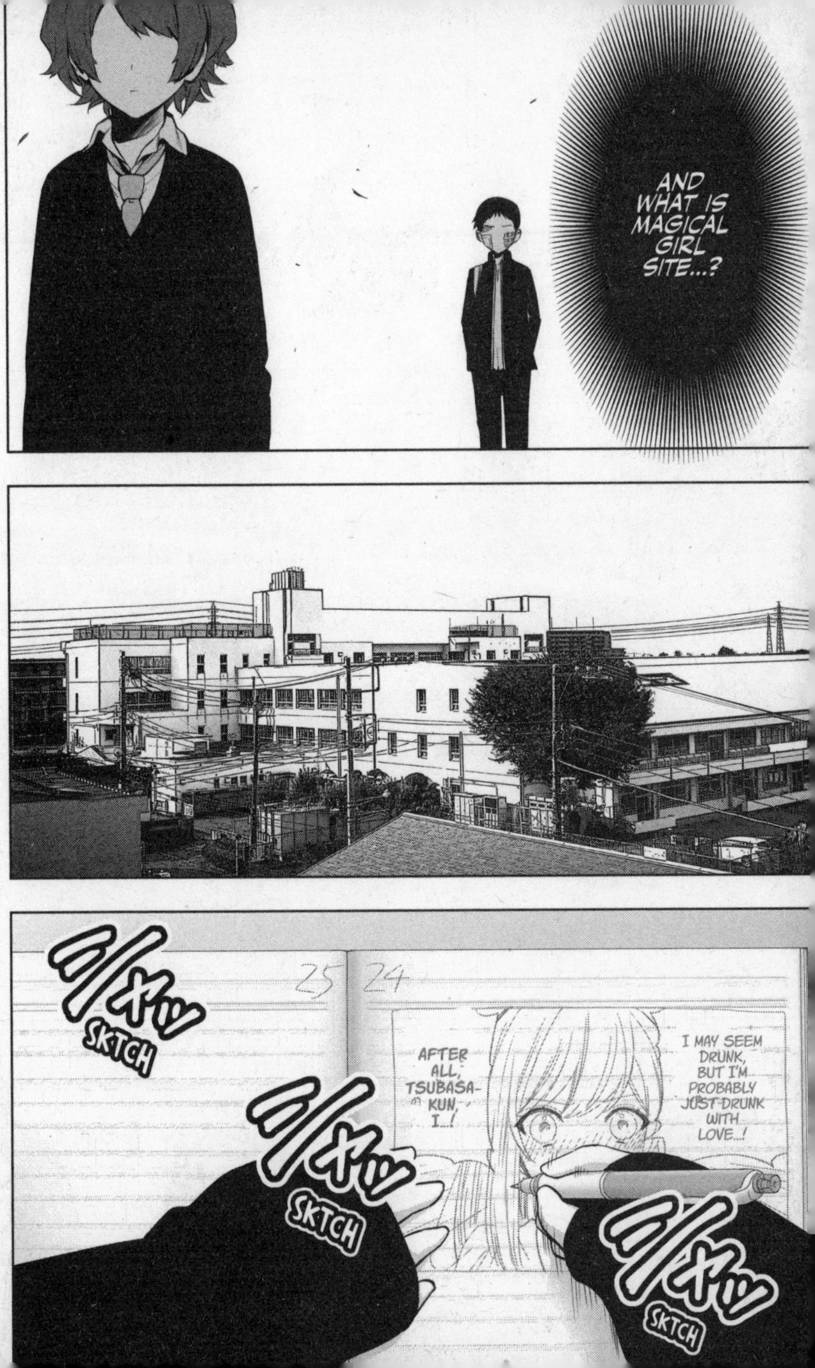
AND WHAT IS MAGICAL GIRL SITE...?
24
25
SKTCH
I MAY SEEM DRUNK, BUT I'M PROBABLY JUST DRUNK WITH LOVE...!
AFTER ALL, TSUBASA-KUN, I...!
SKTCH
SKTCH

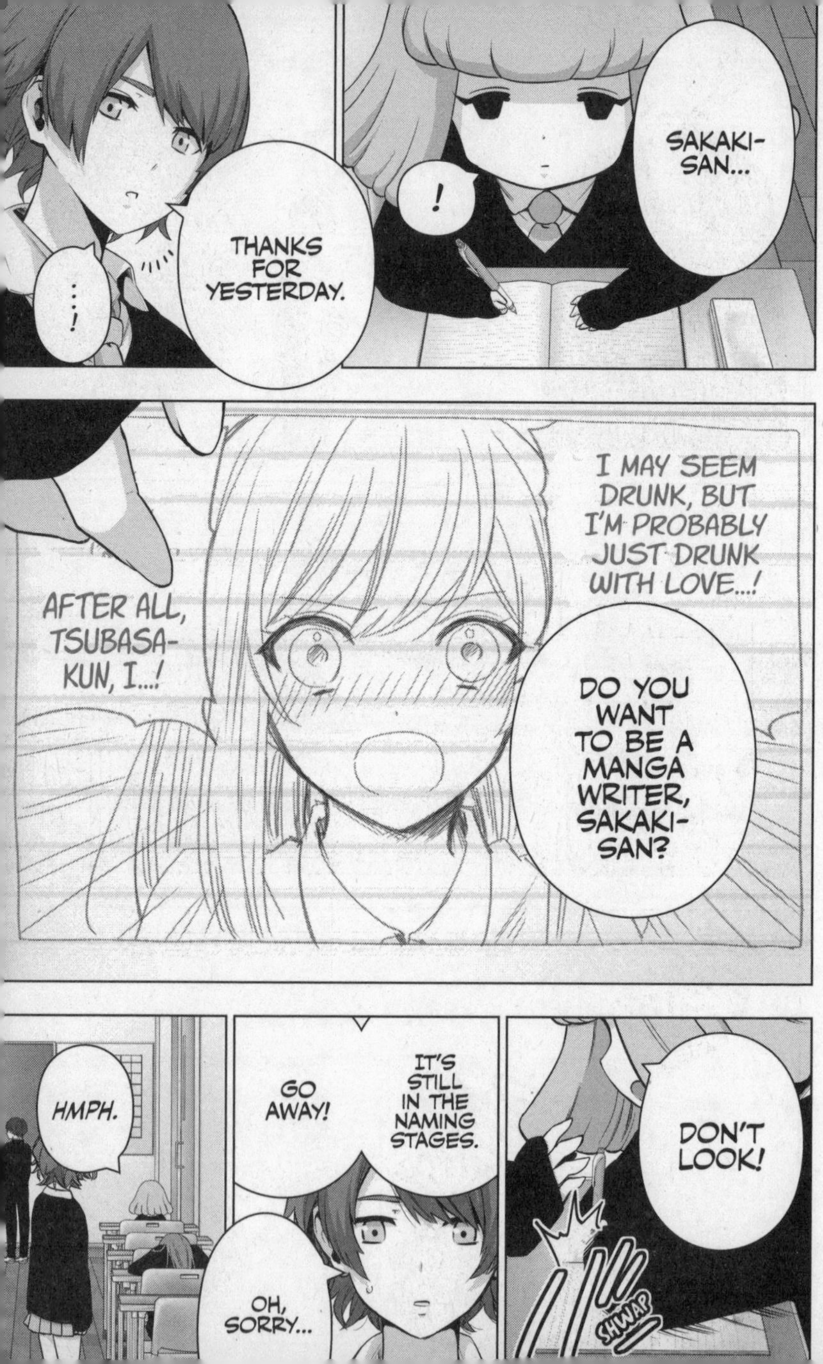
SAKAKI-SAN...
!
THANKS FOR YESTERDAY.
...!
I MAY SEEM DRUNK, BUT I'M PROBABLY JUST DRUNK WITH LOVE...!
DO YOU WANT TO BE A MANGA WRITER, SAKAKI-SAN?
AFTER ALL, TSUBASA-KUN, I...!
DON'T LOOK!
SHWAP
IT'S STILL IN THE NAMING STAGES.
GO AWAY!
OH, SORRY...
HMPH.

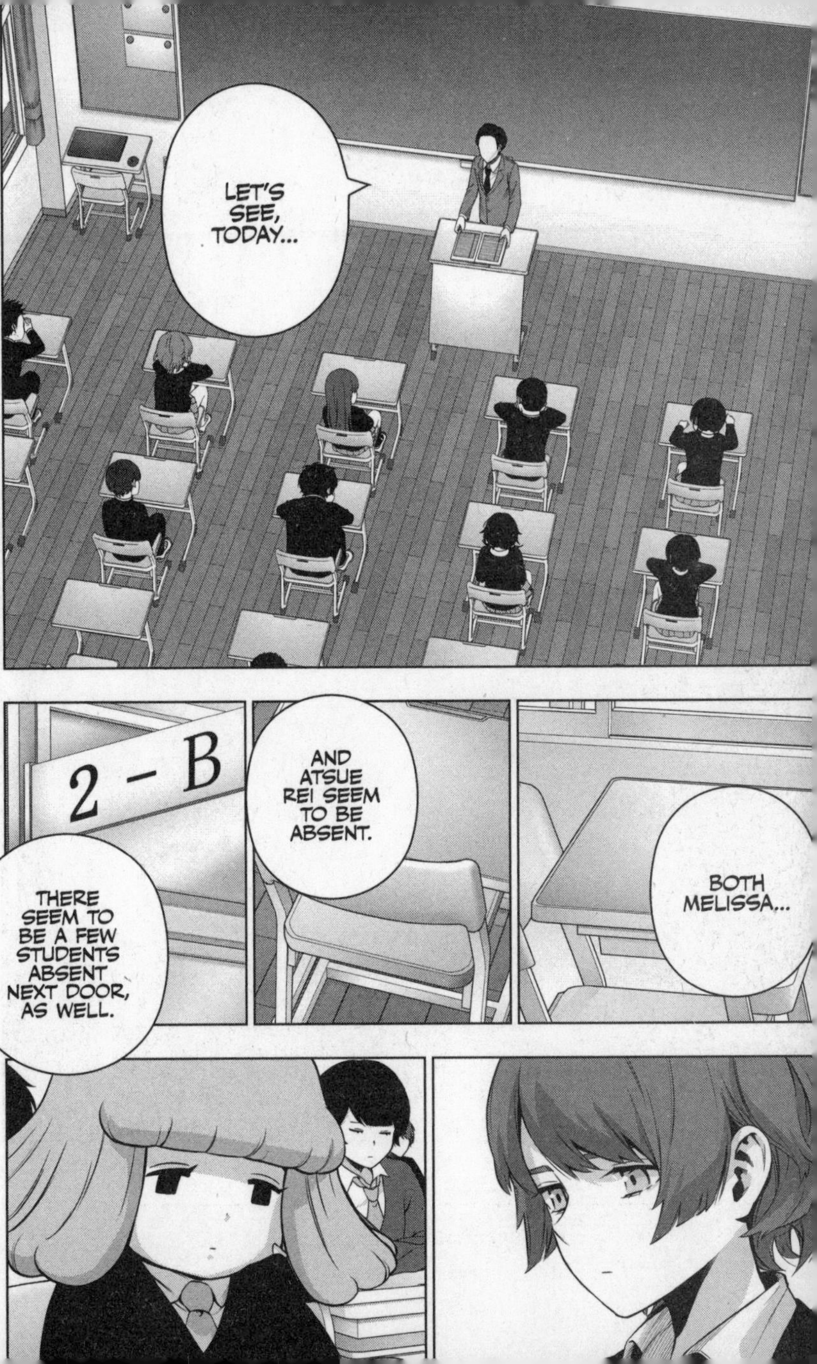
LET'S SEE, TODAY...
BOTH MELISSA...
AND ATSUE REI SEEM TO BE ABSENT.
2 - B
THERE SEEM TO BE A FEW STUDENTS ABSENT NEXT DOOR, AS WELL.

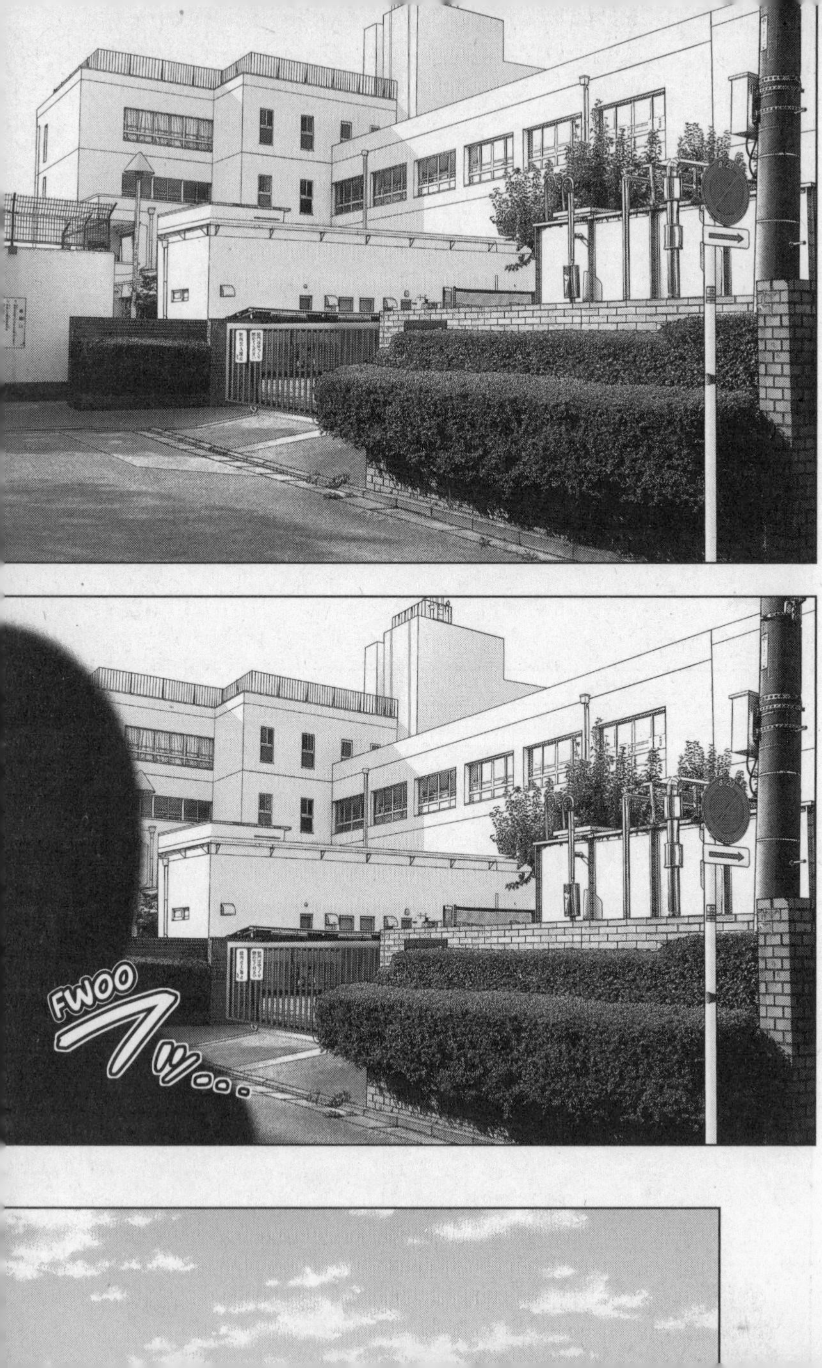
FWOO

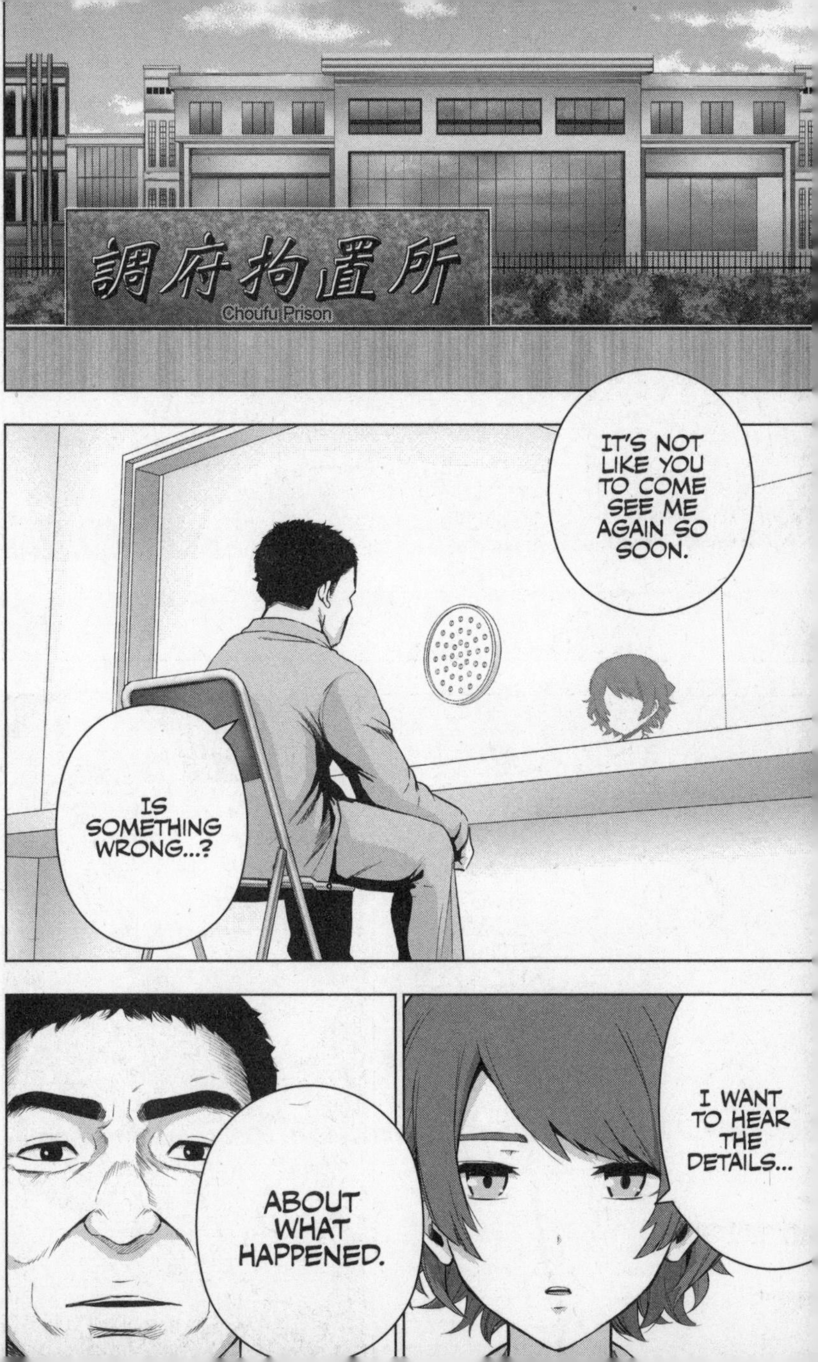
調府拘置所
Choufu Prison
IT'S NOT LIKE YOU TO COME SEE ME AGAIN SO SOON.
IS SOMETHING WRONG...?
I WANT TO HEAR THE DETAILS...
ABOUT WHAT HAPPENED.

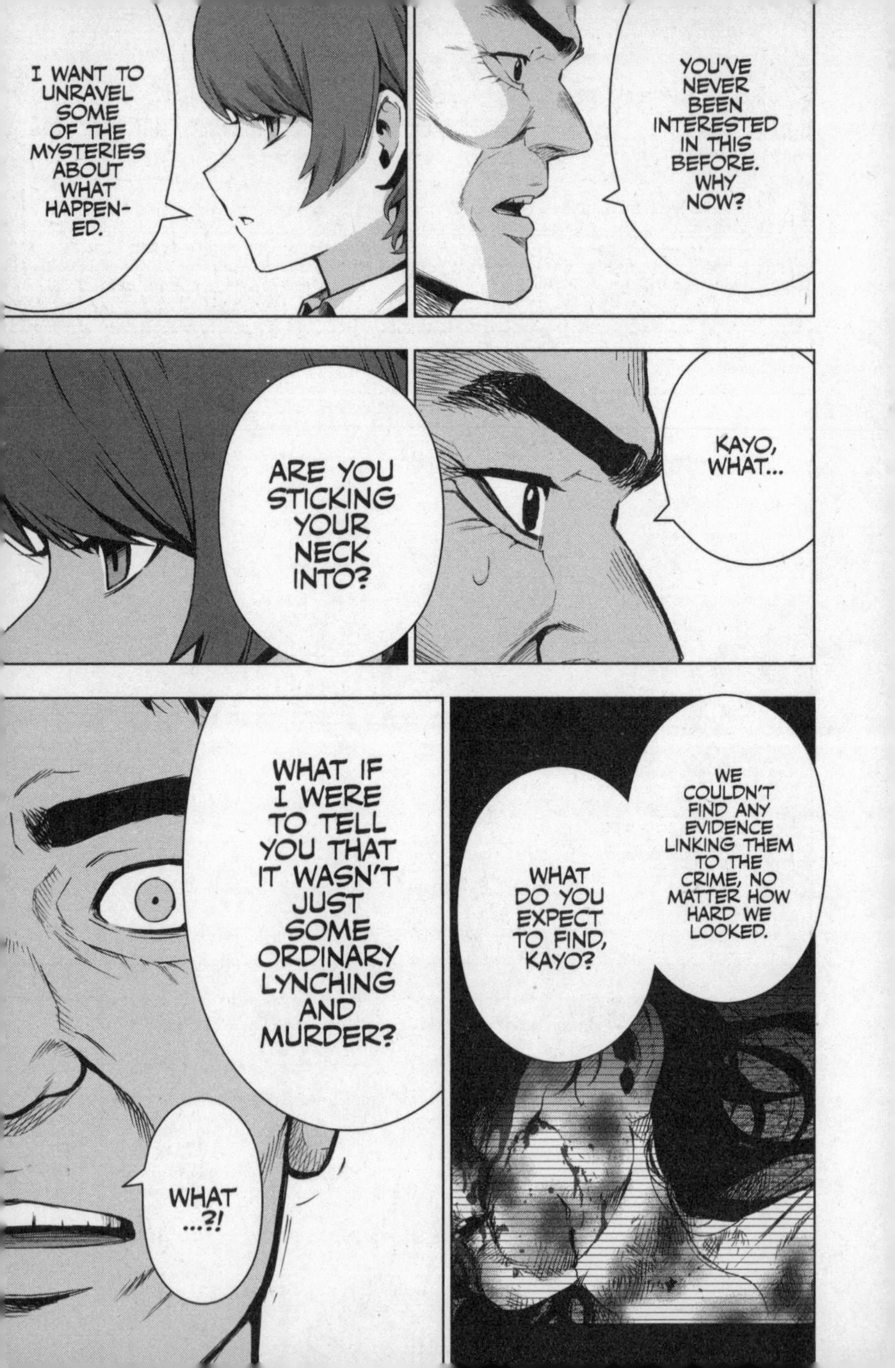
YOU'VE NEVER BEEN INTERESTED IN THIS BEFORE. WHY NOW?
I WANT TO UNRAVEL SOME OF THE MYSTERIES ABOUT WHAT HAPPEN-ED.
KAYO, WHAT...
ARE YOU STICKING YOUR NECK INTO?
WE COULDN'T FIND ANY EVIDENCE LINKING THEM TO THE CRIME, NO MATTER HOW HARD WE LOOKED.
WHAT DO YOU EXPECT TO FIND, KAYO?
WHAT IF I WERE TO TELL YOU THAT IT WASN'T JUST SOME ORDINARY LYNCHING AND MURDER?
WHAT ...?!

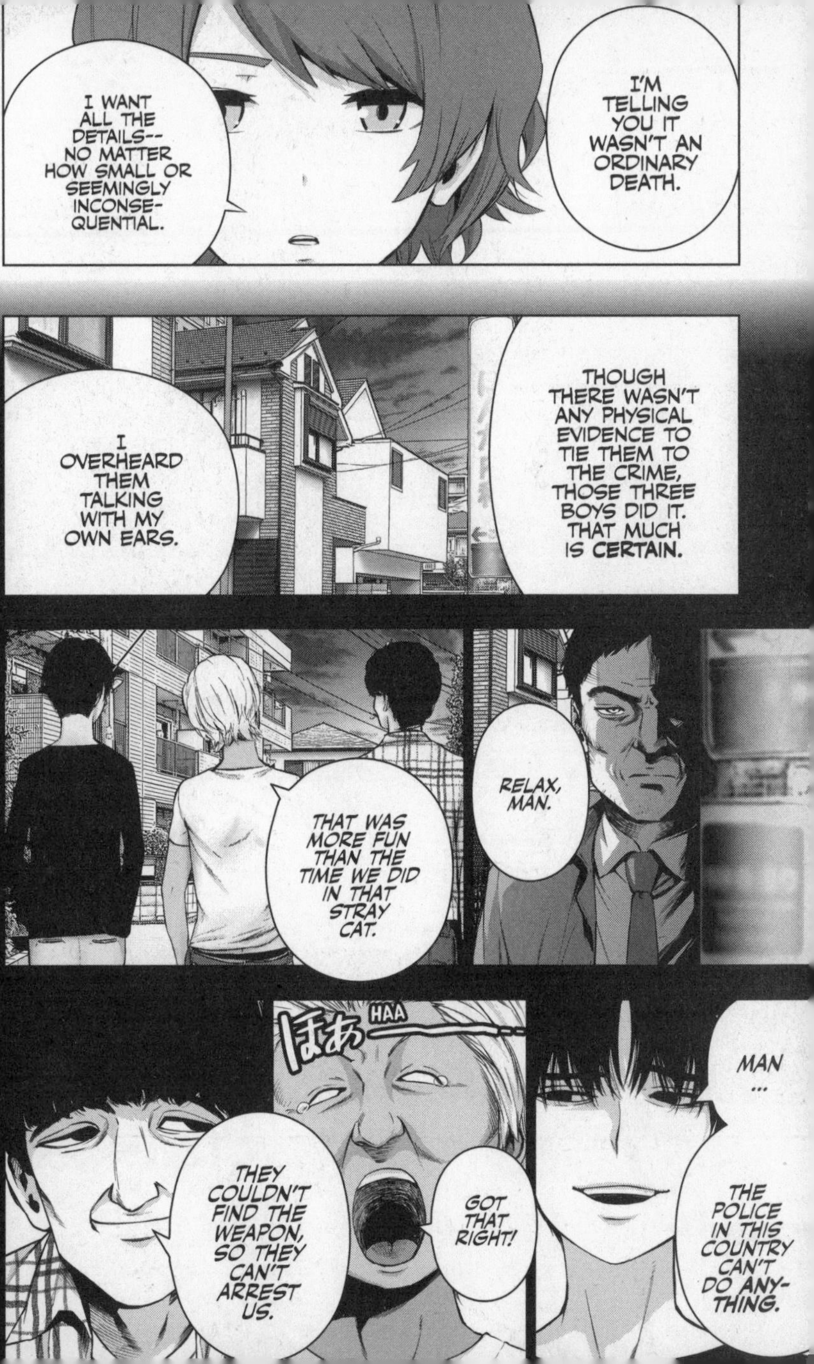
I'M TELLING YOU IT WASN'T AN ORDINARY DEATH.
I WANT ALL THE DETAILS-- NO MATTER HOW SMALL OR SEEMINGLY INCONSE-QUENTIAL.
THOUGH THERE WASN'T ANY PHYSICAL EVIDENCE TO TIE THEM TO THE CRIME, THOSE THREE BOYS DID IT. THAT MUCH IS CERTAIN.
I OVERHEARD THEM TALKING WITH MY OWN EARS.
RELAX, MAN.
THAT WAS MORE FUN THAN THE TIME WE DID IN THAT STRAY CAT.
MAN ...
THE POLICE IN THIS COUNTRY CAN'T DO ANY-THING.
ほあ
HAA
GOT THAT RIGHT!
THEY COULDN'T FIND THE WEAPON, SO THEY CAN'T ARREST US.

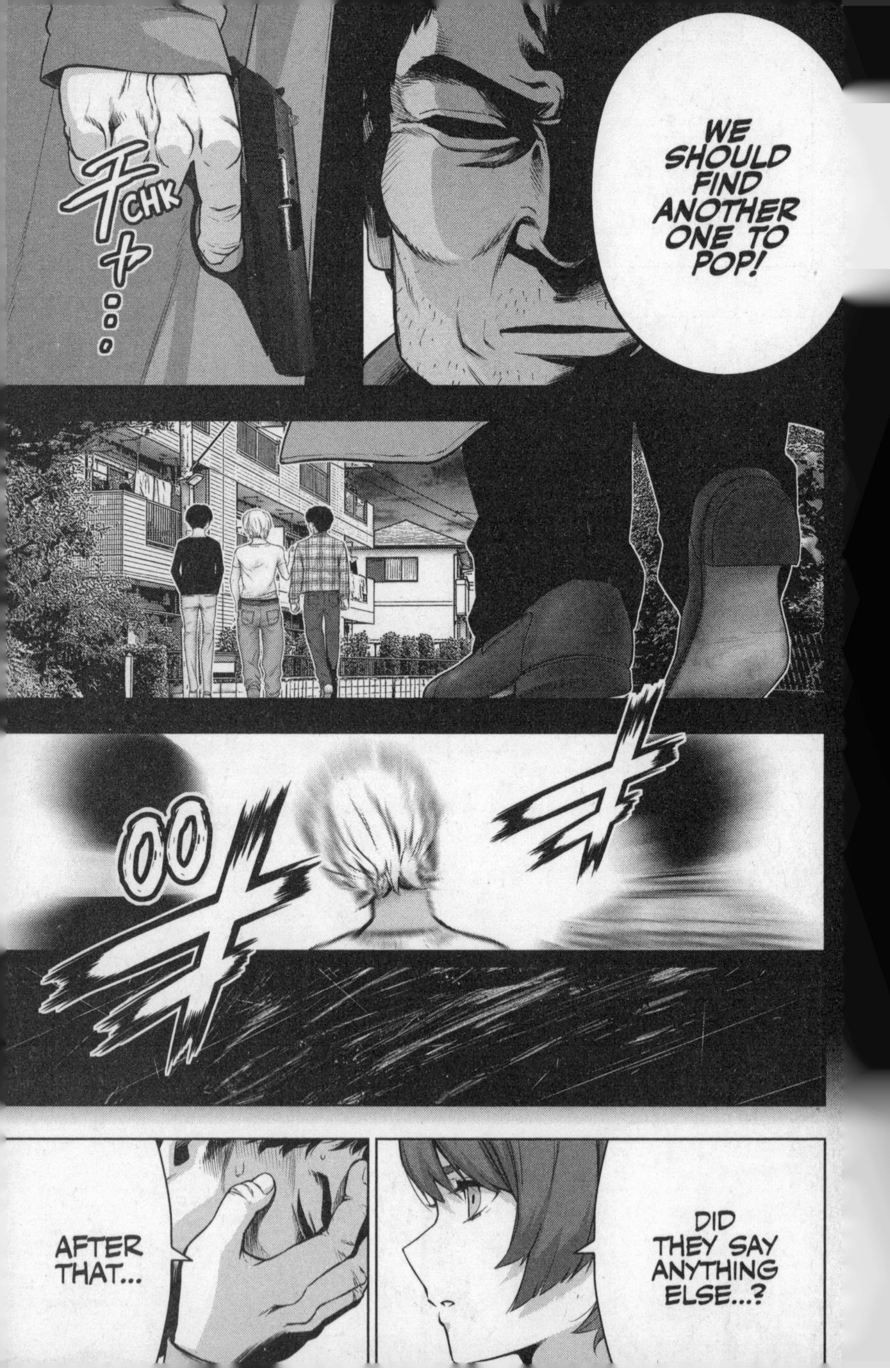
WE SHOULD FIND ANOTHER ONE TO POP!
CHK
OO
DID THEY SAY ANYTHING ELSE...?
AFTER THAT...

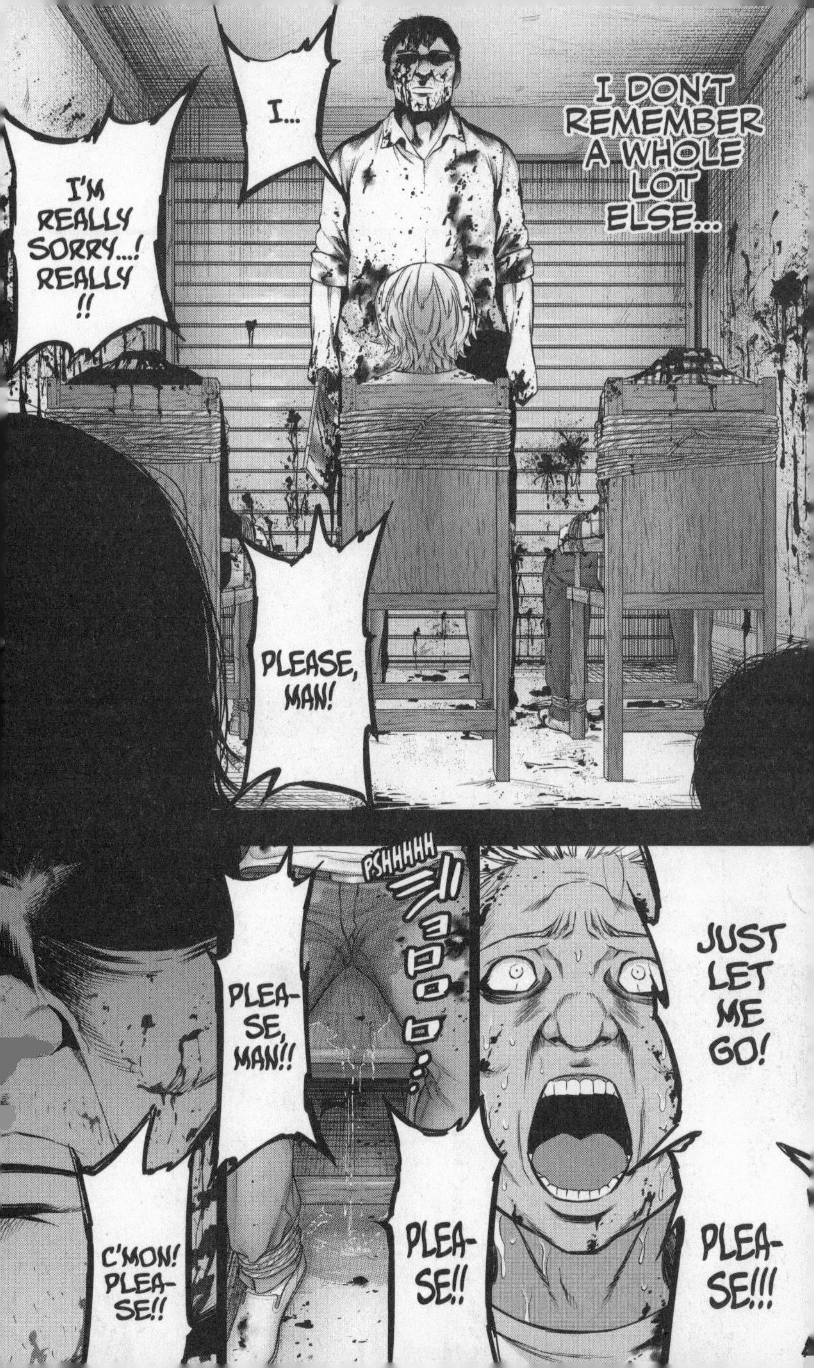
I DON'T REMEMBER A WHOLE LOT ELSE...
I...
I'M REALLY SORRY...! REALLY!!
PLEASE, MAN!
JUST LET ME GO!
PLEA-SE!!!
PSHHHHH
PLEA-SE, MAN!!
PLEA-SE!!
C'MON! PLEA-SE!!

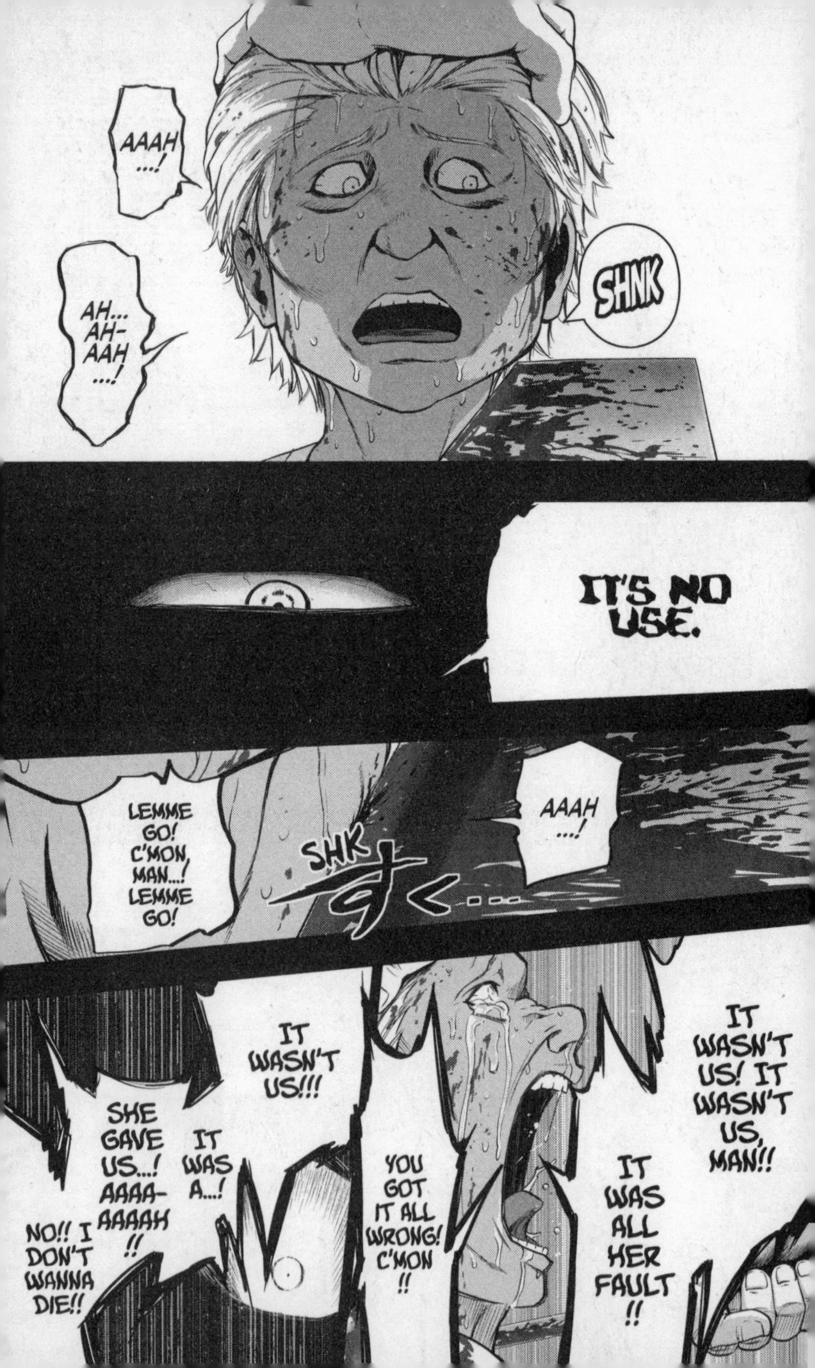
AAAH...!
SHNK
AH... AH-AAAH...!
IT'S NO USE.
AAAH...!
SHK すく...
LEMME GO! C'MON, MAN...! LEMME GO!
IT WASN'T US! IT WASN'T US, MAN!!
IT WAS ALL HER FAULT!!
IT WASN'T US!!!
YOU GOT IT ALL WRONG! C'MON!!
IT WAS A...!
SHE GAVE US...! AAAA-AAAAH!!
NO!! I DON'T WANNA DIE!!

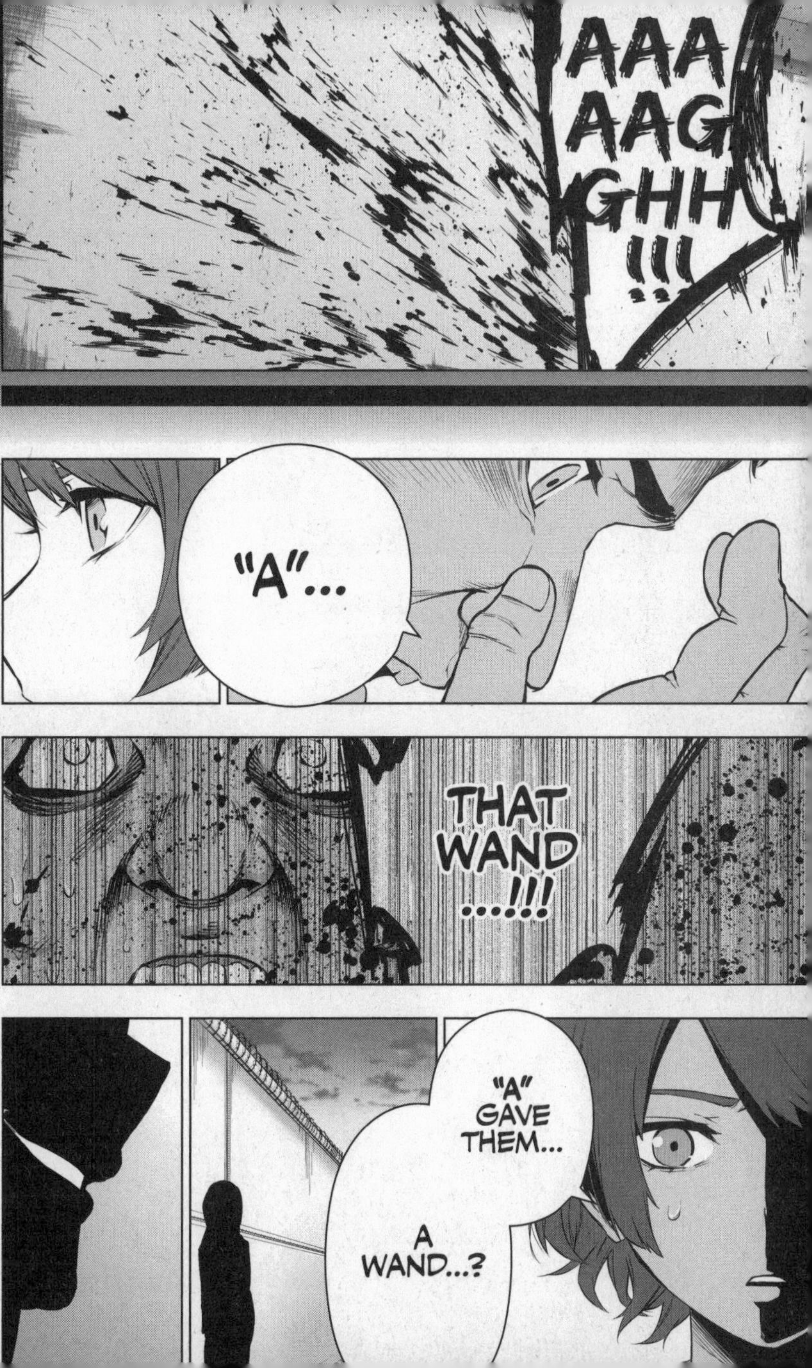
AAAAAGGHH!!!
"A"...
THAT WAND ...!!!
"A" GAVE THEM...
A WAND...?

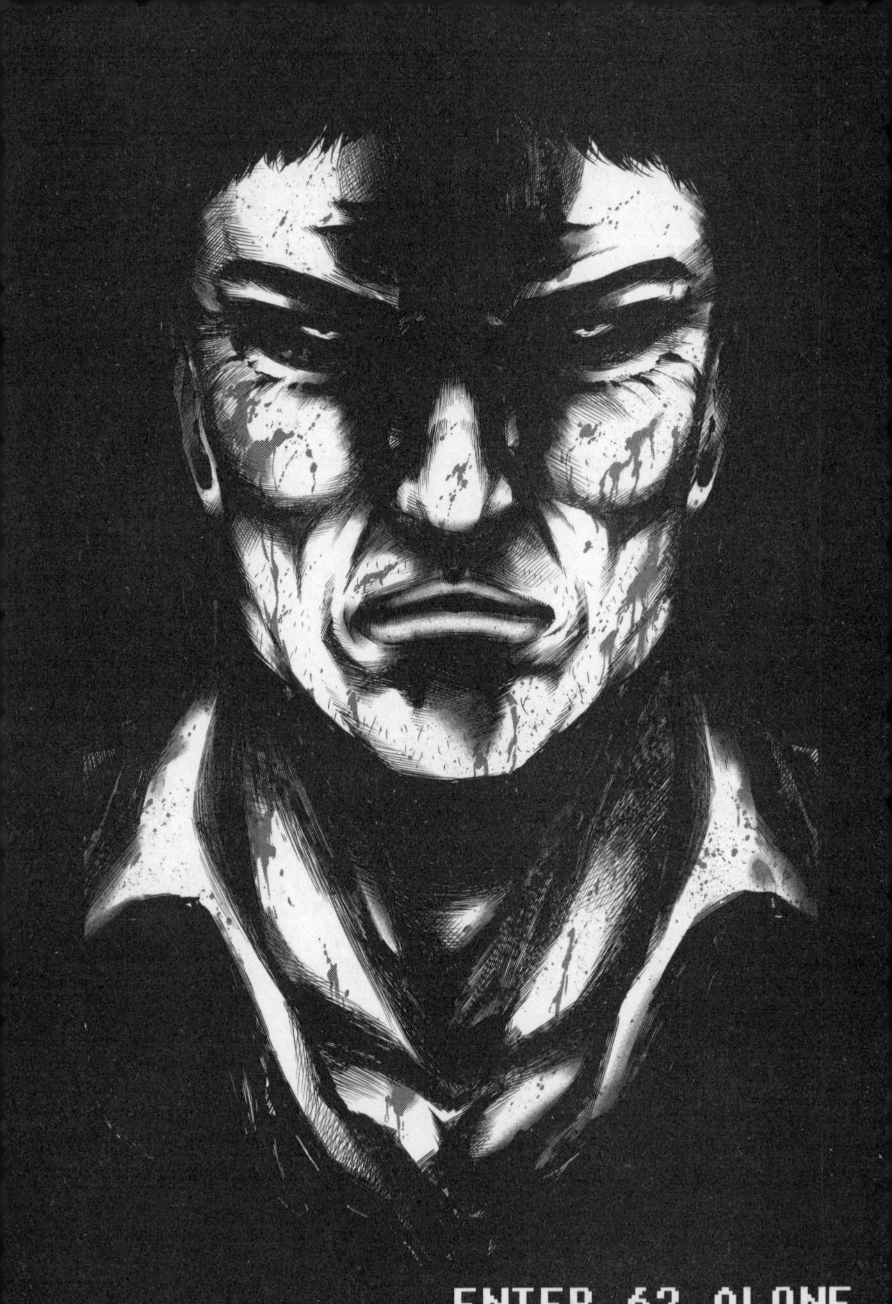

ENTER.62 ALONE

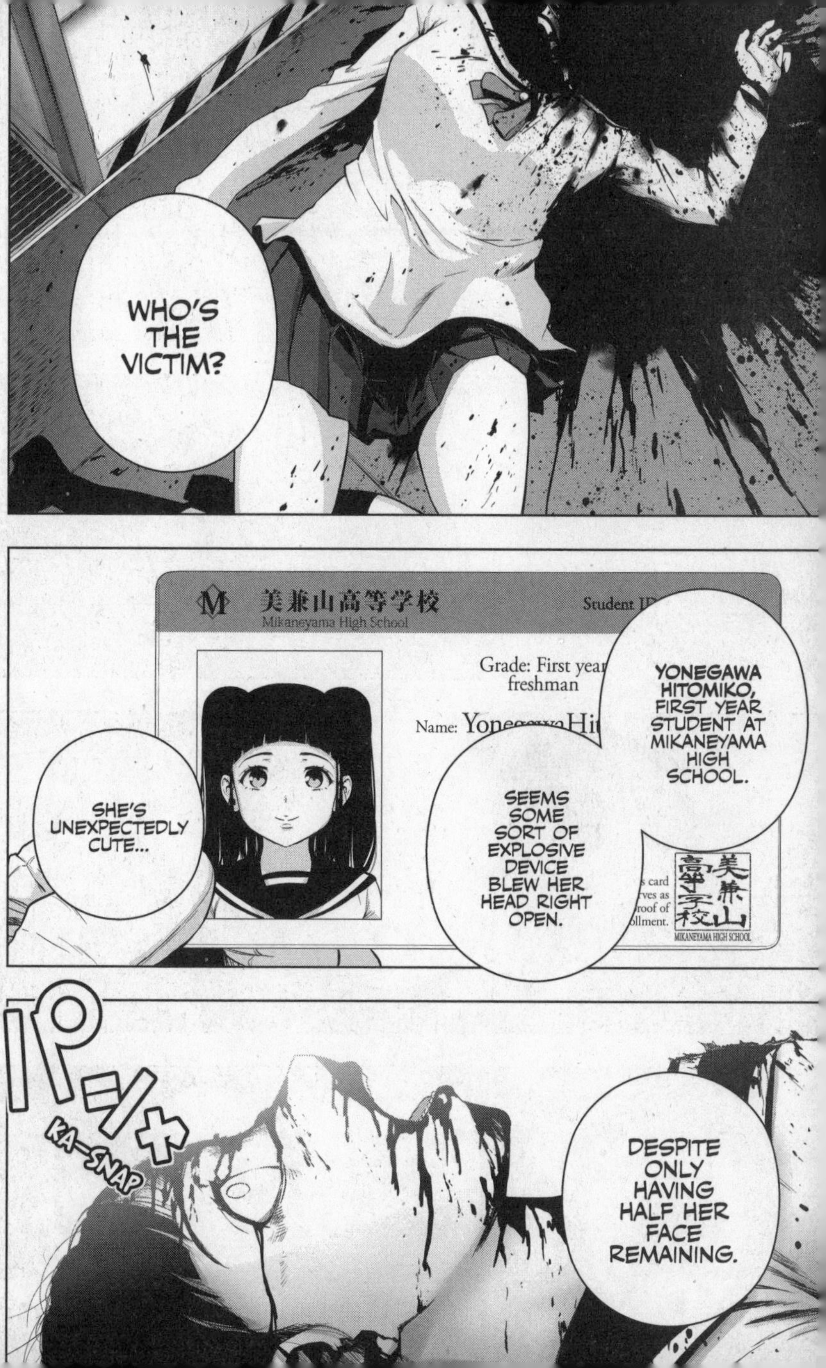

WHO'S THE VICTIM?
美兼山高等学校
Mikaneyama High School
Grade: First year
freshman
美兼山高等学校
MIKANEYAMA HIGH SCHOOL
YONEGAWA HITOMIKO, FIRST YEAR STUDENT AT MIKANEYAMA HIGH SCHOOL.
SEEMS SOME SORT OF EXPLOSIVE DEVICE BLEW HER HEAD RIGHT OPEN.
SHE'S UNEXPECTEDLY CUTE...
DESPITE ONLY HAVING HALF HER FACE REMAINING.
パシャ
KA-SNAP

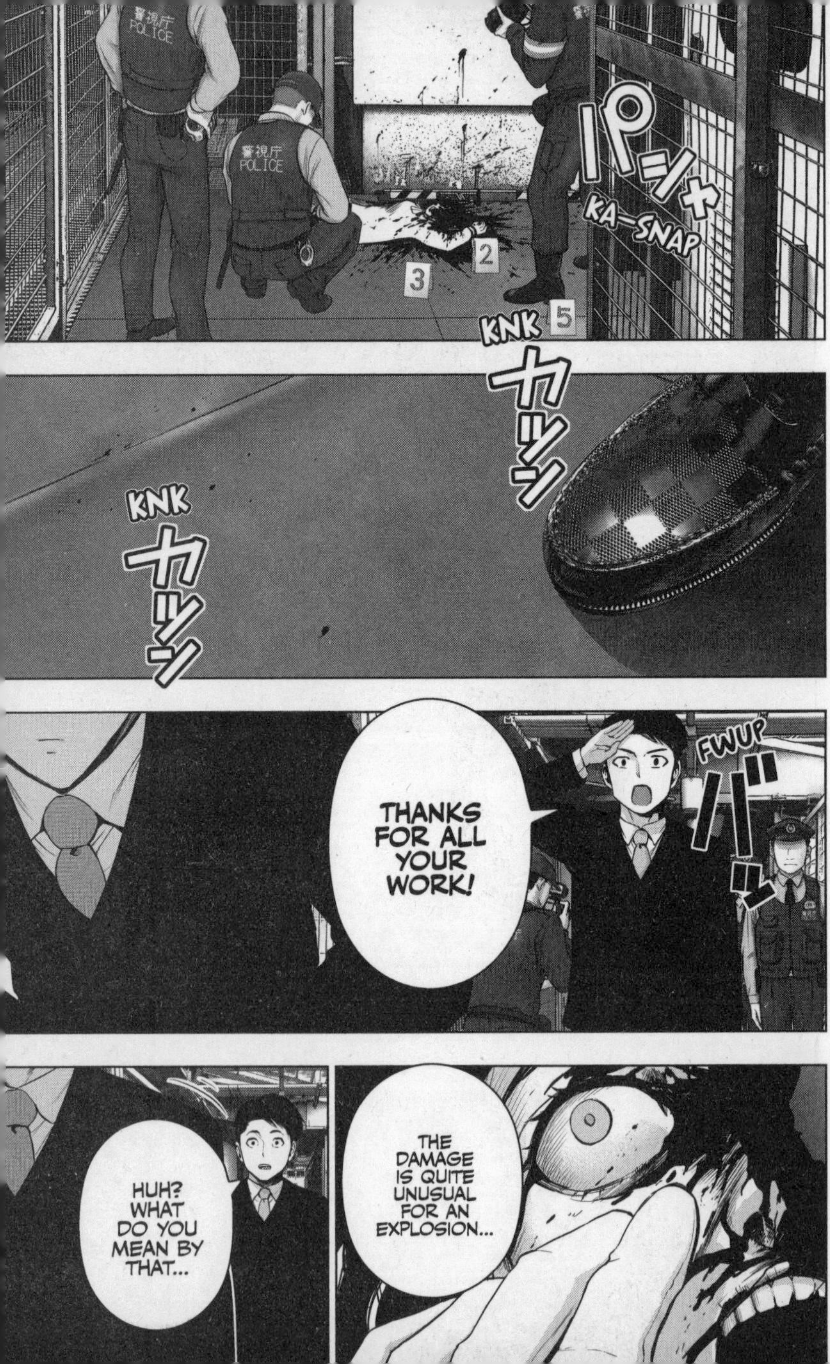

パシャ
KA-SNAP
KNK
カッン
KNK
カッン
FWUP
バッ
THANKS FOR ALL YOUR WORK!
THE DAMAGE IS QUITE UNUSUAL FOR AN EXPLOSION...
HUH? WHAT DO YOU MEAN BY THAT...

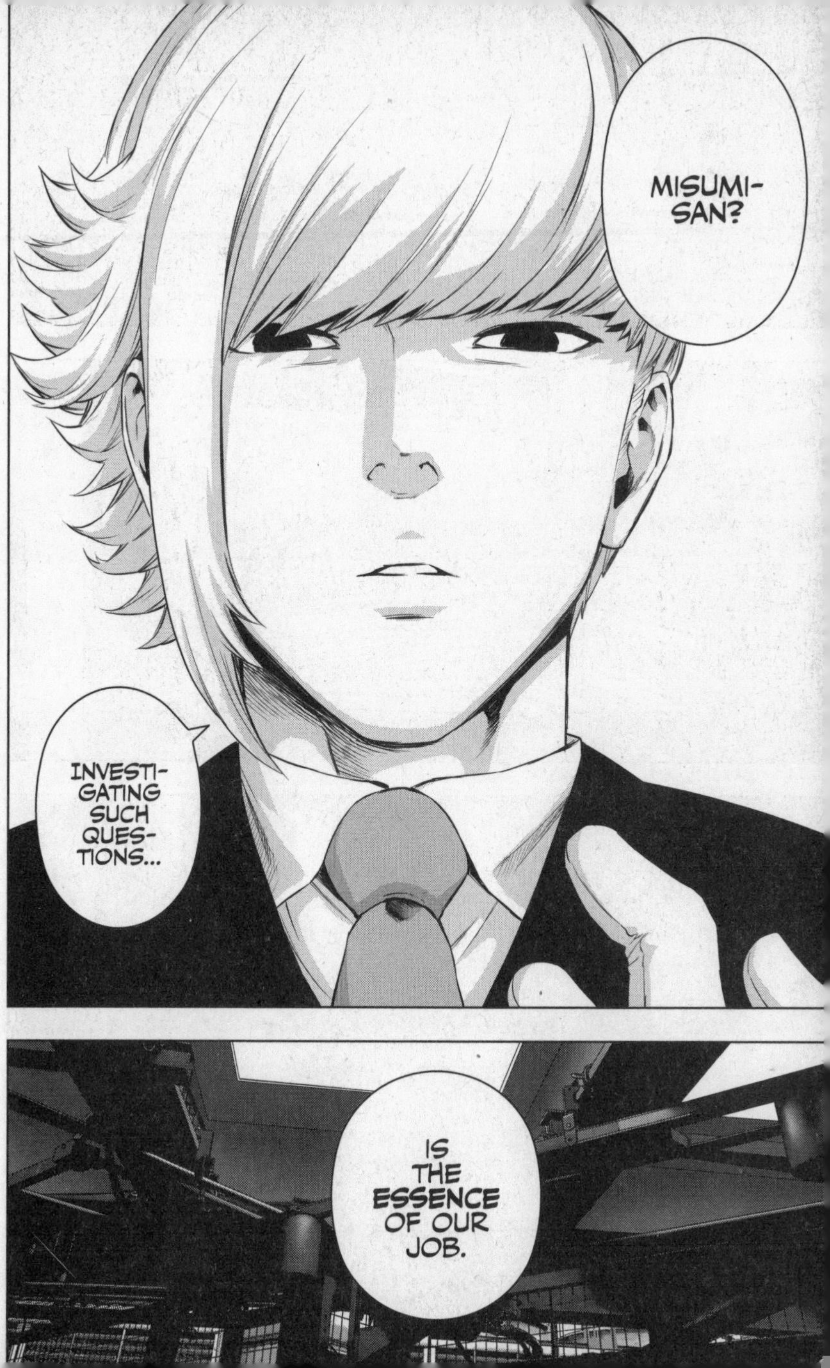
MISUMI-SAN?
INVESTIGATING SUCH QUESTIONS...
IS THE ESSENCE OF OUR JOB.

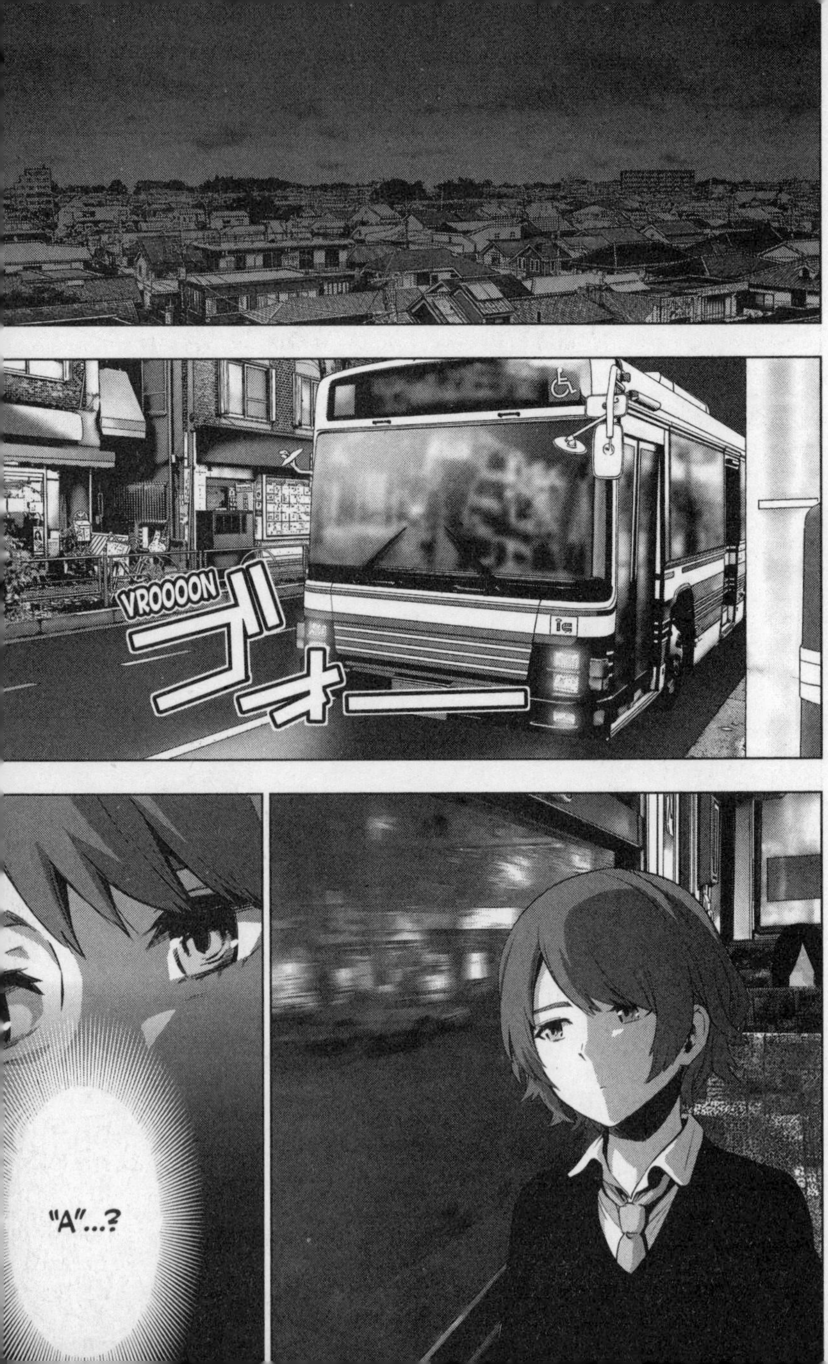
VROOOON
ブォー
"A"...?

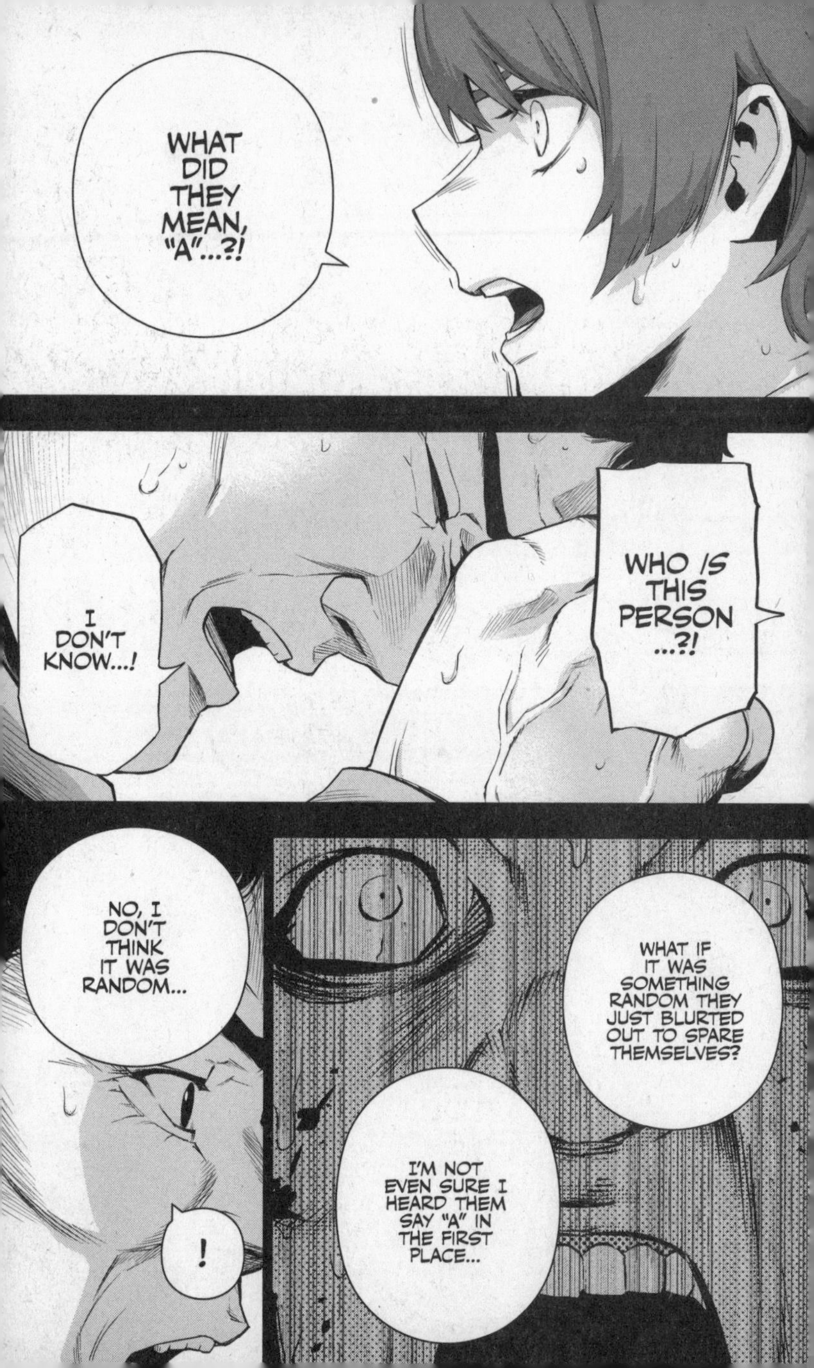
WHAT DID THEY MEAN, "A"...?!
WHO *IS* THIS PERSON ...?!
I DON'T KNOW...!
WHAT IF IT WAS SOMETHING RANDOM THEY JUST BLURTED OUT TO SPARE THEMSELVES?
I'M NOT EVEN SURE I HEARD THEM SAY "A" IN THE FIRST PLACE...
NO, I DON'T THINK IT WAS RANDOM...
!

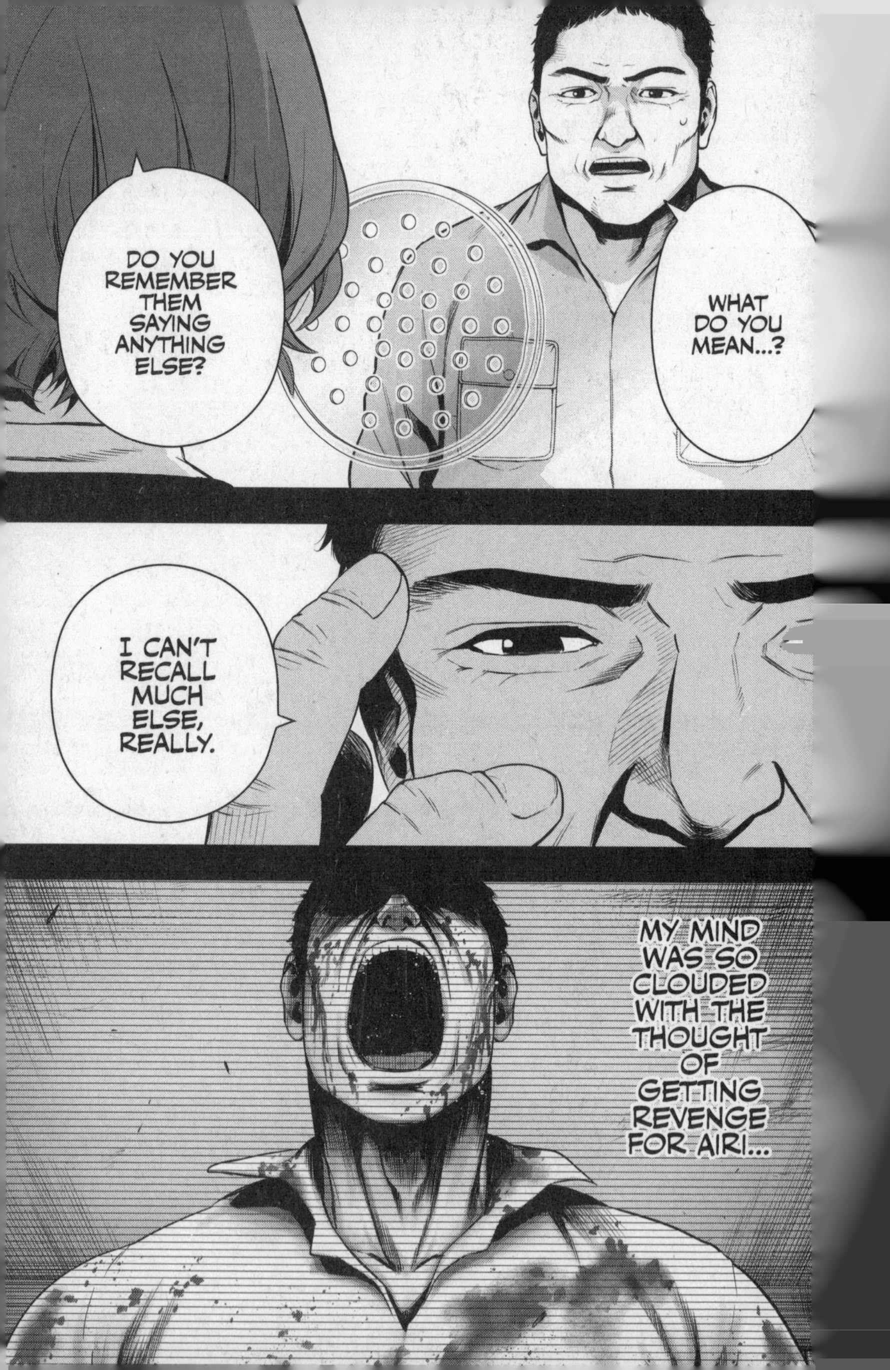
WHAT DO YOU MEAN...?
DO YOU REMEMBER THEM SAYING ANYTHING ELSE?
I CAN'T RECALL MUCH ELSE, REALLY.
MY MIND WAS SO CLOUDED WITH THE THOUGHT OF GETTING REVENGE FOR AIRI...

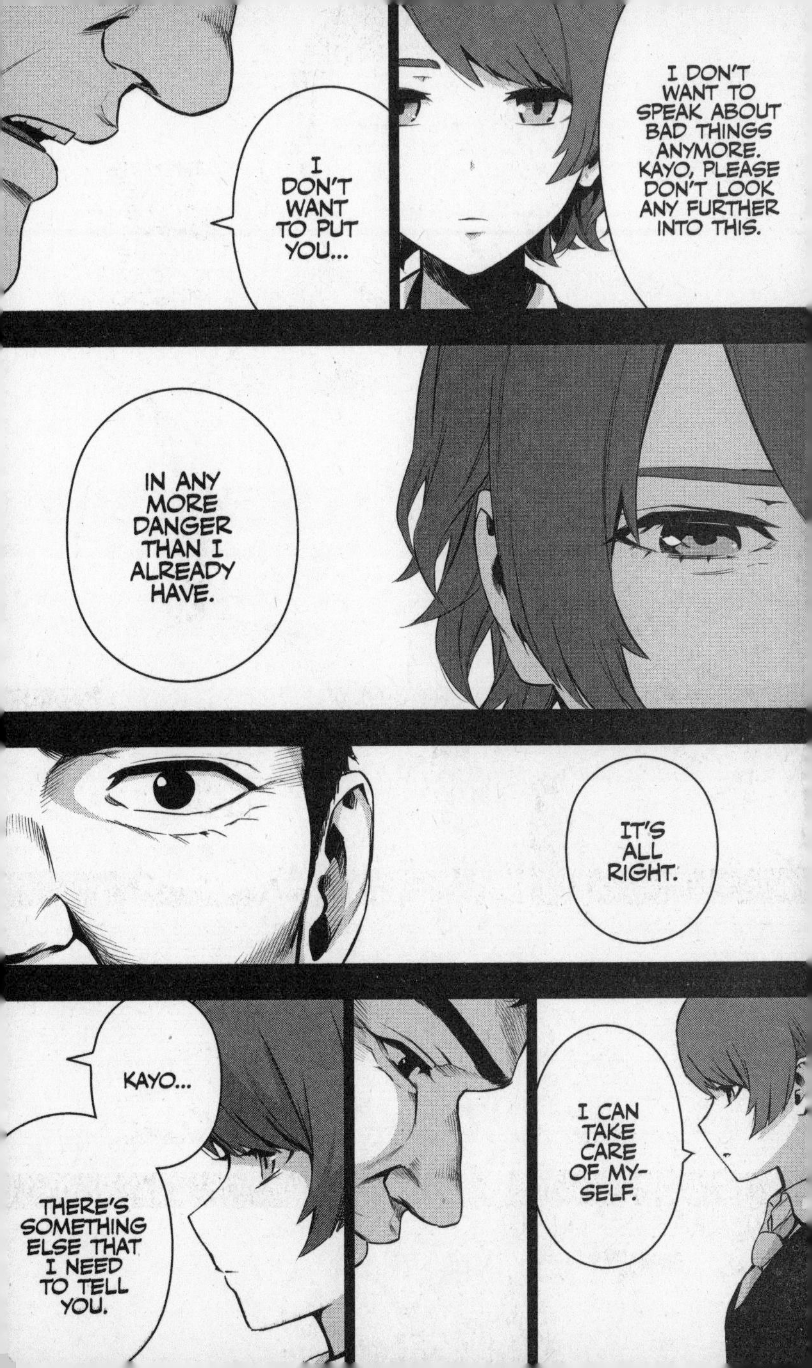
I DON'T WANT TO SPEAK ABOUT BAD THINGS ANYMORE. KAYO, PLEASE DON'T LOOK ANY FURTHER INTO THIS.
I DON'T WANT TO PUT YOU...
IN ANY MORE DANGER THAN I ALREADY HAVE.
IT'S ALL RIGHT.
I CAN TAKE CARE OF MY-SELF.
KAYO...
THERE'S SOMETHING ELSE THAT I NEED TO TELL YOU.

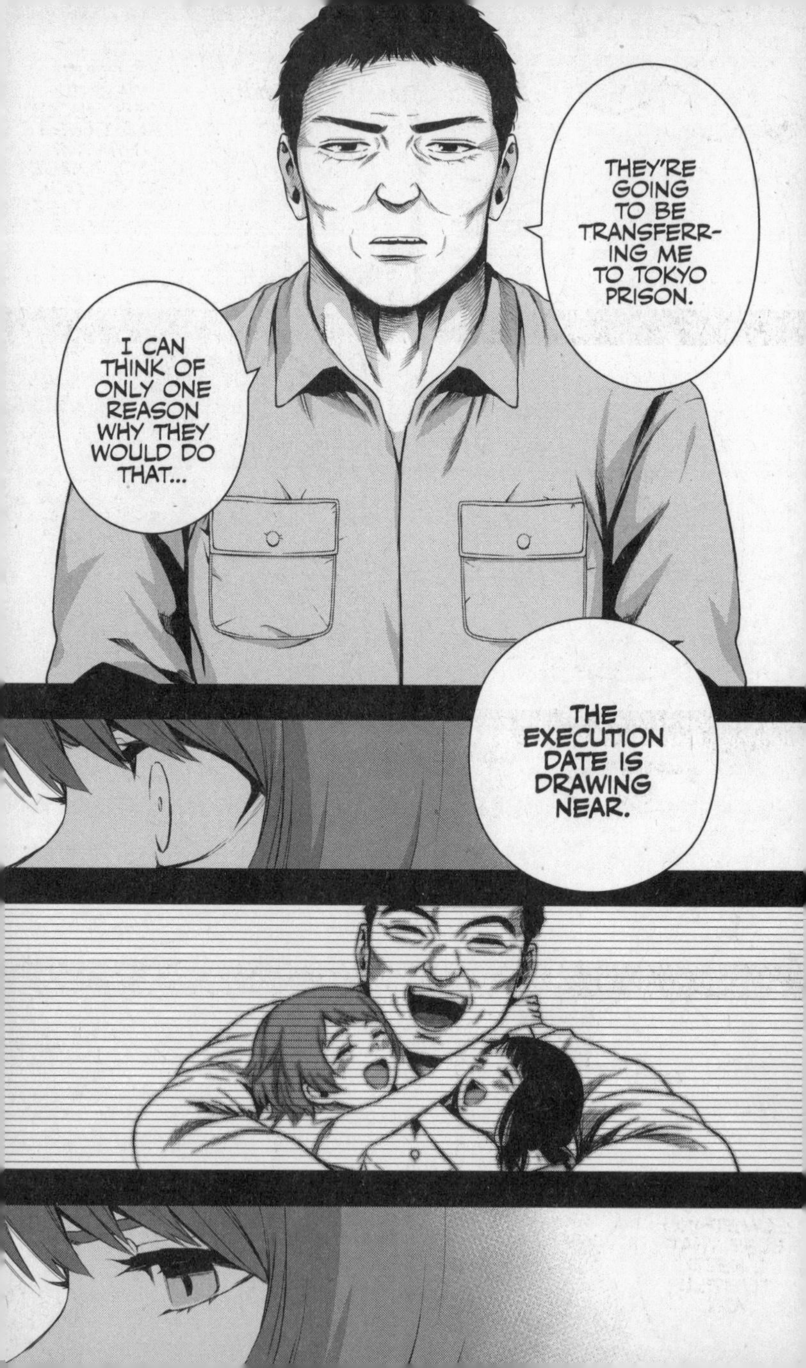
THEY'RE GOING TO BE TRANSFERR-ING ME TO TOKYO PRISON.
I CAN THINK OF ONLY ONE REASON WHY THEY WOULD DO THAT...
THE EXECUTION DATE IS DRAWING NEAR.

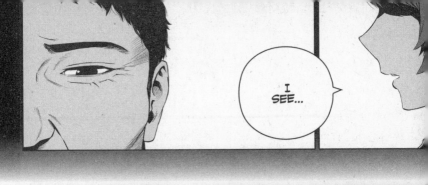

I
SEE...

PSHOO

SHWF

MOM...

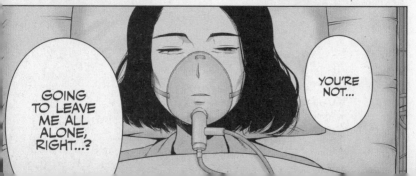

GOING TO LEAVE ME ALL ALONE, RIGHT...?

YOU'RE NOT...

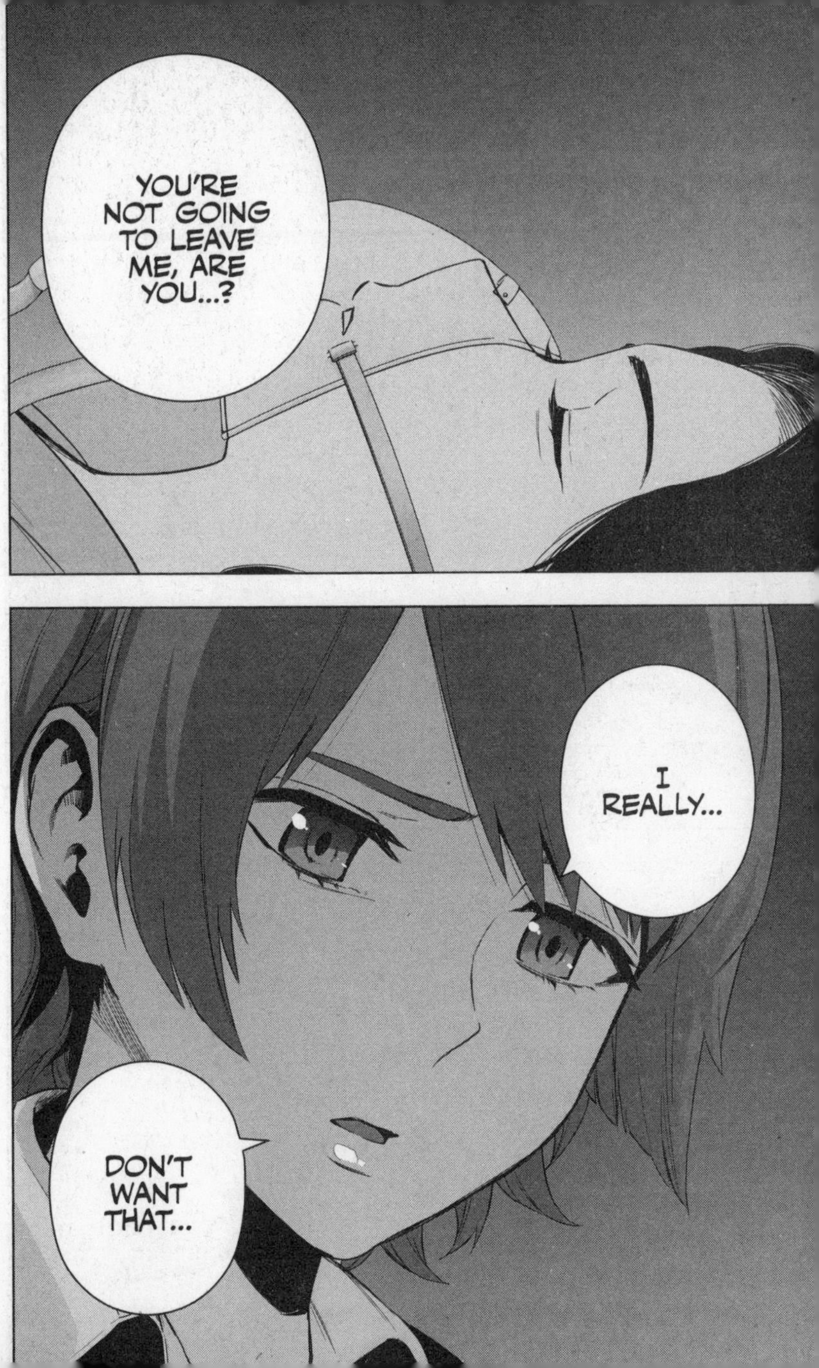
YOU'RE NOT GOING TO LEAVE ME, ARE YOU...?
I REALLY...
DON'T WANT THAT...

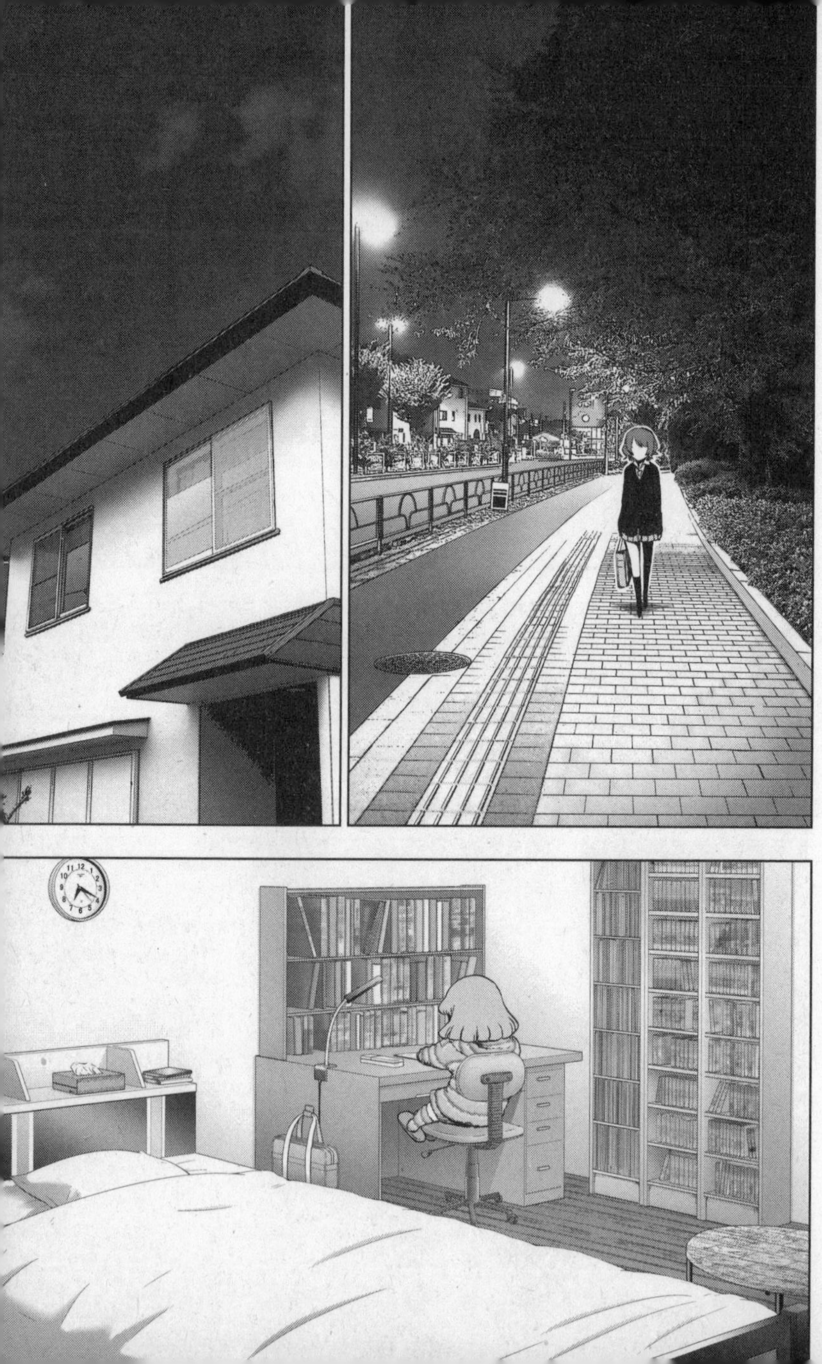

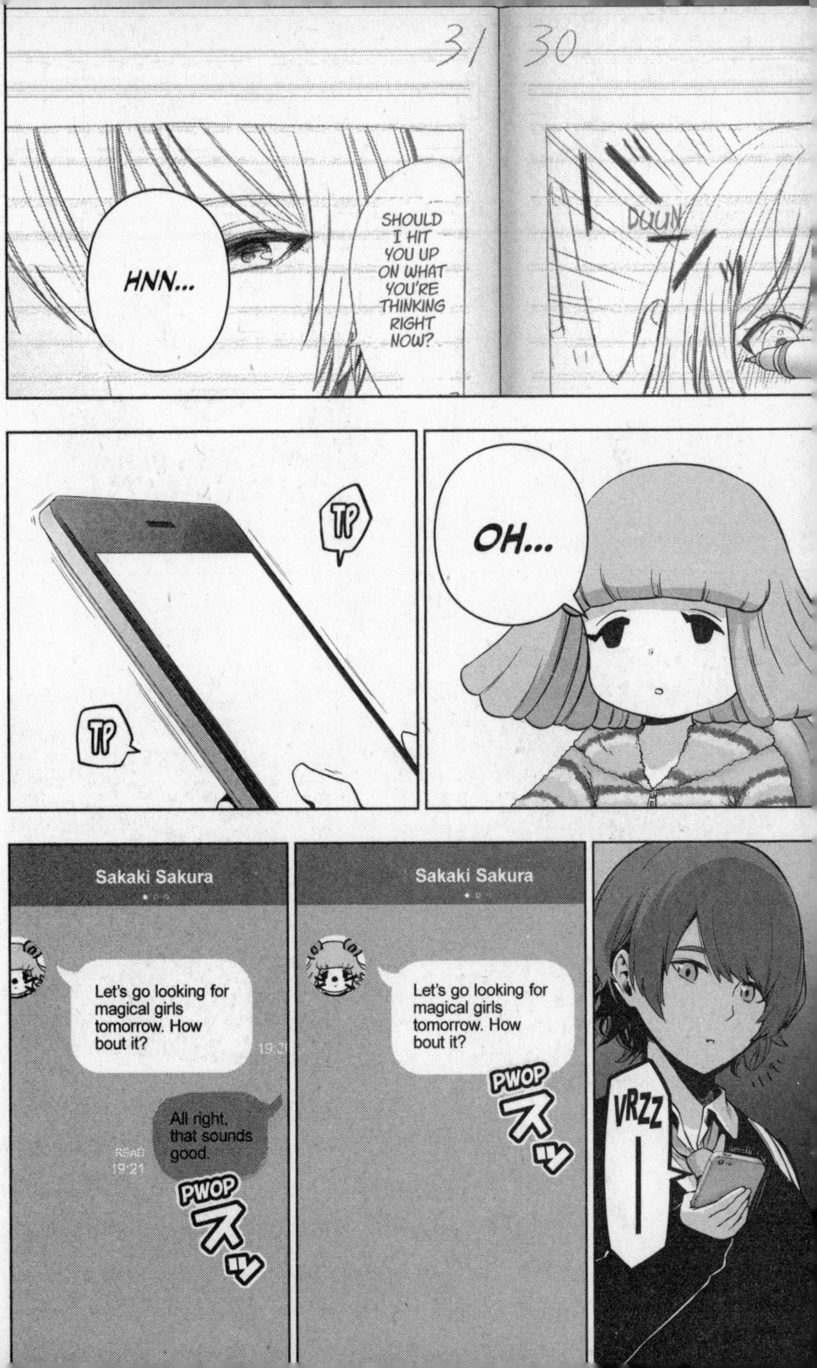
30
DUUN
31
SHOULD I HIT YOU UP ON WHAT YOU'RE THINKING RIGHT NOW?
HNN...
OH...
TP
TP
VRZZ
Sakaki Sakura
Let's go looking for magical girls tomorrow. How bout it?
PWOP
スッ
Sakaki Sakura
Let's go looking for magical girls tomorrow. How bout it?
All right, that sounds good.
READ
19:21
PWOP
スッ

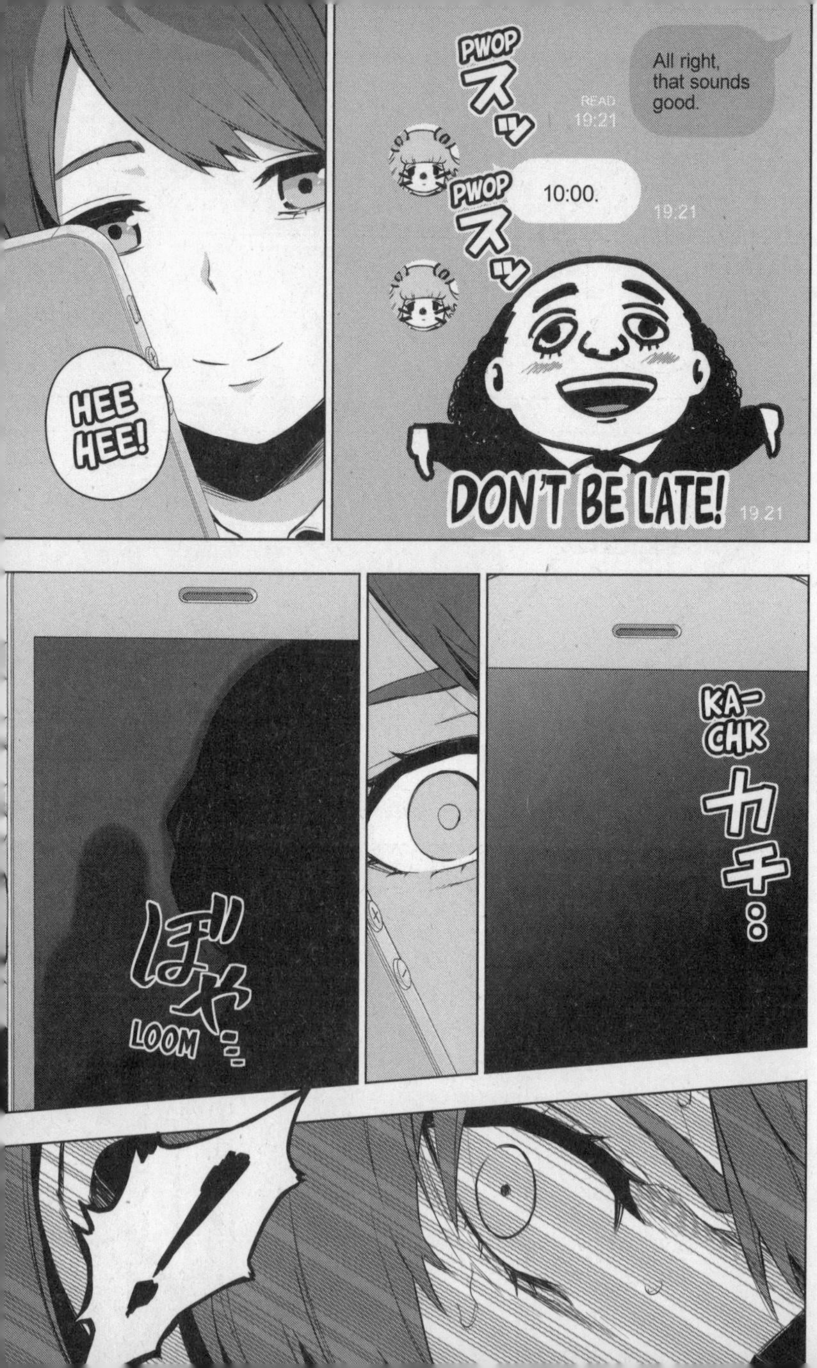
All right, that sounds good.
READ
19:21
PWOP
スッ
10:00.
19.21
PWOP
スッ
DON'T BE LATE!
19.21
HEE HEE!
KA-CHK
カチ…
ぼや…
LOOM

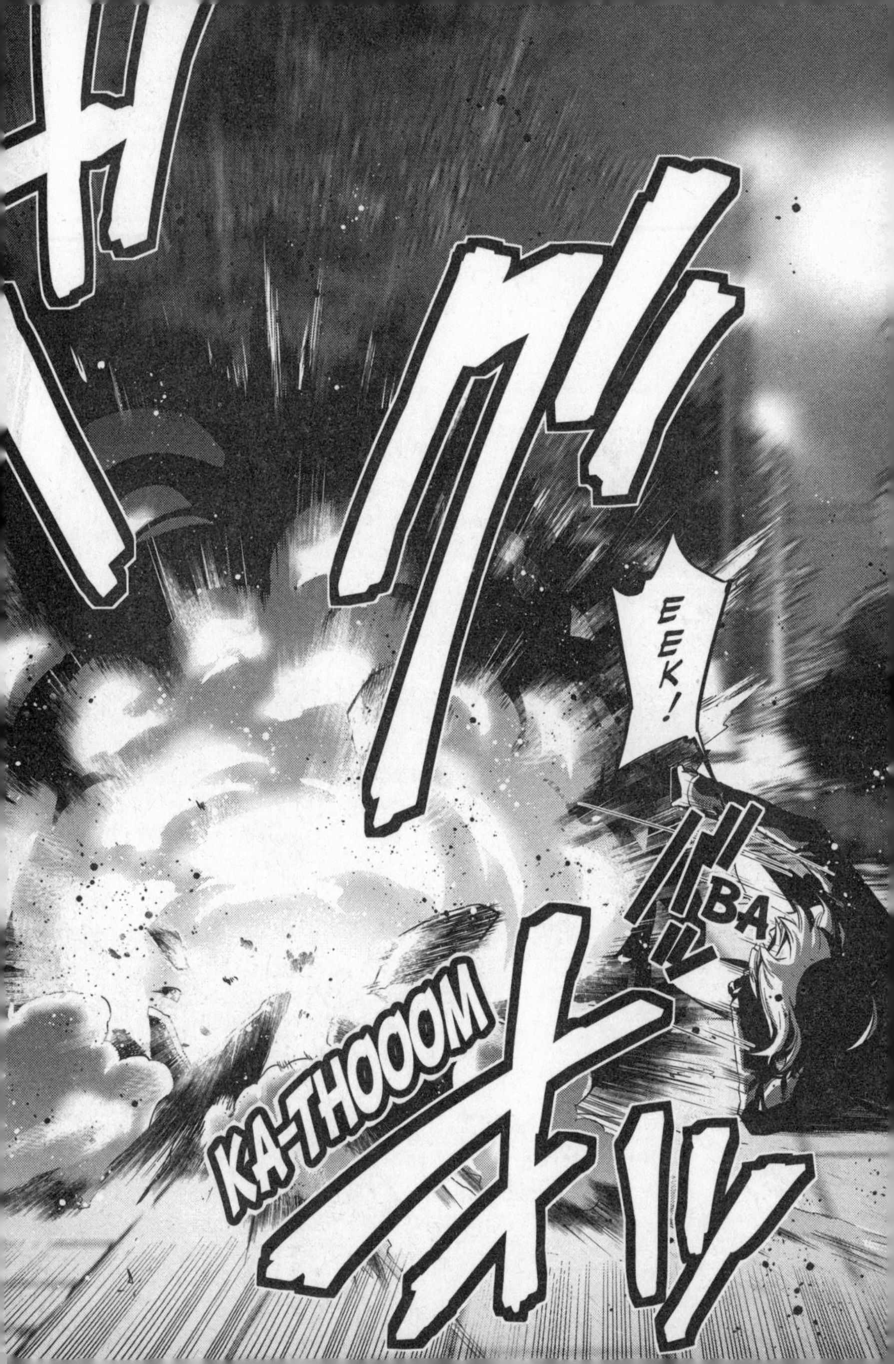
EEK!
BA
KA-THOOOM

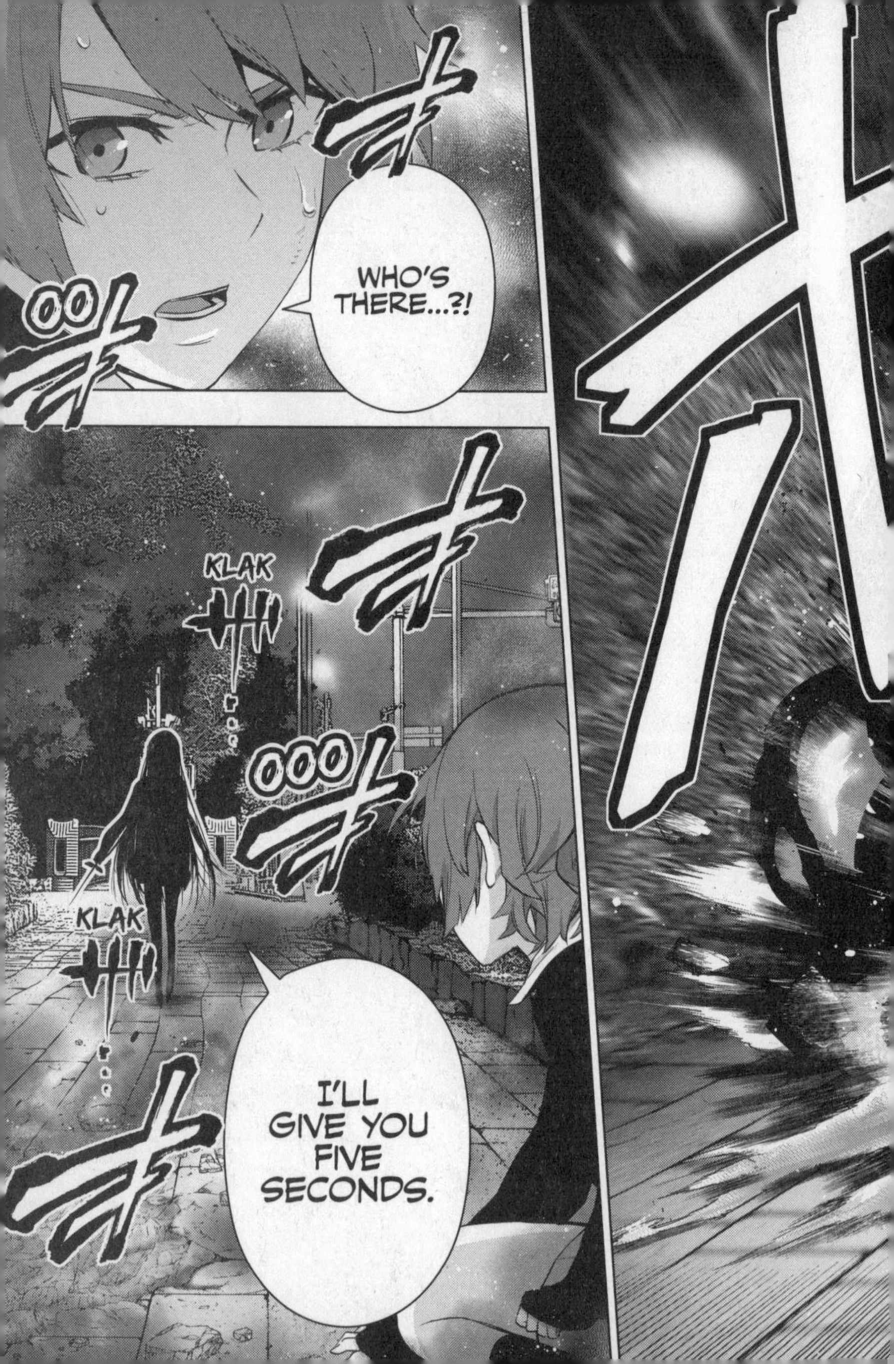
WHO'S THERE...?!
KLAK
I'LL GIVE YOU FIVE SECONDS.
KLAK

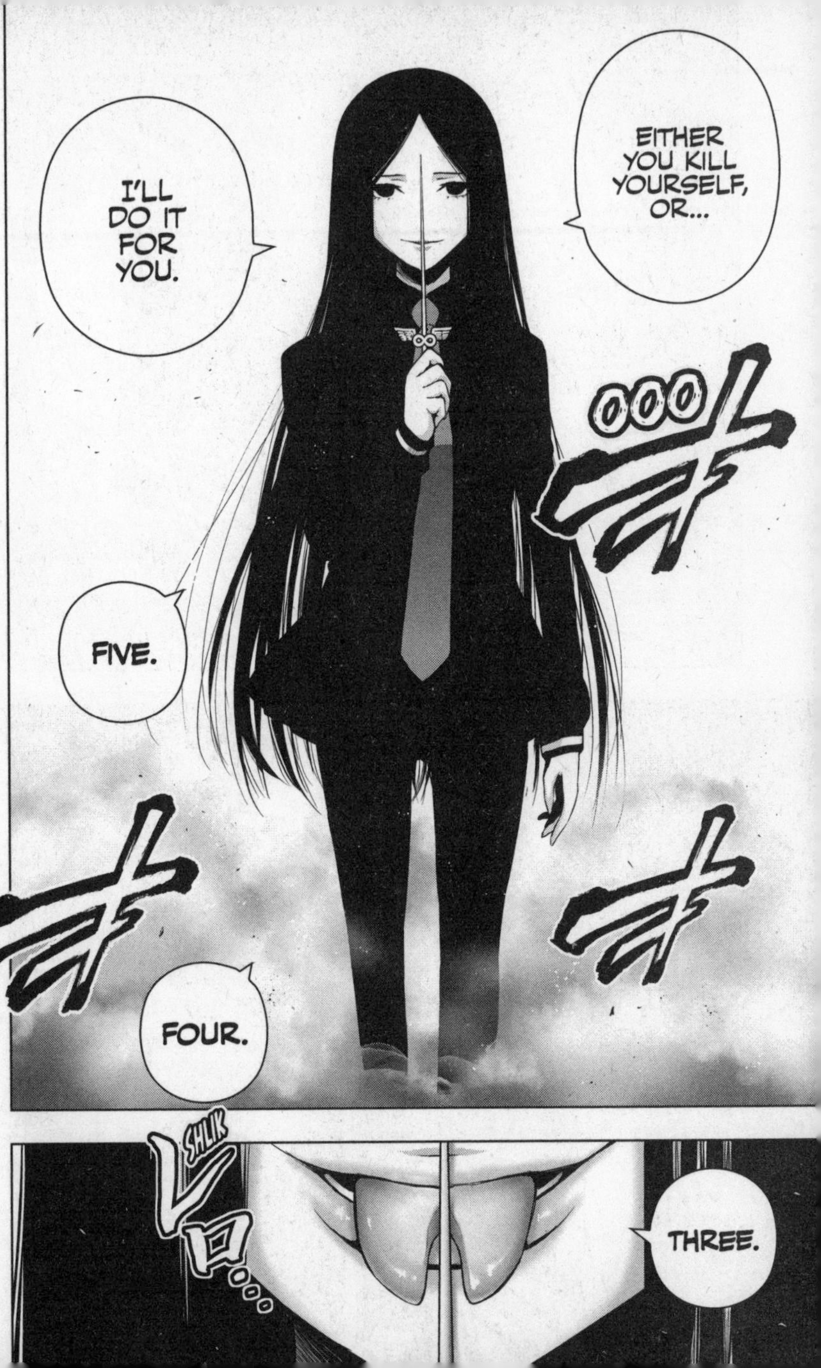
EITHER YOU KILL YOURSELF, OR...
I'LL DO IT FOR YOU.
OOO
FIVE.
FOUR.
THREE.
SHLIK

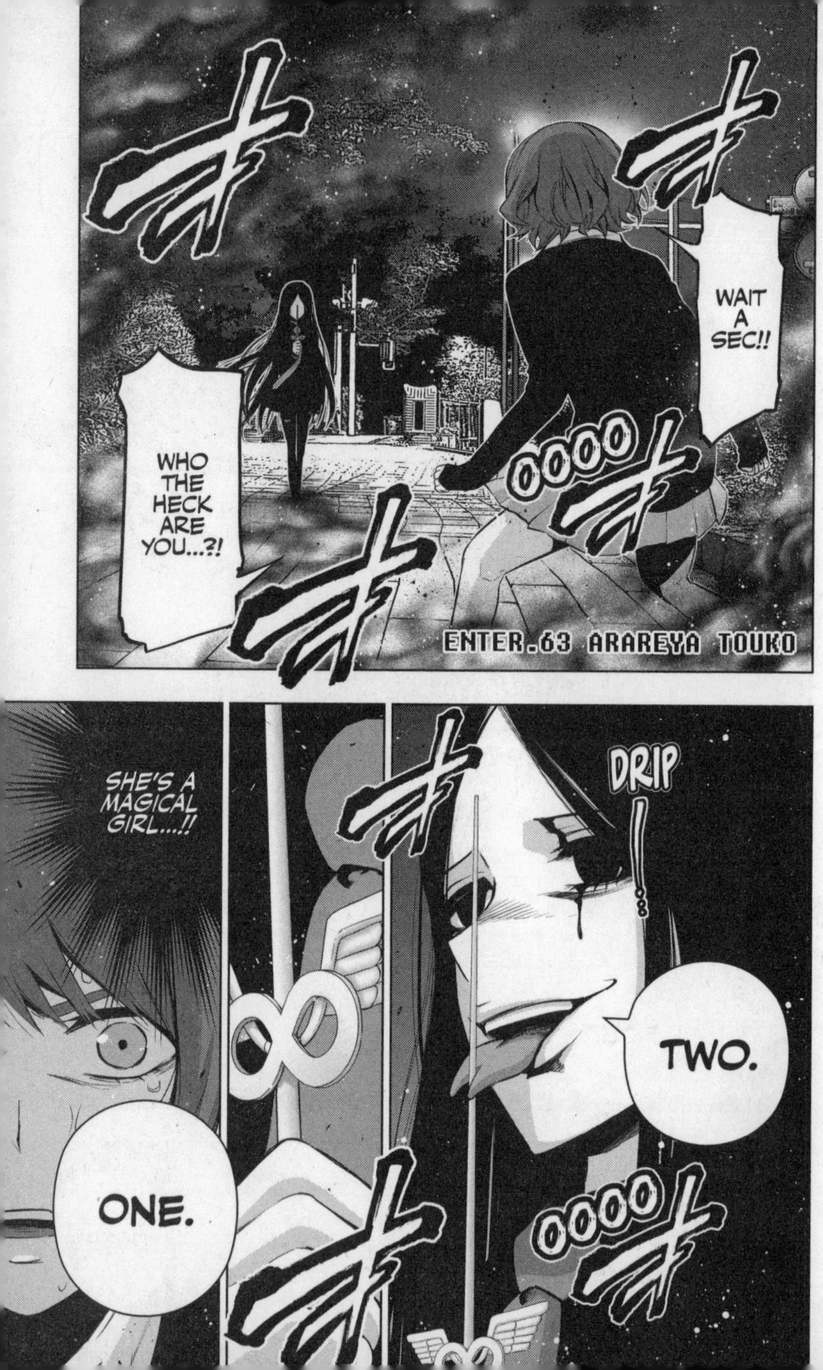
WAIT A SEC!!
OOOO
WHO THE HECK ARE YOU...?!
ENTER.63 ARAREYA TOUKO
DRIP
TWO.
OOOO
SHE'S A MAGICAL GIRL...!!
ONE.

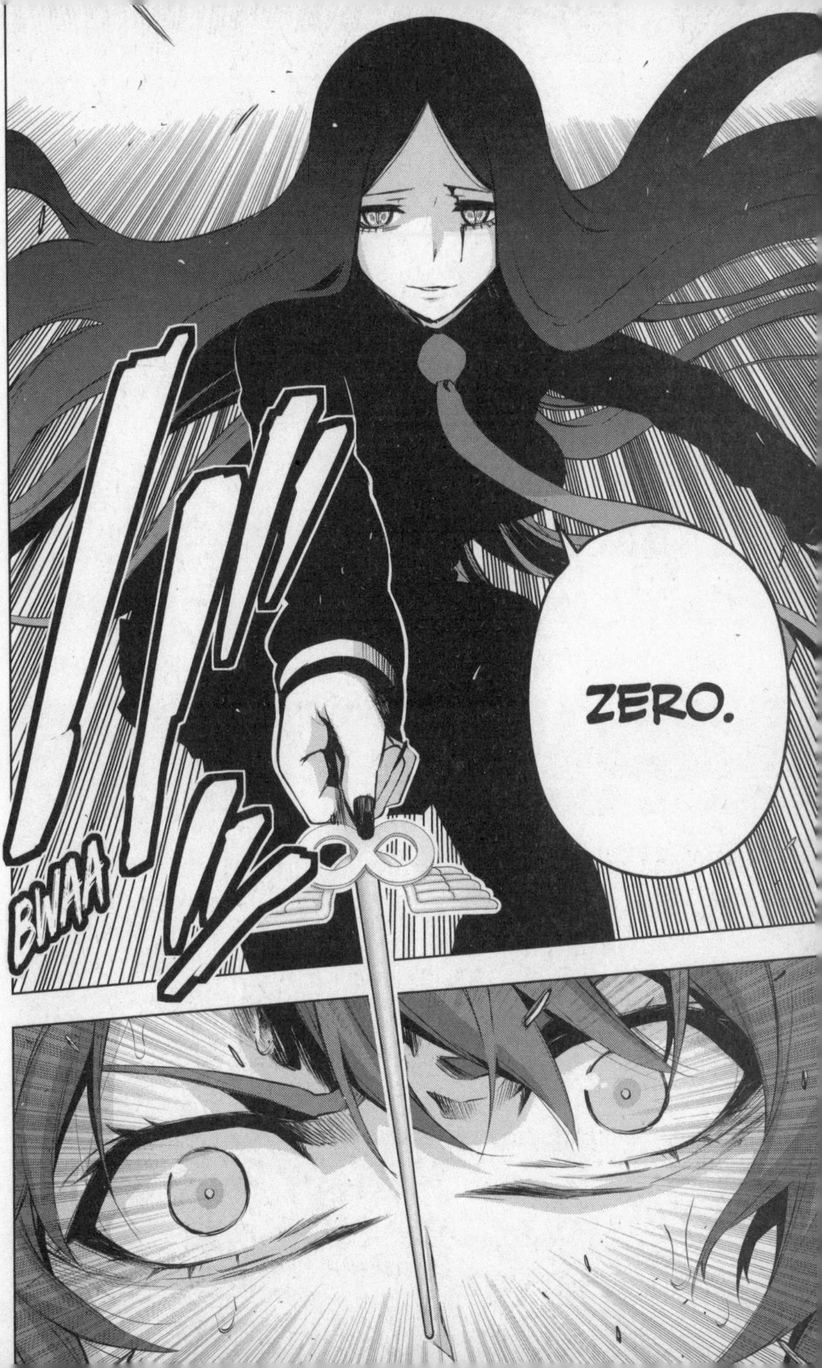
ZERO.
BWAA

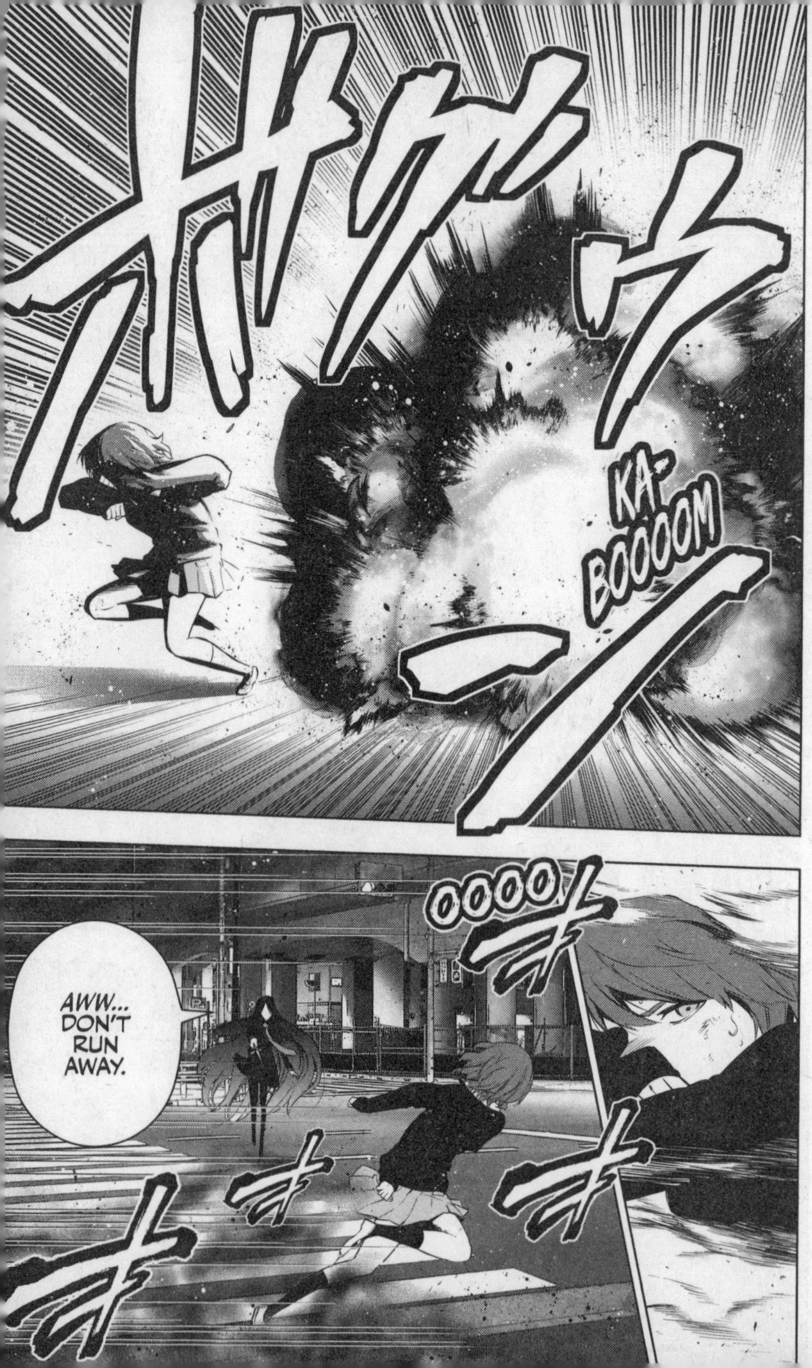
KA-BOOOOM
OOOO
AWW... DON'T RUN AWAY.

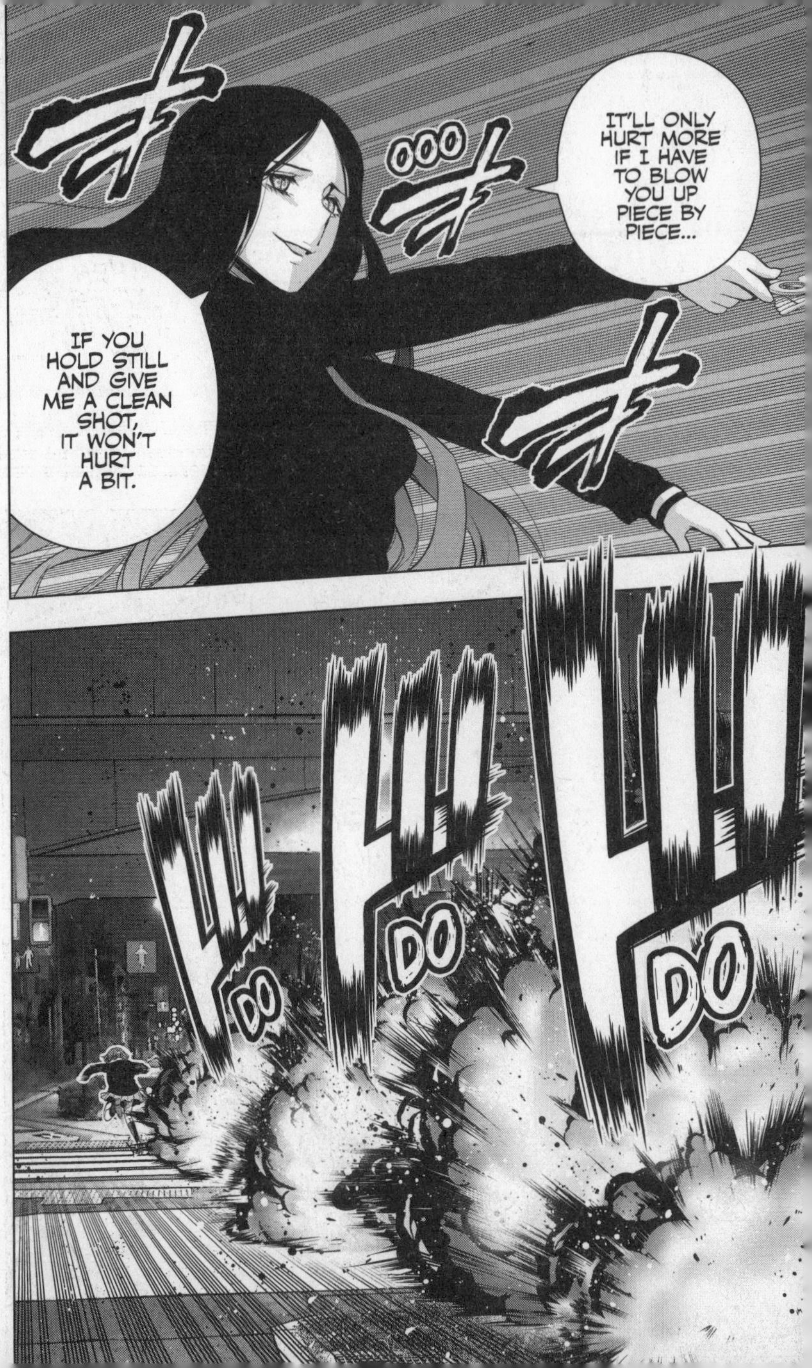
IT'LL ONLY HURT MORE IF I HAVE TO BLOW YOU UP PIECE BY PIECE...
OOO
IF YOU HOLD STILL AND GIVE ME A CLEAN SHOT, IT WON'T HURT A BIT.
DO
DO
DO

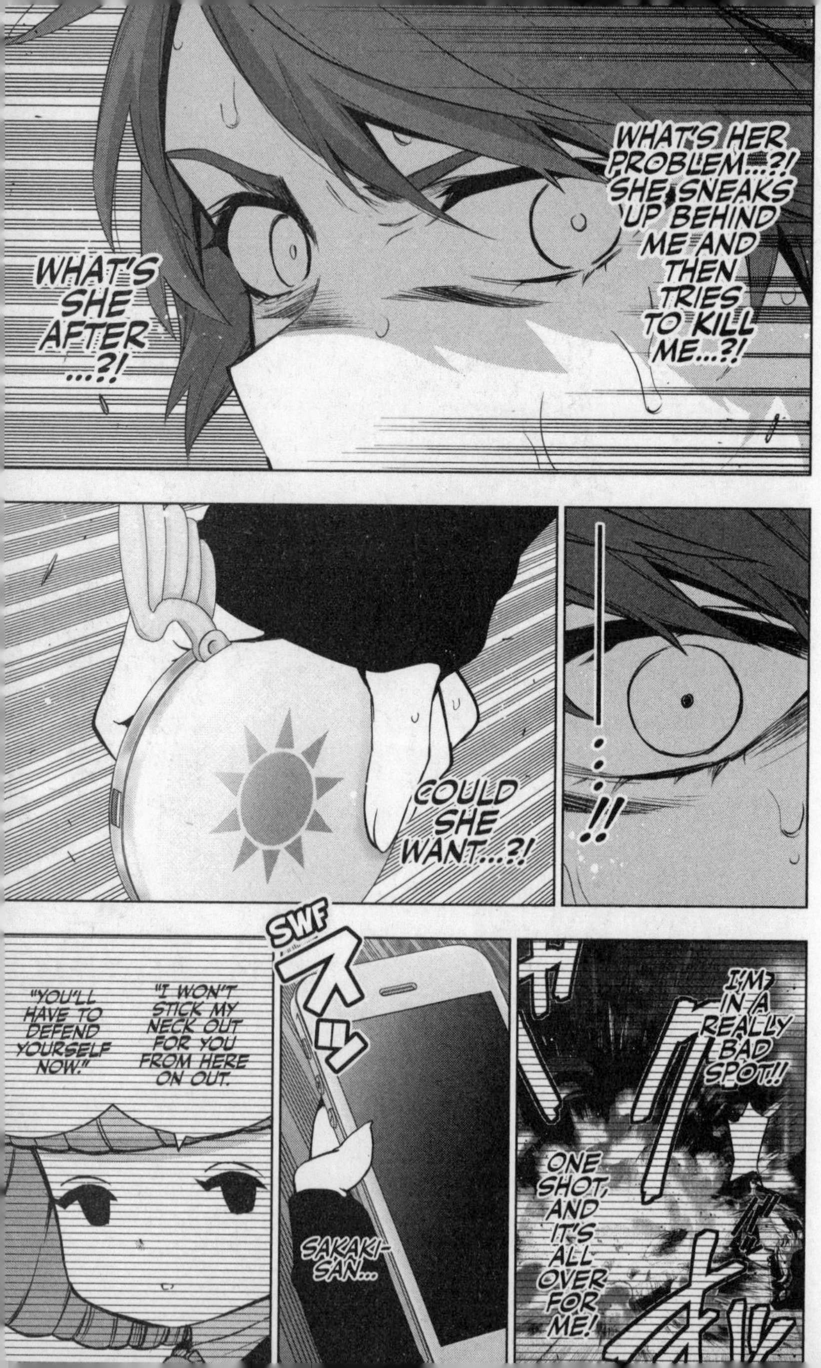
WHAT'S HER PROBLEM...?! SHE SNEAKS UP BEHIND ME AND THEN TRIES TO KILL ME...?!
WHAT'S SHE AFTER ...?!
——...!!
COULD SHE WANT...?!
I'M IN A REALLY BAD SPOT!!
ONE SHOT, AND IT'S ALL OVER FOR ME!
SWF
SAKAKI-SAN...
"I WON'T STICK MY NECK OUT FOR YOU FROM HERE ON OUT.
"YOU'LL HAVE TO DEFEND YOURSELF NOW."

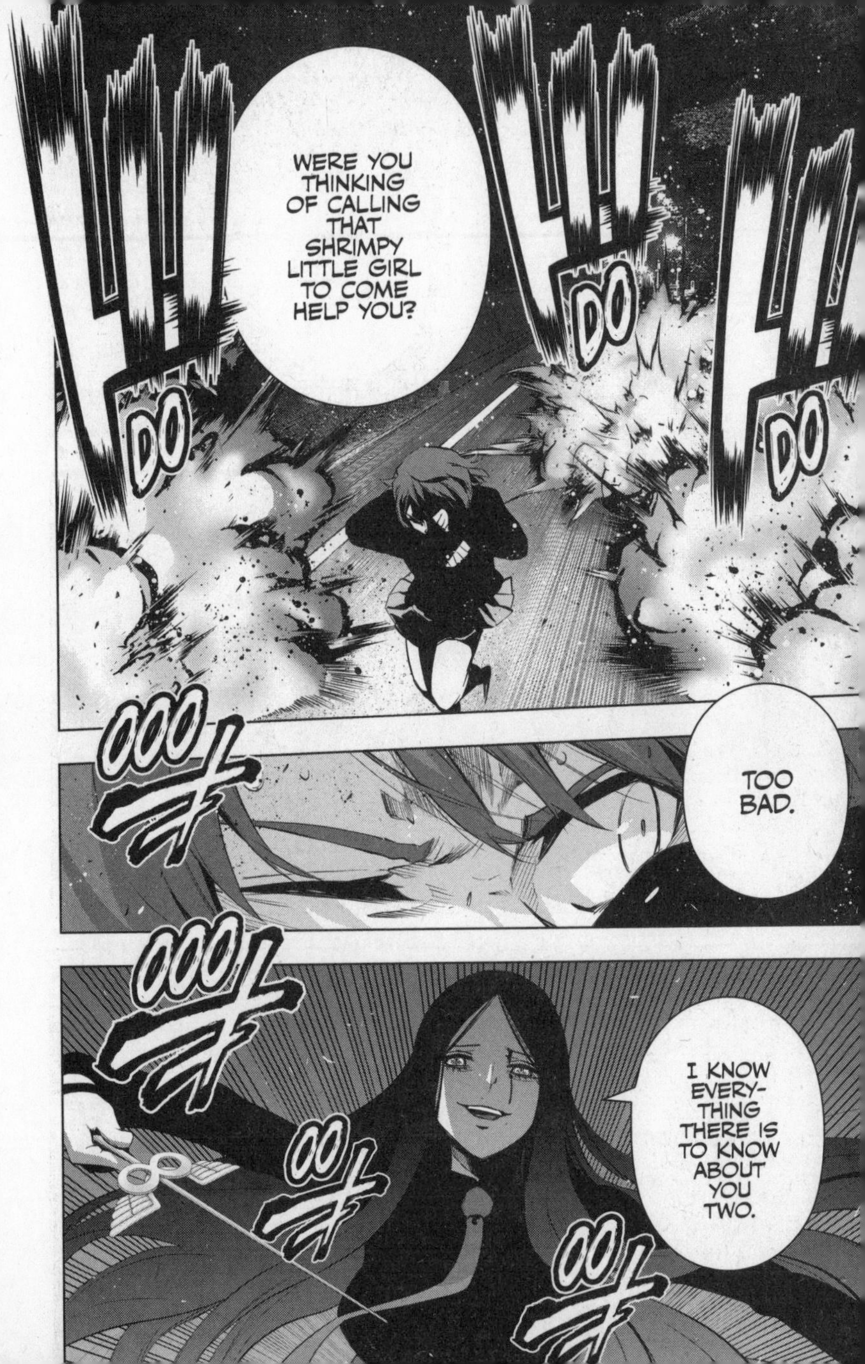
DO
DO
WERE YOU THINKING OF CALLING THAT SHRIMPY LITTLE GIRL TO COME HELP YOU?
DO
TOO BAD.
I KNOW EVERY-THING THERE IS TO KNOW ABOUT YOU TWO.

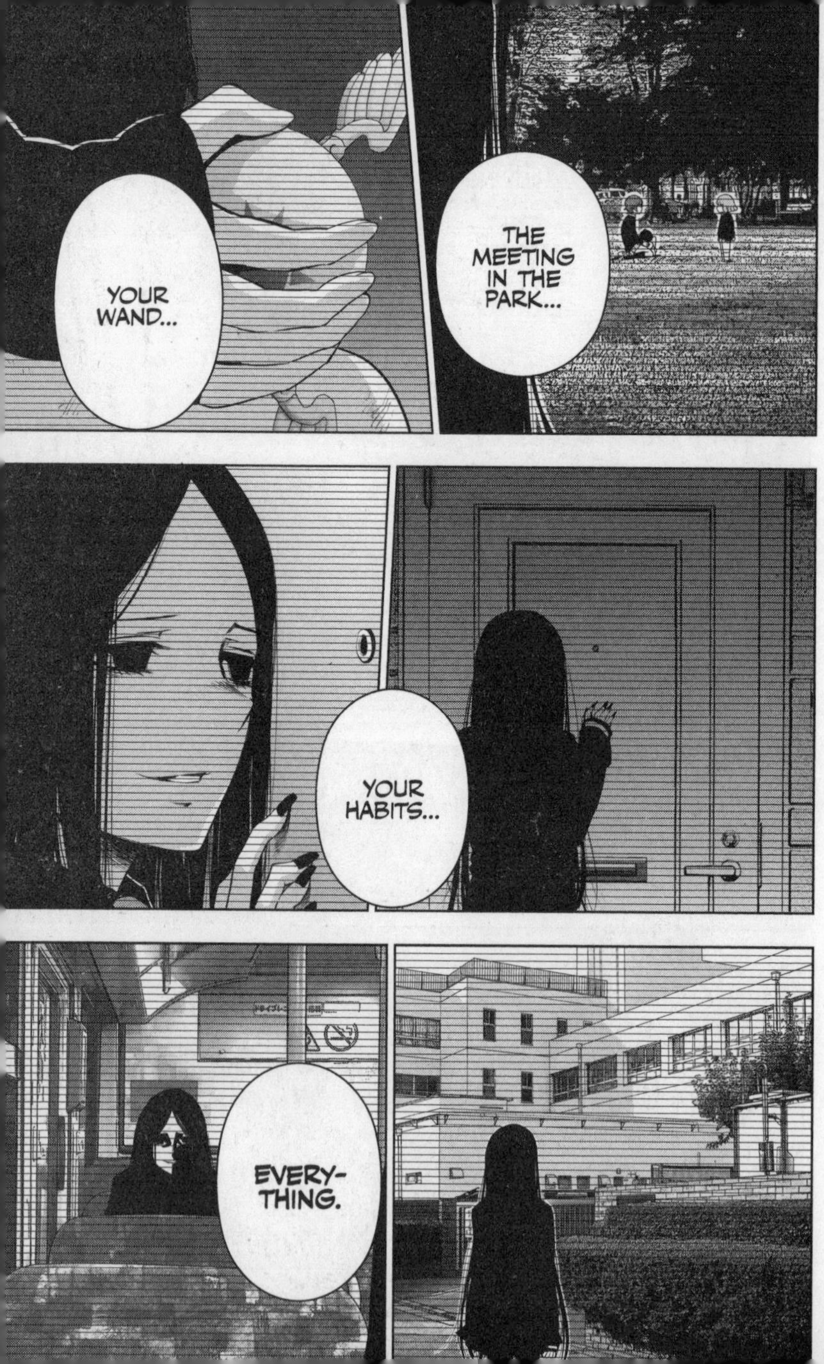
THE MEETING IN THE PARK...
YOUR WAND...
YOUR HABITS...
EVERY-THING.

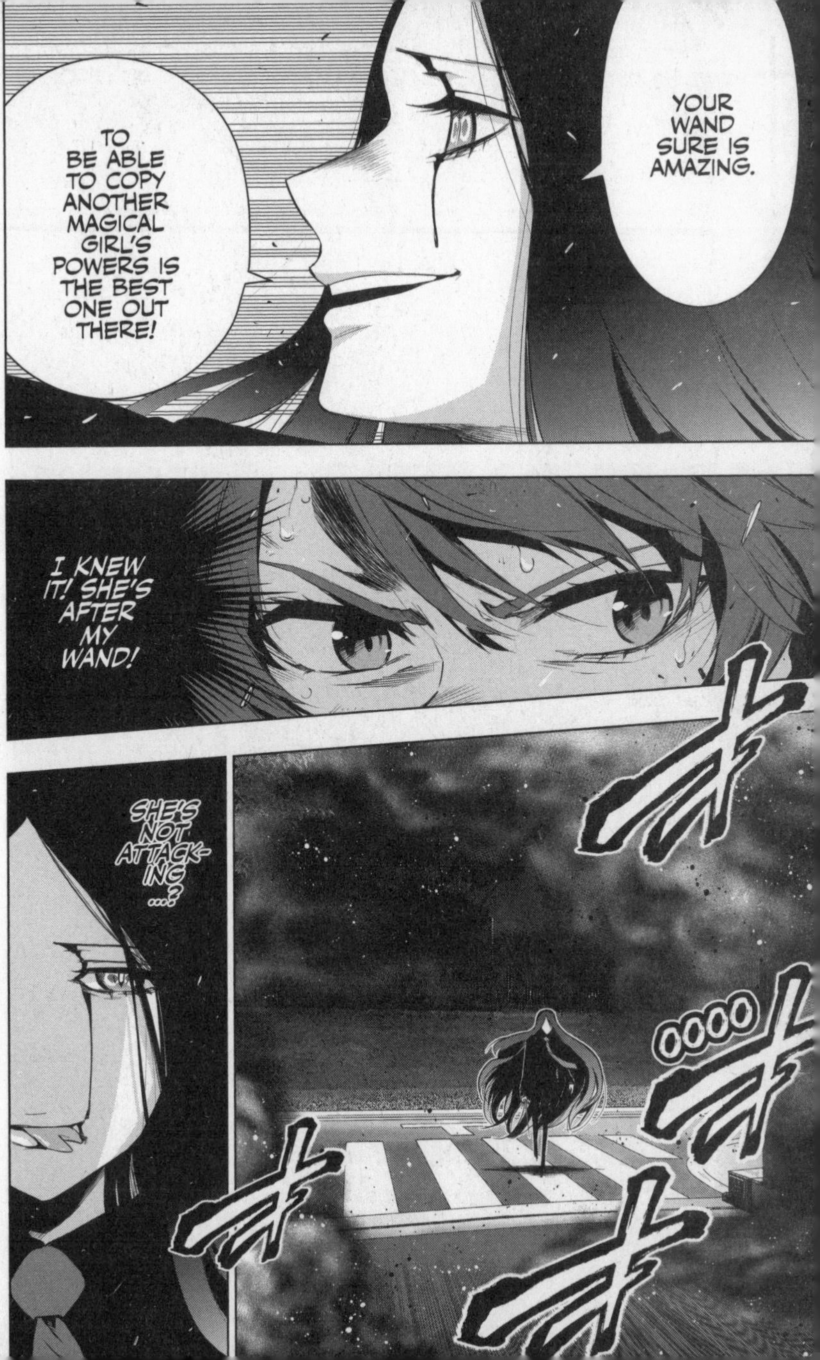
YOUR WAND SURE IS AMAZING.
TO BE ABLE TO COPY ANOTHER MAGICAL GIRL'S POWERS IS THE BEST ONE OUT THERE!
I KNEW IT! SHE'S AFTER MY WAND!
OOOO
SHE'S NOT ATTACK-ING...?

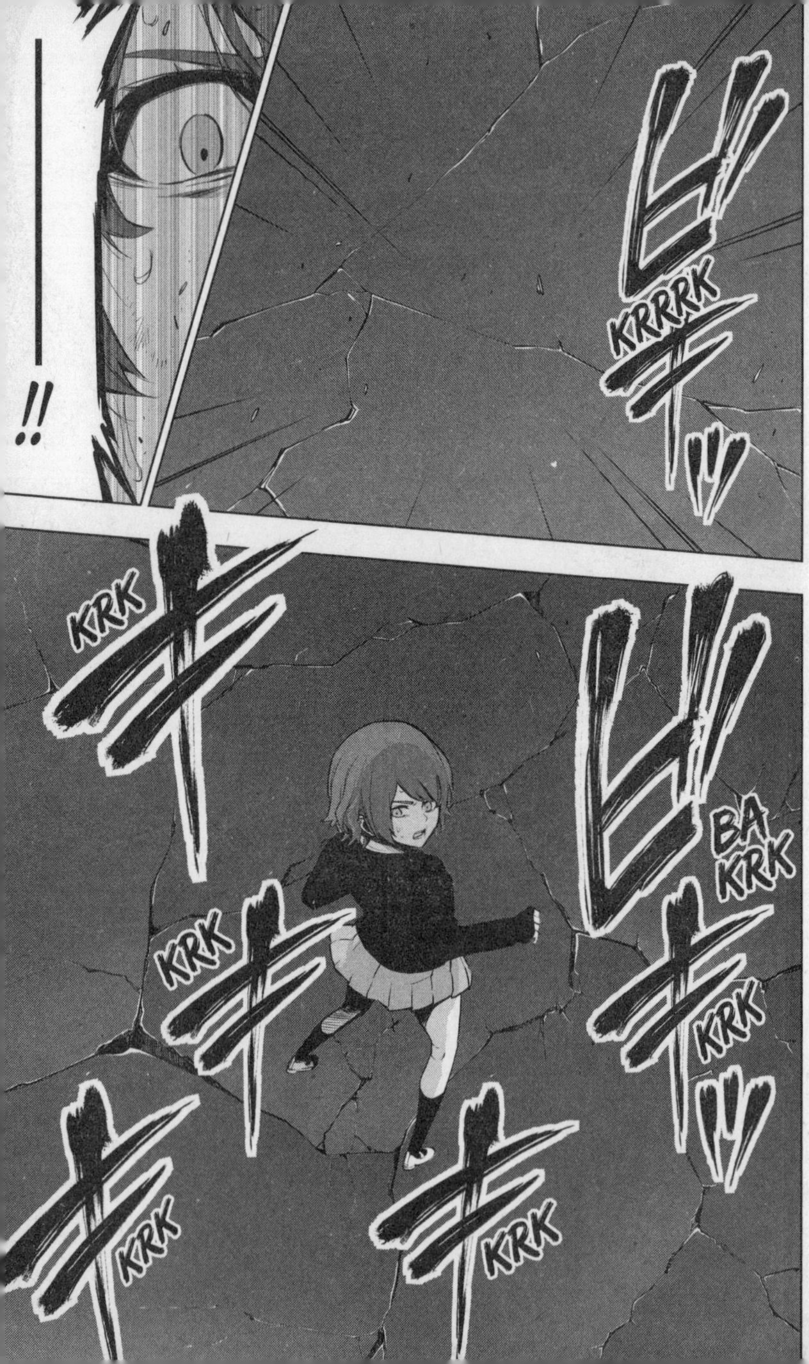
KRRRK
——!!
BA KRK
KRK
KRK
KRK
KRK
KRK

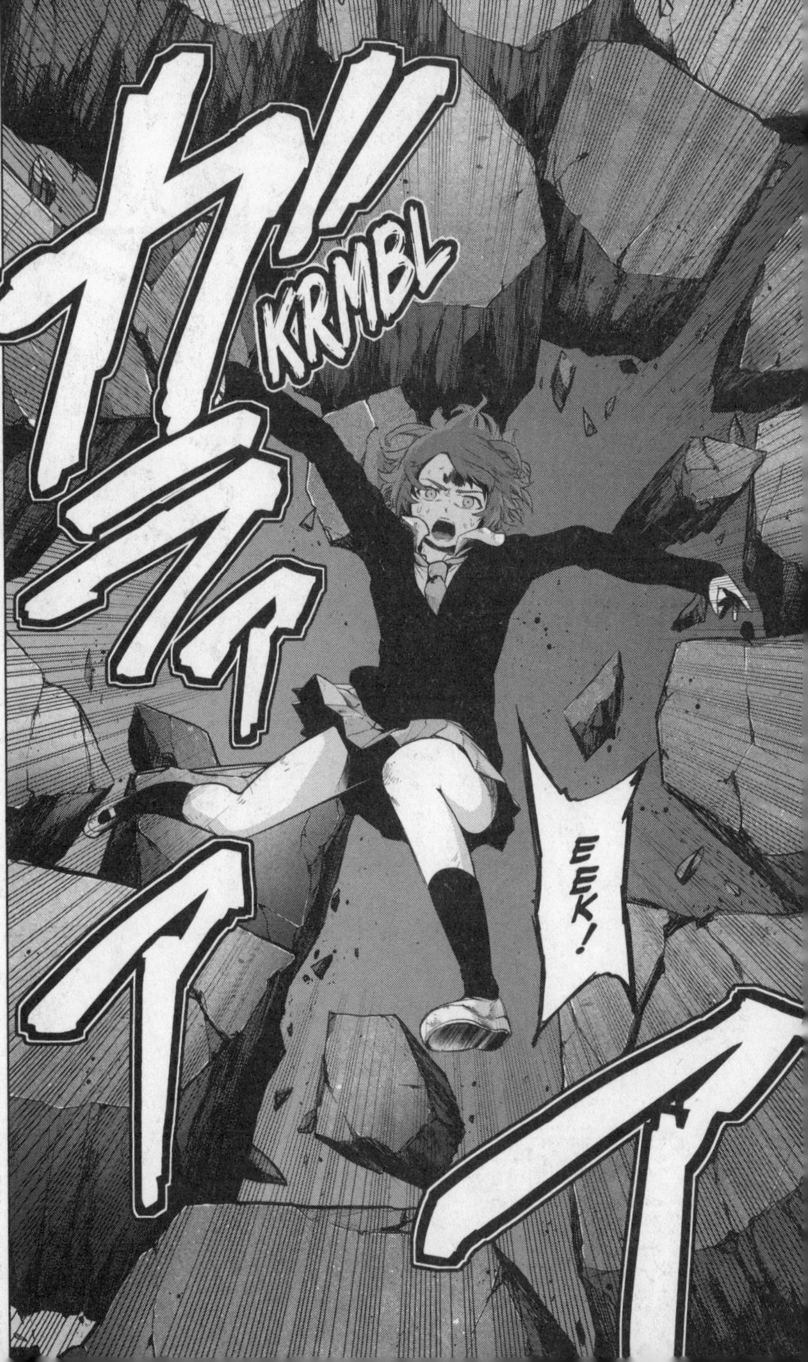
KRMBL
EEK!

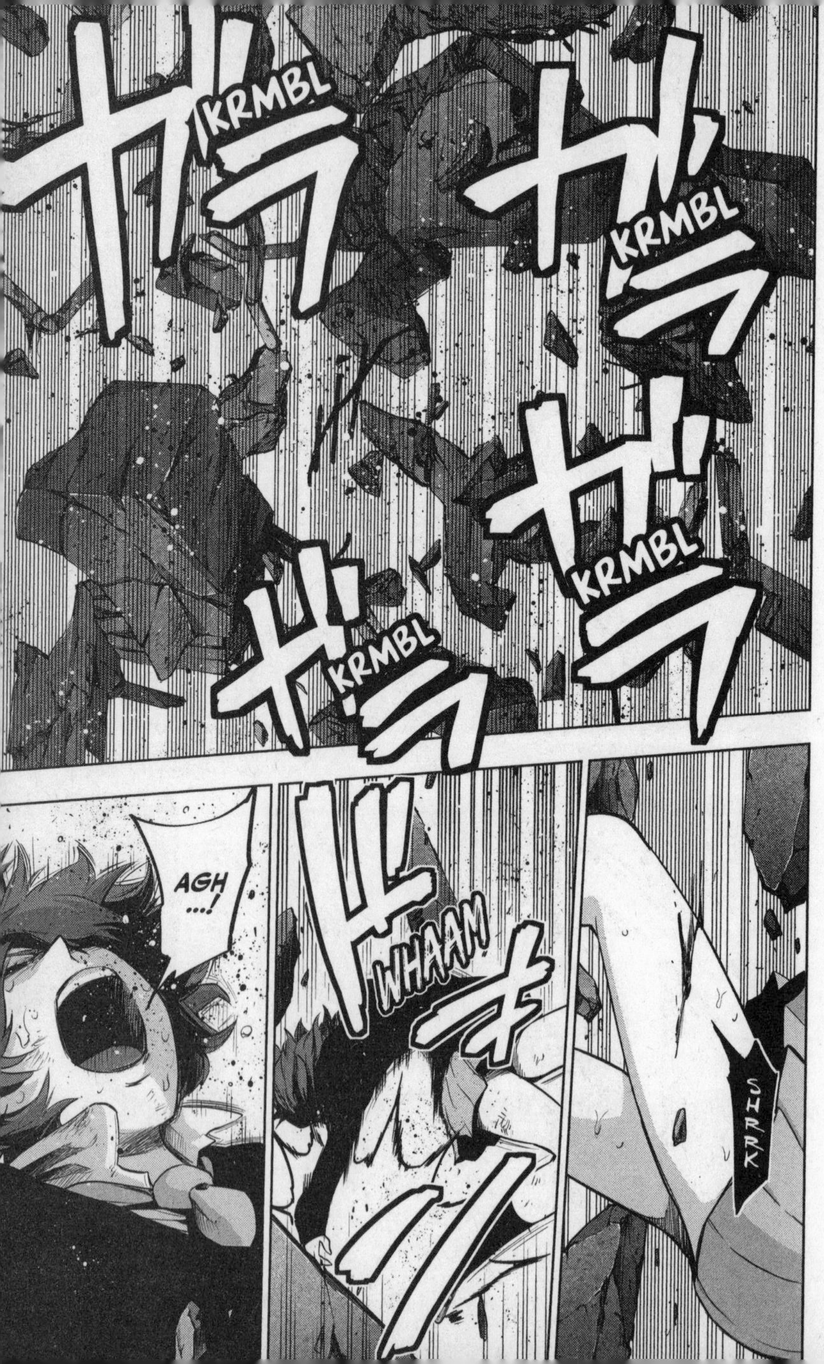
KRMBL
KRMBL
KRMBL
KRMBL
SHRRK
WHAAM
AGH ...!

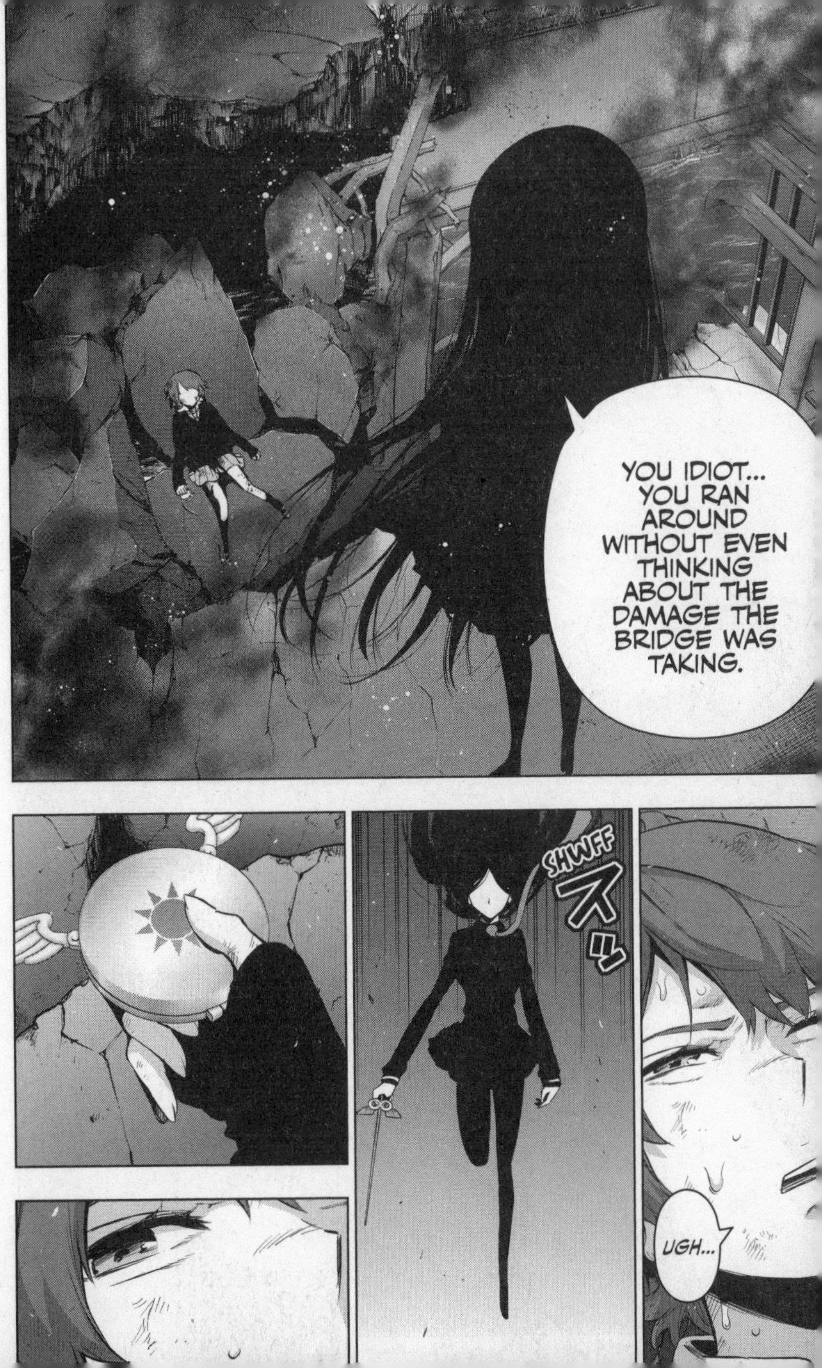
YOU IDIOT... YOU RAN AROUND WITHOUT EVEN THINKING ABOUT THE DAMAGE THE BRIDGE WAS TAKING.
UGH...
SHWFF
スッ

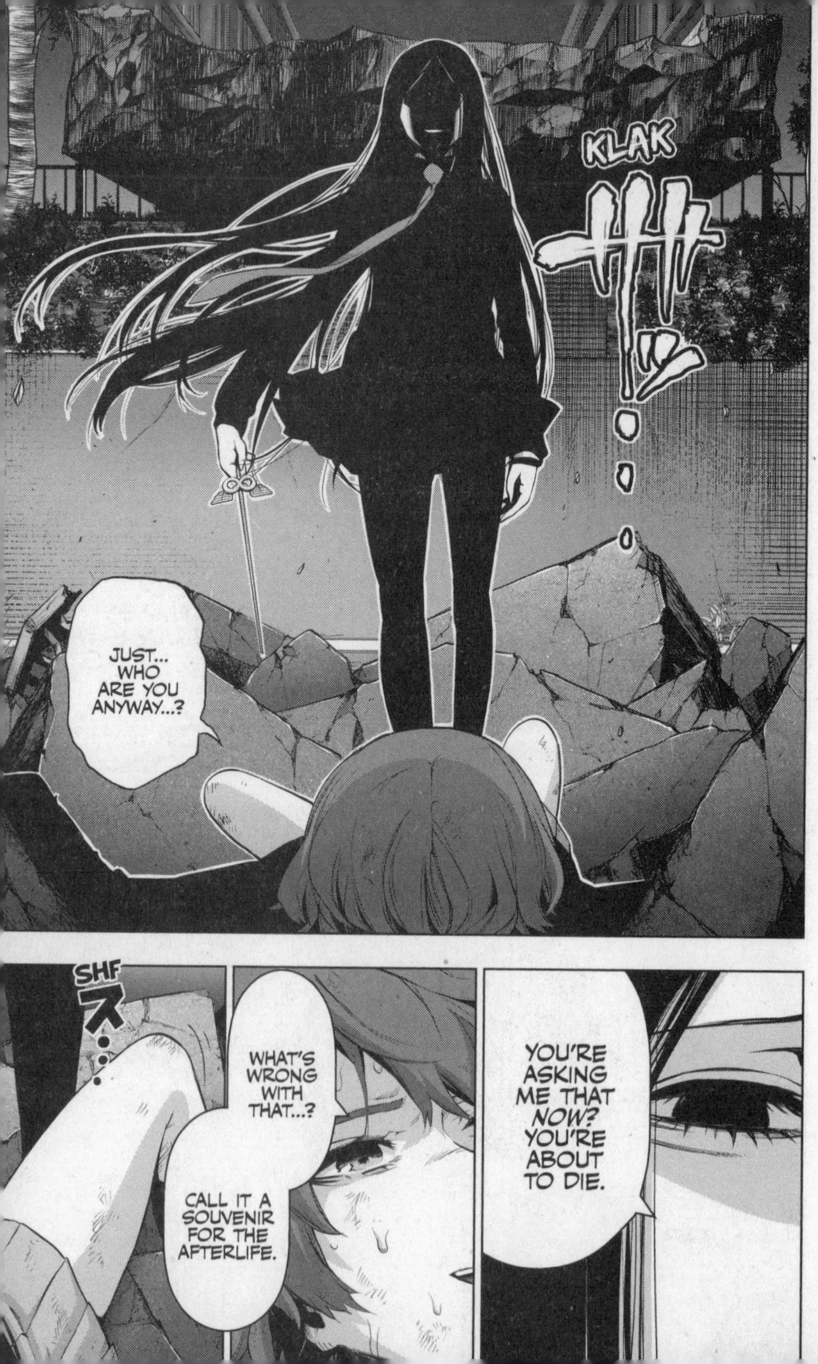
KLAK
JUST... WHO ARE YOU ANYWAY...?
YOU'RE ASKING ME THAT *NOW?* YOU'RE ABOUT TO DIE.
WHAT'S WRONG WITH THAT...?
CALL IT A SOUVENIR FOR THE AFTERLIFE.
SHF

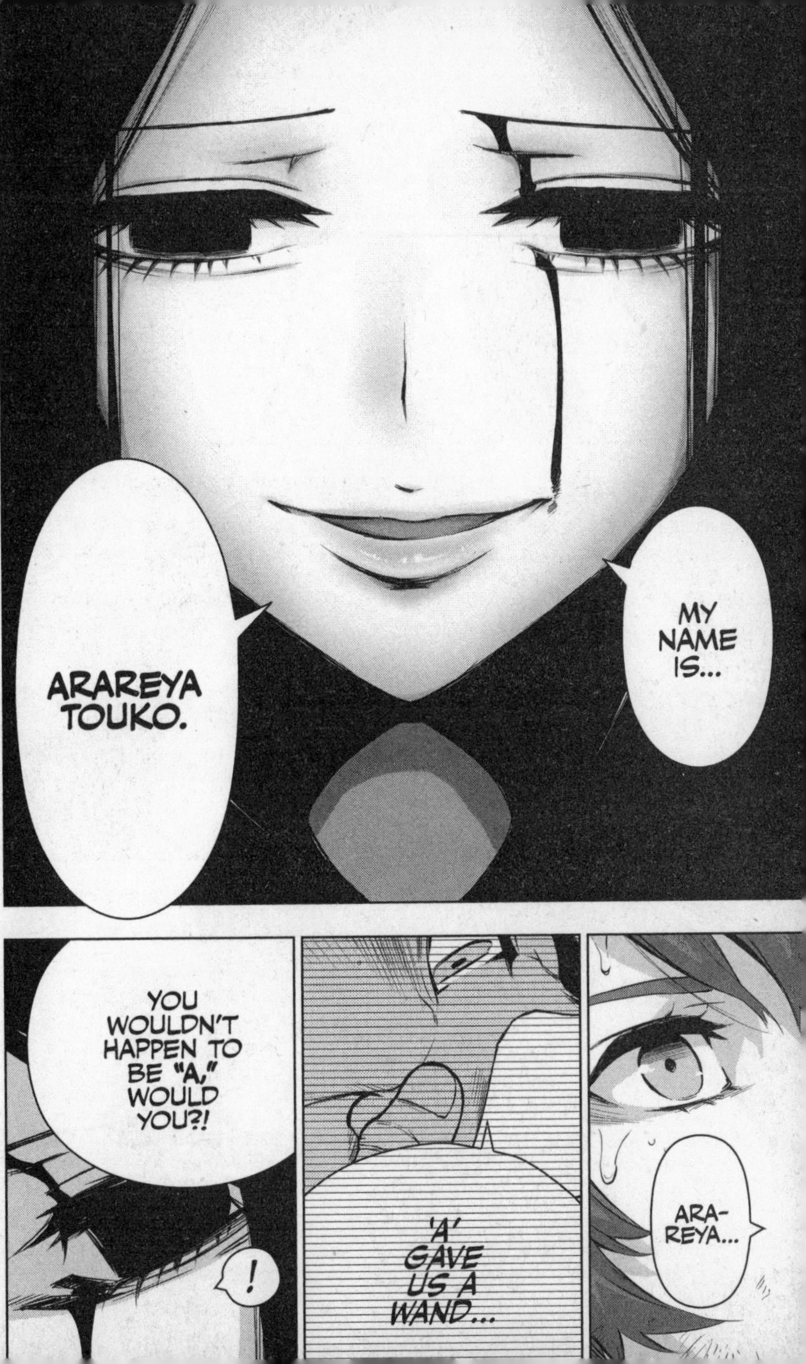
MY NAME IS...
ARAREYA TOUKO.
ARA-REYA...
'A' GAVE US A WAND...
YOU WOULDN'T HAPPEN TO BE "A," WOULD YOU?!
!

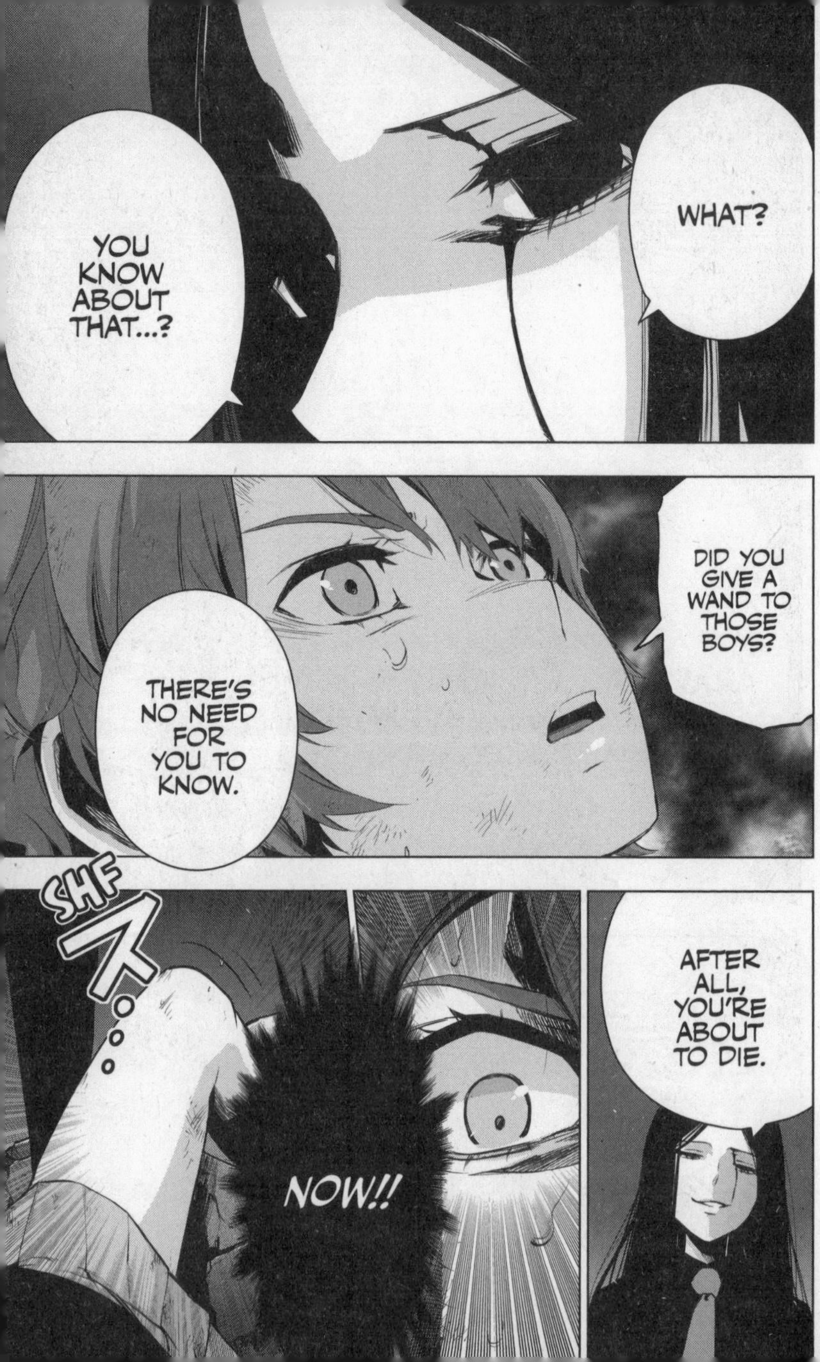
WHAT?
YOU KNOW ABOUT THAT...?
DID YOU GIVE A WAND TO THOSE BOYS?
THERE'S NO NEED FOR YOU TO KNOW.
AFTER ALL, YOU'RE ABOUT TO DIE.
SHF
NOW!!

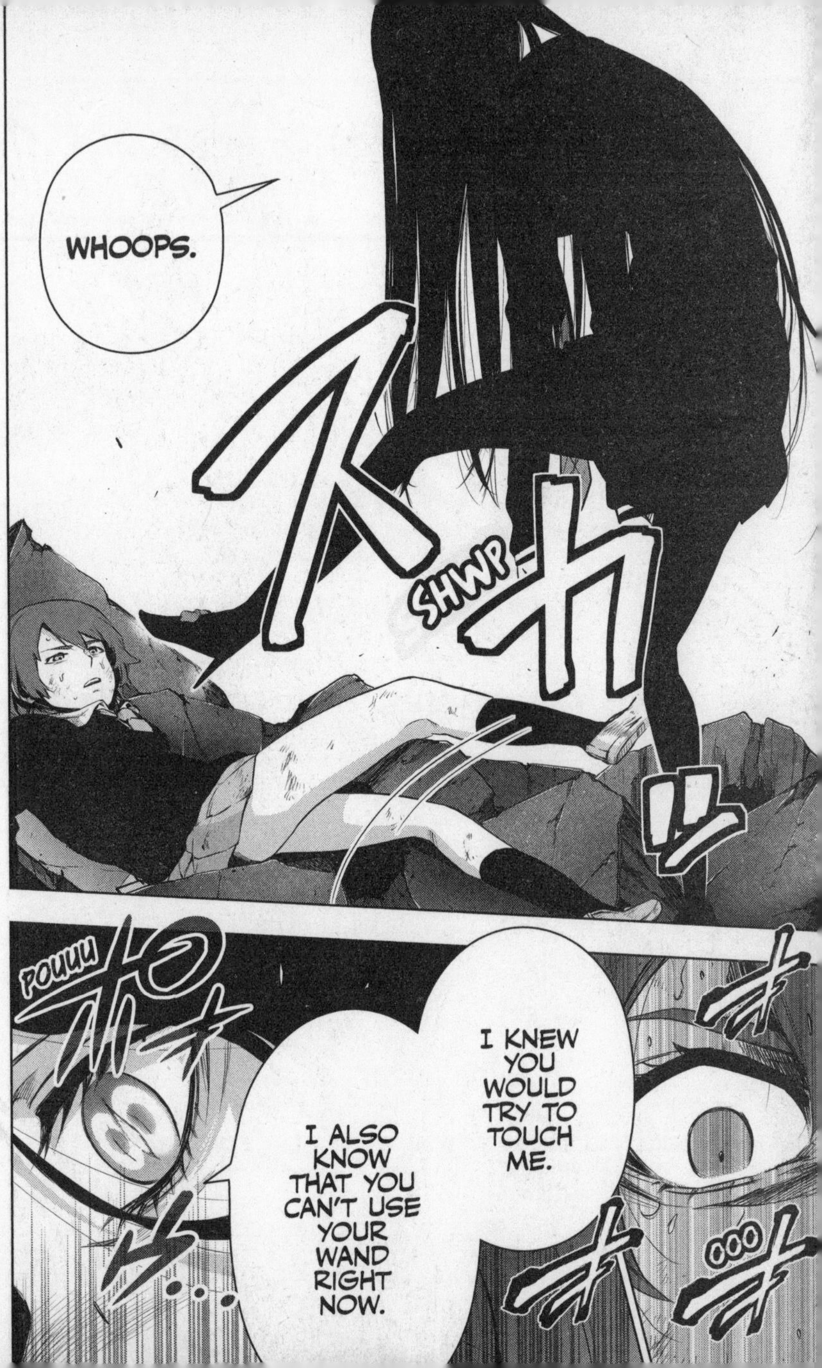
WHOOPS.
SHWP
OOO
I KNEW YOU WOULD TRY TO TOUCH ME.
I ALSO KNOW THAT YOU CAN'T USE YOUR WAND RIGHT NOW.
POUUU
...

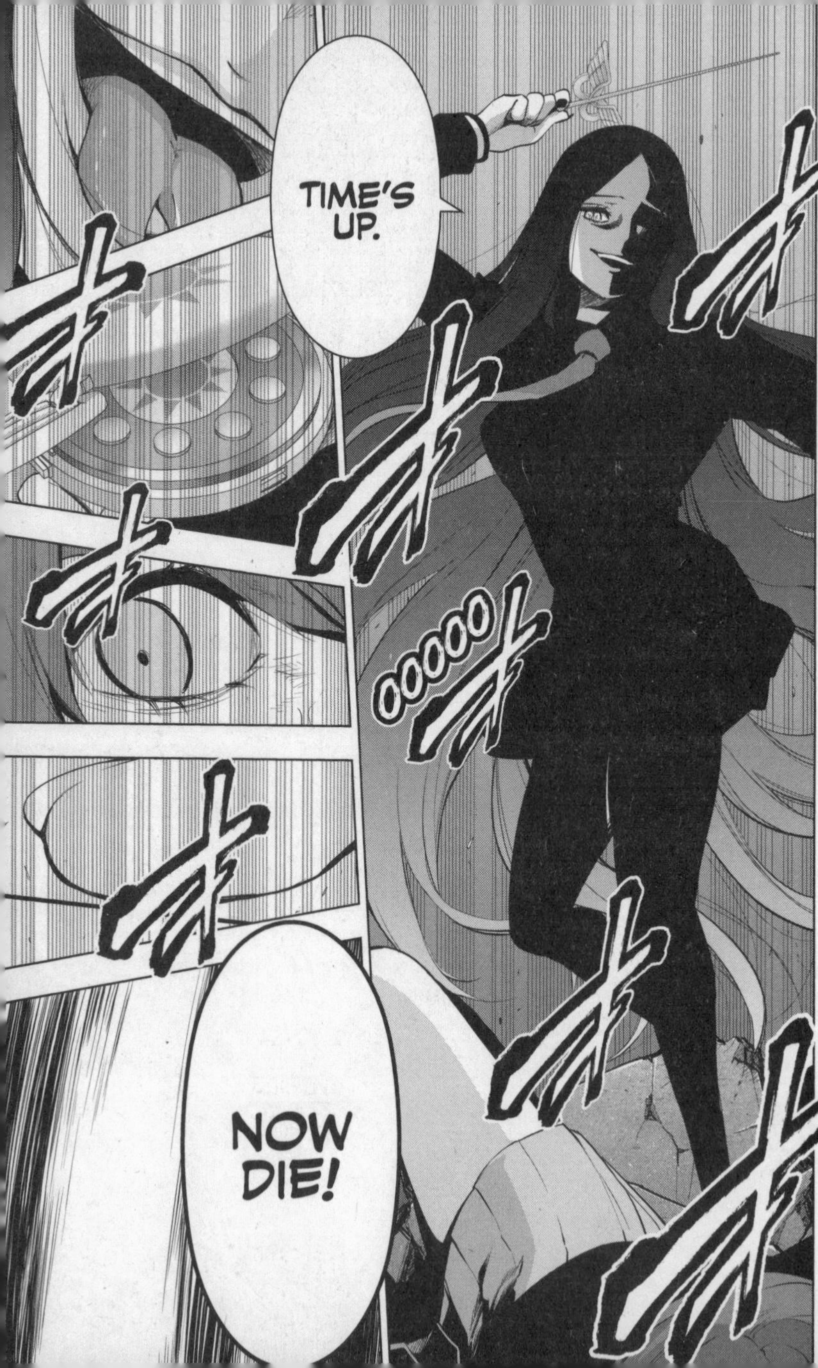
TIME'S UP.
OOOOO
NOW DIE!

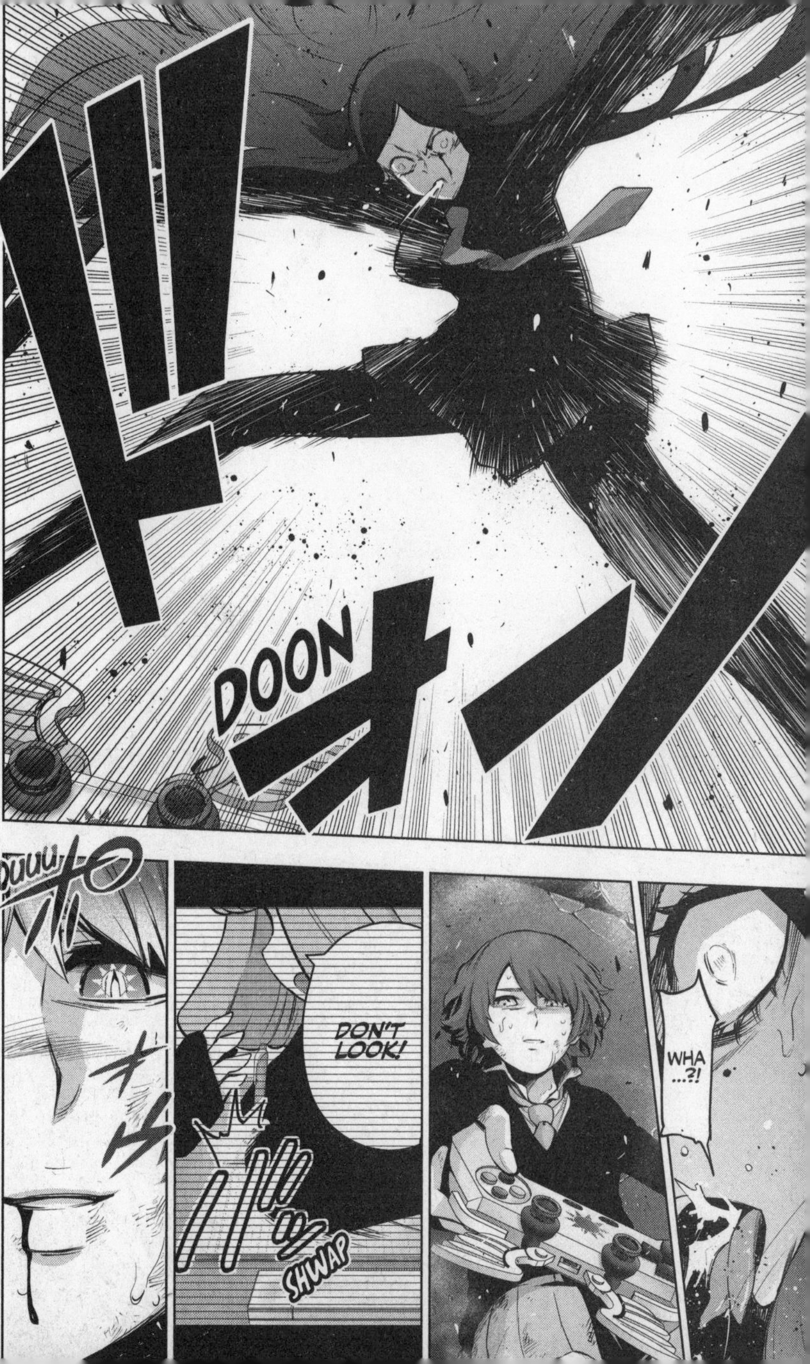
DOON
WHA ...?!
DON'T LOOK!
SHWAP
POUUU

ENTER.64 GAIN

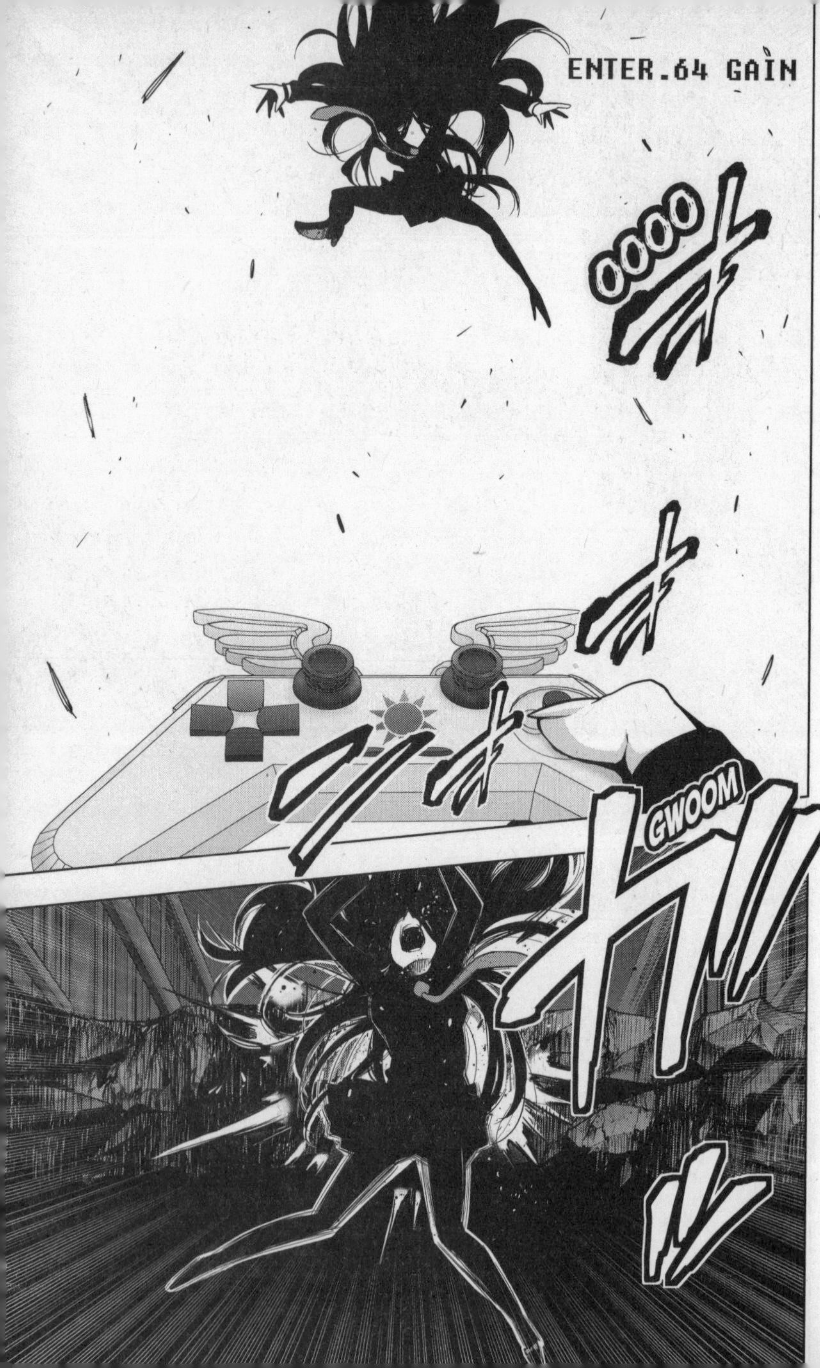
GWOOM

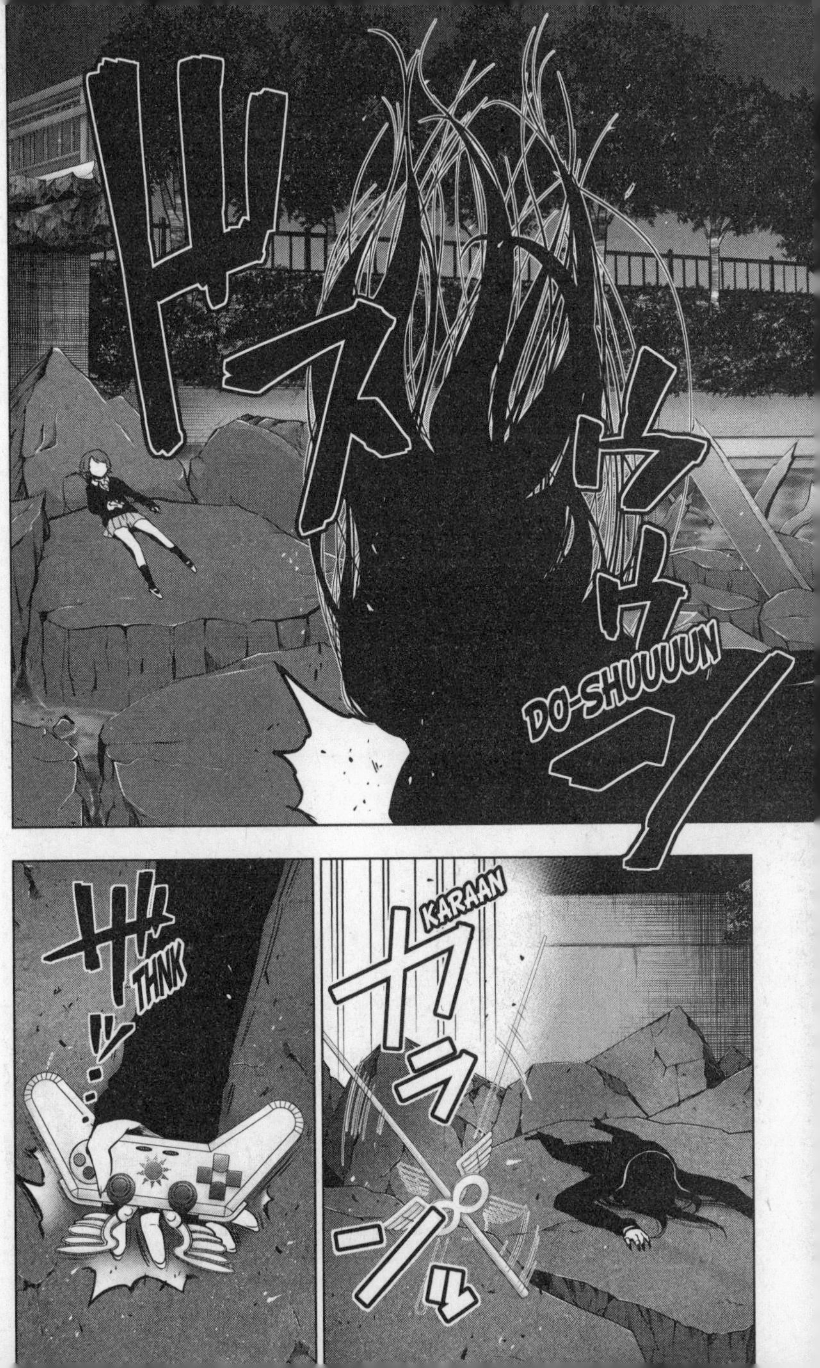
DO-SHUUUUN
KARAAN
THNK

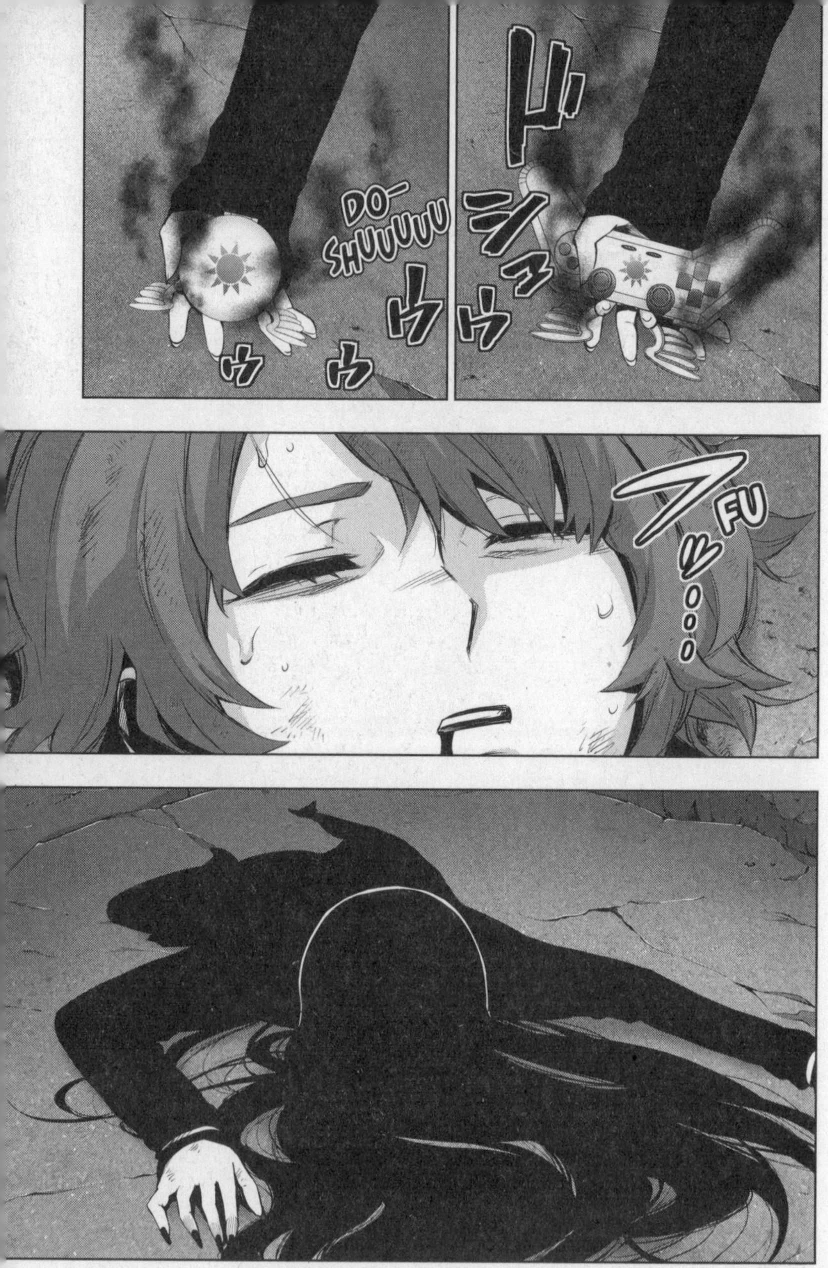

ドシュウ
DO-SHUUUUU
ウウウ
フッ…
FU

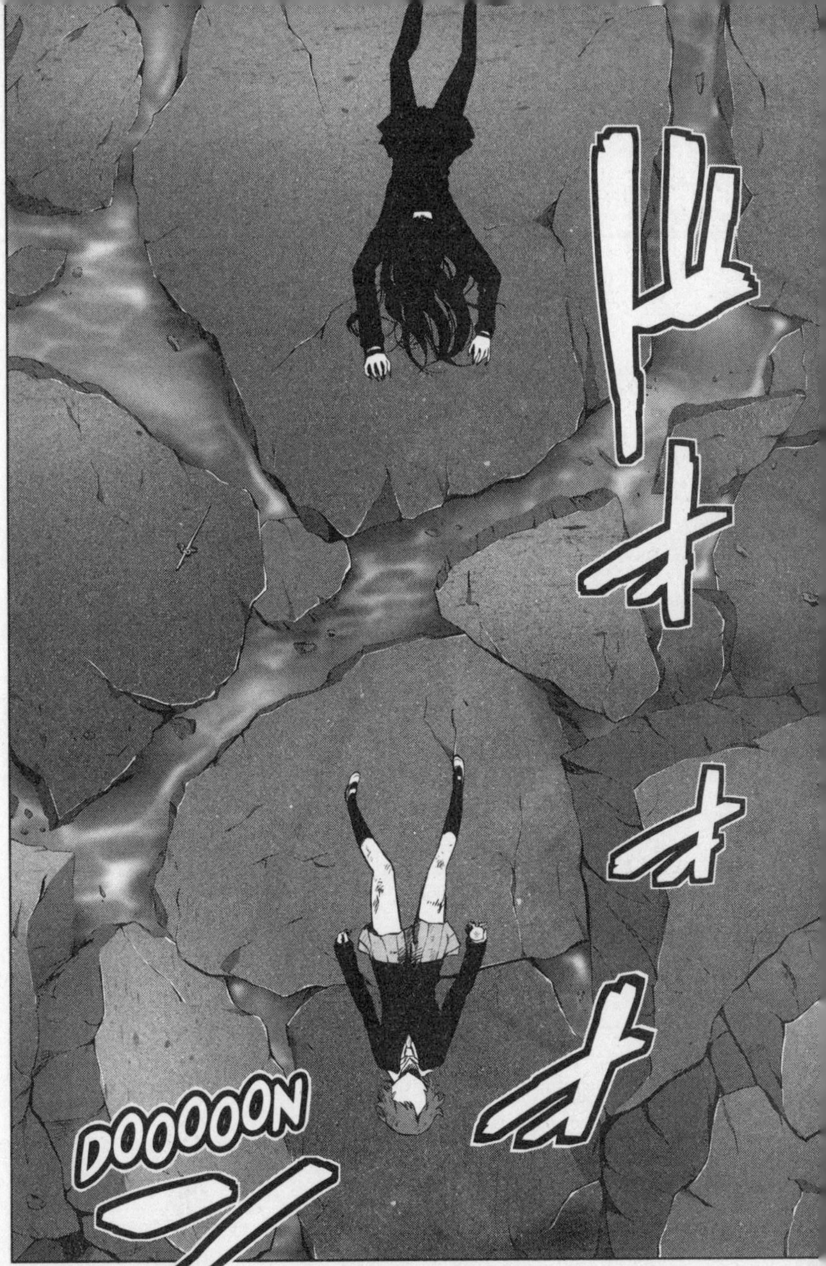
ドオオオン
DOOOOON

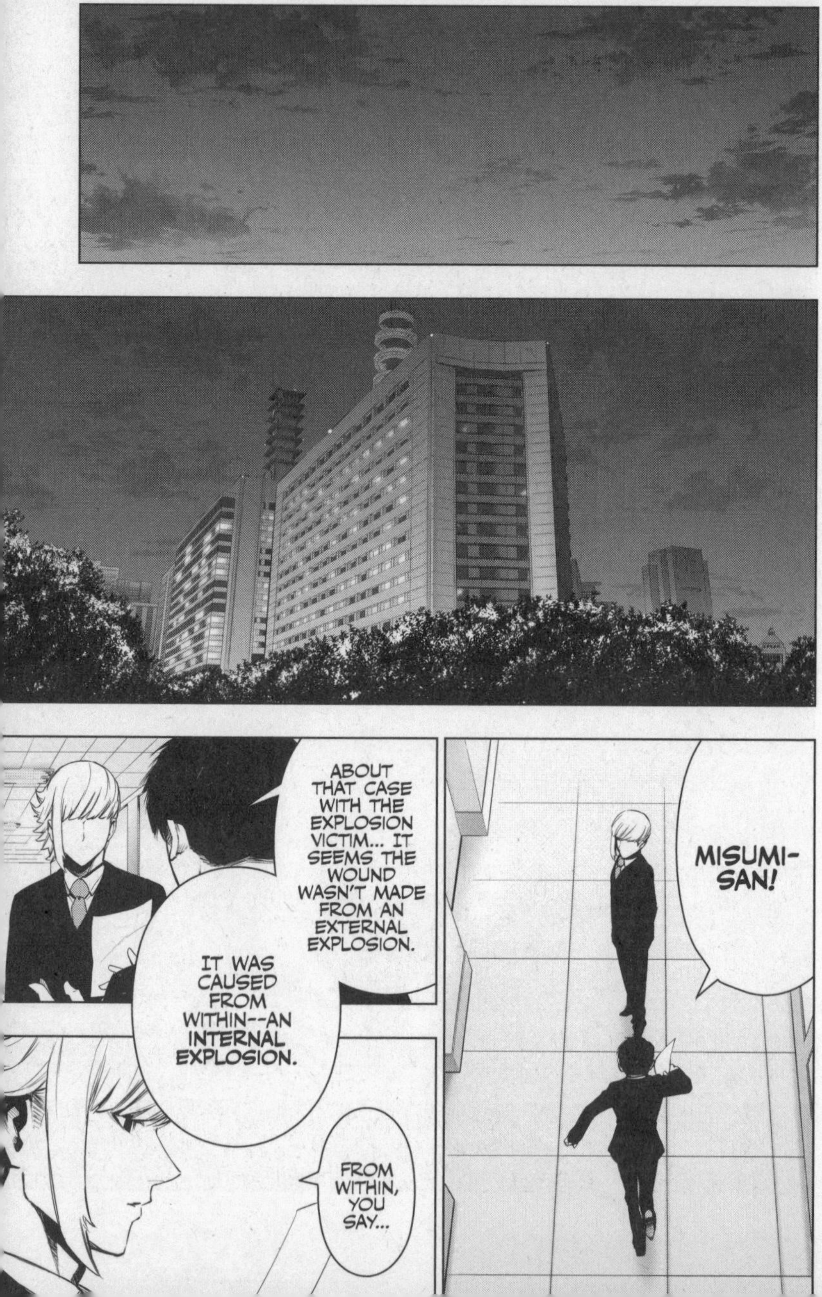
MISUMI-SAN!
ABOUT THAT CASE WITH THE EXPLOSION VICTIM... IT SEEMS THE WOUND WASN'T MADE FROM AN EXTERNAL EXPLOSION.
IT WAS CAUSED FROM WITHIN--AN INTERNAL EXPLOSION.
FROM WITHIN, YOU SAY...

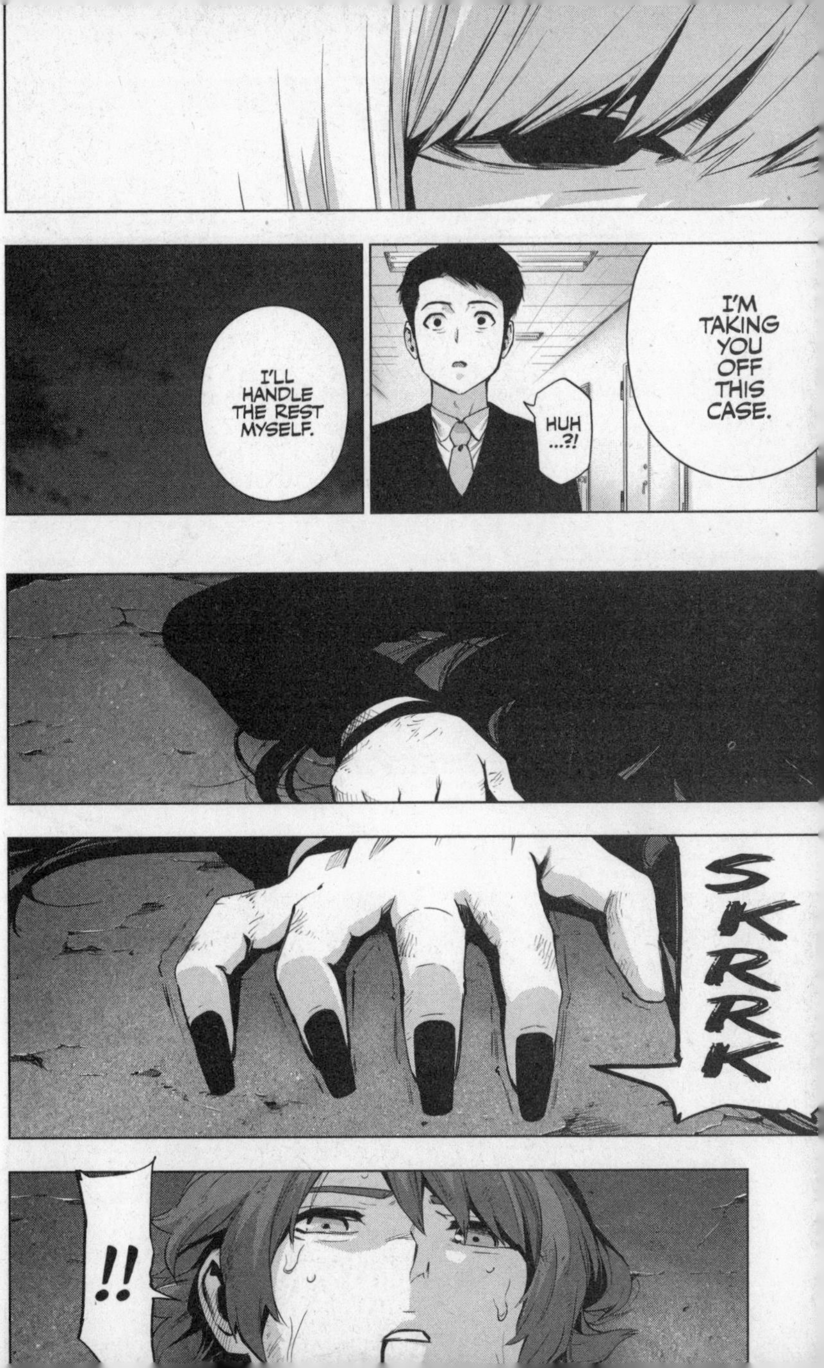
I'M TAKING YOU OFF THIS CASE.
HUH ...?!
I'LL HANDLE THE REST MYSELF.
SKRRK
!!

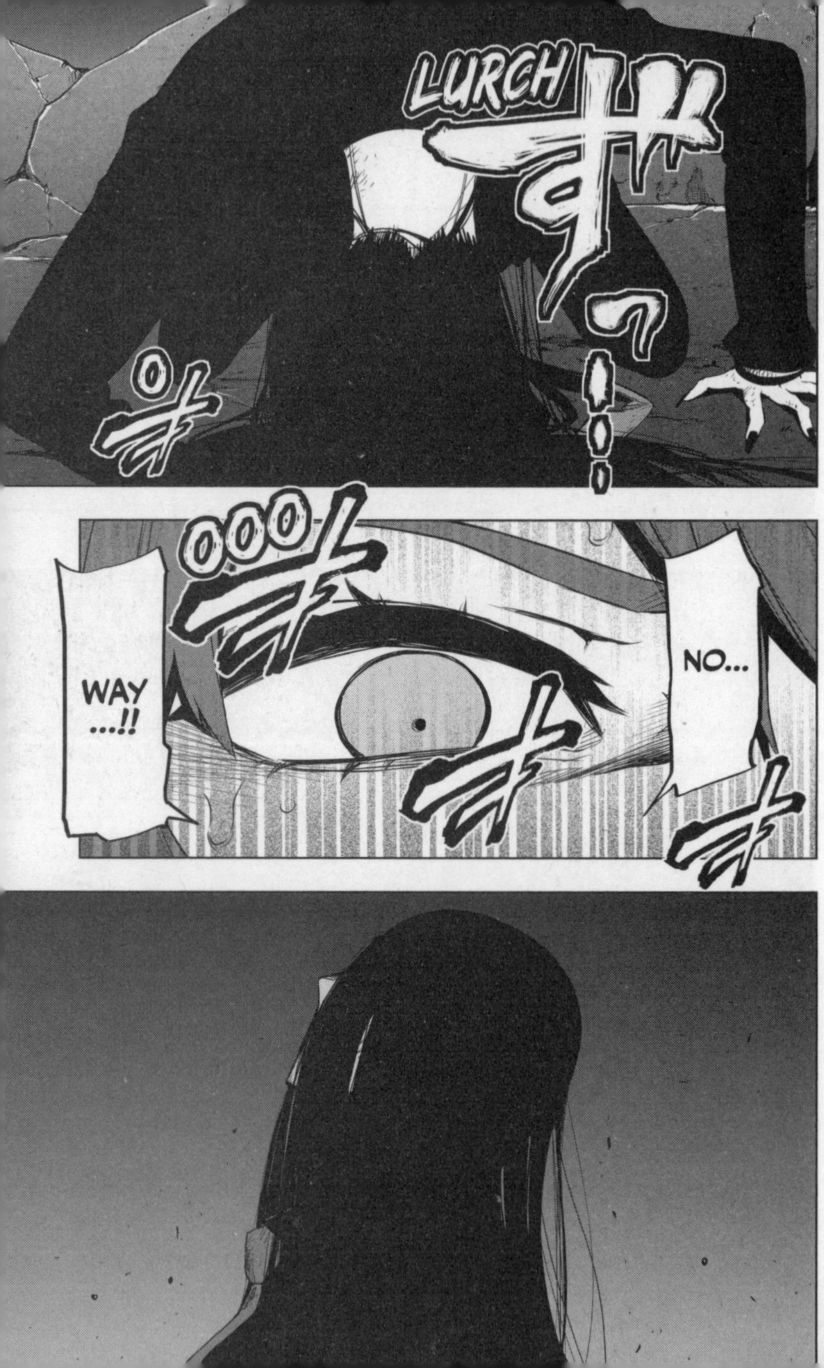
LURCH
OOO
NO...
WAY
...!!

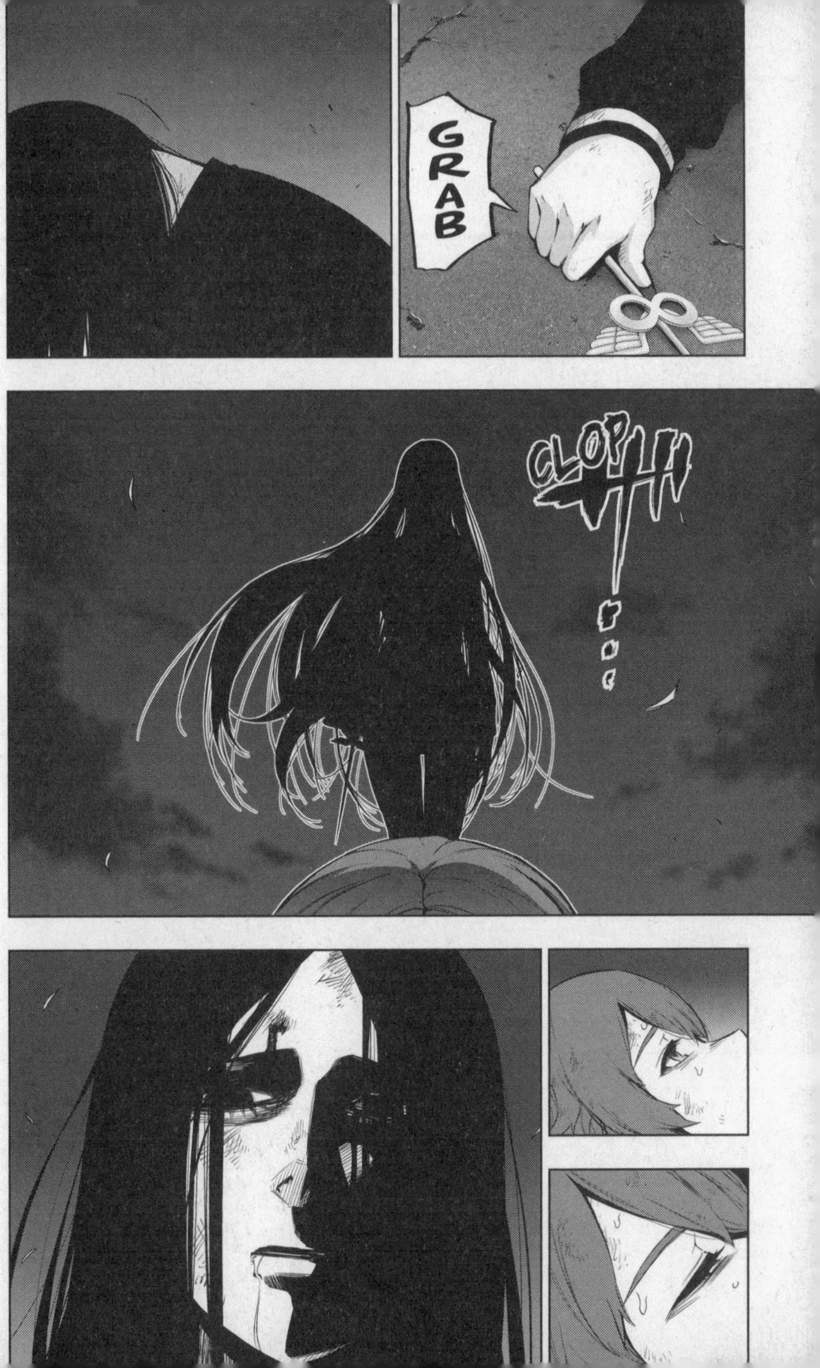
GRAB
CLOP

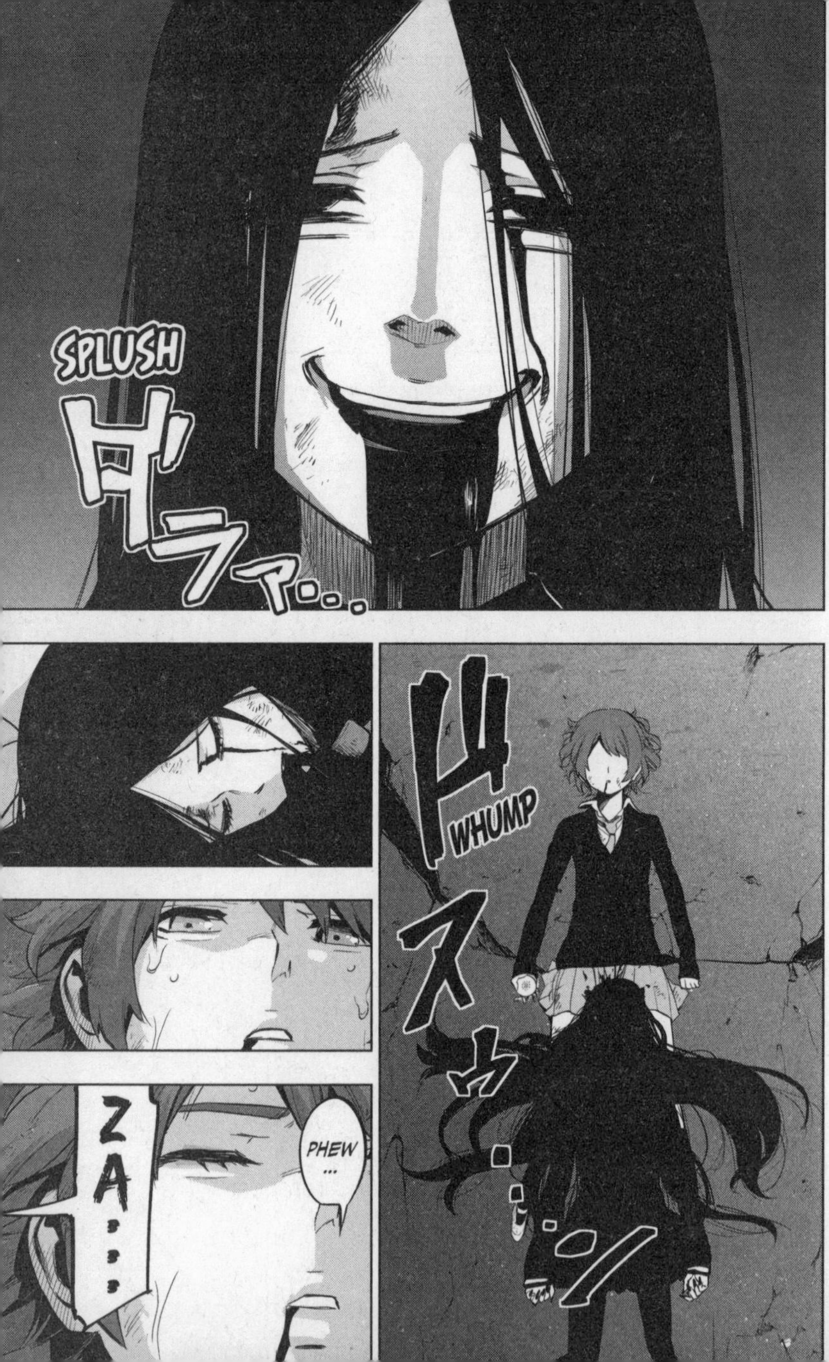
SPLUSH
WHUMP
PHEW...
ZA...

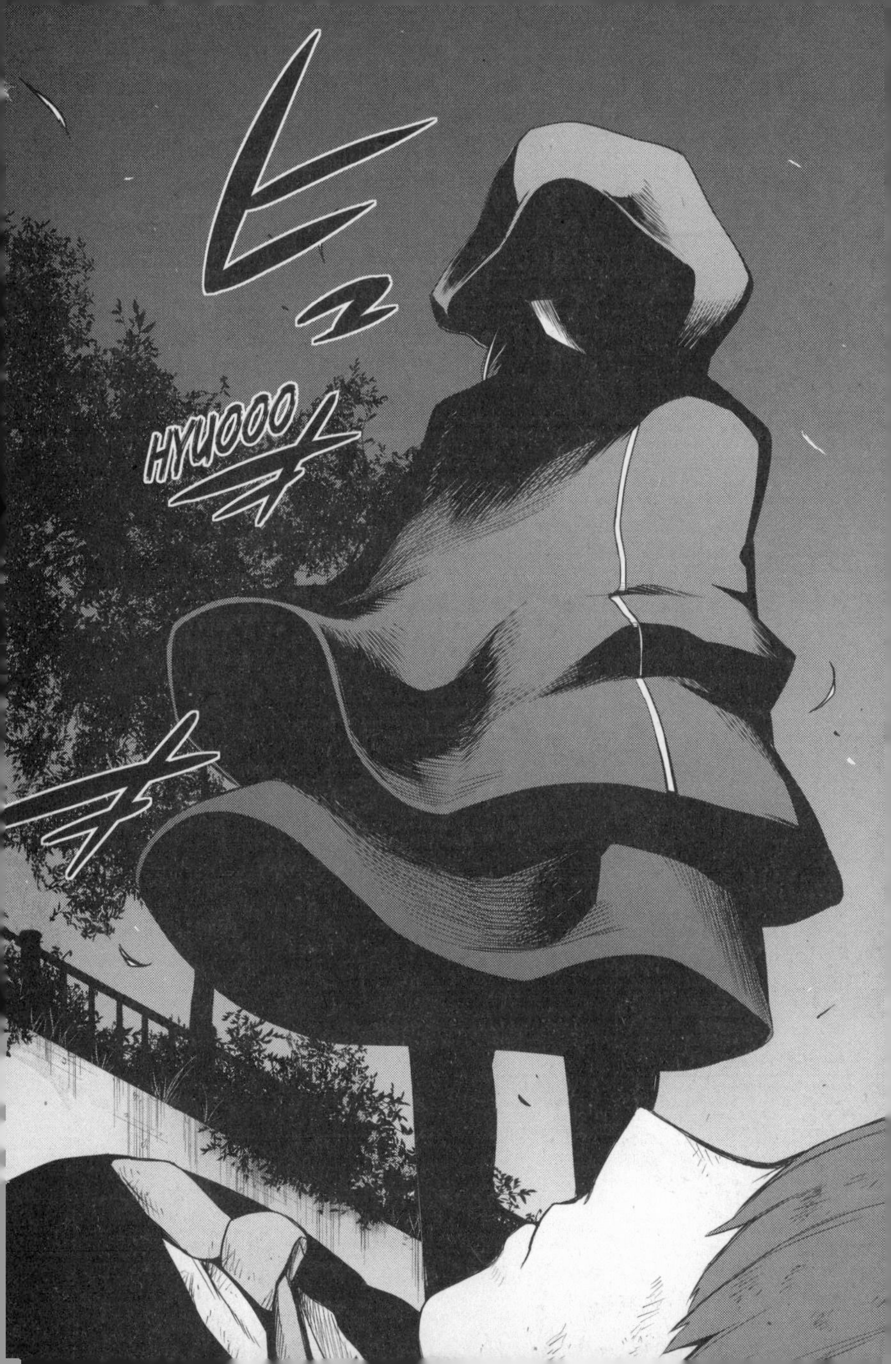
ヒュ
HYUOOO
オ
オ

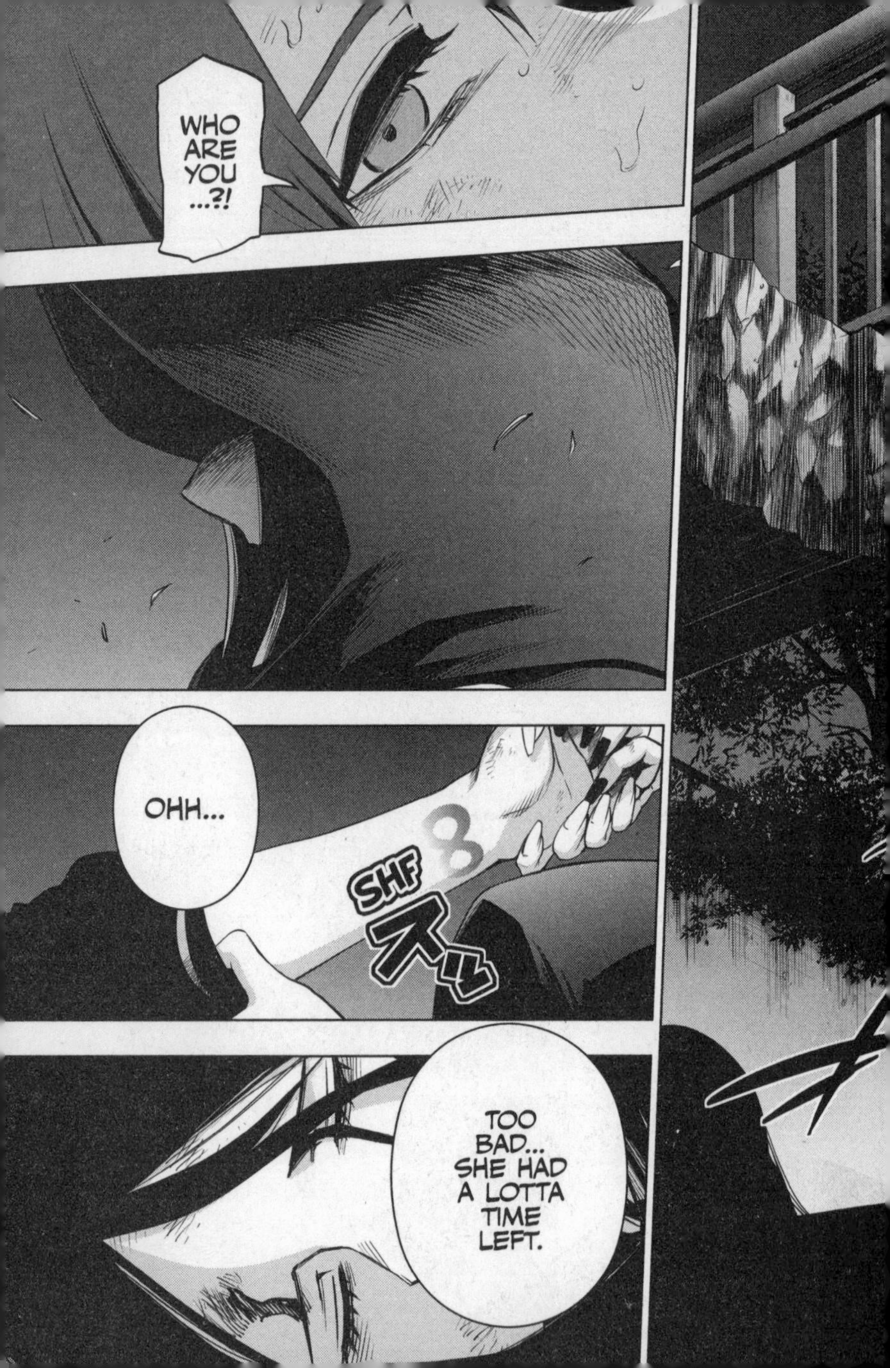
WHO ARE YOU ...?!
OHH...
SHF
TOO BAD... SHE HAD A LOTTA TIME LEFT.

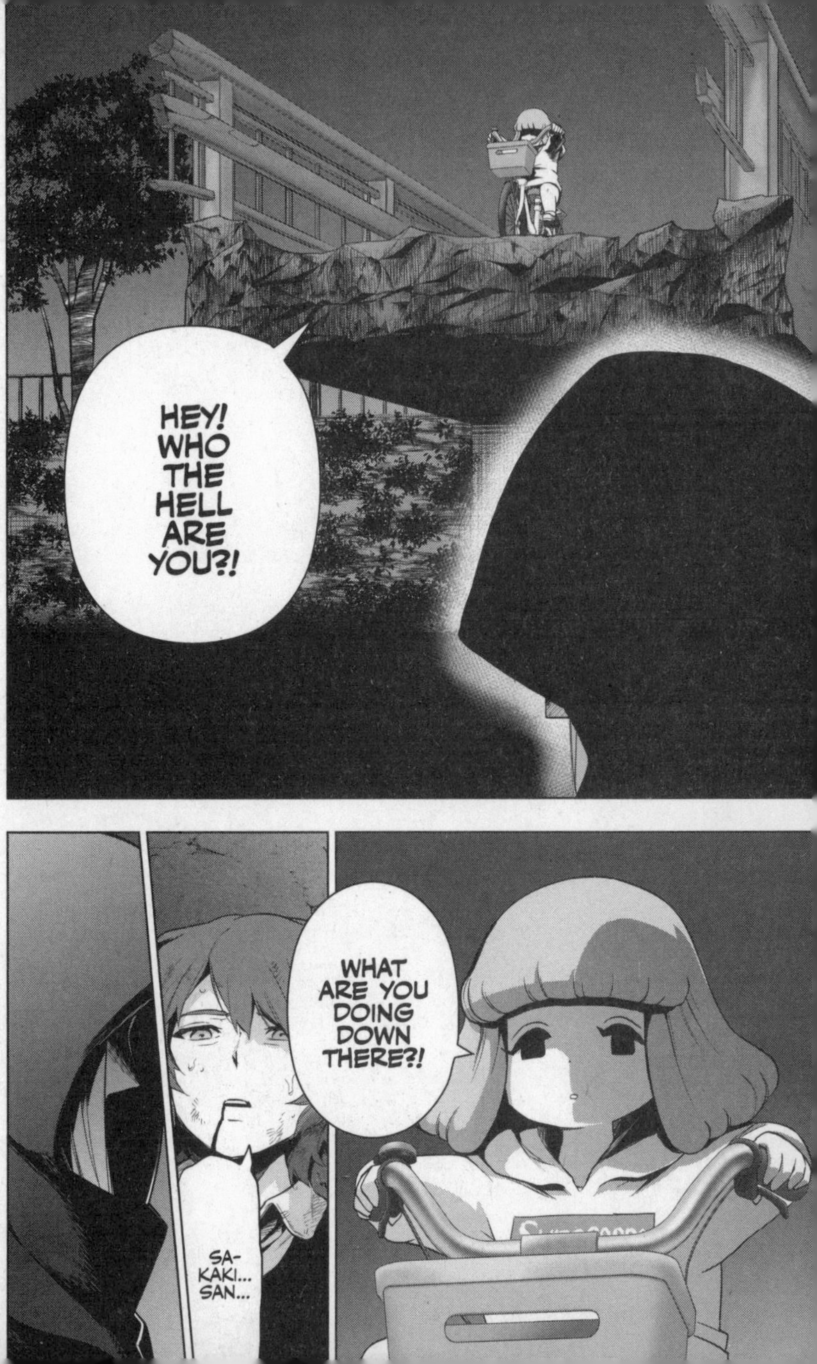
HEY! WHO THE HELL ARE YOU?!
WHAT ARE YOU DOING DOWN THERE?!
SA-KAKI... SAN...

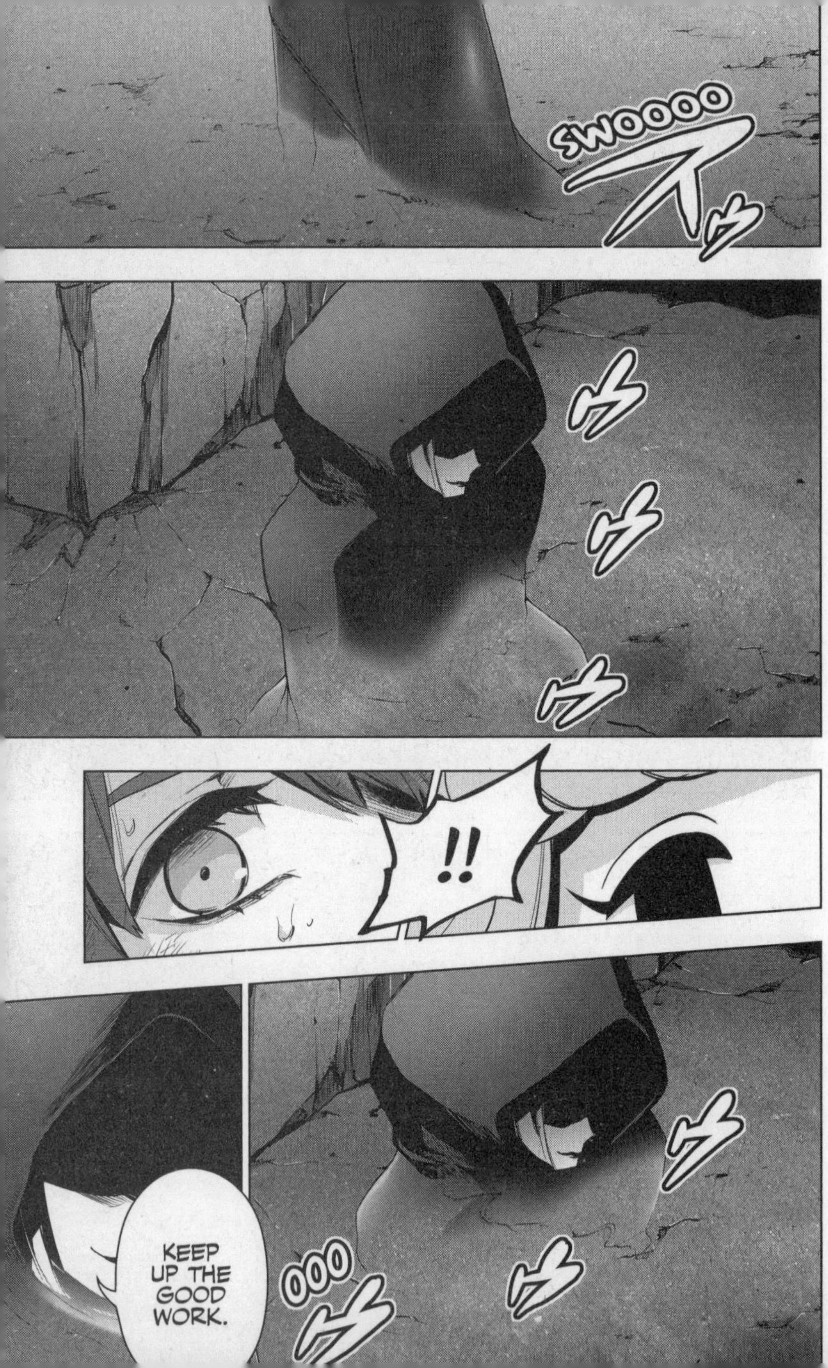
SWOOOO
!!
OOO
KEEP UP THE GOOD WORK.

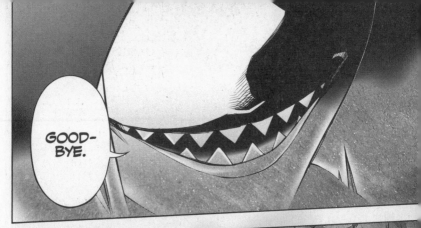

GOOD-
BYE.

GA-
SHANK

WHO
WAS
THAT
...?

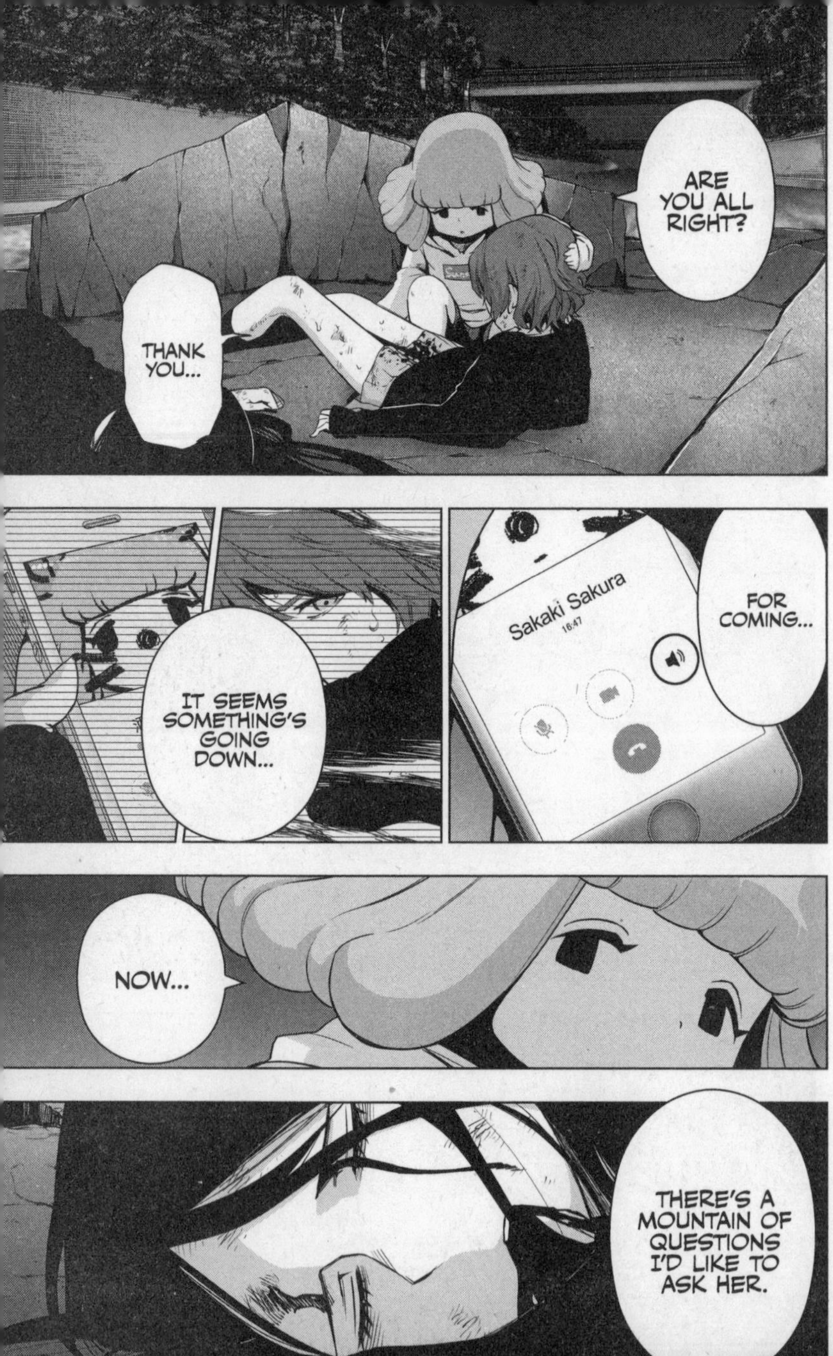
ARE YOU ALL RIGHT?
THANK YOU...
FOR COMING...
Sakaki Sakura
16:47
IT SEEMS SOMETHING'S GOING DOWN...
NOW...
THERE'S A MOUNTAIN OF QUESTIONS I'D LIKE TO ASK HER.

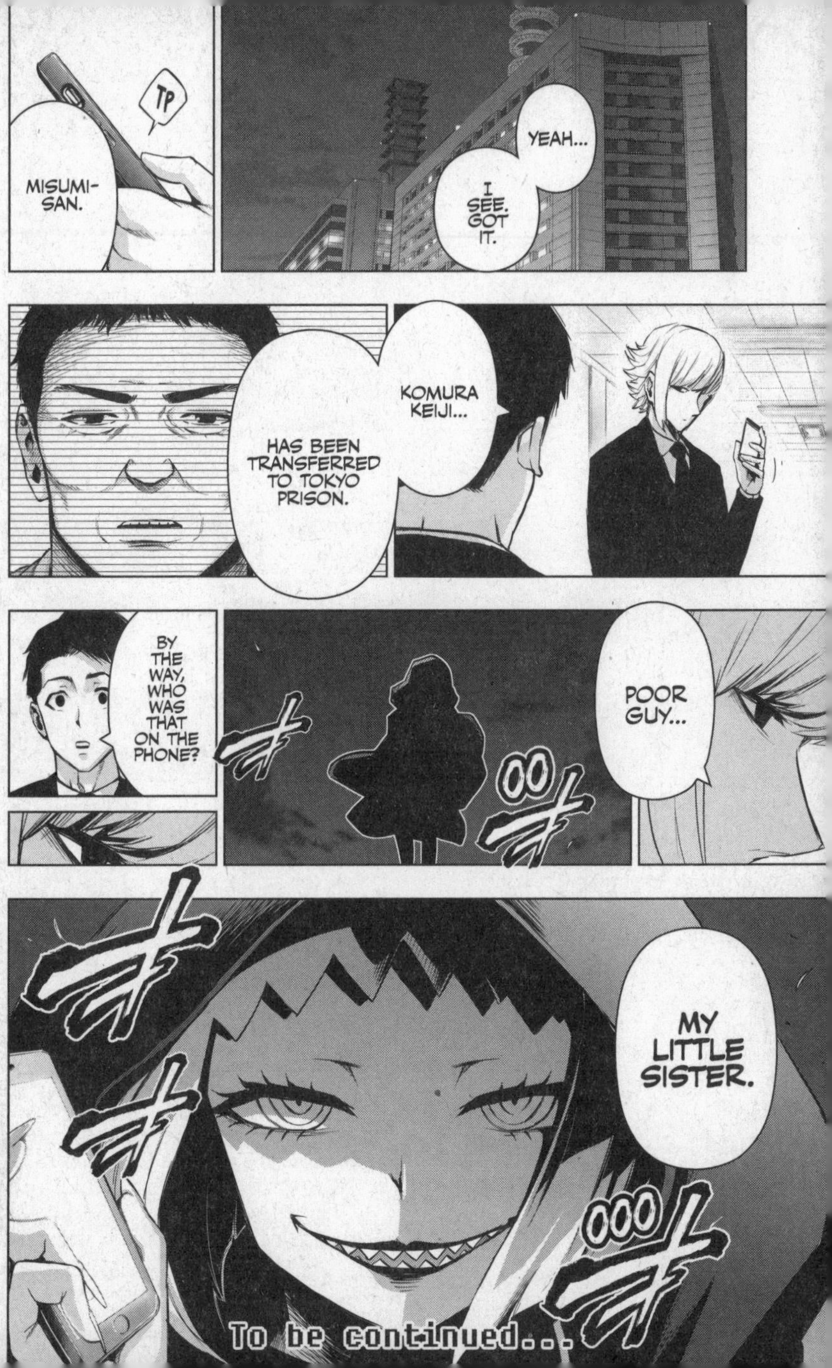
YEAH...
I SEE. GOT IT.
TP
MISUMI-SAN.
KOMURA KEIJI...
HAS BEEN TRANSFERRED TO TOKYO PRISON.
POOR GUY...
OO
BY THE WAY, WHO WAS THAT ON THE PHONE?
MY LITTLE SISTER.
OOO
To be continued...

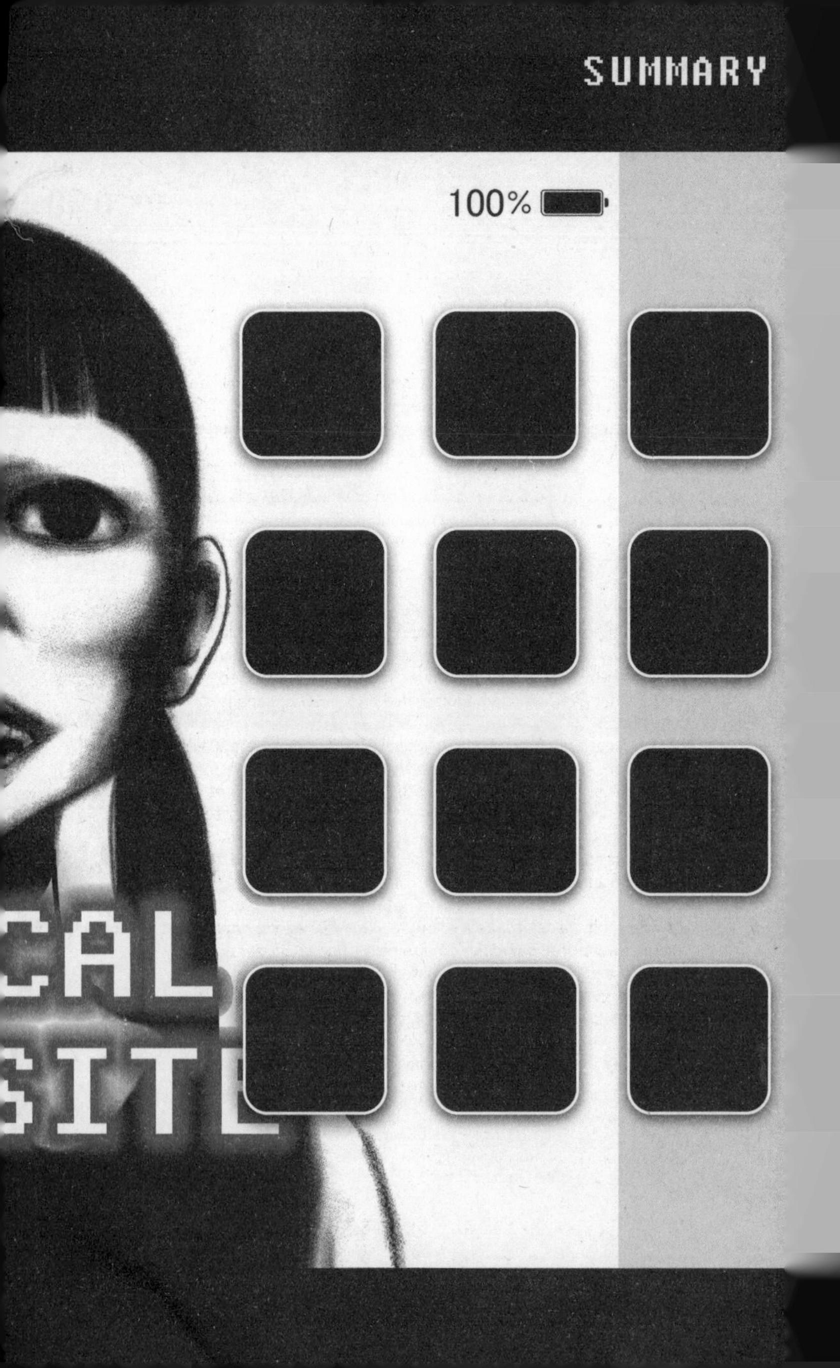
SUMMARY
100%
CAL
SITE

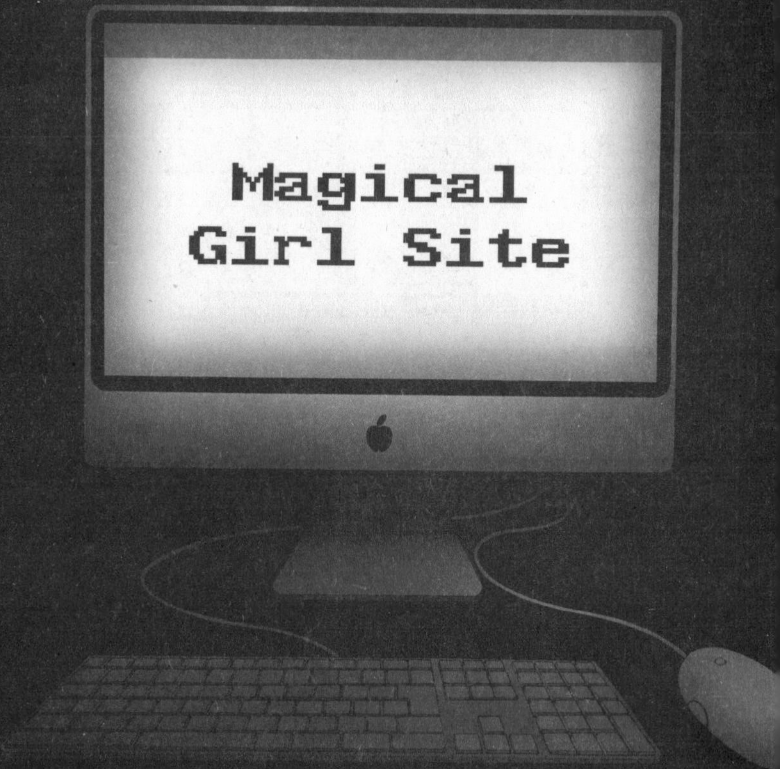
Magical
Girl Site

VOLUME 9

AUTHOR
KENTARO SATO